Working Girls

Working Girls

*Sex, Taste, and Reform in the Parisian
Garment Trades, 1880–1919*

PATRICIA TILBURG

OXFORD
UNIVERSITY PRESS

Great Clarendon Street, Oxford, OX2 6DP,
United Kingdom

Oxford University Press is a department of the University of Oxford.
It furthers the University's objective of excellence in research, scholarship,
and education by publishing worldwide. Oxford is a registered trade mark of
Oxford University Press in the UK and in certain other countries

© Patricia Tilburg 2019

The moral rights of the author have been asserted

First Edition published in 2019

Impression: 1

Published in the United States of America by Oxford University Press
198 Madison Avenue, New York, NY 10016, United States of America

British Library Cataloguing in Publication Data

Data available

Library of Congress Control Number: 2019946071

ISBN 978–0–19–884117–3

DOI: 10.1093/oso/9780198841173.001.0001

Printed and bound by
CPI Group (UK) Ltd, Croydon, CR0 4YY

To Juliette, Madeleine, and Thomas

Acknowledgments

One of the exceptional joys of working on a history of Parisian culture is the ability to spend so much time in and around the city's library and archival collections: the Centre de Recherches des Archives Nationales, Archives de Paris, Archives de la Préfecture de Police de Paris, Bibliothèque de l'Opéra, Bibliothèque du Musée des Arts Décoratifs: Mode et Textile, Bibliothèque Forney, Bibliothèque Historique de la Ville de Paris, Bibliothèque Marguerite Durand, Bibliothèque Nationale de France, Musée de la Mode et du Textile, and the Gaumont Pathé Archives. I am grateful to Mme Grouard Charpentier for granting access to the Fonds Charpentier at the Bibliothèque historique de la ville de Paris, as well as to the library's conservators Claude Billaud and Juliette Jestaz for their invaluable assistance. Special thanks also to Annie Metz at the Bibliothèque Marguerite Durand, Monsieur Thomas and Monsieur Nicolas at Diktats bookstore, Sabina Robert at the Musée national de l'Éducation, and Emmanuelle Blandinières Beuvin at the Musée des Arts Décoratifs. Thanks to Sophie Ververken for providing me with letters from *poilus* to her grandmother Marcelle Bouyeron. Months in Paris were only a small portion of the years spent writing this book, and two wonders allowed me to pursue this project when I could not be in France: the Bibliothèque Nationale de France's digital library Gallica, and Davidson College's Interlibrary Loan Service, especially Joe Gutekanst.

Grants, sabbatical leave, and other funding for this research have been generously provided by Davidson College, as well as the National Endowment for the Humanities, and the Institut Français de la Mode. The Western Society for French History, the Society for French Historical Studies, the Nineteenth-Century French Studies Association, and the American Comparative Literature Association all provided space for me to present this work as it developed. Thanks to Maude Bass-Krueger and Sophie Kurkdjian for organizing the "Mode et Guerre Europe, 1914–1918" conference at the Institut français de la Mode. Thanks also to the editorial staff at Oxford University Press for their keen eyes and production assistance throughout this process, especially Christina Wipf Perry, Cathryn Steele, Kayalvizhi Ganesan, and Dorothy McCarthy.

My colleagues at Davidson College, especially in the Departments of History and Gender & Sexuality Studies, have provided years of extraordinary intellectual camaraderie and support, and many of them have helped shepherd this book through its various stages with incisive comments, mentorship, library co-working, and pomodoro writing solidarity: Alison Bory, Patricio Boyer, Vivien Dietz, Melissa González, Katie Horowitz, Sarah Luna, Jane Mangan, Sally McMillen,

Taimoor Shahid, John Wertheimer, Alice Wiemers, and Sarah Waheed. Nine years ago, Christine Haynes and I founded the Charlotte Area French Studies Workshop, and since that time she and the workshop have been a vital local space to connect my own writing with other French and Francophone studies scholars in the region including Michèle Bissière, Denise Davidson, Elizabeth Everton, Caroline Fache, Félix Germain, Carol Harrison, Carole Kruger, Alan Singerman, Allison Stedman, Phil Slaby, Catherine Slawy-Sutton, Natalia Starostina, Homer Sutton, and Ellen Welch. Numerous scholars have provided suggestions and input on this book along the way: Elinor Accampo, Martin Bruegel, Eleanor Courtemanche, Brad Deane, Carolyn Eichner, Sima Godfrey, Kate Hamerton, Deanna Kreisel, Andrea Mansker, Scott MacKenzie, Richard Menke, Jean Pedersen, Claude Pennetier, Tyler Stovall, Geoff Read, Charles Rearick, Debora Silverman, Willa Silverman, Mary Lynn Stewart, Carol Symes, Steve Zdatny, and the late Rachel Fuchs.

Family and friends in France have made me a second home in their country, and I am forever grateful, especially to Loic LeGuerhier, Céline Clavel, Hélène Merle, Adrian Amezcua, Emmanuelle and Ludovic Portois, Cédric and Sophie Diez, Alain and Sandra Ricard, Marie-Angèle Barzani, Demetrio and Maryse Nozal, Laura De Souza, Olivia De Souza and Antoine Chateau, and all the Barzani, Ricard, and Nozal clans. Back on this side of the Atlantic, friends and family have made sure the years spent on this project were filled with much more than book writing: my sister-in-law Deborah Ricard and her husband Jorge Molina, as well as Laurian Bowles, Alison Bory, Caroline Fache, Dave Frantzreb, Adam Levine, Matt Nichols, Jennifer Munroe, Annie Seier, Josh Seier, Jenny Ward, and Alice Wiemers. My *beaux parents* Sarah and Jean-Pierre Ricard have provided childcare, meals, and countless *apéros*. My siblings Will Tilburg, Nadia Barbar, and Karen Tilburg make me endlessly thankful for group texts. Deanna Kreisel and Scott MacKenzie consistently remind me of the curative power of a feast with old friends, wherever the table. Sheila Callaghan and Kirstin Ohrt have given decades of rollicking sisterhood. Melissa González modeled for me her eccentric and fortifying brand of feminist communicative ethics. Patricio Boyer is an accomplice of the first order, and has taught me there is always time for a matinée. The years spent on this book saw the loss of my family's two matriarchs, my grandmother Mary Reilly and my grandmother-in-law Suzanne Ricard, indomitable women whose lives began in the interwar years where this book ends.

My parents Kathleen and William Tilburg are the first people to whom I owed a debt of gratitude, and the debt has grown now too large ever to repay adequately, certainly not with just a line in this book. I continue to learn from them every day and to draw inspiration from their partnership, their parenting, and their grandparenting. The research and writing of this book coincided with the births and early childhoods of my daughters Madeleine and Juliette Ricard-Tilburg, and thus, have coincided with almost a decade of my efforts to learn to be a decent parent to them. Their fierce sense of justice and bountiful capacity for joy have nourished and emboldened me in these years (even if I wish they had slept a little more). It is to them that I dedicate this book, as well as to their father Thomas Ricard, my partner in all things, the Parisian exile whose tenderness, complicity, humor, and love provide the moorings for our life in North Carolina and make all adventures beyond it possible.

Contents

List of Illustrations

List of Abbreviations

AN	Archives Nationales de France
APPP	Archives de la Préfecture de Police de Paris
BMD	Bibliothèque Marguerite Durand
BNF	Bibliothèque Nationale de France
BNF-L	Bibliothèque Nationale de France, Richelieu (Louvois) Musique
BNF-R	Bibliothèque Nationale de France, Richelieu, Arts du Spectacle
FC	Fonds Charpentier

Introduction

In a 1908 study of Frenchwomen's philanthropic organizations, novelist and journalist Paul Acker acknowledged the difficulty of accessing the real lives of working women in Paris:

> The Parisian workingwoman has had spun around her a kind of legend, charm-ing and false like all legends. The workingwoman is the joy of Paris and one of its prettiest jewels, dressed up as she is with bits of nothing, and, despite her simple clothing, always seductive with her light step, her little, amused face, her lively gestures, her merry laugh ... We also say that she is a little fairy who weaves marvels, while being nourished only by fashion. We compare her to a carefree bird, happy as long as she is singing. We find her touching because she lunches on a morsel of bread under the trees of the Tuileries. We find her new and picturesque names like *midinette* ... The poets have celebrated her from time immemorial, and, through the generations, she remains, with minor changes, the Mimi Pinson of Musset, or Jenny with the flowerpot ... The reality is less beautiful, and should be better known ... But lies are more pleasant than the truth ...[1]

My book takes the mythos of the Parisian midinette as its primary field of investi-gation—not merely to record the plethora of fanciful commentary about female garment workers in the capital during the belle époque, but also to understand this whimsical Parisian imaginary as a fantasy with political intention. This narra-tive of Parisian working-class femininity defined significant aspects of French popular culture, philanthropy, and labor reform from the fin de siècle through the First World War, and became an essential means of representing and coping with the early twentieth-century encounter between labor and modern capitalism.

From the late eighteenth century, the Parisian garment worker held a singular place in French popular culture as a sign of working-class erotics and of France's global supremacy in fashion and luxury craft. In the 1830s and 1840s, these women became common cultural currency with the indelible *grisettes* of Romantic literature: Murger's Mimi, Sand's Marthe, Musset's Mimi Pinson. I assess the legacy and meaning of this archetype in its later Third Republican incarnation, when the working Parisienne became a national icon and a fulcrum for concerns about women's work, labor reform, and French taste. As the

---

[1] Paul Acker, *Oeuvres sociales des femmes* (Paris, 1908). Acker (1874–1915) was a novelist and journalist.

Working Girls: Sex, Taste, and Reform in the Parisian Garment Trades, 1880–1919. Patricia Tilburg, Oxford University Press (2019). © Patricia Tilburg.
DOI: 10.1093/oso/9780198841173.001.0001

twentieth century dawned and France entered an era of extraordinary industrial competition and labor activism, politicians, reformers, and culture makers deployed an insistently romantic vision of the Parisian fashion worker to manage anxieties about economic and social change. The *midinette*—the ideal Parisian garment worker who took her name from the noon lunch hour—loomed large in the social imaginary of early twentieth-century Paris. This capacious and yet readily legible term was used widely in the belle époque to refer to any (but typically young, typically unmarried) woman in the Parisian garment trades: milliners, seamstresses, flowermakers, shop girls, and laundresses; poorly paid pieceworkers or relatively better paid couture dressmakers. But it also had a secondary usage, a "[y]oung girl who was simple and frivolous, and of naïve sentimentality."[2] These two significations, a figure of labor and a figure of pleasure and feeling, would be used to characterize the garment workers of Paris throughout this period.

Turn-of-the-century Paris was home to approximately 80,000 female garment workers, living and working largely in grim conditions. Malnutrition, disease, and regular unemployment were part and parcel of couture work in the capital. The garment industry resisted regulation that came to other industries in this same period, and so garment laborers faced poorly ventilated and even toxic workshops, mandatory night work, arbitrary firing, and insufficient wages. As a result, female garment workers went on strike in Paris repeatedly from 1901 through World War I. Yet, throughout these years, Parisian midinettes were imagined as naïve and cheerful, laboring for the love of fashion and for the pleasures of pocket money.

The attractive, young, single garment worker with a ready smile and inimitable Parisian taste was featured in countless novels, films, songs, social commentary, and even reform campaigns from the era as an inescapable urban type. This working girl stood in for, at once, the superiority of French taste and craft, and the political (and sexual) subordination of French women and labor. From the 1880s through the Great War, nostalgia about a certain kind of France was written onto the bodies of workingwomen across French popular culture. And the midinette was written onto the geography of Paris, by way of festivals, monuments, historic preservation, and guide books. She was also the public face of tens of thousands of real workingwomen (many of them not "girls" at all) whose demands for better labor conditions were modulated, distorted, and, in some cases, amplified by this ubiquitous Romantic type.

For Anglo-American Victorianists, there will be much here that is unfamiliar. The narratives of sexual danger and fateful misery that mark British and American turn-of-the-century urban literature and philanthropy dealing with seamstresses—that "city of dreadful delights" to use Judith Walkowitz's phrase—find a different

---

[2] *Trésor de la Langue Française.*

inflection in the French context.[3] The Victorian seamstress was a figure of pure tragedy: the ill-fated unwed mother, the consumptive spinster, the soon-to-be prostitute.[4] Of course, these same images were ubiquitous in French Romantic and social realist literature as well; the economic precarity and sexual availability of Paris' garment worker were represented as melodramatic danger, and the single workingwoman was viewed with ambivalence. But the female garment worker's sexuality also was heralded as part of the aesthetic and physical pleasure of Paris, and crucial to the French cultural and industrial *patrimoine*, even as she was perceived as vulnerable in many of the same ways as her laboring sisters in London and New York. The threat to these women was certainly believed to be a moral one, but their friable virtue elicited less anxiety than did concerns about threats to a French way of life grounded in these workers' pre-industrial craft and innate fashionability. Even philanthropic initiatives that took the female garment worker's moral exposure in the city as a problem to be solved were limited by notions of their adorable frivolity and nationally-useful taste.

The midinette, then, was a cultural type that diverged from an earlier nineteenth-century trope in which garment workers' poverty and overwork lead inexorably to sex work and/or death.[5] This narrative persisted at the turn of the century, but in France it was now accompanied by a fusion of the doomed Romantic seamstress and the sunny New Woman. Whereas the benighted Victorian seamstress was a woman who avoided the male gaze,[6] the Parisian midinette was understood and represented as an appealing urban spectacle, a site of male pleasure and national pride. Scholars remark the distinct sexualization of workingwomen in the public spectacle of Parisian life (as contrasted to London), as well as the transformative participation of women in that spectacle.[7] I join with revisionist

[3] Judith R. Walkowitz, *City of Dreadful Delights: Narratives of Sexual Danger in Late-Victorian London* (Chicago, 1992).

[4] On representations of the Victorian seamstress, see Lynn Alexander, *Women, Work, and Representations: Needlewomen in Victorian Art and Literature.* (Athens, OH, 2003); Christina Walkley, *The Ghost in the Mirror: The Victorian Seamstress* (London, 1981); Beth Harris, *Famine and Fashion: Needlewomen in the Nineteenth Century* (Burlington, VT, 2005); Catherine Gallagher, *The Industrial Reformation of English Fiction: Social Discourse and Narrative Form, 1832–1867* (Chicago, 1985); Lisa Tickner, *The Spectacle of Women: Imagery of the Suffrage Campaign, 1907–14* (Chicago, 1988).

[5] Beth Harris, "Introduction," in *Famine and Fashion*, 1–10, 3; Rohan McWilliam, "The melodramatic seamstress: interpreting a Victorian penny dreadful," in *Famine and Fashion*, 99–114.

[6] Beth Harris, "All that glitters is not gold: the show-shop and the Victorian seamstress," in *Famine and Fashion*, 115–39, 117.

[7] Elizabeth Wilson writes that, unlike London, Paris's "atmosphere of pleasure and excess, both sexual and political, did create an environment in which women were able to gain certain freedoms—even if the price of this was their over-sexualisation…" *The Sphinx in the City: Urban Life, the Control of Disorder, and Women* (Berkeley, 1991), 56. Sally Ledger sees workingwomen as novel urban participants who challenged the notion of urban space as masculine. She re-reads the fictive shopgirl "as a more sexually significant and imposing figure…who inhabits the metropolis in a more self-confident and disruptive way" than previously imagined. "Gissing, the shopgirl, and the new woman," *Women: A Cultural Review*, Vol. 6, No. 3 (1995), 263–74, 268. Parsons argues for the possibilities of urban identification beyond the male *flâneur*, noting both the convention of urban workingwomen as "publicly available tropes for masculine literary and theoretical discourse," and attention to these women's pleasures which accompanied a gendering of the nineteenth-century crowd as female. Deborah L. Parsons, *Streetwalking the Metropolis: Women, the City, and Modernity* (Oxford, 2000), 154.

feminist scholars who posit a primary role for the public woman in understanding fin-de-siècle modernity. Elizabeth Wilson, Deborah Parsons, and Sally Ledger all assert the possibility of a turn-of-the-century *flâneuse,* a female corollary to the deracinated, modernist male spectator of the *flâneur,* and have urged scholars of this period to understand the ambiguities and potential of a public sphere increasingly defined by the presence of workingwomen.[8] But few have moved the workingwoman to the center of discussions of modernity. By centering the working Parisienne in the cultural and social histories of this period, I reframe these histories, and reveal the way that the figure of the midinette inflected labor policy, reform efforts, and the daily lives of Paris's workingwomen. No longer (or not only) the martyred seamstress in a garret, the midinette, with her relentless cheer, was a forcible capitalist fantasy, her smile and her fashionably encased body a living testament to the aspirations and will to power of the solidarist Third Republic. Tracing her history and that of the women she represented allows us to unveil the Republic's own tortured relationship with transformed modes of production, modern labor activism, and the specter of national decline from the beginnings of movements for a "social Republic" in the 1880s through the war.[9]

Working Parisians have long been a prime site for scholars drawn to urban typology as a way of understanding social and economic change. Already in 1939, Walter Benjamin used the symbols and language of nineteenth-century Paris to explain the relation between urban culture and modernity; he wrote of "images in the collective consciousness in which the new is permeated with the old. These images are wish images; in them the collective seeks both to overcome and to transfigure the immaturity of the social product and the inadequacies in the social organization of production."[10] The grisette and midinette were just such images. Louis Chevalier writes of the myth of the Parisienne as "the most ancient, the most immutable, the most sacred" of Paris's myths, taking a more substantial place in the city's history than "monuments, more than the great events, more than Notre-Dame or the French Revolution."[11] In his study of early twentieth-century Parisian popular culture, Adrian Rifkin similarly refers to "Parisianism...as the

---

[8] Griselda Pollock and Janet Wolf see little room for a female *flâneuse.* Wolff called for investigation of "the very different nature of the experience of those women who *did* appear in the public arena." Janet Wolff, "The invisible flâneuse: women and the literature of modernity," *Theory, Culture & Society,* Vol. 2, No. 37 (1985), 37–46. Griselda Pollock, *Vision and Difference: Femininity, Feminism and the Histories of Art* (New York, 1988). Arguing on behalf of the possibility of a fin-de-siècle *flâneuse,* see Wilson's *The Sphinx in the City,* Parsons' *Streetwalking the Metropolis,* and Walkowitz's *City of Dreadful Delights.* Rita Felski's *The Gender of Modernity* (Cambridge, 1995). See also Ruth Iskin, "The flâneuse in French fin-de-siècle posters: advertising images of modern women in Paris," in *The Invisible Flâneuse?: Gender, Public Space and Visual Culture in Nineteenth Century Paris,* ed. Aruna D'Souza and Tom McDonough (Manchester, 2008).

[9] Charles Sowerwine, *France since 1870* (New York, 2001).

[10] Walter Benjamin, "Paris, the capital of the nineteenth century," in *The Arcades Project,* trans. Howard Eiland and Kevin McLaughlin (Cambridge, 1999), 4.

[11] Louis Chevalier, *Les Parisiens* (Paris, 1967) 12.

supreme category of the national" in France.[12] In some ways, the enticing nature of the midinette type has made her so familiar to scholars of nineteenth- and twentieth-century France as to become hidden in plain sight. As ethnographer Anne Monjaret puts it, the midinette is "at once present and absent...Profusion killed the object, or at least veiled it from the eyes of our contemporaries to the point of forgetting it."[13] Rifkin insists that scholars "release some of the repressed materials of the mythologies of Paris, to free them from those conventions that constrict them in the cruel objectivity of glamour."[14] The midinette type could, in the guise of fanciful nostalgia, be employed as a means of accommodation to a novel system of economic and social relations. Here Charles Rearick's elucidation of the "Parisian imaginary" is useful, a concept referencing centuries of "awestruck description of Paris...crystallized as collective memories" that "[structure] how Paris has been viewed, described, and admired."[15] Rearick asks scholars to "pay close attention to the distinctive mundane particulars" of the Parisian picturesque— among them, the "pretty midinette"—which made up a national consumer culture which "sent Parisian folklore" out to the suburbs and provinces.[16]

But the pretty midinette was not simply one in a cavalcade of picturesque Parisian stock characters; she was a central figure in France's story about itself as the twentieth century began. My book apprehends "distinctive mundane particulars" related to the midinette like song, joyfulness, taste, sexual availability, under-eating, and fashion consumption, as elements of a powerful type from the turn of the century through the end of the Great War. I interrogate the way this image worked on the ground, in the street, in the workshop, in the corner café, on the floor of the Bourse du Travail, or in the editor's room of the Parisian dailies both to magnify and muffle workingwomen's claims for better working and living conditions and an expanded civic voice. To so insistently imagine Parisian workers as cheerful young fashionplates at a time which saw, in the words of Gérard Noiriel, "more intense working-class militancy than any other period in recent French history," seems particularly perverse.[17] These cultural fantasies had a political import underanalyzed by scholars of this period in French history, some of whom even replicate the wistful tone of their primary sources when examining the Parisian picturesque. In this way, I offer a new kind of labor history, one that attempts to bridge, in Lenard Berlanstein's words, the "lasting division" between

---

[12] Adrian Rifkin, *Street Noises: Parisian Pleasure, 1900–1940* (New York, 1993) 70.

[13] Anne Monjaret, Séverine Dessajan, Francine Fourmaux, Michela Niccolai, and Mélanie Roustan, *Le Paris des "midinettes": Mise en culture de figures féminines, XIX–XXIème siècles, ethnologie des traces et mémoires d'ouvrières parisiennes* (Paris, 2008).

[14] Rifkin, *Street Noises*, 3.

[15] Charles Rearick, *Paris Dreams, Paris Memories: The City and its Mystique* (Stanford, 2011), 3.

[16] Ibid. 224, 95.

[17] Gérard Noiriel, *Workers in French Society in the 19th and 20th Centuries* (New York, 1990), 73. Noiriel refers here to 1890–1910.

historians "who examine discourse and those who examine experience."[18] On one side, cultural historians have interrogated the Parisian picturesque as a modernist invention framed by bourgeois anxieties about urbanism and industrialization; on the other, labor historians have produced voluminous research on working-class political movements and social reform. My study joins these planes of research, and puts them in raucous dialogue with one another: a letter by a 19-year-old seamstress and a speech by a government minister; a frothy Parisian guide by a bon vivant and the minutes of a union meeting; a bawdy café-concert song and a policy brief on garment working conditions.

The nineteenth century saw the discovery of the workingwoman as a social problem, "a principal character in the historical tableau," as European states moved from a pre-industrial economy in which female labor was a given, to an industrial economy in which it was endlessly debated and surveilled.[19] On the eve of the First World War, the rate of women's participation in paid labor in France was one of the highest in the world at 35–40 per cent; Jean-Louis Robert writes that "it may not be too fanciful to suggest that France was *the* land of women workers at the beginning of the twentieth century."[20] Scrutiny of the wage-earning woman intensified just as (and because) the skilled male artisan found his economic and social status diminished, and as the homebound middle-class woman became the ascendant feminine ideal. The female garment worker was an especially convenient figure for tracking the growing pains of late nineteenth- and early twentieth-century industrialization, labor organization, and the place of women in those processes.[21] The midinette took her place on the French cultural stage in the context of a dramatic shift in manufacturing in which the dominance of a highly skilled artisan class was ceded to a new kind of urban worker: specialized and less expert "semi-craftspeople" or "petites mains" (as they were called in Paris' couture workshops).[22] Women in the needle trades were some of the first to feel the pinch of these broader transformations, and were on the frontline of

---

[18] Lenard Berlanstein, "Introduction," in *Rethinking Labor History*, ed. Berlanstein (Urbana, 1993), 1–14, 12.

[19] Deborah Valenze, *The First Industrial Woman* (New York, 1995), 85.

[20] Jean-Louis Robert, "Women and work in France during the First World War," in *The Upheaval of War: Family, Work, and Welfare in Europe, 1914–1918*, ed. Richard Wall and Jay Winter (Cambridge, 1988), 253.

[21] Deborah Cherry marks nineteenth-century seamstresses as Foucaultian figures, "sites of the crossings of multiple discourses on class, gender, and sexuality . . ." "Surveying seamstresses," *Feminist Arts News*, Vol. 9 (1983), 27–9.

[22] Berlanstein writes of the emergence of "the specialized laborer who lacked the technical expertise and multiple proficiencies of the full artisan" and who represented the majority of the Parisian workforce by the turn of the century. *The Working People of Paris, 1871–1914* (Baltimore, 1984), 15. Noiriel similarly refers to "a fundamental crisis of identity at the heart of the working class" in this period, with "the substitution of machinery and scientific knowledge for traditional forms of expertise was very deeply felt by trained workers." Noiriel, *Workers in French Society*, 84. See also Roger Magraw, *A History of the French Working Class*, Vol. II: *Workers and the Bourgeois Republic* (Oxford, 1992).

France's struggle with increasingly competitive international markets for luxury fashion goods.[23]

Parisian industry had, on average, smaller workshops than in the suburbs,[24] and was home to prominent trades which depended upon skilled handiwork: *haute couture*, artificial flowers, feathers, hats, corsets, leather and fur goods. The term *midinette*, however, was also applied to poorly paid pieceworkers (often working at home with tasks provided by contractors), laundresses, errand girls, saleswomen, and less skilled *confection* workers creating ready-to-wear clothing by machine. Even seamstresses in luxury couture firms worked twelve-hour days in the first decade of the twentieth century; in moments of press requiring extended nightwork, often around society events like the Grand Prix, work could stretch to seventeen to thirty hours straight.[25] Garment workers were paid by the day or by the piece, and thus suffered months of seasonal unemployment during the *morte-saisons* when fashion orders slackened (several months mid-winter and several months in early summer). During the six months of annual regular work, better-paid *haute couture* workers could make 5–6 francs per day at the turn of the century; most made around 3 francs a day.[26] Homeworkers paid by the piece often made even less.[27]

The belle époque Parisian workforce had one of the largest populations of immigrant workers in the country.[28] Russian Jews and other Eastern European immigrants were an increasingly large part of the Parisian garment workforce by 1901, and this must be understood as a significant context for the nostalgic promotion of the thoroughly "French" and "Parisian" midinette in these decades.[29] As Tyler Stovall has demonstrated, local Parisian labor history in this period is a post-colonial and raced history, even if actual discussion of race was "muted."[30] Thus, the (white, French, female) garment worker in Paris served as a perfect stand-in for questions about massive transformations in and traditional understandings of the French economy.

Garment workers also stood, physically, in the middle of post-Haussmann Paris, as visible participants in and producers of the city's globally-renowned consumer pleasures. They tended to live in the outer arrondissements of the capital in

[23] Berlanstein, *The Working People of Paris*, 84–90.
[24] Tyler Stovall, *Paris and the Spirit of 1919: Consumer Struggles, Transnationalism and Revolution* (New York, 2012), 89.
[25] Caroline Milhaud, *L'Ouvrière en France* (Paris, 1907), 18–19.
[26] Pierre Du Maroussem, *La Petite Industrie: salaires et durées du travail, Tome II: Le Vêtement à Paris* (Paris, 1896) 660–3.
[27] Milhaud, *L'Ouvrière*, 35.   [28] Stovall, *Paris and the Spirit of* 1919, 122.
[29] Nancy Green, *The Pletzl of Paris: Jewish Immigrant Workers in the Belle Epoque* (New York, 1986); James R. Lehning, *To Be a Citizen: The Political Culture of the Early French Third Republic* (Ithaca, 2001).
[30] Stovall, *Paris and the Spirit of* 1919, 18, 22. On the linkage of whiteness, French femininity, and national identity in Paris, see Robin Mitchell, "'Ourika mania': interrogating race, class, space, and place in early nineteenth-century France," *African and Black Diaspora*, 10, No. 1 (2017), 85–95.

the neighborhoods of Batignolles, Belleville, Charonne, Montmartre, and Ménilmontant, and worked in the city center where the garment industry was based: the Sentier, rue de la Paix, Opéra, Place Vendôme, and workshops within the major Parisian department stores like the Galeries Lafayette. As we shall see, the daily "rivers" of garment workers walking to work and lunching in the capital's luxury center became one of the quintessential sights of the belle époque Parisian landscape.[31] Much contemporary writing on changing working conditions tended to concentrate on the female garment worker,[32] with Parisian consumer culture widely imagined to rest on their labor and taste.

From the 1830s, working Parisiennes were eyed with a concern, skepticism, and disdain born of the anxieties attendant upon a shifting industrial landscape. Paris's seamstresses especially were imagined to be emblematic of the modern city as morally compromised and compromising.[33] From Parent-Duchâtelet's *De la Prostitution dans la ville de Paris* (1836) to Jules Simon's *L'Ouvrière* (1861), workingwomen (particularly those in the Parisian needle trades) were conjured in works of political economy, social scientific inquiries, and moralist reform tracts as a pressing threat to the urban moral order and its first victims, both the symptom and the disease of socio-economic change.[34] Social theorists and critics endlessly repeated the story of the fallen seamstress; indeed, it became, in the words of Joan Scott, "a folk tale or morality play with a predictable plot and outcome. The theme of the destruction of innocence by rape or death served as a stark physical analogue of capitalism's impact."[35] If, in Simon's aphoristic formulation, "the woman, once a worker, is no longer a woman,"[36] the female garment laborer was uniquely positioned to ease fear of gender dissolution given her connection to the fashion industry.[37] Needle workers, Simon warned however, were also susceptible to the call of the Parisian goods they helped make: "From the first step she takes in the street, all the luxury of the world enters her eyes at once…" Simon also described the pleasure of reading garment workshop exposés: "Nothing is more

[31] Susan Hiner, quoting Arsène Alexandre, *Les Reines de l'aiguille*, on the geography of garment work. "Picturing the catherinette: reinventing tradition for the postcard age," in *French Cultural Studies for the Twenty-First Century*, ed. Masha Belenky, Kathryn Kleppinger, and Anne O'Neil-Henry (Newark, 2017), 132.

[32] Berlanstein, *The Working People of Paris*, 202.

[33] Judith DeGroat, "Women in the Paris manufacturing trades at the end of the long eighteenth century," in *Women and Work in Eighteenth-Century France*, ed. Nina Kushner and Daryl Hafter (Baton Rouge, 2015), 202–22.

[34] See Joan Wallach Scott, *Gender and the Politics of History* (New York, 1988).

[35] Scott, *Gender and the Politics of History*, 109.

[36] Jules Simon, *L'Ouvrière* (Paris, 1861), p. vi.

[37] As a wage worker whose associations with fashion meant she remained pleasingly femininity, the seamstress "allowed for a reassuring image of the separatedness and difference of masculinity and femininity at a time when those categories seemed to be collapsing." Beth Harris "Introduction," in *Famine and Fashion*, 1–10, 5.

appealing than reading some of these works... [possessing] both the charm of a voyage of discovery and the weight of a morality book."[38]

Labor reformers at the turn of the century filtered anxieties about industrial capitalism and the perceived fraying of the social fabric through their overdetermined and eroticized rhetoric around the midinette. A number of French historians have excavated the material challenges of Parisian workingwomen's lives and dominant discourses about women's labor by way of philanthropic, judicial, and administrative archives.[39] Several studies of Anglo-American workingwomen's philanthropy in this same period have tried to understand the psycho-sexual and social politics of reform work.[40] My research makes plain that French reformers, philanthropists, labor activists, and feminists doggedly exposed the backbreaking conditions of the sweated garment trades, all the while eroticizing, romanticizing, and infantilizing the women they had committed to save. Across the pages of government inquiries, meeting minutes, speeches, and policy briefs, reformers muted workingwomen's own efforts to articulate labor grievances by resorting to pop cultural notions of midinette frivolity.

Perhaps in part due to the persistence of this image to this day, the midinette has played merely a supporting role in scholarly studies of this period.[41] Only recently have scholars considered the midinette as a historical phenomenon in her own right.[42] Ethnographers Anne Monjaret and Michela Niccolai trace the literary *physiologie* of the midinette, "a figure on the border between the worlds of the worker and the bourgeois, inseparable from Paris" and "a hybrid character

---

[38] Simon, *L'Ouvrière*, 275, 16–17.

[39] Judith Coffin, *The Politics of Women's Work: The Paris Garment Trades, 1750–1915* (Princeton, 1996); Rachel G. Fuchs, *Poor & Pregnant in Paris: Strategies for Survival in the Nineteenth Century* (New Brunswick, 1992); James McMillan, *France and Women, 1789–1914: Gender, Society and Politics* (New York, 1999); Christine Adams, *Poverty, Charity, and Motherhood: Maternal Societies in Nineteenth-Century France* (Urbana, 2010); Lorraine Coons, *Women Home Workers in the Parisian Garment Industry, 1860–1915* (New York, 1987); Eliza Ferguson, *Gender and Justice: Violence, Intimacy, and Community in Fin-de-siècle Paris* (Baltimore, 2010).

[40] Seth Koven, *Slumming: Sexual and Social Politics in Victorian London* (Princeton, 2004); Shannon Jackson, *Lines of Activity: Performance, Historiography, Hull-House Domesticity* (Ann Arbor, 2000).

[41] Well into the 1990s, women's ready-to-wear was the second-largest Parisian employer, yet there has been relatively little historical assessment of Parisian fashion as an industry. Nancy Green, *Ready-to-Wear and Ready-to-Work: A Century of Industry and Immigrants in Paris and New York* (Durham, 1997), 3.

[42] Of particular value is Anne Monjaret's authoritative compilation of midinette terminology, types, and locales: Monjaret et al., *Le Paris des "midinettes."* See also Anaïs Albert, "Les midinettes parisiennes à la Belle Époque: bon goût ou mauvais genre?," *Histoire, Économie, et Société* (September 2013), 61–74; Monjaret and Michela Niccolai, "La Midinette en chansons: représentations masculines d'un idéal féminin populaire (1830–1939)," in *Représentations: Le genre à l'œuvre, Tome 3*, ed. Melody Jan-Ré (Paris, 2012; Claude Didry, "Les Midinettes, avant-garde oubliée du prolétariat," *L'Homme et la Société*, nos. 189–90 (July–December 2013). On labor activism and midinettes, see Patricia Tilburg, "Mimi Pinson goes to war," *Gender & History*, Vol. 23, No. 1 (April 2011), 92–110; Maude Bass-Krueger, "From the '*union parfaite*' to the '*union brisée*': the French couture industry and the *midinettes* during the Great War," *Costume*, Vol. 47, No. 1 (2013), 28–44.

borrowing her features from older ones, inscribing herself in a historic continuity across time."[43] For sociologist Claude Didry, the midinettes of this period are the "forgotten avant-garde of the proletariat," crucial by way of their activism to the structuring of modern labor relations in France, despite decades of dismissal as a frivolous character from the "masculine imaginary."[44] In line with these studies, I propose the midinette as a fundamental type in the early twentieth-century Parisian imaginary, and interrogate the symbolic work performed by this type in French popular culture.

My study is embedded within a growing historiography around the New Woman, girlhood, and the category of singleness.[45] The midinette was a version of the belle époque New Woman that, far from an unsexed virago bent on castrating political independence, was attractively modern and liberated, and yet also sexually and socially submissive. The Third Republic was, after all, in the words of Charles Sowerwine, not only the "longest" Republic in French history, but also the "most masculine"; "the political exclusion of women was so profoundly integrated into republican (fraternalist) language and thought, it was practically invisible."[46] As David Pomfret argues, the working-class Muse of turn-of-the-century France was "positioned somewhere between the barricades, the boutique, and the boudoir" and contained the "iconic power of the young female body, its exploitation for political and commercial ends, and the opportunities for individual empowerment that lay therein."[47] By way of the ephemera of popular Parisian entertainment, the midinette, argues Anaïs Albert, "enter[ed] into the pantheon of the fin-de-siècle erotic imaginary."[48] As an unattached woman who was relatively independent,

[43] Monjaret and Niccolai, "Elle trotte, danse et chante, la midinette! Univers sonore des couturières parisiennes dans les chansons (XIXe–XXe siècles)," L'Homme 215–16 (2015), 47; Monjaret and Niccolai, "La Midinette en chansons," 101.

[44] Didry, "Les Midinettes," 64.

[45] Andrea Mansker, Sex, Honor and Citizenship in Early Third Republic France (New York, 2011). On the French middle-class New Woman, see Mary Louise Roberts, Disruptive Acts: The New Woman in fin-de-siècle France (Chicago, 2002); Rachel Mesch, Having It All in the Belle Epoque: How French Women's Magazines Invented the Modern Woman (Redwood City, 2013). Beyond France, see Catherine L. Dollard, The Surplus Woman: Unmarried in Imperial Germany, 1871–1918 (New York, 2009); Rita Kranidis, The Victorian Spinster and Colonial Emigration: Contested Subjects (New York, 1999); Tani E. Barlow et al., "The modern girl around the world: a research agenda and preliminary findings," Gender & History, Vol. 17, No. 2 (August 2005), 245–94.

[46] Charles Sowerwine, "La Politique, 'cet élément dans lequel j'aurais voulu vivre': l'exclusion des femmes est-elle inhérente au républicanisme de la Troisième République?," Clio: Histoire, Femmes, et Sociétés 24 (2006), 171–94, 173, 180. See also Karen Offen, "Exploring the sexual politics of French republican nationalism," in Nationhood and Nationalism in France, ed. Robert Tombs (London, 1991), 195–209.

[47] David M. Pomfret, "'A muse for the masses': gender, age, and nation in France, fin de siècle," American Historical Review 109, No. 5 (December 2004), 1439–74, 1473–4. See also Helen Harden Chenut, The Fabric of Gender: Working-Class Culture in Third Republic France (University Park, 2005). Kathy Peiss argues that many American workingwomen at the turn of the century "affirmed a heterosocial culture that incorporated some aspects of the 'New Woman' without subverting the institutions upholding male power and control." Cheap Amusements: Working Woman and Leisure in Turn of the Century New York (Philadelphia, 1986), 158.

[48] Albert, "Les Midinettes parisiennes," 67.

but who also could be sexually and economically dominated, the midinette evoked the feminine submission and Parisian charm of yesteryear, even as she embodied modern urban consumer culture. While midinette literature presented the seduction of workingwomen as nearly effortless urban delight, such representations tempered anxieties about the proletarianization of labor on one hand and the challenge of the *femme nouvelle* on the other.

Yet, even as her body was imagined again and again as a consumable piece of the urban pleasure landscape, the midinette was also armed with a nationally-significant tastefulness that endowed her, in principle, with individuality and even genius. Since at least the eighteenth century, argues Jennifer Jones, French men and women of all social levels had seen a nationalistic "stake...in French taste... and in the elevation of Paris as the commercial and artistic capital of Europe."[49] Historians have traced the exceptionally close connections made between women, taste, and national identity in nineteenth-century France.[50] Lisa Tiersten demonstrates that worries about the debasing nature of the capitalist market and concerns about philistine bourgeois tastelessness by the 1870s led to increased attention to and promotion of the bourgeois Parisienne's chic as a national duty.[51] According to Debora Silverman, fin-de-siècle proponents of French decorative arts reform hoped to diffuse the threat of the New Woman by offering bourgeois women in particular a "special role and responsibility" in national regeneration through the patronage and production of tasteful interior décor.[52] At Paris's 1900 Exposition Universelle, the bourgeois Parisienne took on monumental proportions, literally, as a queenly statue topping the entry gates and clad in a gown by couture designer Jeanne Paquin.[53] Thus, at the turn of the century, the burden of safeguarding national style seemed to rest squarely on the shoulders of the bourgeois Frenchwoman (if clad in a dress crafted by Parisian midinettes). Such discourse around French taste largely excluded working-class women, whose class, writes Leora Auslander, was thought to "[produce] an absence where taste ought to have been."[54] While republican taste theorists created an "imagined community" of democratized taste in which all Frenchwomen

[49] Jennifer Jones, *Sexing La Mode: Gender, Fashion and Commercial Culture in Old Regime France* (New York, 2004), 115. Katherine Hamerton explores the Enlightenment-era eroticization of feminine taste. "A feminist voice in the Enlightenment salon: Madame de Lambert on taste, sensibility, and the feminine mind," *Modern Intellectual History*, 7, No. 2 (2010), 209–38.

[50] See Debora Silverman, *Art Nouveau in Fin-de-Siècle France* (Los Angeles, 1989); Leora Auslander, *Taste and Power: Furnishing Modern France* (Los Angeles, 1996); Lisa Tiersten, *Marianne in the Market: Envisioning Consumer Society in Fin-de-Siècle France* (Los Angeles, 2001); Whitney Walton, *France at the Crystal Palace: Bourgeois Taste and Artisan Manufacture in the Nineteenth Century* (Los Angeles, 1992).

[51] Tiersten, *Marianne in the Market*, 219.

[52] Silverman, *Art Nouveau*, 186. See also Ruth Iskin, *Modern Women and Parisian Consumer Culture in Impressionist Painting* (Cambridge, 2007).

[53] See Silverman's discussion of 1900's *Parisienne* in *Art Nouveau*; Iskin, *Modern Woman*, 215–19.

[54] Leora Auslander, "Perceptions of beauty and the problem of consciousness: Parisian furniture makers," in *Rethinking Labor History*, 158.

could in principle take part, this ideal "aesthetic democracy" was, according to Tiersten, "not true in any meaningful sense for working-class women," who "surely understood taste to be a form of cultural capital based on social and economic capital."[55]

But was this the case? My research suggests that by the early twentieth century, the working-class Parisienne had assumed a central symbolic role as guardian of French taste—a role overlooked in most studies of the belle époque. This working Parisienne was valued as a cultural ideal not because she rose above her class limitations, but rather because she joined decorousness with diligent labor, bourgeois-style consumption with republican virtue, and political deference with erotic submission. For the (predominantly male) journalists, politicians, and philanthropists who commented on the midinette, these women thus operated as an image of Paris and of the nation that was at once more fortifying than the bourgeois Angel in the House, and less threatening or politicized than the female allegory of the French Republic, Marianne (or worse still, the Paris Commune's militant fire-starter, the *pétroleuse*, or the unsexed bluestocking).[56]

Workingwomen were not merely included alongside bourgeois women in paeans to French taste at the turn of the century, but occasionally were elevated above bourgeois feminine taste. While middle-class women could cultivate an aesthetic disinterestedness that was symbolically valuable in the fight against crass commercialism, garment workers, because of their restricted budgets, per-ceived political fatalism, and luxury labor, could be easily portrayed as creatures of effortless inborn taste, disconnected from social status or worse, social climbing. Far from occasional or peripheral figures in this aesthetic program, Parisian garment workers were presented at times as an antidote to bourgeois feminine consumption. What is more, many couture workers understood themselves as key participants in the "imagined community" of Parisian chic. This book, by putting the fantasy midinette of this period into dialogue with actual garment laborers through workingwomen's magazines, letters, and memoirs, sheds new light on the tremendous cultural power assigned to popular feminine taste in belle époque Paris.

Workingwomen's tastefulness was also fundamental to social scientific inquiries and government interventions in the garment trades at the turn of the century. French couture tradesmen, manufacturers, and government officials held up the Parisian worker as an irreplaceable source of French creativity, in need of protec-tion from foreign competitors and yet also the nation's greatest hope for besting those competitors. They also trumpeted the national import of Parisian women's

---

[55] Tiersten, *Marianne in the Market*, 219.

[56] See Silverman, "The 'New Woman,' feminism, and the decorative arts in fin-de-siècle France," in *Eroticism and the Body Politic*, ed. Lynn Hunt (Baltimore, 1991); Gay L. Gullickson, *Unruly Women of Paris: Images of the Commune* (Ithaca, 1996); Hollis Clayson, *Paris in Despair: Art and Everyday Life under Siege (1870–1871)* (Chicago, 2002).

taste to silence pressing demands on the part of their workers—for humane working conditions or against health hazards in the couture industry. In these debates, the Parisian garment worker was repeatedly promoted as a nostalgic throwback to pre-industrial handicraft and as a less troubling version of the New Woman and the unionized laborer.

When possible, I have amplified the voices of the Parisian garment workers themselves. As Mary Jo Maynes notes in her study of European working-class autobiographies in the long nineteenth century, there is a "telling" dearth of French workingwomen's autobiographies from the high era of syndicalism, in contrast to the relative plenty of such documents in the German workers' movement. Maynes surmises that "the scarcity of autobiographies suggests a lack of institutional support for certain—specifically female—patterns of becoming working class."[57] Midinette pop culture offers access to one pattern of "becoming working class" for Parisian garment workers at the turn of the twentieth century. As Monjaret and Niccolai note, theses tropes were not solely entertainment for the middle-class men who produced midinette songs, novels, poems, and images.[58] Working Parisiennes were also consumers of and performers of these cultural products; they lived, worked, and developed as subjects in a cultural and physical landscape that pronounced them attractive but promiscuous, tasteful but careless, overworked but uncomplaining. Kathy Peiss has helpfully called for "a doubled vision" when studying workingwomen's culture, one which apprehends the ways in which "women's embrace of style, fashion, romance, and mixed-sex fun could be a source of autonomy and pleasure as well as a cause of their continuing oppression."[59]

To this end, I scrutinize the gendered and romanticized cultural screens through which Parisian workingwomen were understood while also excavating their lived experience. Many garment workers lamented the contrivance of the gay midinette, foregrounded their own experience and demands, and pushed against dominant understandings of their labor, their political commitments, and their sexuality throughout this period. Some working Parisiennes referenced the midinette to criticize the moral failings or frivolity of their fellow workers and affirm their own integrity; others critiqued the type itself as reductive. Some women recounted the daily reality of the working and living conditions idealized in midinette pop culture, with harrowing descriptions of street harassment, sexual assault, unemployment, and hunger. Others expressed pride in couture work and

---

[57] Mary Jo Maynes, *Taking the Hard Road: Life Course in French and German Workers' Autobiographies in the Era of Industrialization* (Chapel Hill, 1995), 194. Marilyn Boxer also refers to the lack of women's voices in such histories. "Protective legislation and home industry: the marginalization of women workers in late nineteenth and early twentieth-century France," *Journal of Social History*, 20, No. 1 (1 October 1986), 52. See also Nan Enstad, *Ladies of Labor, Girls of Adventure: Working Women, Popular Culture, and Labor Politics at the Turn of the Twentieth Century* (New York, 1999).

[58] Monjaret and Niccolai, "Elle trotte, danse et chante, la midinette!," 73.

[59] Peiss, *Cheap Amusements*, 6, 8.

identification with the tastefulness assigned to them in pop culture. In some cases, garment workers even used the popular understanding of "midinettisme"[60] to their advantage, as a means of accessing free classes, as justification for labor demands, as a defense of their craft skill, or even as strike tactic.

Chapter 1 traces the genealogy of the early nineteenth-century *grisette* as a Romantic literary type from her inception in the 1820s to her spectacular reappearance on the cultural scene as a figure of fanciful nostalgia at the turn of the century, a sign of romantic longing for a lost Paris. At the same time, the grisette's high-spirited granddaughter the midinette exploded as a pop culture staple, inseparable from the erotic and entertainment landscape of Paris in this period. This chapter traces the constituent parts of the midinette type, and understands her as a liminal figure at the border between old Paris and the new.

Chapters 2, 3, and 4 explore the interaction between the midinette ideal and efforts to regulate and reform garment work at the turn of the century. Concerned reformers from the government and the private sector built lunchrooms, founded a popular conservatory, and fought for better working conditions, all with the goal of protecting and fortifying the Parisian workingwoman. Yet such initiatives depended on an understanding of couture workers born of bourgeois male fantasy and nostalgia for pre-industrial social and gender relations. When the French cemented the bonds of the entente cordiale with Great Britain by way of the Franco-British Exhibition of 1908, they placed the Parisian garment worker front and center as an exemplar of national taste and luxury craft supremacy. When a persistent labor inspector attempted to signal the danger to artificial flowerworkers of the double-faced rose, the so-called *mauvais rouge*, she faced bureaucratic inertia fueled by rhetoric about the significance of the artificial flower industry to France's taste renown. With Gustave Charpentier's charitable association the Oeuvre de Mimi Pinson, the romantic idyll of the nineteenth-century student/artist and the cheerful seamstress was adapted into a wholesome project of social philanthropy aimed at raising up working-class women with free performing arts classes. Other reformers relied upon one of the constituent fantasies of midinette fiction, the seduction of the lunching (but adorably undereating) midinette, to drive the development of workingwomen's restaurants and improved facilities in garment workshops for food preparation.

Chapter 5 examines the waves of strikes in Parisian couture from 1901 through 1919. During these strikes, as thousands of couture workers took to the streets and won, over time, substantial victories for French labor, the image of the midinette, with all of her soothing eroticism and playfulness, intensified rather than diminished. The full power of this bourgeois fantasy was realized as couture strikers were framed by the press, the police, and their own male labor partisans as

---

[60] The term was used by Maurice d'Arcus in "Le Règne du midinettisme," *c.*February 1914. FC, No. 449: *Mimi-Pinson: Remise de l'épée d'Academicien à Gustave Charpentier.*

careless girls out for a lark. Yet the strikes also saw the articulation of a powerful counterimage, the militant midinette, a new brand of activist female garment worker, workingwomen who at once appropriated and defied popular perceptions of the midinette to win unprecedented labor reforms.

The book ends with a chapter dedicated to the fate of the midinette ideal in the cataclysm of World War I, when, among other national disasters, many garment workers were thrown out of work or saw their wages cut. At the same time, the midinette was embraced by the press, government agencies, and trench soldiers as a comforting and eroticized image of the homefront. The body of the wartime midinette was a charged link between the homefront and the trenches, and a physical manifestation of the supremacy of French culture. She was used by bourgeois philanthropists, social commentators, and even trench soldiers to assuage early anxieties about the homefront. While working Parisiennes were imagined as merrily resigned to their work, some pushed beyond the limits of this cultural role by initiating their own charitable campaign for soldiers on the front, and by taking advantage of free nursing programs to take up positions in military hospitals around France.

The belle époque midinette marked an important evolution of the image of the Parisian workingwoman from the fin de siècle through the end of the Great War. Forever drawn back into the Romantic frame of the nineteenth-century grisette, Parisian garment workers were employed to render social change more palatable by reducing them to objects of bourgeois delectation. But these women and their defenders sometimes were able to leverage this nostalgia into cultural capital. By the time war came, Mimi Pinson was more than a colorful urban type—she had become a contested body upon which French men and women across the political spectrum attempted to project concerns about women's emancipation, about national taste, about the labor movement, about industrial competitiveness, about labor reform, and about the nation itself.

1

From Grisette to Midinette

The Garment Worker in French Popular Culture

Around 5 o'clock in the evening on 14 December 1884, 25-year-old milliner Lucie Nicard approached her estranged lover, law student Eugène Bonichon, on the rue Gay-Lussac in Paris and shot him in the neck. Seized by Bonichon's companions immediately, Nicard cried: "You disarmed me too soon! Otherwise, I would have put six bullets in his head."[1] In letters found on her person, Nicard avowed her intention to kill Bonichon and then herself. The couple had met a year before, sharing the same landing of a Parisian apartment building. In the breathless press coverage of Nicard's acquittal for attempted murder the following spring, journalists described the defendant as the last of the dying breed of the Parisian grisette, and compared her story to that of fictional grisettes from the Romantic era decades before. Bonichon's and Nicard's love letters were presented at the trial and published in press coverage, with the unaffected sentiment of Nicard's letters making "a great impression on the jury."[2] In these letters, we hear of Nicard's abandonment by a careless lover and her reliance on sweated garment work to feed and clothe her illegitimate daughter, a toddler who subsequently died of a throat infection while staying with her mother in Saint-Lazare prison.[3] Nicard told the judge of her loneliness and despair, and that she had intended to kill herself rather than be forced into prostitution after Bonichon's desertion.

Despite Nicard's bleak tale, trial observers largely were charmed by the hat-maker's passion, and by her story's evocation of memories of their own youthful indiscretions with garment workers in the Paris of yesteryear. Nicard's defense attorney pleaded for her acquittal on the grounds that her love was "sincere" and that her only crime was being born "forty years after Mimi Pinson."[4] Critic Édouard Hémel wrote that Nicard conjured "an entire world that disappeared some thirty years ago...a type vanished, dead, and, we thought, buried: the grisette."[5] Jules Claretie agreed that Nicard's story made him wistful for the fleeting romances of his youth. Back then, he recalled, rather than a bullet to the neck, all one had to

---

[1] "Bulletin judiciaire: une descendante de Mimi Pinson," *Journal des débats: politiques et littéraires*, 12 April 1885, p. 3.
[2] "Chronique judiciaire," *Le Radical*, 15 April 1884, p. 3.
[3] "Bulletin judiciaire: une descendante de Mimi Pinson," 3.   [4] Ibid. 3.
[5] Édouard Hémel, "Notes et souvenirs," *La Revue générale: littéraire, politique et artistique*, 15 April 1885, pp. 166–8.

Working Girls: Sex, Taste, and Reform in the Parisian Garment Trades, 1880–1919. Patricia Tilburg, Oxford University Press (2019). © Patricia Tilburg.
DOI: 10.1093/oso/9780198841173.001.0001

fear from sexual encounters with garment workers was "watching Mimi die in the hospital, which was sometimes a poetic riddance...Mimi was more agreeable in the old days, I admit...No more grisettes? That would really be too bad. They are necessary for one's youth to pass...There aren't any more of those poor girls that we loved in passing, that we abandoned running, that we spoke of laughing, and who died at the hospital behind white curtains or who suffocated in an isolated attic room."[6] Claretie waxed nostalgic for a youth spent shrugging off the deaths of his discarded lower-class lovers, women "who work a lot, who love well, who are loyal and who don't cost very much." Writer Alexandre Hepp was one of the few to castigate the rose-colored filter through which the public perceived Nicard's crime:

—It's perfect, declares the jury; it's ravishing, says the public. Why?

Because Mlle Nicard takes advantage of *Scènes de la Vie de Bohème*, because she attaches herself to Murger, because she evokes Mimi...I'm all for making a clean break from these deceptive remembrances.[7]

Regrettably for Hepp, this particular remembrance of the Romantic grisette only gained in potency as the new century dawned.[8]

I interrogate the revived usage of this early nineteenth-century literary type as a balm to disruptions in gender norms and in the labor market from the fin de siècle through the Great War. I situate my reading within a typology of nostalgia devised by Svetlana Boym. Boym classifies two types of nostalgia. One, restorative nostalgia, is government-directed and aimed at affirming invented national traditions; the other, reflective nostalgia, embraces the feeling of longing and makes a collective embrace of things seen to be slipping away. The grisette seems to have been employed in and to have activated both forms of nostalgia in the decades straddling 1900. If, per Boym, the modern city was "an ideal crossroads between longing and estrangement, memory and freedom, nostalgia and modernity," the grisette lived at this same intersection.[9]

This chapter begins with an examination of the early nineteenth-century grisette as a literary type, and traces her reappearance on the cultural scene as a figure of nostalgia at the turn of the nineteenth century as the foundation of a French "garment imaginaire," to use Nancy Green's term.[10] I then develop a physiognomy

---

[6] "La Vie à Paris," *Le Temps*, 17 April 1885.

[7] Alexandre Hepp, *Les Anges parisiens* (Paris, 1886), 222.

[8] Nicard's story was still used as shorthand for nostalgic romance in 1932. See Pierre-Barthélemy Gheusi, "À l'Opéra Comique," *Le Figaro*, 24 April 1932, p. 4. "On se rappelle la comédie d'Henry Bataille. Lolette, gentil modèle, sentimental grisette du temps de Lucie Nicard."

[9] Svetlana Boym, *The Future of Nostalgia* (New York, 2002), 76.

[10] Nancy L. Green, *Ready-to-Wear and Ready-to-Work: A Century of Industry and Immigrants in Paris and New York* (Durham, NC: Duke University Press, 1997).

of the grisette's belle époque descendant, the midinette—a modernized version of the type, and inheritor of both the grisette's cultural significance and her limitations. From pulp novels to cabaret songs to monuments, the Parisian garment worker found eroticized and socially useful shades of herself promoted around her city and nation in these years—shades which more often than not moved backward in time to the *grisette* of the 1830s and 1840s.

La Grisette

From the seventeenth century, the term *grisette* was used to refer to young working women (so called for the coarse grey material commonly making up their outer garments); the term also carried connotations of coquettishness, frivolity, and casual romance.[11] By the end of the eighteenth century, the grisette was further understood as a young woman who supported herself by wage labor (see Mercier's *Tableau de Paris*).[12] The 1820s witnessed the expansion of the occasional figure of the grisette into a familiar literary type, a giddy, emancipated working-class foil to the cosseted bourgeois girl.[13] Representative of this type were songs by Pierre-Jean de Béranger such as 'Les Infidélités de Lisette' (1813), and Restoration-era novels and plays such as Auguste Ricard's *La Grisette, roman des moeurs* (1826), Paul de Kock's *Mon Voisin Raymond* (1822), and Eugène Scribe's *Les Grisettes* (1823). Under the July Monarchy, in what Alain Lescart calls the "great age of *tableaux parisiens*," the grisette became a key figure in Romantic literary physiognomies that mapped the modern city for an ascendant bourgeoisie.[14] It was then that the term additionally began to denote a workingwoman in the garment trades linked romantically to Bohemian students and artists—as muse, painters' model, and/or cheerful mistress.[15]

---

[11] Alain Lescart, *Splendeurs et misères de la grisette: évolution d'une figure emblématique* (Paris, 2008), 19.

[12] Catherine Nesci, *Le Flâneur et les flâneuses: les femmes et la ville à l'époque romantique* (Grenoble, 2007), 283.

[13] Lescart, *Splendeurs*, 43, 47.

[14] Ibid. 43. See also Ruth Amossy, "Types ou stéréotypes? Les 'physiologies' et la littérature industrielle," *Romantisme* 19, No. 64 (1989); Anne O'Neil-Henry, Mastering the marketplace: popular literature in nineteenth-century France (Lincoln, 2017); Victoria Thompson, *The Virtuous Marketplace: Women and Men, Money and Politics in Paris* (Baltimore, 2000).

[15] On the Romantic-era grisette see Lescart's superb *Splendeurs*. See also Séverine Dessajan, "The Grisette," in Anne Monjaret et al., *Le Paris des "midinettes,"* 61–83; *Elle coud, elle court, la grisette!* [exposition catalogue], Maison de Balzac, 14 October 2011–15 January 2012, ed. Nathalie Preiss and Claire Scamaroni (Paris, 2011), Bibliothèque des Arts Décoratifs; Joëlle Guillais-Maury, "La grisette," in *Madame ou mademoiselle? Itinéraires de la solitude féminine XVIIIe–XXe siècle*, ed. Michelle Perrot (Paris, 1984), 233–52; Thompson, *The Virtuous Marketplace*, 36–51; Courtney Ann Sullivan, "Classification, containment, and the courtesan: the grisette, lorette, and demi-mondaine in nineteenth-century French fiction," PhD Dissertation (Austin, 2003); Elizabeth Erbeznik, "Workers and wives as legible types in Eugène Sue's *Les Mystères de Paris*," *Nineteenth-Century French Studies* 41, No. 1 (2012), 66–79. On workingwomen as models, see Marie Lathers, *Bodies of Art: French Literary Realism and the Artist's Model* (Lincoln, 2001).

This was a period in which urban female garment workers were increasingly associated with clandestine prostitution and low morality, and "the repository for anxieties generated by industrial capitalism."[16] Following the abolition of the guilds and the introduction of mechanization and other industrial innovations, the early decades of the nineteenth century saw the "emergence" of women's labor as "a social problem" in the "new regime of marketplace liberty" and "one of the crucial proving grounds for liberal political economy and its critics."[17] By 1848, nearly half of the women working in Paris labored in the clothing industry.[18] Judith Coffin argues that the clothing trades were a "particularly tumultuous" site for "battles" over the gendering of and modernization of French labor, with the advent of ready-made clothing and new modes of manufacture and selling.[19]

Catherine Nesci puts a point on the inseparability of the grisette type from bourgeois mastery of the new Paris, with "the woman as an object of desire through which knowledge of the city and fantasies of its control are constituted."[20] This expansive genre included the fiction of Musset, Janin, Balzac, Sand, Murger, Sue, and Dumas; plays by Mélesville, Désaugiers, Decourcelle, and Barbier. Louis Huart's *Physiologie de la grisette* (1841), with illustrations by Gavarni, became one of the more influential definitions of the grisette, setting the tone for later representations of the type.[21]

Arguably the most popular *grisette* of the Romantic era was the protagonist of Alfred de Musset's 1845 story "Mademoiselle Mimi Pinson. Profil d'une grisette."[22] Musset had first referenced the grisette in *Confessions d'un enfant du siècle* (1836) and more substantially in his novel *Frédéric et Bernerette* (1838), a romance between a Parisian law student and a *grisette*.[23] "Mimi Pinson" tells the story of a young seamstress who charms two medical students in the Latin Quarter when she pawns her only dress to feed a hungry friend and then artfully manufactures a shawl and dress out of curtains and a petticoat to attend mass. This story, and an accompanying song popularized by composer Frédéric Bérat, helped to define the grisette as a workingwoman of uncommon compassion and a degree of virtue (perhaps not chaste, but never mercenary). Sunny resignation to work, sentimental and erotic dalliance with bourgeois men, and preternatural fashion skill became the trio of characteristics that Mimi Pinson carried into the next century.

---

[16] Judith De Groat, "The public nature of women's work: definitions and debates during the revolution of 1848," *French Historical Studies* 20, No. 1 (Winter 1997), 41–2. See also Henriette Vanier, *La Mode et ses métiers: frivolités et luttes des classes, 1830–1870* (Paris, 1960).

[17] Judith G. Coffin, *The Politics of Women's Work: The Paris Garment Trades, 1750–1915* (Princeton: Princeton University Press, 1996), 46.

[18] Vanier, *La Mode*, 75.   [19] Coffin, *Politics*, 53–4.   [20] Nesci, *Le Flâneur*, 113.

[21] Louis Huart, *Physiologie de la grisette, vignettes de Gavarni* (Brussels, 1841).

[22] Alfred de Musset, "Mademoiselle Mimi Pinson. Profil d'une grisette," in *Diable à Paris*, Vol. 1 (Paris, 1845).

[23] Alfred de Musset, *Frédéric et Bernerette* (Paris, 1840). Originally published in 1838. On the grisette in Musset's oeuvre see Gilles Castagnès, *Les Femmes et l'esthéthique de la féminité dans l'oeuvre de Musset* (Bern, 2004), 95–101.

Often referred to as the "smile" or "laughter" of Paris, the grisette is habitually merry, despite her desperate economic plight. Musset's Bernerette is "a girl who only thinks of laughing," and has a "talent" for "being content with everything and having for all opinions only the desire to please others."[24] Bernerette and Mimi Pinson both captivate their male listeners by singing romantic tunes. This gaiety is understood throughout grisette fiction first and foremost as a boon to male observers. Frédéric is complimented on his choice of Bernerette as mistress after she enlivens a rainy Sunday excursion to the countryside : "I cannot tolerate a gloomy woman...one has to admit that gaiety is a great good...Your grisette found a way to transform an hour of ennui into a pleasure, and that alone gives me a better opinion of her than if she had written an epic poem."[25] Bernerette's value is her ability to please her bourgeois admirers, maintaining joy and insouciance in spite of poverty. This gaiety was associated across the genre with a feather-brained improvidence and made the grisette a creature of transitory pleasures. Huart describes the grisette as "Carefree and altruistic, this nice girl never thinks of the future; she will stay who she is."[26]

In spite of her professional identity, the Romantic grisette was rarely represented laboring—a considerable contrast to her later incarnation, the midinette. Henri Monnier's 1829 lithographs *Les Grisettes* depict only scenes of romantic entanglements between a bourgeois man and his grisette mistress.[27] Also typical of the genre was the 1834 song "Les Tribulations de Mlle Flore, couturière en robe," in which a mournful seamstress sings of her parade of unfaithful lovers: a painter, a drummer, a hussar, gendarmes, cooks, infantrymen. Flore never hints at her own work; we only know she is a seamstress because of the song's title.[28] The grisette, rather than actually working, was instead often pictured as a devotee of popular fiction, especially sentimental Parisian novels like those of Paul de Kock.[29]

The grisette was also imagined as a young woman of singular fashionability and taste. Already in the eighteenth century, she was seen to hold more cultural capital in the form of Parisian fashion sense than many noblewomen.[30] Jules Janin's entry on "La Grisette" for 1840's "moral encyclopedia" *Les Français peints par eux-mêmes* defined the grisette's taste as both a contrast to the idle luxury of bourgeois women and as a national heritage. The grisette

beautifies her poverty when other women can't even beautify their opulence... the grisettes of Paris perform as many wonders as armies. Their industrious hands ceaselessly and forever shape gauze, silk, velvet, linen...this innocent and

[24] Musset, *Frédéric et Bernerette*, 14, 68.   [25] Ibid. 54.   [26] Huart, *Physiologie*, 15.

[27] Henri Monnier, *Les Grisettes, dessinées d'après nature* (Paris, 1829).

[28] *Les Tribulations de Mlle Flore, couturière en robe* (Clermont, 1834). BNF YE-55472 (4435).

[29] See Huart, *Physiologie*, 53–4.

[30] Claire Haru Crowston, *Fabricating Women: The Seamstress of Old Regime France, 1675–1791* (Durham, NC, 2001), 11, 41, 49.

continual conquest at the point of a needle is a thousand times more durable than all of our conquests at the point of a sword...They reign as despots over European finery...And must this French taste be universal so that these girls, these children of the poor, who will die poor like their mothers, become the omnipotent representative of fashion in the entire universe?[31]

The grisette's labor is here posited as a sacral national duty, her dexterous hands and native taste weapons in the French cultural arsenal. Janin applauds this dichotomous state of affairs, in which impoverished girls toil not for their own advancement (they will, he assures us, die poor) but for French industry and renown. Caught between the misery of her labor and the opulence she creates by her skill, "the noble heroine, without grumbling, will hand over this finery to the one that pays for it, and she will console herself with her songs, her gaiety, and her youth [ses vingt ans]."[32] Thus, the grisette was a new breed of single, female, urban laborer, a woman who evinced a novel degree of independence and fashionability, lived for the pleasures of the new city, and yet never made demands for her own profit.

The grisette appears in French literature almost always as a romantic companion to bourgeois men. As early as the seventeenth century, La Fontaine mentioned the grisette as an easily won "treasure."[33] Late eighteenth-century writers and engravers linked the women of the Parisian needle trades with seduction.[34] Crowston argues that this reputation came out of the "distinctly female world" in which seamstresses moved: "as one of the culture's main creators of femininity and the female power of seduction, seamstresses were themselves seen as essentially sexualized beings possessed of a heightened femininity...Seamstresses knew perhaps too much about the female body, and its transition from gross nature to elegant culture, to be entirely honorable."[35]

The grisette's sexual availability went virtually unquestioned in Romantic-era fiction.[36] Ernest Desprez counseled young men in search of a grisette mistress that, "the virtuous grisette is the one that has only one lover." Most, he insisted, had at least three: a working-class ami de coeur, an older wealthy ami de raison, and a student or bohemian ami des dimanches.[37] When Musset's Frédéric spies Bernerette through a window, they begin a sexual relationship after only a brief

---

[31] Jules Janin, "La Grisette," in Les Français peints par eux-mêmes: encyclopédie morale du dix-neuvième siècle, Tome 1 (Paris, 1840), 10.

[32] Ibid. 11. Castagnès also notes this theme in Musset's grisettes (Les Femmes, 97–8).

[33] Jean de La Fontaine, Joconde ou l'infidelité des femmes, Nouvelles en vers tirée de Boccace et de l'Arioste (Paris, 1665). See Huart's quoting of this verse, Physiologie, 12.

[34] Crowston, Fabricating Women, 113, 143.   [35] Ibid. 143–4.

[36] Jerrold Seigel, Bohemian Paris: Culture, Politics, and the Boundaries of Bourgeois Life (Baltimore, 1986), 39–42.

[37] Ernest Desprez, "Les Grisettes de Paris," in Paris, ou Le Livre des cent et un, Tome 6 (Paris, 1832), 235, 215.

exchange. While the grisette could sometimes move from casual love affair to venal sexual relationships as courtesan, prostitute, or *lorette*, most representations insisted upon her good and loyal heart. Huart's oft-repeated line clarified that the grisette "gives herself always and sells herself never."[38] Given her sexual availability, the Romantic grisette could sometimes change station with relative ease, from chaste worker to kept woman to streetwalker, or to wife or shopkeeper. Nathalie Preiss and Claire Scamaroni write, "Always at the edge of herself like she is at the edge of her window, the grisette of the first half of the nineteenth century is something of a borderline personality, at once prisoner and fugitive."[39]

While grisettes could hail from any French town or city, they were most associated with Paris; Huart pronounced the Parisian grisette, "the QUEEN OF THE GRISETTES!"[40] The love affairs of grisette literature relied on a precise set of Parisian geographies: the promiscuous mixing of bourgeois men and young garment workers in the streets, parks, open-air balls, and apartment buildings of the Latin Quarter (and later, Montmartre). Marcel and Eugène meet Mimi Pinson because she is their neighbor; Frédéric meets Bernerette by glimpsing her in an apartment window facing his. The social promiscuity of the pre-Haussmann mixed class apartment building and the fact that many of these women lived independently was imagined to facilitate love affairs.

Merely a bawdy character in the eighteenth century, by the beginning of the nineteenth century, the grisette, while still primarily a figure of erotic charm, took on, in the words of Alain Lescart, "a new nationalist status." Under the Restoration, she became associated with social and political resistance to Bourbon pretentions, and was seen to triumph along with the values of 1789 and with her male bourgeois companions in the Revolution of 1830. Thus, the grisette came to be vaguely associated with republican values. In Musset's 1845 ballad, the eponymous heroine is referred to as having taken part in the so-called "Trois Glorieuses," three days of popular uprising in the Revolution of 1830: "Mimi does not have a common soul, | but her heart is republican. | She waged war during the Trois Glorieuses… | Happy is he who will pin his cocarde on Mimi Pinson's bonnet."[41] Sand's grisette Eugénie from *Horace* (1842) similarly exemplified the popular republican and Saint-Simonian values of the early 1830s.[42] Lescart places the grisette within the "the entire system of republican images," and explains the explosion of pop cultural interest in her around the July Monarchy as part and parcel of "a change in mentality regarding independent women and the

[38] Huart, *Physiologie*, 47.

[39] Nathalie Preiss and Claire Scamaroni "La Grisette au temps de Balzac (1815–1850)," in *Elle coud, elle court, la grisette!*, 12.

[40] Huart, *Physiologie*, 24.

[41] Musset, "Mademoiselle Mimi Pinson," 232. In July 1830, the repressive regime of King Charles X collapsed in the face of liberal opposition, leading to a new constitutional monarchy under Louis-Philippe.

[42] George Sand, *Horace* (Paris, 1842). See Nesci's discussion of *Horace*, *Le Flâneur*, 293–308.

institution of marriage," that is, with the swelling of the Parisian population in these decades by rural migrants and the increasing number of women, especially single women, living independently if precariously in the urban workforce of the *pétits métiers*.[43] According to Thompson, the grisette was employed by republican writers and journalists as a contrast to the increasingly "relentless pursuit of self-interest" seen to characterize the July Monarchy.[44] In this way, male republican writers used the grisette "to paint themselves as spokesmen for the people, without tainting themselves with the brush of radical revolution," and to appear to resist the hardening influence of the capitalist marketplace.[45]

While associated with republican values, the grisette was also, paradoxically, imagined as politically passive, and resigned to her punishing labor and poverty. In his 1840 entry on "La Grisette," Janin defined the ideal grisette as a "a charming little creature, content with little, who produces and works." Labor was crucial to this equation: "the grisette is like an ant...these slender, little beings, busy and poor..." He underscored the importance of the grisette's acceptance of her fate: "with so little, virtually nothing, she is much more than rich. She is gay, she is happy; she only asks along her way for a little benevolence, a little love." Janin followed with a line which would be repeated about the Parisian garment worker for decades to come: "She is satisfied with little; she is satisfied with nothing." ("Elle est contente de peu, elle est contente de rien.")[46]

This gay passivity also made the grisette an ideal figure as artist's model and muse. Janin praised the grisette's value to Bohemian creators, "Be mute and calm, let me wrap you up in art and poetry. You will be my idol for the day... Stay right there, Jenny, under my paintbrush, on my canvas, in my soul, under my enchanted regard; what metamorphoses you will undergo!...And Jenny comes, docile as I imagined, docile and supple, and ready for anything, for all the candor and poetry that art possesses."[47] A static figure of inspiration subordinated to the artist's vision, the grisette makes his art possible, but is an "idol" only "for the day."

By 1850, the grisette had become an object of melancholic nostalgic longing, harkening back to an earlier Paris, such as Deslys' *La Dernière Grisette* (1853), and Hugo's Fantine in *Les Misérables* (1862).[48] Yet even earlier grisette literature already lamented her disappearance.[49] Nesci suggests that this nostalgic turn was essential to the function of the grisette as type, representing "the passage into modernity: first as a new aesthetic, that of debris and ruins...then as an existential feeling, that of the loss of the city as a physical and spiritual home..."[50]

---

[43] Lescart, *Splendeurs*, 7, 45–6.
[44] Thompson, *The Virtuous Marketplace*, 47. See also Victoria Thompson, "Splendeurs et misères des journalistes: female imagery and the commercialization of journalism in July Monarchy France," *Proceedings of the Annual Meeting of the Western Society for French History*, 23 (1996), 361–8.
[45] Thompson, *The Virtuous Marketplace*, 48.   [46] Janin, "La Grisette," 10, 12.
[47] Ibid. 14.   [48] Lescart, *Splendeurs*, 44.
[49] Seigel, *Bohemian Paris*, 41–2.   [50] Nesci, *Le Flâneur*, 160.

In Huart's 1841 *Physiologie,* the typical grisette disappears by the age of 30: "the grisette is dead, long live the grisette!"[51] Huart bemoaned the increasing scarcity of adorable *trottins* (garment errand girls). These attractive teenage garment workers once had been "the joy of the Parisian flâneur, maybe the only one that remained to him since the coming of the omnibus, the policemen, and the gutters." For the bourgeois Parisian, the grisette's scopophilic and nostalgic charge was thus fixed early in her existence as a type, inextricable from the transformations of mid-nineteenth-century Paris.[52]

In one of his Paris sketches from 1878, German critic and adopted Parisian Max Nordau mourned the passing of the Latin Quarter of forty years before, "formerly a world by itself; a romantic island in the midst of an ocean of philistinism... if Paul de Kock and Henri Murger should leave their graves to-day, and return to this upper world, they would seek in vain their beloved 'Latin land' with its ever-trilling, light-hearted grisettes and its extravagant bohemians, full of genius."[53] The grisette looms large in Nordau's eulogy for 1830s and 1840s Bohemia, with a working-class mistress one of the first steps in bourgeois formation. Nordau imagines the meeting of the grisette and the student, who hears his future mistress singing a tune by Béranger from the window of her garret room. The student finds release from his university studies in her company; she finds respite from her daily labor. Here is a perfectly symbiotic relationship for early industrial capitalism: the young female worker and the ambitious young bourgeois, both temporarily freed from the responsibilities of family and marriage as they satisfy their ancillary roles in the new urban economy. For this relationship to be a salutary one for the young bourgeois, however, it was essential that his temporary sexual companion graciously recede once he entered a profession and married a woman of his class:

> [The grisette] lived only for the day, and thought no more of the future than a bright-winged butterfly sporting in the sunshine on a midsummer day...Three, perhaps four years, she jogged through life at the side of her friend; then the moment came when his studies were finished, and he must enter the ranks of the Philistines. She understood that they must part...Some suppressed tears, some sleepless nights, some sorrowful days—then all was past, and she looked for a new friend to whom she confided the whole undiminished capital of tenderness...[54]

If, as Nordau and so many other grisette connoisseurs insisted, it is indeed in the grisette's nature to "[live] only for the day," her middle-class lover is conveniently

[51] Huart, *Physiologie,* 115. Desprez situated the end of the grisette at age 30 too. "Les Grisettes de Paris," 216.
[52] Huart, *Physiologie,* 29.
[53] Max Nordau, "The Quartier Latin," in *Paris Sketches from the German of Max Nordau* (Chicago, 1895). Original title *Pariser Studien und Bilder* (Leipzig, 1878).
[54] Ibid. 83–4.

released from any social or emotional responsibility for her. Nordau's turn of phrase "the whole undiminished capital of tenderness" is telling; he figures the working-class woman as an inexhaustible supply of affection for young bourgeois men. Nostalgia for the grisette bolstered a vision of an urban economy in which labor (uncomplainingly) provided the productive capacities of bourgeois industry, *and* an endlessly renewable (and cost-effective) sexual and romantic outlet for bourgeois men in their formative years. The grisette as a type served as a kind of sexual doula for bourgeois masculinity, demanding little in return, and taking her powers as muse and delightful companion to her next "friend" once her lover graduated from this transitory stage and assumed his proper station.

Nordau makes plain that this profitable state of affairs (for bourgeois men) has been irreparably damaged by the social transformations of the later nineteenth century. Along with the "old lanes and the old houses...a whole labyrinth of little lanes and squares, replete with memories" obliterated by Haussmannization, the student and the grisette have been vitiated. The student is now stiff and affected, no longer fiercely independent and defiant of convention, and thus desires a woman with more flash than the simple working girl: "The species of the grisette of former times has, consequently, died out, and might sooner be found in a paleontological museum, beside the antediluvian mastodon, than in the modern 'quartier latin.'" She was replaced by a new mercenary brand of mistress, who "despises love and jeers at poetry; she sings no songs of Béranger and tends no flower pots; she looks down upon the working-girl with inexpressible disdain, and boasts of having no other occupation than ruining silly youths."[55] One of the Romantic grisette's most attractive traits was her ability to be at once a dutiful (and picturesque) cog in the social and sexual economy, an ever renewable font of affection and sexual outlet, and yet to remain somehow disinterested. The cocotte, by contrast, evacuates her affair of all sentiment and affection, laying bare the cash nexus of the connection. This endangered version of Parisian femininity was set against Nordau's perception of the modern bourgeois Parisienne, a repulsively artificial and calculating figure to whom men are unnaturally subordinated. Paris, Nordau laments, is now a "society governed by woman," and a woman who has completely abandoned her natural station as dutiful wife and mother: "while in other countries the emancipation of woman is one of the dreams of the social reformers, here in France the more intelligent class is sighing for the emancipation of men."[56]

André Chadourne also used the grisette as an emblem of a transformed Latin Quarter in 1884. He woefully informed his male readers that the grisettes of their university days were gone: "These adorable creatures represented youth, gaiety, and pure and sincere affection to you. Alas! They have vanished. A lot of writers have even claimed to have thrown the last shovelful of dirt on the grave of the last

---

[55] Ibid. 86–7.   [56] Ibid. 52.

Lisette swept away by the omnibus."[57] Especially in the quartiers of the new bourgeoisie, "the grisette has completely disappeared." Mimi Pinson has been replaced by pretty but tasteless "escapees from the workshop…a vulgar class of women" "who "are exhausted after only two days of work."[58] Chadourne casts blame on the "material transformation" of the city, with the demolition of old neighborhoods and buildings in favor of a new "false grandeur."[59] Thus, from her inception through the fin de siècle, the grisette as a fictional type developed out of concerns about the social and economic transformation of urban France—new patterns of labor, Haussmannization, the rise of the New Woman, and an increasingly immersive consumer economy.[60] As the new century dawned, and these changes intensified, so to did the rhetorical deployment of the grisette and of her belle époque granddaughter, the midinette.

Mimi Pinson Lives!

By the turn of the century, the grisette still regularly appeared throughout popular culture as a sign of heightened romantic longing for a lost Paris, a France of small-scale industry, sentiment, and elegance. She was frequently conflated with contemporary garment workers, tethering living belle époque workingwomen to a figure of literary wistfulness. Parisian garment workers in this period inhabited new post-Haussmann city spaces with novel freedom of movement, increased access to the consumer economy, and (for some) newfound political activism. At the same time, these women were repeatedly cast in the mold of a pleasing throwback, a woman at once thoroughly embedded in the modern Parisian landscape and yet, also, out of time, carrying within her the essence and soul of a lost or endangered France. The most popular grisette at the turn of the century was Musset's Mimi Pinson, who was featured in songs, poems, postcards, ballet, vaudeville shows, short stories, novels, films, and even a series of dolls ("a sort of avant-Barbie" according to Michela Niccolai).[61]

Musset's fictional heroine (and the nostalgic and static working-class femininity she exemplified) was built into the monumental landscape of Paris.[62] In 1906, a statue of Musset by Antonin Mercié was dedicated with great fanfare in front of the Théâtre Française (Figure 1.1).[63]

---

[57] André Chadourne, Le Quartier latin (Paris, 1884), 25.

[58] Ibid. 28, 30, 29.   [59] Ibid. 45, 47.

[60] On the nostalgia for "Old Paris" that comes with Haussmannization, see Harvey, Paris, Capital of Modernity, and Rearick, Paris Dreams, Paris Memories.

[61] Niccolai, La Dramaturgie de Gustave Charpentier, 307.

[62] On commemoration and "statuomania" from 1870 to 1914, see Neil McWilliam, "Conflicting manifestations: Parisian commemoration of Joan of Arc and Etienne Dolet in the early Third Republic," French Historical Studies 27, No. 2 (Spring 2004), 381–418; Rosemonde Sanson, "Fête de Jeanne d'Arc" en 1894: controverse et célébration," Revue d'histoire moderne et contemporaine 20, No. 3 (July–Sept. 1973), 444–63.

[63] This statue is currently in the Parc Monceau in Paris.

Figure 1.1. Antonin Mercié, statue of Alfred de Musset, 1906. Parc Monceau, Paris.

Though only a minor character from Musset's oeuvre, Mimi Pinson stands alongside the poet in the monument. In inaugurating the statue, novelist Marcel Prévost credited Musset's stories for creating a vital type: "thanks to them, a feminine sensibility of an era was glimpsed and forever fixed…Mimi Pinson is immortal."[64] The press was quick to observe that a real-life "Mimi Pinson," a Parisian artificial flowerworker, had posed for the sculptor. Director of the Théâtre Français Jules Claretie (who began this chapter wistfully recalling the death of his grisette mistresses) witnessed this workingwoman's affection for Musset during her modeling sessions: "it is well and truly Mimi Pinson in person. A pretty blond girl who Mercié discovered in Belleville…overwhelmed with emotion and very happy and proud to pose alongside the image of the poet who she loved like a posthumous lover."[65] Claretie recasts this real workingwoman as the embodiment of a fictional character from sixty years before, and transmutes

---

[64] "Discours de Marcel Prévost," in "Inauguration du monument d'Alfred de Musset," 22 March 1906, supplément au *Bulletin municipal officiel*, 1049–1055, 1052. In dossier *Monument d'Alfred de Musset*, BNF-R, 8-RF-31966.

[65] Jules Claretie, "La Vie à Paris: Alfred de Musset et sa statue," 24-2-1906. In dossier *Monument d'Alfred de Musset*, BNF-R, 8-RF-31966.

her admiration into a sexual relationship. After quoting lines from Musset, Claretie describes the flowerworker sitting for Mercié every evening after her workday, first placing flowers she had made at the foot of the statue. She was, muses Claretie, "Musset's last lover—and the most faithful."[66] Here, as in so many belle époque renderings, the workingwomen of Paris are principally lovers and muses for bourgeois men, and their labor a decorative accompaniment to those functions.

Around 1911, Mimi was honored with her own statue, "La grisette de 1830" by sculptor Jean-Bernard Descomps, erected in the working-class neighborhood around Canal St-Martin (Figure 1.2).[67] Commissioned by the municipal government in 1903[68] and alternately titled the Monument of Mimi Pinson, is a prime example of what Anne Monjaret calls the Third Republican "masculine imaginary"

Figure 1.2. "La Grisette de 1830," sculpture by Jean Descomps, *c.*1911. Canal St-Martin, Paris.

---

[66] Claretie, "La Vie à Paris: Alfred de Musset et sa statue."
[67] Thompson refers to the statue as "an appeal to a time when love, rather than materialism, ruled society…" *Virtuous Marketplace*, 51.
[68] Thompson, "Splendeurs et misères des journalists," 364.

of the working Parisienne.[69] This grisette smiles broadly, a profusion of roses spilling from her uplifted apron.[70] A beaming and nostalgic vision of the working Parisienne of eighty years before, Mimi's hair is arranged in pleasing period ringlets, her dress is embellished with Romantic-era puffed sleeves and a profusion of frills and ribbons, and an equally festooned wide-brimmed hat hangs from her arm. When the statue was inaugurated in 1912 with the boulevard Jules-Ferry, the ceremony was attended by the president of the municipal council, the Prefect of Police Lépine, and the mayors of the 11th and 12th arrondissements.[71] Miniot, a municipal councillor from the Folie-Méricourt neighborhood, explained the monument to the assembled dignitaries and locals, repeatedly identifying the nineteenth-century fictional grisette with contemporary working-women in the neighborhood. The statue would be "at the same time a souvenir of an already distant era, and a lasting symbol of our gracious, lively, and vivacious little workingwomen."[72] Descomps' Grisette, insists Miniot, with her "girlish grace, her impish charm, her delicate youth," was the "total personification of the Parisienne of yesteryear and of today."[73] He compares the working-class faubourg to a rushing river, with crowds of laborers hurrying to work and back home again day after day, always surrounded by "our kind little workingwomen, nimble, gay, and elegant, whose amiable chatter makes the journey go faster" and "lightens the weariness of the day." These young women's gaiety and prettiness are the bulwarks that quiet the "tumultuous river" of the workers' neighborhood. Miniot underscores the modern garment worker's admirable qualities: "Our pretty midinettes carry on the tradition of their older sister, the grisette of 1830, the grisette sung by Béranger, Paul de Kock and Musset, who wanted to celebrate her sensitive and tender soul, her immutable good humor, her cheerful insouciance and her profound selflessness." He imagined that each time one gazed upon the statue, "the graceful Parisienne of olden days will allow us...to even better appreciate the charm and goodness of today's Parisienne."[74] The statue served as a daily reminder to the neighborhood's workingwomen of the early nineteenth-century ideal of the female worker (cheerful, fashionable, and good). To accentuate the

---

[69] Anne Monjaret, "À l'ombre des jeunes filles en pierre. Des ouvrières dans les jardins parisiens," *Ethnologie française*, XLII, No. 3 (2012), 503–15.

[70] The Ville de Paris purchased another sculpture of beaming workingwomen in 1908, Julien Lorieux's *Sainte-Catherine. À l'Ouvrière Parisienne*, a marble statue of five smiling midinettes, linking arms. "Les Achats de la Ville de Paris aux salons," *La Chronique des arts et de la curiosité: supplément à la Gazette des beaux arts*, 18 July 1908, p. 264. The statue seems not to have found a home until its installation in the Square Montholon in 1923.

[71] "On a hier inauguré le Boulevard Jules-Ferry, la Statue de Mimi Pinson," *Le Radical*, 25 March 1912, p. 1.

[72] "Inauguration du boulevard Jules-Ferry et du monument de la Grisette de 1830," *Bulletin municipal officiel de la Ville de Paris*, 23 April 1912, 2137–2138, 2137.

[73] Ibid. 2137–8.   [74] Ibid. 2138.

national import of this reminder, the 128th infantry band played the Marseillaise as the statue was unveiled.[75]

Paris saw no dearth of songs acclaiming Mimi Pinson in this period; Musset's verses on Mimi were set to music regularly from the 1840s through the 1920s and her name graced waltzes in 1904, 1907, and 1914.[76] Hers was an image that proved popular beyond Paris. The theatrical schedule for the Kursaal music hall in Algiers from 1910 included a run of a film *Mimi Pinson* and a polka of the same name. In 1901, songwriter Edmond Teulet, who himself later authored two songs about Mimi Pinson, published an anthology of sentimental songs from the previous century. In his adulatory preface to the collection, Jules Claretie declared that romance was "deeply anchored in the French population. Every Gaul has a grisette spirit lying dormant in his heart." Indeed, Marianne, allegory of the Republic, should wear "the bonnet of Bernerette and Mimi Pinson," because it was "just as symbolic" of the nation as the Phrygian cap.[77]

So pervasive was Mimi Pinson as a figure of historical memory in this period, consumers could avail themselves of any number of romantic postcards featuring pretty garment workers named "Mimi Pinson." One such series of photographs depicts Mimi in her modest but tastefully appointed garret apartment (complete with ubiquitous hat box and canary in a cage), picturesquely rising from bed in her nightgown and brushing her hair, her feminine (but humble) décor as much a part of her allure as her physical attractiveness.[78] Such postcards reproduced Mimi Pinson as an object of erotic consumption, mixing equal parts sexual desirability, nostalgia, and industrious simplicity, all as part of the touristic landscape of Parisian pleasure.

Parisian guides often directed visitors to enjoy the capital's garment workers as a touristic site. A.-P. de Lannoy's 1900 *Les Plaisirs et la vie de Paris: Guide du flâneur* instructed curious men where to find garment workers for amorous adventures. This search was both a sexual pursuit and an act of nostalgia for conquests from the imagined reader's youth: "If Paulus's songs intoxicated your younger years, you will have a vague craving to meet a nice hatmaker. An exceptional range of

[75] "On a hier inauguré…," 1.

[76] Félix Mortreuil. "Les Amoureux de Mimi Pinson, chansonette," music by Bunel-Lud (Paris, c.1904), BNF-L 4-VM7-2066(21); L. Bergeret, "Idylle d'une Mimi Pinson, romance," Music by A. Alteirac (Paris, 1907), BNF-L VM7-127210; N. Pitois. "Jolies Mimi-Pinson, chanson," music by Rémy d'Arbelle (Paris, 1914), NUMM-386947. For some examples of Musset's verses set to music, see "Mimi Pinson!," lyrics by d'Alfred de Musset (Paris, 1875), BNF-R VM7-72796; "Mimi Pinson. Chanson," lyrics d'Alfred de Musset, music by Arthur Coquard (Paris, c.1890); "Mimi Pinson! Couplet avec choeur ad libitum," lyrics by Alfred de Musset, music by A. Guéroult (Paris, 1897); "Mimi-Pinson, mélodie," lyrics by Alfred Musset, music by S. Grangeon (Paris, 1912), BNF-L FOL-VM7-8009; "Mimi Pinson," lyrics by Alfred Musset, music by Gustave Bautz (Paris, 1914). BNF-L NUMM-386431.

[77] Jules Claretie, "Preface: Béranger et la chanson," in Edmond Teulet, *Chansons du Siècle dernier* (Paris, 1901), p. xii.

[78] A subsequent card from the series shows Mimi Pinson dressed and sitting at a sewing machine. "Mimi Pinson [image fixe]: [carte postale]," 1903. BMD CP 1181a.

products for export have made the Rue de la Paix the meeting point of all desires. You have only to suffer the inconvenience of buying her one of those sparking jewels, or one of those petticoats embroidered with Valencienne lace, that gleam in the sun."[79] Introducing a section on the sexual pleasure sites of Montmartre, Lannoy mused, "Charming inns of time gone-by, where are your elegant lieutenants, like Mimi Pinson, and your arbors under which we kissed to the sound of a barrel organ."[80] He goes on to recommend the Moulin Rouge as "the temple of Aphrodite of the Butte," where "At the stock market of hearts, the cheerful workingwoman displays her mischievous nose, the grisette her purse..."[81] Armand Silvestre's guide to the 1900 Exposition Universelle counsels that readers get to know Paris by meeting "the real Parisienne" who wears "Mimi Pinson's bonnet and the joyful cocarde of Liberty. The Parisienne! O reader who I already think of as a friend, if you take away from your trip this exquisite worship and the appreciative memory she deserves, you will not have wasted your time." One can recognize the real Parisienne by her seductive walk: "one cannot encounter her without having a passionate desire to follow her...those who have experienced her will tell you that she is loyal when she loves, and she loves often."[82]

Mimi Pinson reappeared frequently in theatrical period pieces evoking the July Monarchy. In 1882, Maurice Ordonneau and Arthur Verneuil staged a popular operetta, *Mimi Pinson: Vaudeville-Opérette en trois actes*, at the Théâtre de Cluny. This light-hearted romantic comedy follows a merry band of grisettes and university students in Paris's Latin Quarter just a month after the Trois Glorieuses. The adorable heroine Mimi Pinson "turns the heads" of students and aristocrats alike; indeed, the entire cast sings Musset's verses in her honor.[83] Mimi makes clear that while good-natured and seducible, she is not wanton: "Grisette, but honest. I am saving my heart for the one that will understand me..." The appeal of the show was evidently in part its backward gaze. Critic Arthur Heulhard included a line of Musset's verse in his review of the show, ("Mimi Pinson is a blonde, | That we know, | She has only one dress in the world | And only one bonnet"), and added, "We don't know blondes like this anymore, happy with only one dress and one bonnet..."[84] Thus, Mimi Pinson was conjured on stage as a sign of an endangered, less avaricious femininity. Indeed, verses from Musset's Mimi Pinson song were

---

[79] A.-P. de Lannoy, *Les Plaisirs et la vie de Paris (guide du flâneur)* (Paris, 1900), 17. Lannoy was the pseudonym of Auguste Pawlowski. Preface by Georges Montorgueil.

[80] Ibid. 98–9.   [81] Ibid. 101.

[82] Armand Silvestre, *Guide Armand Silvestre de Paris et de ses environs et de l'Exposition de 1900* (Paris, 1900), 9–10.

[83] Maurice Ordonneau and Arthur Verneuil, *Mimi Pinson: vaudeville-opérette en trois actes*, music by Michiels (Paris, 1882). First performed in Paris at the Théâtre de Cluny, 12 March 1882. BNF 8-YTH-20608.

[84] Arthur Heulhard, "Chronique des ateliers," *Courrier de l'art: chronique hebdomaire des ateliers, des musés, des expositions, des ventes publiques, etc.* 30 March 1882, 2.

repeated in numerous belle époque novels and songs, at times as a non-sequitur in the middle of more contemporary plots. The song was reprinted in its entirety in Edmond Ladoucette's 1904 novel *Les Amours de Mimi-Pinson*; the heroine, a contemporary seamstress named Mimi Pinson, boosts the morale of her fellow seamstresses *en atelier* with the song.[85] In Eugène Baillet's 1883 song "As in the time of Mimi Pinson," contemporary garment workers take Musset's heroine as their model in an existence devoted to "Joyful love and song."[86] The song envisages a weekend excursion to the countryside by workingwomen with their male "friends," drinking wine under the arbors of a *guingette* (an open-air dance hall): "We are those joyous girls | Who know that they are twenty years old! | Our grandmothers were those crazy ladies | Who came to drink at Porcherons, | And launched saucy retorts | Into the glass of frank lads."[87] The bond between these young women and their grandmothers is not labor or craft (never mentioned), but an amorous youth, a resolutely apolitical genealogy.

Catullle Mendès and Reynaldo Hahn's 1910 ballet *La Fête chez Thérèse* (whose heroine is "Mimi Pinson (grisette)") presented the public with an immersive, frothy voyage back to the July Monarchy, along with a vision of the Parisian garment worker as a cheerful sexual companion to bourgeois Bohemians and of a remarkably quiescent Parisian garment trade.[88] Stage directions for the first act in a Parisian fashion house included this notation for set designers: "See: Musset, Balzac and others, passim."[89] The seamstresses take their cues from early nineteenth-century literature as well: "They wear the outfit of a grisette—little bonnet, gingham dress and silk apron, like in the novella by Musset." Thus from the outset, the inspiration of this period ballet is not a historical epoch, but a literary one. The ballet opens with a picturesque dance by a workshop of seamstresses in front of their lovers, and a song by Mimi in which she details romantic Sunday outings with long-haired poets and students to the country or to popular dances.[90]

La Fête chez Thérèse debuted on the Parisian stage as the city's garment industry experienced its most substantial strikes to date (discussed in Chapter 5). Musicologist Lavinia Caddy suggests that Hahn's and Mendès's Mimi Pinson may have been a nod to the increasing visibility of independent and vocal workingwomen in the social scene. Mimi, suggests Caddy, is endowed with "feminine

---

[85] Edmond Ladoucette, *Les Amours de "Mimi-Pinson"* (Paris, 1904). BNF 4-Y2-3158, 10–11.

[86] Eugène Baillet, "Comme au temps de Mimi-Pinson" (*La Petite Muse: chansons et poésie d'Eugène Baillet*, 1901), 117–19. Music by Abel Queille. The song appears in the *Bibliographie de la France: journal général de l'imprimérie et de la librairie*, 50 (15 December 1883).

[87] Ibid. 118.

[88] Catullle Mendès and Reynaldo Hahn, *La Fête chez Thérèse: ballet-pantomime en deux actes* (Paris, 1910).

[89] Ibid. 1.

[90] Ibid. 4. Mimi's poet lover Theodore falls in love with her client, the duchesse Thérèse. During an Old Regime costume ball, Theodore tries to win the duchess. Mimi's sincere plea convinces Thérèse to reject Theodore, who reluctantly returns to Mimi.

authority, assertiveness, even aggression," much like the *femme nouvelle*.[91] Caddy also notes the historical nostalgia of this ballet, its "retrospective impulse," but puts it somewhat in tension with its advanced social message.[92] I argue that these two themes are not incidental contrasts, but necessary pendant pieces. If the seamstress was an icon of newly emancipated French womanhood, hers was an iconic power delimited by her recollective sexuality and political obedience.

To thoroughly associate garment trade workers with joyful, pre-industrial labor and transitory cross-class romance could defuse concerns about less palatable female types at the fin de siècle, particularly the striking worker or the unsexed New Woman.[93] Henri Boutet's 1896 cartoon foregrounded this latter function (Figure 1.3). Here, a pretty milliner stands on a roadside, while a New Woman in bloomers runs down an infant Cupid with her bicycle. The cartoon's caption announces: "THIS WILL KILL THAT." The denatured *femme nouvelle* murders love and romance. Boutet's caption alerts the attractive onlooker: "Blessed be your poverty, Mimi Pinson; it keeps you from the bicycle."[94] The burden of maintaining pre-feminist romantic love and gender order is placed squarely on the shoulders of a diminutive hatmaker. For Boutet, Mimi Pinson's low wages are a blessing, safeguarding her from the missteps of her more privileged bluestocking *concitoyennes*. Though garbed in contemporary dress, Mimi personifies a femininity frozen in time, comfortingly immutable as both her poverty and her erotic availability endure. Boutet pointedly dedicates the cartoon to "our trottins." Both the grisette's winsome political apathy and her role as submissive plaything to young bourgeois men were underscored by contrasting her to the New Woman. Montorgueil similarly contrasted the unsexed and emancipated "Bicycliste" of the 1890s to the gentle florist, "Will not a day come when the florist will vainly offer her flowers? An implacable enemy is born to all that makes up the auxiliary grace of Woman: the bicycle. More brutal than any revolution...the lady Quixotes of feminine demands."[95] Montorgueil again assured male readers of his 1899 guide to Montmartre that the lovely workingwomen of the Butte were not easy converts to feminism: "The demands of their sex, so loud in this fin de siècle, have not moved them. Feminism has recruited few militants among them."[96]

---

[91] Davinia Caddy, "On ballet at the Opéra, 1909–14, and *La Fête chez Thérèse*," *Journal of the Royal Music Association* 133, No. 2 (2008), 261. See also Annegret Fauser, "*La Guerre en dentelles*: women and the *Prix de Rome* in French cultural politics," *Journal of the American Musicological Society* 51, No. 1 (1998).

[92] Caddy, "On ballet," 232.

[93] Sullivan suggests that early nineteenth-century writers used the "apolitical nature of the grisette" as a "foil to the feminist movement of the 1830s and early 1840s." Sullivan, "Classification," 98.

[94] Henri Boutet, "Etrennes aux dames de la part de Henri Boutet: Ceci Tuera Cela.—Bénis ta pauvreté, Mimi Pinson, elle te préserve de la bicyclette." *La Plume*, 1 January 1896.

[95] Georges Montorgueil, *La Parisienne, peinte par elle-même* (Paris, 1897), 183.

[96] Georges Montorgueil, *La Vie à Montmartre* (Paris, 1899), 57.

Figure 1.3. "Etrennes aux dames de la part de Henri Boutet: Ceci Tuera Cela.—Bénis ta pauvreté, Mimi Pinson, elle te préserve de la bicyclette." *La Plume*, 1 January 1896.
Source: Bibliothèque Nationale de France.

Another monument to Mimi Pinson, her purported house on the rue Mont-Cenis in Montmartre, became a tourist attraction in this same period (though Musset's story was set on the Left Bank), and was the subject of numerous paintings, sketches, photographs, and postcards through the interwar. Odes to Mimi Pinson's house were often made in the service of evoking not only "Old Paris" but the youthful dalliances of the city's culture makers with delightfully unemancipated workingwomen.[97] Maurice Utrillo, whose mother, the painter Suzanne Valadon, was herself a former garment worker and painters' model (and mistress), completed a series of paintings of this house over the course of his career beginning in 1914. Utrillo continued to paint the house from memory even after its demolition in 1926. A number of *hommes des lettres* opposed the demolition as the loss of something essential to Parisian character and history, especially in this period "when women are mostly interested in the Charleston!"[98] In 1926, journalist Gaëtan Sanvoisin defended the house as a piece of Parisian and French mythology: "Immortal and universal, because Mimi Pinson has symbolized, for several generations, a French figure, the little affectionate and industrious workingwoman. Gay as a bird... she loved flowered shawls, sunny arbors, idealism, and sentimental songs. She remains, within us all, the pastel-tinted Muse of the younger days of our fathers... Will not the strength of feeling, along with real practical arguments, save the house of she who smiled at the dawn of our first excitements, our first desires?"[99] Sanvoisin here reaches the crux of his attachment to the crumbling house: that it represents a crucial nostalgic site for his own sexual history. Mimi Pinson's house memorializes the author's sexual initiations and those of his male cohort. *Le Temps* reported that a group of real workingwomen joined a demolition protest in September 1926 and presented a garland of flowers to "Mimi Pinson" at the doomed house: "This invocation in the presence of a past that is slipping away concluded with songs more romantic than funereal."[100]

Eighteen-year-old silent film star Simone Vaudry played the titular role in 1924's *Mimi Pinson* ("d'après Musset"), which reviewers noted for its old Paris locations: "What is remarkable... is the choice of spots from old Paris, the delightful locales that the director was able to find and that gave to much of his scenes

---

[97] See *Recueil factice d'articles de presse: La Maison de Mimi Pinson à Montmartre, articles divers, Sept 1926*, BNF-R, Salle des Arts du spectacle, 8-RF-31915. See also Niccolai, "Mimi Pinson"; Niccolai, *La Dramaturgie de Gustave Charpentier*, 101, 306. Rearick includes the demolition with several unsuccessful battles for Old Montmartre in this period (*Paris Dreams, Paris Memories*, 47–51). In 1925, Gaumont Pathé filmed the house in a newsreel, "Le vieux Montmartre disparaît. La maison qu'habita Berlioz va tomber prochainement sous la pioche des démolisseurs de même que celle qui abrita la Mimi Pinson de Murger," 0:27 min. Paris: Journal Gaumont, 1925. Ref. 2502GJ 00004. www.gaumontpathéarchives.com.

[98] "La Maison de Mimi Pinson," *Volonté*, 2 Sept. 1926, in *Recueil factice d'articles de presse*. See also Monjaret et al., *Le Paris des "midinettes,"* 34–5.

[99] Gaëtan Sanvoisin, "La Vie qui passe: la maison de Mimi Pinson," *Gaulois*, 2 Sept. 1926, [3].

[100] G.M., "La Maison de Mimi Pinson," *Le Temps*, 4 Sept. 1926. *Recueil factice d'articles de presse*, 10–11.

the value, originality, and color of old etchings."[101] Another reviewer enthused that "*Mimi Pinson* contains all the spirit and grace of the modest workingwoman, the grisette as we used to say. It represents an entire Parisian world whose setting has quite changed since then, but without affecting the essential soul."[102]

Physiology of a Midinette

While the grisette was still a familiar figure of Parisian lore by the fin de siècle, her cultural valence was redirected to the figure of the midinette. While the grisette correlated closely with the political and social change of the July Monarchy, the midinette as a type, according to Anne Monjaret, "belongs to the Third Republic...and incarnates it."[103] The term came into usage at the fin de siècle, meaning a young female worker in the couture industry who had her lunch (*dinette*) at noon (*midi*). While its first connotation was of the relatively better paid young women working in Parisian haute couture, in practice, the term could be applied to any female worker in couture and its related industries. The term was also associated with these women's supposed frivolity and sentimentality.[104] The midinette was in many ways an updated version of the grisette; she carried with her the grisette's romantic guilelessness, and was principally an object of bourgeois male pleasure. Indeed, many contemporaries and some scholars have treated the midinette and grisette as interchangeable, one of those constantly reborn "myths" of French "popular sensibility."[105] Yet despite sharing many qualities with her grisette predecessor, the midinette came to be definitively identified with the production of finely-made couture goods and with post-Haussmann urban spectacle and public space.

The first known print usage of the term "midinette" was an 1888 essay in *Gil Blas* by Paul Arène called "Les Oiseaux de Paris," and it already bore all of the elements that would become standard in midinettes depictions.[106] Arène observes three teenage garment workers playing in the snow at noon: "Because of the hour that they usually appear, these little workingwomen of couture, hatmaking, and flowers are called by this pretty name of midinettes in certain neighborhoods

---

[101] Untitled clipping, "Mimi Pinson," *Recueil factice d'articles de presse sur "Mimi Pinson" (d'apres Musset) [FILM]*. BNF-R, 8-RF-3194.

[102] Untitled clipping, *Eve*, 12 Oct. 1924. *Recueil factice d'articles de presse sur "Mimi Pinson" (d'apres Musset) [FILM]*.

[103] Monjaret et al., *Le Paris des "midinettes,"* 15.

[104] The *Trésor de la langue française* defines a midinette as "Jeune fille simple et frivole, à la sentimentalité naïve."

[105] Chevalier, *Les Parisiens*, 379.

[106] Paul Arène, "Les Oiseaux de Paris," *Gil Blas*, 3 Feb. 1888, p. 1. A week later, Arène gave credit for the term to a writer named Laforet. "Bibliothèques et Gens de lettres," *Gil Blas*, 10 Feb. 1888, pp. 1–2. Arène (1843–96) was a journalist, novelist, and playwright. The *Trésor de la langue française* incorrectly cites a *Journal Amusant* sketch from 17 May 1890 as the first usage. Monjaret et al., *Le Paris des "midinettes,"* 16.

devoted to elegant industries." At this hour, the boulevards are a public space the midinettes possess, despite their youth and class: "In large numbers, they imagine themselves *chez elles*...Between 11 and noon, the street belongs to the midinette." The young women return breathlessly to the workshop and set to "improvising" the fine-fingered work that comprises Parisian elegance. Arène envisions the rest of their working day: a joyful walk home, window-shopping arm-in-arm with their comrades, and, possibly, encounters with lovers. Arène slips effortlessly from these women's leisure hours to recalling a countryside excursion in his youth with a midinette named Armandine one Sunday to pick violets. He ends his essay lost in this nostalgic digression: "But why this distant memory? And why, with my heart seized by a retrospective melancholy, did I think I saw Armadine once again...trembling with her violets?"[107] Thus, from the genesis of the term, the midinette was characterized by girlish joy, romantic possibility, and tasteful labor, all apprehended through the nostalgic and desiring eye of the bourgeois male writer/artist.

Like the grisette before her, the midinette's gaiety was part and parcel of a cheerful resignation to the hardship of working life. André Vernières's 1908 novel *Camille Frison*, an attempt at an accurate if fictional study of Paris's sweated garment trades, offered a succinct portrait of the midinette. "Her physiognomy," he wrote, "is alert, at times cheeky, her eyes sparkle with spirit. She is bright, lively, and impulsive; she is always joking, and seems indifferent to even the most painful events. At heart, she is very sensitive, sentimental even, and goes from laughter to tears like a child."[108]

Though the word was used widely in the belle époque,[109] *midinette* was not included in official French dictionaries until the late 1940s.[110] When the Académie Française refused to admit the word in 1927, columnist Sergines ardently defended it:

> Midinette is perhaps the most charming word in our language, by the grace that it evokes and by the joyous sound it makes...It is really the Parisian essence, born of a ray of sunshine idling in our public gardens...It was coined at the beginning of the century and was quickly adopted, and quickly conquered our hearts. I ask you, how could one better label the amiable little girls who, at the strike of noon, shared their lunch with the sparrows of Paris? Plays, cartoons, sketches, songs, books, and magazines have popularized both object and the word.[111]

---

[107] Arène, "Les Oiseaux de Paris," 1.

[108] André Vernières, *Camille Frison, ouvrière de la couture*, 29–30 (Paris, 1908), BNF 8-Y2-56916. Vernières was the nom de plume of Lucien-François-Joseph-André Delpon Vissec.

[109] A definition for "midinette" appears in the *Revue Universelle* in 1903 in a section on new slang. "Mots et Locutions," *Revue Universelle*, 1903, p. 568.

[110] Monjaret et al., *Le Paris des "midinettes,"* 15–16.

[111] Sergines, "Les Midinettes à la porte," *Les Annales politiques et littéraires: revue populaire*, 15 Apr. 1927. Sergines was the pseudonym of Adophe Brisson, who died in 1925. It is unclear who used the name in 1927. See also Figaro (Junior), "Nos Echos: refusé par l'Académie," *Journal Amusant*, 10 Apr. 1927, p. 18.

All Parisian charm and sun-soaked urban joy, the term was also inseparable from the besotted attention of male writers, composers, and journalists.

Sex and the City

In the Parisian imaginary, the belle époque midinette tended, like her grisette grandmother, to inhabit a liminal moral space between libertinage and bourgeois feminine virtue. Often surrounded by carefree coquettes who toil alongside her in the couture workshop and encourage her romantic follies, the midinette heroine is, more or less, a good girl. She might take a lover, or be seduced or raped, but she is generally a young woman of romantic loyalty and goodness. While melodramatic tragedy was one possible trajectory for fictive midinettes, they were often represented as unchaste, but, ultimately, content, either happily married, en concubinage, or managing their own couture shops.[112] In Louis Artus's 1911 play Les Midinettes, the pretty seamstress Julie (played by Mistinguett) ends as the happy consort of a former client's husband. The 1917 film Midinettes starred Suzanne Grandais as the modest milliner Rosette who is thrown into the world of chic and materialist aristocrats by an unexpected inheritance. She ends up gratefully returning to her garret room overlooking the Seine and to her honorable mechanic fiancé Jacques.[113]

The belle époque couture workshop was conjured consistently as a site of erotic display and promise.[114] In his novel Les Amours de Mimi Pinson (1904), Ladoucette explains that couture houses "are places for rendezvous, where at certain hours, in singularly suggestive proximity to one another, the aristocratic ladies of the faubourg and the demi-mondaines, along with men who are the husbands of the former and the lovers of the latter meet one another, brush against one another..."[115] George Sibre and Albert Verse's 1905 operetta Couturière sans aiguilles the main action takes place in a Parisian couture workshop populated by amorous seamstresses who spend their work day singing of their affairs and entertaining lovers. The last riotous scene finds the seamstresses stripping down to their underwear and bursting into song before a male admirer. One woman reassures a reluctant comrade that such behavior is standard at places like the Moulin Rouge.[116] Thus, a garment workshop is converted into a music-hall and its workers into enticing performers.

---

[112] See, for example, the 1905 operetta Couturière sans aiguilles by Georges Sibre and Albert Verse; the 1913 film Oscar et Kiki la midinette.

[113] Louis Mercanton and René Hervil, Midinettes: scénario (1917), 4-MY-1187 BNF-R.

[114] Zylberberg-Hocquard notes the positive image in nineteenth-century popular fiction of the luxury Parisian workshop as opposed to negative portrayals of factories and their female workers. Zylberberg-Hocquard, "L'Ouvrière," 613.

[115] Ladoucette, Les Amours de "Mimi-Pinson," 11.

[116] Georges Sibre and Albert Verse, Couturière sans aiguilles: vaudeville-opérette en un acte (Paris, 1905), 19. BNF 4-YTH-7713. Performed for the first time at the Bobino Music Hall. Direction by Eugène Dambreville and music by J. Deschaux.

Midinette literature takes as a given that female garment workers are sexual prey, particularly in the workplace. Defossez's 1904 play *Les Midinettes* martyred its seamstress heroine for five acts as she is pursued by her employer. Ultimately, after she is forced to cede to him to save her dying mother, she becomes a nun and sits in a disquieting vigil at the deathbed of her rapist.[117] In the 1912 film *Les Amoureux de la couturière*, a seamstress arrives at the home of a wealthy client for a fitting and almost instantaneously is set upon by the randy men of the household.[118] The couture boss in 1916's *Irène, grande première* refers jovially to his "droit de cuissage" over his female employees.[119]

While the grisette was a deracinated figure, secluded in her Latin Quarter garret with her lover and disconnected from working life (indeed her precise occupation was, to a certain extent, irrelevant to her romantic progress), the new Mimi Pinson was most often depicted moving in a boisterous flock with her comrades in and around the sites of their labor, especially the luxury workshops along the Rue de la Paix, an essential part of the geography of the capital's commercial and carnal pleasures.[120] Indeed, the term *midinette* referenced the moment in the workday when these young women were best observed by lubricious flâneurs, the noon lunch hour. The midinette, more than the grisette, was a spectacular urban figure, inseparable from the commercial delights of post-Haussmann Paris. The pretty garment worker was omnipresent in representations of the Parisian picturesque as a modern urban attraction, like an enchanting species of city bird (to which she was regularly compared),[121] her natural habitat the parks and boulevards of the capital, and the luxury garment workshops. Lannoy's 1900 *flâneur* guide gives an entirely typical description of the midinette:

Before she heads home with a lively step, the Parisian errand girl leaving the workshop wanders, happy to breathe in freedom. Nothing is more seductive than the workingwoman of Paris, with her turned-up nose seeming to check for rain, her 25-sous blouse, so simple and so fashionable, that gives her the air of a little princess, her worn shoes…ravishing hair and laughing, mischievous eyes. On rainy days, you have to see her hiking up her skirt with the casualness sung by all the chansonniers of the cafés-concerts.[122]

---

[117] Alfred Desfossez, *Les Midinettes: drame en 5 actes et 7 tableaux* (Paris, 1904). First performed at the Théâtre des Fantaisies Saint-Martin, 1 Jan. 1904. Reprised at the Théâtre de Belleville, 31 Jan. 1904 and at the Théâtre Montparnasse, 14 May 1904.

[118] *Les Amoureux de la couturière* [film scénario], BNF-R, 4-COL-4(2163). Paris: Pathé Frères, 1912.

[119] Olivier Diraison-Seylor, *Irène, Grande Première, roman* (Paris, 1916), 95.

[120] Nancy Troy notes the belle époque theatrical trend of using couture houses as a "narrative frame." *Couture Cultures: A Study in Modern Art and Fashion* (Cambridge, 2003), 94.

[121] On the association between Parisian garment workers and birds, see Monjaret and Niccolai, "Elle trotte, danse et chante, la midinette!"

[122] Lannoy, *Les Plaisirs*, 26–7.

This pseudo-anthropological description brings together the most persistent elements of the midinette type: a nod to her labor and poverty, and a celebration of her physical attractiveness, fashion sense, and cheerfulness. Lannoy frames the whole with the popular songs of the café-concert, thereby assuring his male readers that these real women are a flawless representation of their fictional type. The text is accompanied by a sketch of a pretty *modiste* lifting her skirt ever so slightly and carrying a hatbox.[123]

In the sumptuously illustrated 1899 *La Vie à Montmartre*, Montorgueil treats the morning commute to the city center of Montmartois garment workers as a scene of erotic flirtation. These women "get dressed in such a hurry, always late, that they finish their morning toilette outside. Little movements of their fingers smooth their blouses...pat down their skirt while walking, straightening the plain undergarments that fill it out, they raise the skirt with a studied gesture, especially if their ankle boots are presentable—because they know that a well-turned ankle, in black stockings, entertains the *messieurs* following them. Shop windows are their cheval mirrors..."[124] The text was accompanied by fetching illustrations of chic garment workers on a street. Montorgueil, like so many midinette observers, inverts the common artistic trope of the woman dressing in her boudoir. The garment worker conducts her captivating toilette on the street and in the windows of the capital's stores, a living urban spectacle, existing only as an object of the flâneur's voyeuristic attention: "to please is their constant concern—to please for the delight of pleasing."[125] The women confide in one another, making explicit to the voyeur-reader their readiness for easy sexual encounters, "Each one is her own novel, lived day by day, as she recounts comic, sometimes sad, events: the passing romance and its consequences, the dates, the woodland scenes on a summer Sunday, the dresses rumpled on a green lane...the fears of pregnancy overcome at the cost of an indulgence revealed by the pallor of the next day."[126]

When Gérard Baüer set about conducting an "inventory" of love in Paris in 1922 to trace the great changes in sexual relations since the war, he devoted an entire chapter to a wistful paean to the effortless sexual encounters of the Rue de la Paix, the "training ground" where one "provisioned oneself with a mistress," in this "nursery" of pretty garment workers, "from the head saleswoman to the errand girl."[127] Literary trope and reality are here identical:

Head saleswomen, models, workshop *prémieres* make up the base of this little troupe of pretty girls who nicely represent "Parisian grace"...In the olden days, a formula summed up well the mores in favor: "They had an old guy." They also had a young guy. The "old one" for the money and the young one for the "pleasure." This was assuredly true for a long time and upon this an entire

---

[123] Ibid. 25.   [124] Montorgueil, *La Vie à Montmartre*, 47.   [125] Ibid. 48.
[126] Ibid. 48–9.   [127] Gérard Baüer, *Recensement de l'amour à Paris* (Paris, 1922), 52.

popular literature was based, and upon which comedy and vaudeville were built for years.[128]

Baüer presents these mores as superior to the new relations of the interwar, when men seeking pre- and extramarital sex partners scorn simple women. Female garment workers, in this vision, are easily available for sex, but, significantly, are not prostitutes, a perfect midpoint between the entangling romance of bourgeois women and the mercenary relations of sex workers. Bauer credits these women's endemic promiscuity with generating the pop cultural interest in midinettes. In a review of the 1911 play *Les Midinettes*, a reviewer for the *Journal Amusant* begins by stipulating that the romantic interludes depicted therein were a faithful version of the bourgeois male audience's own sexual history: "We've all been twenty, we've all known errand girls…And all of us have cruelly dumped the little mistress with her fingers dotted with needle pricks."[129]

Thus, the looming sexual danger of the city street, while unquestionably present in belle époque popular culture, was tempered in much of midinette literature with the garment worker as a knowing and even cheerful participant in her own seduction. The midinette was seen as a young woman who used her daily commute to exhibit herself for amorous encounters and for the delectation of male observers. The chic and curvaceous hatmaker in "A Midinette's Thought," a cartoon from 1903, recognizes the inutility of hurrying to work: "What good is it to rush; they wouldn't be able to follow us then."[130] This boulevard pursuit is represented again and again in the belle époque, making Paris an arena of sexual conquest and the midinette a compliant and even eager quarry in this hunt. In a 1910 postcard, a midinette piloting a monoplane (stocked with hatboxes) is pursued by an older, elegantly dressed gentleman in top hat and frock coat in his own monoplane. The midinette straddles the plane, her skirts blown back to reveal shapely calves and heeled shoes, ribbons and foulard catching the air playfully, as she smiles back at her pursuer.[131] *Mamzelle Trottin*, a 1909 film short, features another coquettish garment worker who is chased around Paris by "a flock of old rakes" who are "attracted to her fresh youth." Every time the men seem poised to catch her, on the metro platform or on the boulevard, Mamzelle disappears into her seemingly enchanted hat box, frustrating their desire with a "teasing laugh."[132] A cartoon by Jehan Testevuide from around 1901 inverts this pursuit, making plain the willingness of Parisian garment workers for short-term sexual engagements with wealthy men. In the first panels, we see little boys affix a sign to the back of an unwitting gentleman on a park bench. As he walks away, he is

[128] Ibid. 59.
[129] "Entre cour et jardin: variétés—les midinettes," *Le Journal Amusant*, 11 Feb. 1911.
[130] Mars, "Pensée de midinette" [caricature], *Le Journal Amusant*, 21 Nov. 1903.
[131] E.L.D., "Monoplan de course pour midinettes" [postcard], 1910. BMD CP 1188 a.
[132] *Mamzelle Trottin, modiste* (1909) [film scenario]. BNF-R, 4-COL-4/4097.

shadowed by a crowd of smiling garment workers, identifiable by their delivery cartons and stylish dress. In the final panel, a police officer reveals the sign to the befuddled gentlemen: "SEEKING YOUNG WORKINGWOMEN FOR EASY WORK (AT NIGHT)." The gentleman is shocked, while the young women laugh uproariously.[133]

In the 1907 film *The Trottin's Dream*, an apprentice seamstress delivering a large dress box across the city is pursued by "an older and very chic gentlement who offers to satisfy all her desires." She runs away, but while resting on a bench, dreams that the man presents her with consumer objects emerging magically from the box—shoes, hats, dresses, jewelry, and even a car. He finally transforms into Satan after plying her with champagne and trying to kiss her. The film ends with the *trottin* being awakened by an honorable gendarme, and then returning to work.[134] The silent film *Oscar et Kiki la Midinette* (1913) makes comic hay of the garment worker's incessant stalking by libidinous bourgeois men. When elegant suitor Oscar disguises himself as a midinette to finish the deliveries of his milliner girlfriend Kiki, he is trailed by a lewd flâneur as he crosses the Champs de Mars in front of the Eiffel Tower.[135] Pioneering film director Alice Guy produced a fascinating twist on this common trope in *Les Résultats du féminisme* of 1906, which depicts an upside-down Paris of female rule. The film opens in a hatmaking workshop of prettily coiffed male milliners. A male hatmaker giggles and makes himself up in the mirror before making a delivery, and once on the street is accosted by a female *flâneuse* (lounging with wine outside a café with a straw boater and cane). Another woman rescues the diminutive hatmaker, only to aggressively kiss and grope him on a park bench in the next scene.[136]

Innumerable popular songs in the belle époque described dapper older gentlemen ogling midinettes; such songs were so pervasive as to be a genre unto themselves. Anne Monjaret and Michela Niccolai have traced some of the major themes in this genre, from the 1840s through the late twentieth century, and have noted the complexity of the songs' narrative perspective. Often written by men to be sung by women, grisette and midinette songs were "a kind of mirror game that facilitates the integration of an imposed ideal and permits its identification."[137]

---

[133] Jehan Testevuide "L'Ecritau" [cartoon, c.1901], *Collection iconographique Maciet: métiers. mi-mod.* Maciet 330/59. Bibliothèque des Arts Décoratifs. Testevuide was the pseudonym of cartoonist Jean Saurel (1873–1922).

[134] *Rêve du trottin: scénario* [film scenario]. 4-COL-3 (0154) (1907) Paris: Gaumont, 1907. Bibliothèque Nationale de France.

[135] Léonce Perret, dir., *Oscar et Kiki la midinette* (Paris: Gaumont Pathé, 1913), 9:50 mins. 1913CNCGFIC 00038 1/280441, Gaumont Pathé Archives, www.gaumontpathearchives.com.

[136] Alice Guy, dir., *Les Résultats du féminisme* (Paris: Gaumont Pathé, 1906), 7:25 mins. 1906 GFIC 00012, Gaumont Pathé Archives, www.gaumontpathearchives.com. I am grateful to Elinor Accampo for letting me know about this film. Alice Guy-Blaché (1873–1968) directed hundreds of films from the 1890s to the 1920s.

[137] Monjaret and Niccolai, "Elle trotte, danse et chante, la midinette!," 73. See also Monjaret and Niccolai, "La Midinette en chansons."

The songs invariably reflect that desiring male gaze, with midinette bodies presented for consumption by both the imagined flâneur and listeners. *March of the Hatmakers* (1894) finds the Parisian flâneur on a daily hunt: "When I glimpse a milliner | Who passes by on the street in the mornin' | I am immediately on the trail | Of the charming errand girl | I dare to whisper in her ear | I adore ya, beautiful child…." The song ends with night falling as he wraps an arm around his chosen *modiste*.[138] *Les Midinettes* (1895) by Émile Bessière and Henri d'Alverne imagines

> Little girls with impish sweet faces,
> Who put themselves together with care,
> They go about in twos or threes,
> Just as noon strikes.
> Ardent old men, on the sidewalk,
> Lie in wait for these sweet young things,
> Dreaming of giving them a boudoir,
> Jewels, money, pleasures, caresses.

The songbook cover depicts two well-dressed midinettes (one with a hatbox, lest we mistake her class) followed closely by a smirking man in a gleaming top hat and monocle. One midinette wears a feathered hat, feather stole, and fur muff. The second wears a polka-dotted dress, puffed sleeves, and lifts her skirt to reveal her calf, beribboned heeled shoes, and a bit of a frilly undergarment.[139] Émile Lafitte's 1903 composition "Les Midinettes" was sold with an eye-catching cover depicting a gentleman in a white suit with a red carnation, biting the tip of his cane and lubriciously eyeing a line of attractive young women rounding a large clock striking noon. The two women at the front of the line ever so slightly raises the edges of their skirts to reveal petticoats and heeled boots (Figure 1.4).[140]

That same year, the song *Les Joyeuses Midinettes* imagined young garment workers streaming into the Tuileries at noon with their "perky gait…to make you wild." The song follows the young women to a *guignette* on Sunday where "Warmly, | Wildly, | She gives herself to her lover | Without a worry…." The final verse finds the midinettes abandoned, as a matter of course, by wealthy lovers, but happily returning to couture work: "They know well, | That a day comes, | Where none of this is left | In love, | The good days, | Are, alas, often really short. | That's

[138] Goubert and Félix Marty, "Marche des modistes, chansonette," music by Roger de Fabry (Paris, 1894). BNF-L VM7-54758.
[139] Emile Bessière, "Les Midinettes (Croquis Parisien)," music by Henri d'Alverne (Paris, 1895). BNF-L, VM7-27193.
[140] Émile Lafitte, "Les Midinettes: marche pour piano" (Paris, 1903). BNF-L VM12 15,893. Lafitte was *chef d'orchestre* of the Jardin de Paris.

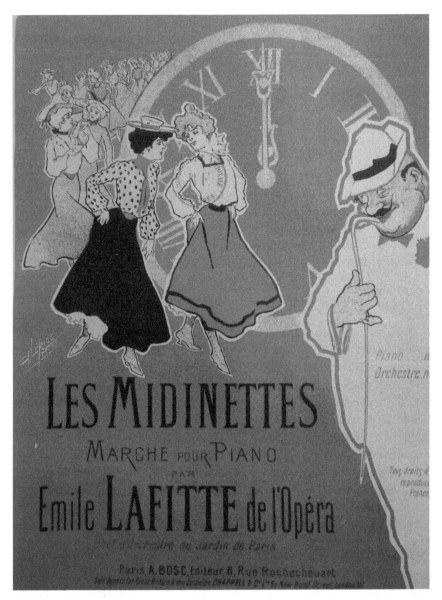

Figure 1.4. *Les Midinettes: Marche pour piano.* By Émile Lafitte (Paris: Imp. Chaimbaud & Cie, 1903).
Source: Bibliothèque Nationale de France.

why, | Their ten fingers | Will work like before... They'll return to the workshop."[141] Some midinette songs did posit street encounters in which bourgeois pursuers are rejected by a garment worker, often in favor of a working-class suitor. These

---

[141] P. Bades and V. Mignon, "Les Joyeuses Midinettes," music by P. Bades and H. Tarrelli (St Denis, 1903). BNF-L, VM7-112393.

songs nonetheless portray the Parisian street as a space of near-constant harassment for young workingwomen and presuppose their sexual availability.[142]

This trope of the Parisian garment worker as seduction-prone and easy victim of failed romance unsurprisingly bled through into representations of real-life events. In July 1911, boatmen on a lake in the suburbs of Paris discovered the drowned body of "a young workingwoman, a midinette" wearing a black dress and "traces of make-up." Identification papers found on the body gave the woman's address in Paris's 17th arrondissement. Though her legs had been tied together with rope, the police concluded she had died by suicide, since she had not been robbed. "The cause?" conjectured Le Figaro, "Love, probably."[143]

Belle époque Paris hosted numerous fêtes and sporting events that staged the midinette as the embodiment of urban pleasure. In part, this represented a shift traced by W. Scott Haine in which the "upper tier" of working-class youth "participated in the opulent and elaborate leisure culture of central Paris rather than in the inexpensive and impoverished one of the outer boulevards."[144] Scholars have detailed the annual fête of Sainte-Catherine in which unmarried Parisian garment workers under the age of 25 marched about the city wearing fanciful hats and costumes of their own creation, danced, and drank champagne in their ateliers.[145] The Catherinettes were a perfect demonstration of midinette taste, labor, and sexual availability. The Fête de la Couronnement de la Muse, while more highly stage-managed and moralistic, served a comparable function.[146]

In 1903, the journal Monde Sportif sponsored a 12-kilometer midinette (walking) foot race from Paris to Nanterre. Some 2,500 garment workers took part; the winner was a milliner's assistant named Jeanne Cheminel.[147] The race provoked commentary in many Parisian dailies, and seems to have been understood as both a beauty pageant, as an extension of the eroticized boulevard contact of flâneur and midinette, and, finally, by the midinettes themselves, as a sporting event. The list of prizes gives some sense that race organizers were less interested in athleticism than femininity. Winning participants were provided "20,000 fr. worth of gifts, jewelry, cloth, and lace." The last place walker received a lace collar, and the oldest participant a subscription to the women's magazine La Beauté. A prize was awarded for the most beautiful walker; the prettiest of the first twenty blondes to

---

[142] See, for example, these songs in the BNF-Louvois collection: Antoine Garofalo, "J'suis modiste, chansonette," music by Michel Frendo (Paris, 1895); Lucien Naulrès, "Trottin et vieux monsieur," music by Ernest Lerwile (Paris, 1903); Lerda, "La P'tit' Modiste, chansonette," music by R. Mancini (Paris, 1909); Léon Boureau, "L'Amour des midinettes, chansonnette," music by Paul Beaume (Paris, 1911).

[143] "Suicide d'une jeune femme à Enghien," Le Figaro, 5 July 1911.

[144] W. Scott Haine, "Development of leisure and the transformation of working-class adolescence, Paris 1830–1940," Journal of Family History, Vol. 17, No. 4 (Sept. 1992), 451–76, 463.

[145] See Anne Monjaret's extensive ethnography of this topic, especially La Sainte-Catherine: culture festive dans l'entreprise (Paris, 1997).

[146] Pomfret, "'A muse for the masses'."

[147] Haine, "Development of leisure," 464–5; Stewart suggests that the race was not repeated in subsequent years because of criticisms of the display of women's bodies. Stewart, For Health and Beauty, 164. The race seems not to have been run again until the 1920s.

finish the race could have her portrait painted. The first blue-eyed brunette to cross the finish line received a box of candy.[148]

Composer Louis Gueidan thrilled to the sensual attractions of the race in his song 'Paris-Nanterre: Marche des midinettes' (1903): "In front of the [male] gawker, astonished | By their performance | By their elegance, | Brunettes and blondes, | Skinny ones and [round ones]...And the Gentlemen | Young and old | Intoxicated by the lace | Turn and turn around them." He concludes with a wish that the participants had worn more revealing clothing: "Tight and suggestive leotards? | Eve's outfit | Would be my dream."[149] Journalists also complained that the race participants were not attractively enough garbed, or at least provided copious detail on the wide variety of garments on display.[150] Poet Henry Lafragette described the sight of the racers, "Like a sweet but fleeting vision, | You pass by, smiling, oh, sublime Chimeras," who would make admiring poets swoon and beg for kisses.[151] The seamstress heroine of the potboiler Irène, grande première (1916) meets her bourgeois lover at a belle époque marche des midinettes when he and his dandy friends stalk the finish line for garment workers to bed.[152]

In fact, during the 1903 marche des midinettes, onlookers became so unruly in their pursuit of the racing garment workers that the police had to intervene.[153] Photographs of the race show mostly male crowds closely surrounding the walkers.[154] Le Figaro's Frantz Reichel noted overflowing crowds, but characterized the assembly as "deliciously disordered": "[The midinettes] run by in packs, in knickers and short skirts, dressed in dark colors or in light, wearing a polo hat or a beret or a felt hat gently planted in blond or black masses of braided tresses. There are exquisite impish faces, adorable smiles, in outfits that are delicious, stylish, and elegant, or just gracefully original. They are joyful, with a brazen but not impolite air, quite simply Parisian; they pass through the amiable, gay, and courteous crowd."[155] He marveled at this scene, "mad, unbelievable, an amazing picturesqueness, a phenomenal gaiety."[156] This was, it was noted, a crowd that included two Barons de Rothschild, an archdeacon, the grand couturiers Redfern, Doeillet, Worth, Paquin, and Rouff, as well as numerous deputies.[157] A concert celebrating the race in Nanterre that evening was organized by composer Gustave

[148] "La Marche 'des midinettes,'" Journal des débats politiques et littéraires, 26 Oct. 1903, p. 2.

[149] Paris-Nanterre: Marche des midinettes, chanson-marche. Paroles de Louis Gueidan. Air: Marche des petits pierrots (Paris, 1903). BNF 4-YE PIECE-1259.

[150] "La 'Marche des midinettes,'" La Lanterne, 27 Oct. 1903, p. 1.

[151] Henry Lafragette, "Midinettes et chansonniers," La Presse, 27 Oct. 1903.

[152] Diraison-Seylor, Irène.

[153] "La Marche 'des midinettes,'" Journal des débats politiques et littéraires, 26 Oct. 1903, p. 2; "La 'Marche des midinettes,'" La Lanterne: journal politique quotidien [Le Supplément], 27 Oct. 1903, p. 1.

[154] Photographs by Jules Beau, Marche des Midinettes, Paris-Nanterre, organisée par le Monde Sportif, 25 octobre 1903, F.1v [Collection Jules Beau. Photographie sportive]: T. 24. Années 1903 et 1904. BNF IFN-8448930.

[155] Frantz Reichel, "La Marche des midinettes," Le Figaro, 26 Oct. 1903, pp. 1–2, 1.

[156] Ibid. 2.   [157] Ibid. 2.

Charpentier and his workingwomen's Conservatoire de Mimi Pinson. Thus, racers were greeted after the race by other female garment workers performing songs by Paris chansonniers about midinettes, as well as songs by Musset and Bérat about the grisette Mimi Pinson.[158]

Some midinette participants, however, approached the race as a serious sporting event, not a spectacular staging of their femininity. *The Tatler* remarked that "Great amusement was caused by the serious fashion in which the 'midinettes' faced their task." This English correspondent also noted the sporting clothes of the walkers, some wearing "cycling knickerbockers, others divided skirts, others again short dresses of workmanlike trim."[159] *La Presse* reported that several midinettes complained to journalists after the race that the winning walker had been, contrary to the rules, trained by her father and male friends. Months later, three of the winners accepted a challenge from Berliner workingwomen to race. After losing three times to their German counterparts, the midinettes vowed to compete in a rematch the following year. *Le Figaro-Modes* suggested instead that they challenge the German women to a "contest of elegance, of grace, and of seduction" from the Place Vendôme to the Opéra, a "course" along which they would surely triumph. This journalist thereby reinscribed the sporty midinettes in their proper habitat—central Paris and fashionable seduction.[160]

The words of actual Parisian midinettes in this period reveal that lubricious male interest, especially on the street, was a matter of quotidian harassment for workingwomen. In a 1908 letter to the workingwomen's magazine *Journal de Mimi Pinson*, a 20-year-old *ouvrière* named Myrtho described her navigation of Parisian streets with her comrades around the daily grind of their work at a *grand maison* on the Boulevard des Italiens:

> We leave the workshop, jovial, noisy, prattling on with energy about the little twists and turns of the day, making a remark in passing about the *première* who is too authoritarian or who sticks too much to the old routines. Then we talk métier and we admire some new design, then...I don't know, maybe we hatch a surprise for the saint's day of one of our own or contemplate a nice trip to the country on Sunday, whose arrival, consequently, seems to us slow to come.[161]

These conversations about work, fashion, and recreation are followed assiduously by male observers: "Amused, the passers-by watch us and make...their remarks."

---

[158] Françoise Andrieux, "Les Ouvrières parisiennes chantent et dansent dans les banlieues (1903–1939)," in *La Banlieue en fête: de la marginalité urbaine à l'identité culturelle* (Saint-Denis, 1988), 236–7.

[159] "The Paris walking race of sixteen hundred 'midinettes'," *The Tatler*, No. 123, 4 Nov. 1903, p. 165.

[160] "La Défaite des midinettes," *Le Figaro-Modes*, 15 Aug. 1904, p. 18.

[161] Letter from "Myrtho," excerpted in Mussette, "Le Carnet de Mussette," *Le Journal de Mimi Pinson, à l'atelier & dans la famille*, 10 Aug. 1908, No. 2, p. 10.

She notes that some offer gracious flattery, while "libertines" and others with bad taste make "insulting propositions." The young women are practiced in their responses: "a smile thanks the polite and amiable folks, a shrug of the shoulders and a look that can become severe keep the louts in line."[162] The editors received a second letter later that month from another group of garment workers, "expressing their complaints relative to the rudeness and the nasty remarks to which young women whose daily jobs require them to take the Metro, especially at rush hour, are exposed..."[163]

In her memoir, Madeleine Henrey recalled the sexual advances she warded off as a 13-year-old *trottin* running errands for her dressmaker mother in Paris in 1919. She remembered:

My only adventures were to be chased from counter to counter by vicious old gentlemen, to be pinched and fingered rather too often in the crowds of the underground. I became used to this, and the nausea brought on the first few times by these sneaking and not altogether flattering attacks quickly subsided. Paris is thus. Life was beginning. A young woman develops her own defences, but clearly the days of playing on the pavements were finished. I was to know the joys of growing up, the satisfaction of seeing men turn round in the street to take a second look at me.[164]

Henrey here combines the fear and disgust of street harassment with resignation, and, ultimately, excitement and even pleasure in such encounters for women who learned the rules of the street. During her time as a young seamstress, Yvette Guilbert learned from the affairs and harassment of her more experienced colleagues: "They trained me from the time I was fourteen; I heard every sort of story...What tales of seduction have I not heard...What a lesson it was to hear such adventures! By the time I was eighteen I had learned of every masculine trick, of every trap laid by man. If my body remained pure I felt my soul in danger and my mind soiled."[165] Workingwoman Charlotte Davy related a more harrowing version of this tale in her memoir. Followed home by her employer during lunch, Davy was raped repeatedly in a long-term non-consensual relationship which hung upon threats of firing and exposure.[166]

---

[162] Ibid. 10.

[163] Editor's note, *Le Journal de Mimi Pinson, à l'atelier & dans la famille*, 25 Aug. 1908, p. 1.

[164] Mrs Robert Henrey, *The Little Madeleine. The Autobiography of a Young Girl in Montmartre* (London, 1951). Madeleine Henrey (1906–2004), née Gal, was born in Clichy in 1906 to her seamstress mother and miner father.

[165] Guilbert, 21–2.   [166] Charlotte Davy, *Une Femme....* (Paris, 1927).

Taste and Labor

The erotics of the belle époque midinette were inseparable from her diligent wage labor and nationally-useful taste. Pleasure-loving and gay, the new Mimi Pinson was nonetheless a worker of unusual skill, and her labor in the luxury garment trades was a fundamental part of the midinette type. While the natural habitat of the Romantic grisette was her fifth floor room with its flowerpot and caged bird, the belle époque midinette was depicted moving in public spaces closely allied with working life. Zylberberg-Hocquard posits a shift in representations of the French workingwoman at the turn of the century that valorized women's salaried labor and self-sufficiency.[167] While this certainly seems to be the case, this valorization was accompanied by a conservative fantasy of garment work as both a labor of love for fashion-conscious workingwomen, and a charged sign of their alluring sexuality.

Montorgueil assured readers that, in spite of their romantic frivolity, Parisian garment workers were attached to their work. While one might imagine that women devoted to the "art of being beautiful" would become "indolent like female cats" once a supportive lover had been acquired, they actually had a "taste for daily labor" which resisted "the attractions of pleasure." The workingwoman who "grew up at work," was incapable of sustained idleness:

> She gets bored in gilded solitude. In a system of relative luxury, condemned to inaction, she returns to her past melancholically and misses the hard bread that her gaiety bit with such lovely teeth. She misses the activity and the job that sang between her diligent fingers, the calm that came from an automatic exertion, the industrious strength that atavism accumulated in her. Workingwoman, daughter of laborers, always a workingwoman, she returns to work…this loyalty to the workshop keeps her from the degeneration of the prostitutes. She is no longer the vassal of a master; she belongs to herself.[168]

Montorgueil constructs a marvelous vision of the female garment worker that deftly balances sexual dalliance with industriousness. Indeed, in his imagining, those women who escape the necessity of labor by way of a lover will long for the "hard bread" of their impoverished days. They will cast off the shackles of their lover-master and embrace independence, but as loyal workers not fearsome bluestockings: "She will return to the life insured by wages, to her fifth-floor apartment without a fireplace, to her meager pittance, to her four-*sous* dresses."[169]

---

[167] Zylberberg-Hocquard, "L'ouvrière dans les romans populaires du XIXe siècle." *Revue du Nord* 63, No. 250 (July-September 1981), 620–1.

[168] Montorgueil, *La Vie à Montmartre*, 51–2.   [169] Ibid, 53.

While industrious, midinettes were frequently imagined as choosing the garment trade because of their fondness for fashion and their desire to cultivate a pleasing appearance. In Montorgueil's 1897 *La Parisienne*, the garment worker is representative of the quintessential Parisienne in that fashion was not simply her profession, but her passion and art: "she reigns alone and uncontested over the empire of fashion. It is there that she is eminently an artist. There, she invents and creates…She dresses and adorns herself, indulging herself, aspiring not to settle for pleasing enough but to please more. She is her own doll, only experiencing real joy when she is making herself beautiful."[170] This association between style and labor undergirded arguments that midinettes worked out of love for their métier, not material want. Even the lowly trottin was in thrall to her grueling work: "This life, which would be hell for others, is one she aspired to like one aspires to reach Heaven…she used to dream of the blessed day when the schoolgirl's basket weighing down her arm would be the white delivery box of the errand girl. What a dream it is to have a little hat, the freedom of the streets, the *flânerie* of boutiques, to go to see beautiful ladies in beautiful houses, to penetrate behind the scenes of luxury and wealth!"[171] Garment work was not incidental to the midinette's identity; it was constitutive, transforming sweated wage labor into feminine caprice.

This closer association of the midinette with her luxury garment work accompanied a fuller embrace of the midinette as a fairylike tastemaker than was true of the Romantic-era grisette. While the nineteenth-century grisette had been coquettish, her belle époque descendants were more widely commended for their native French tastefulness. Female workers across the garment industry were regularly referenced as women of exceptional, inborn elegance, when their labor involved design work (as with some milliners, flowermakers, and seamstresses), or when their labor involved no design, as with many department store clerks, delivery girls, or industrial clothing manufacture workers.

I propose that notions of working-class feminine taste performed significant cultural work at the turn of the century—not simply as a poor women's version of bourgeois taste, but as a curative to bourgeois luxury and a reimagining of the urban working classes. The midinette ideal helped to reconcile contemporary attitudes about the connection between women, taste, and the nation. Turn-of-the-century Parisian garment workers were read as a new version of the Parisienne in whom consumer luxury was fused with republican ideals of working-class labor and virtue. This Parisienne was not detached from her class, but instead found her cultural value by joining feminine decorousness and diligent work, in contrast to the cosseted and extravagant bourgeois Parisienne.

Working Parisiennes had not always been so thoroughly associated with preternatural tastefulness. Jennifer Jones traces the oscillation in eighteenth- and

---

[170] Montorgueil, *La Parisienne, peinte par elle-même*, 96.   [171] Ibid.

early nineteenth-century fashion and aesthetic theory between positing tastefulness as the purview of the wealthy or as a democratized, national identity, an "economy of taste" organized "around taste and nationality" rather than class.[172] In the nineteenth century, with the ascendance of a self-interested and (it was feared) tasteless bourgeoisie, middle-class women were burdened with new taste duties.[173] Conceptions of workingwomen's taste have been largely absent from such studies, though Ruth Iskin suggests that the myth of the fashionable Parisienne was "seemingly class-transcendent," accessible to at least "some working women" by way of lower-cost department stores and sales.[174] An examination of midinette pop culture suggests that a culture-wide understanding of (some) workingwomen's taste as superior and nationally important developed at the turn of the century, as anxieties about bourgeois feminine consumption intensified.

One trope of midinette fiction was a deepened association of Parisian garment workers with mysterious powers of fashion confection. Sweated labor melts away in representations of the "fées de la couture" (*couture fairies*), as midinettes were habitually called. The expression "doigts des fées (*fairy fingers*)" was ubiquitous in such descriptions—taking the pained point of contact between these women and their labor and transforming it into effortless enchantment, while also distinguishing (often incorrectly) garment work from industrial machine work. The screenplay for the film *Mimi Pinson* of 1909 introduces the heroine as "one of these kind Parisian workingwomen, so hardworking and courageous, whose fairy fingers animate cloth with the dream of elegance scampering about in their little brains."[175] Pierre Alin's song "Les Midinettes" (1911) praised the "Little hands and little fingers" to whom Paris owed its "refined elegance | Exquisite hats, seductive fashions, | All of these little things born magically | From all these fairy fingers."[176] The long-suffering but golden-hearted seamstress heroine of former flowermaker and novelist Simone Bodève's 1908 *Clo* is defined by her extraordinary tastefulness. Clotilde's upper-class lover Maurice notes "that indefinable and light gracefulness that he saw granted so rapidly with a little help, a scalloped ribbon, a pleat in a dress as she sewed next him in the evening…this gracefulness that she was able to spread to every corner of his sad, badly furnished bachelor apartment upon which she managed, he didn't know how, to confer the enchanted secret of her beautiful harmony."[177] After suffering through rape, abortion, and romantic

---

[172] Jones, *Sexing La Mode: Gender*, 195.   [173] Tiersten, *Marianne in the Market*, 3.
[174] Iskin, 193.   [175] Marie Thierry, *Mimi Pinson: scénario*, (1909). 4-COL-4(4729) BNF-R.
[176] Pierre Alin, "Les Midinettes," (Paris, 1911).
[177] Simone Bodève, *Clo*. (Paris, 1908) 68. Bodève (1876–1921) was the pseudonym of Jeanne Chrétien. Born to a Parisian working-class family, she worked as a flowermaker and stenotypist. See Jean Elisabeth Pedersen, "'These Women Who Work:' Simone Bodève, Romain Rolland, and the Politics of Literary Reputation in Paris." Paper delivered at the *Society for French Historical Studies*, March 2012.

travails, Clotilde opens her own shop; after all, "it is an art to dress others."[178] The milliners' workshop in Gustave Le Rouge's *Le Crime d'une midinette* (1917) is a similar site of magical creation: "The work went quickly as if by enchantment and gradually the graceful creations of the little fairies were lined up in the tall show windows where in a few days they would be admired by mondaines and billionaires."[179]

Popular midinette love songs consistently lauded the skill and taste of the attractive garment worker being pursued. Bades and Mignon's "Joyeuses Midinettes" (1903) tells garment workers: "Between your fairy fingers, | A bit of cloth becomes marvelous | And takes on a stunning radiance | A lady who's nicely decked out, | Is really only beautiful through you, | Cause you're the queens of good taste."[180] A 1914 waltz, "Jolies Mimi-Pinson," sandwiched a verse praising midinette taste between others primarily describing the carnal pursuit of these women: "In their little hands, silk, velvet, | All those ribbons and fine laces | Will be transformed into charming finery | That will make all of our fine ladies dreamy. | Thanks to those little hands and their beautiful talent, | Elegant people the world over come to Paris. | Let's love them well, our little bees | Who produce such pretty marvels."[181] Thus the erotic function of the midinette was inextricable from her national role as a diligent producer of taste.

Midinettes were seen to display their tastefulness in their labor as well as in their personal style. Parisian garment workers were repeatedley praised for an ineffable style of the "petit rien"—that is, a style achieved by way of talent and ingenuity, and with relatively modest monetary outlay. The Parisian midinette in Vernières' *Camille Frison* is defined by her economical and superior style: "Even though the workingwoman comes from the most modest social standing, she has an instinctive taste, a native dexterity, which displays itself not simply in her work but which can be sensed in her entire person. She has an elegance that *is made from nothing* and that is striking in its simplicity."[182] She is a woman "who can produce a wonder of elegance from a rag and a bit of nothing, who with her frail fingers creates masterpieces before which foreigners kneel..."[183] In stark opposition to the frivolous bourgeois woman shopper, the midinette produces French luxury dominance with her labor and displays it on her own body, but without ruinous spending or morally suspect idleness.

---

[178] Bodève, *Clo*, 238.

[179] Gustave Le Rouge, *Le Crime d'une Midinette*, (Paris, 1917) 9. The book was reprinted in 1925, 1935, and 1936. Le Rouge was a popular adventure and science fiction writer. His first wife Juliette Torri seems to have been a seamstress-turned-sculptor's model; his second wife was a Parisian umbrella saleswoman. Lacassin refers to Le Rouge as "the Jules Vernes of the midinettes." Francis Lacassin, *A la Recherche de l'empire caché: Mythologie du roman populaire.* (Paris: 1991). 157, 176.

[180] P. Bades et V. Mignon, *Les Joyeuses Midinettes*. Music by P. Bades and H. Tarrelli. (St. Denis, 1903). BNF-L VM7-112393.

[181] N. Pitois, *Jolies Mimi-Pinson, chanson*. Music by Rémy d'Arbelle (Paris, 1914.)

[182] Vernières, 29–30; emphasis added.   [183] Vernières, 23.

Midinette tastefulness was advanced as a national inheritance, a taste not taught but absorbed as part of a biological *patrimoine* and most manifest in the native Parisienne. Vernières called the couture industry "one of the most characteristic manifestations of French genius, one of the most beautiful flowerings of our national commerce."[184] Parisian needle workers revealed the "artistic sense with which our race has been gifted and that no other people possess to the same degree..." The seamstress heroine Camille contrasts the "true workingwoman" to needleworkers trained in professional schools: "She has the métier *in her blood*, and learns it by watching others, whereas the student of a professional school...applies theories and, not having lived in the milieus where fashion is created, where couture is really a living thing, her taste and her initiative do not develop. She is not doing *couture*, but clothing manufacture [*confection*]."[185] This was a common refrain of midinette literature—that garment workers had a taste born of their physical presence in Paris and a native French genius.

Yet, taste for fashion, while a national treasure to be safeguarded, also appears throughout midinette fiction as a frequent cause of the workingwoman's downfall. Camille describes her first seduction by a young fur merchant named Henri (a man she meets on the train during her commute from the suburbs into the city), who overcomes her virtue by complimenting her taste. He tells her that her taste "shone through in [her] despite [her] simplicity" and meant she should wear fine dresses like her clients.[186] Later, working into the night on a fabulous ball gown, Camille experiences the bewitching, virtue-weakening effect of the dress:

> Night had fallen and the moonlight coming in through the windowpanes made the dress sparkle in the darkness. I was spellbound, transported. I sat there for a longtime, dreaming in front of this enchanted spectacle. The words of the fur merchant came back to me. I saw society ladies in gorgeous gowns of all sorts coming and going in salons dazzling with light, followed by handsome gentlemen who fluttered around them. And I was there among them, wearing the lovely dress that I had made whose sequins sparkled brilliantly like gold in the moonlight.[187]

The very next day, Camille agrees to accompany Henri to his apartment where he serves her wine and has sex with her.

One finds this belief in the working Parisienne's tastefulness in workingwomen's writing as well. Madeleine Henrey refers to her dressmaker mother's "inborn taste" and "genius" in couture creation, and to the "inborn gifts" of another seamstress friend.[188] Yvette Guilbert rhapsodized over her milliner mother's skill in her memoir: "God had given my mother fairy fingers, and she could learn in

---

[184] Vernières, 26.   [185] Vernières, 70–1.
[186] Vernières, 91–2.   [187] Vernières, 94–5.   [188] Henrey, 32, 90, 177.

twenty-four hours any trade without having had any training. Her skill and quickness were miraculous."[189] Guilbert herself also worked as a seamstress and was indignant when one client not only failed to pay for the "wonderful evening dresses" she made but also passed off Guilbert's creations as the work of a major couturier, denying her credit.[190] Feminist labor activist and former seamstress Jeanne Bouvier recalled creating a "superb red bodice" for the syndical pavilion at the 1900 Exposition: "I put all of my art into its execution and I was happy to think that my labor would appear in the display case of the Pavilion, that would show the world what the proletariat was capable of."[191] Pathbreaking Parisian couturier and workingwoman Madeleine Vionnet referred to taste as "transmitted from mother to daughter. But some people don't need to be educated; they are innately tasteful. I think I am one of them."[192] After World War I, Vionnet led a legal campaign to protect her designs as precious intellectual property and as a patrimony of French genius. Former flowermaker Simone Bodève insisted that among young garment workers, "there is not one who does not imagine herself at least the equal of the female client who is transformed, decorated, and dressed by her genius, and who does not believe, in spite of everything, that all possibilities are open to her."[193] While some lacked taste or moderation, "you will recognize the very intelligent ones, the very sensible ones by their choice to wear black and to follow the latest fashions according to their means, with an indefinable little bit of imagination that distinguishes them from the woman bragging about being 'comme il faut.'" Indeed, tastefulness could be used as a means of assessing the character of a garment worker: "You will recognize the crazy ones by the inimitable incoherence of their *toilette*."[194] As much as Bodève acknowledged (and spent her career detailing) the miseries of garment work, she concludes that "The workingwoman, and particularly milliners and seamstresses, love their work. How else to explain that she can create such wonders, which only can be found in Paris and which other workingwomen elsewhere can only copy and distort."[195]

However dominant this vision of the garment worker as fashion creator, during the belle époque acts of design creation could be used to set women outside of the legal category of *ouvrière*. A case before the Conseil de Prud'hommes in 1908 found that a *prémiere main* could sue the couturiers who had fired her after only a

[189] Yvette Guilbert, *The Song of My Life: My Memories*, (London, 1929) 16.

[190] Guilbert, *The Song of My Life*, 21.

[191] Jeanne Bouvier, *Mes mémoires: ou 59 années d'activité industrielle, sociale et intellectuelle d'une ouvrière, 1876–1935* (Paris, 1983), 108–9.

[192] *Madeleine Vionnet*, ed. Pamela Golbin (New York, 2009). Exposition Madeleine Vionnet, Musee des Arts Decoratifs, Paris, 24 June 2009–31 January 2010, p. 14. Quotation from Madeleine Chapsal, "Hommage à Madeleine Vionnet," *Vogue Paris*, Apr. 1975, p. 26.

[193] Simone Bodève, *Celles qui travaillent* (Paris, 1913), 7.   [194] Ibid. 8.

[195] Ibid. 64. For a popular but less romanticized version of the midinette tale, see former seamstress Marguertie Audoux's *L'Atelier de Marie-Claire* (1920). Marie-Hélène Zylberberg-Hocquard and Slava Liszek, "Marie-Claire ou la voix des couturières," *Le Roman social: littérature, histoire et mouvement ouvrier* (Paris, 2002), 39–46.

month because she had created designs for them and thus, in the words of the labor relations board, had done the work "of an inventor, and, as it were, up to a certain point, of a creative artist" and that "all of the later material labor had been effected by true workingwomen," who fashioned the raw materials according to her design. As a result, this *première* was legally an "employee," not an *ouvrière*, and could not be fired during the standard trial employment period to which workingwomen in the needle trades were subject.[196]

There is also evidence in workingwomen's memoirs that the midinette's much-trumpeted interest in fashion could be perceived as a legacy one had to reject to reach political maturity. Bouvier distinguished herself from other seamstresses in her memoir, recalling her co-workers' incredulity when she insisted that, rather than buying a new hat or dress, she preferred to save money to be able to contribute to her mutual insurance and to buy a house for retirement.[197] Similarly, Bodève, though a former flowerworker herself, was unsure whether young garment workers, because of their proximity to and interest in the world of luxury fashion, could even be considered of the laboring class. She derided writers for taking so little interest in the real working class, "the true, impoverished People, obscure and hardworking," and instead for being "attached to a poignant art that paints the miseries and struggles of delicate, pretty girls; but are they really of the people? They seem to have somewhat 'passed over to the enemy side'..."[198] Bodève gently criticized those young apprentice seamstresses infected by "the appalling need to be fashionable [*d'être coquettes*]." At the same time, she defended young garment workers from their reputation, "we are quite serious, even if we don't seem to be."[199]

Parisian couture workers in this period seem to have indeed engaged in a style of "the slightest thing [*le petit rien*]"; many workingwomen appear to have understood themselves as purveyors of Parisian taste as much in their own dress as in their labor—an understanding that can be traced in workingwomen's magazines from this period, particularly those with advice columns.[200] *Le Journal de Mimi Pinson* (a magazine provided free to workingwomen at kiosks in Paris's garment districts), included a bi-monthly fashion column by "Miss Teyrieuse" which slipped effortlessly between advice to the new fashions' wearers and professional

[196] "Compétence. I. Premiere de maison de modes. Attributions. Creations de modèles. Oeuvre d'invention. Employée. Justice de paix. Situation antérieure au 27 mars 1908. Compétence. II. Congédiement. Premier mois. Période d'essai applicable seulement aux ouvrières. Indemnité de brusque congédiement due aux employés." Tribunal Civil de la Seine (7e CH). 10 Aug. 1908. *Revue des Conseils de Prud'hommes*, A11 (Dec. 1908), 195–8.
[197] Bouvier, *Mes mémoires*, 98, 112. Orig. 1936.
[198] Bodève, *Celles qui travaillent*, 33–4.   [199] Ibid. 64.
[200] Ann Heilmann and Margaret Beetham note that such journals contained a "heterogeneity of voice" crucial to New Woman identity. "Introduction," *New Woman Hybridities: Femininity, Feminism, and International Consumer Culture, 1880–1930* (New York, 2004), 5.

tips for women sewing and even designing the latest trends.[201] In August 1908, Teyrieuse asked her working readers to speak to each other about fashion via her column, and invited seamstresses and hatmakers to form an "apostolate of the needle and ribbon" that would "uphold...good taste, elegance, as well as economy" for all the female workers of the city, whatever their trade.[202] To this end, the magazine sponsored a competition to honor the "best design" by their seamstress and milliner readers which also incurred "the smallest expense."[203] Teyrieuse's column from October again presumed that her readers are at once the new fashion's wearers *and* its creators. Thus, the new long *jaquette* that season, would include, in some cases, "more than one hundred button holes...This last detail promises to be considerable labor for the workingwomen charged with its execution." And the hatmakers of Paris were debating the size of hats: "Opinion is divided and each class of milliner presents its recommendation on hat design." The new, narrow dress line, however, is described from the perspective of the wearer: "With the gowns we will be wearing this winter, it will be extremely difficult to do ballet steps."[204]

The Confédération générale de Travail's daily paper *La Bataille syndicaliste* approached midinette fashionability as a significant working-class concern. Feminist and syndicalist writer Marcelle Capy penned a piece in May 1914 that connected garment workers' demands for the English work week (a half day off on Saturdays) to the midinette's need to be well-dressed. She praised the "perfect" taste and dexterity of Parisian needle workers, and then pointed out that, "We like to say that the midinette is elegant; we admire her grace and her taste, but we don't ask ourselves what prodigious savings she must achieve to arrive at this. The bosses oblige her to be well-dressed—a poor outfit would arouse the disgust of the rich clients...The English week then would be a great benefit to the midinette" because it would give her time to shop.[205]

La Bataille syndicaliste also had a regular advice column for workingwomen called "Advice to Midinettes," in which a certain "Mimi Pinson" answered letters from readers soliciting, among other things, tips for achieving an *au courant* and affordable style. The columnist regularly refers to the modest means of her readers and to their lives as working women, and, as Anaïs Albert has suggested, did so as a critique of the vulgarity of bourgeois style.[206] Mimi Pinson and her readers share a common devotion to maintaining tasteful style despite limited finances; these columns insist upon the worker-reader's ability to do so: "if means do not

---

[201] The Bibliothèque nationale has three issues of the magazine, all from 1908.

[202] Miss Teyrieuse, "Modes," *Le Journal de Mimi Pinson, à l'atelier & dans la famille*, No. 2, 10 Aug. 1908, p. 13.

[203] Ibid.   [204] Ibid.

[205] Marcelle Capy, "La Midinette et la semaine anglaise," *La Bataille syndicaliste*, 26 May 1914, p. 3.

[206] Albert, "Les Midinettes parisiennes à la Belle Époque." For Albert, the column expresses Parisian workingwomen's engagement with mass consumer culture.

permit it, one can all the same be very much in style."[207] Mimi Pinson often
rejects faddish style in favor of a simpler and more economical elegance—an
elegance achieved by the dexterity and taste of the working Parisienne. In
December 1910 she wrote, "In general, the new shapes are not that pretty...I prefer a simple cuff to these...One can, without great expense, put together a charming ensemble by trimming one's cuff with a small band of fur."[208] In fall 1910, when
a trend for thicker veils was sweeping Paris, Mimi Pinson advised her readers:
"Leave to the *parvenues* the privilege of decking oneself out in amusing fly cages,
if it pleases them. This season we will see many little veils in Chantilly lace, made
with extraordinary finesse. Unnecessary to tell you that the original is beyond our
means, but I have seen some lovely imitations for an entirely affordable price."[209]
One reader explained that she was eager to acquire a sealskin coat "because I have
a job where one has to look good, but I don't think one has to spend so much to
get something that matches up."[210]

Twenty-year-old garment worker Myrtho wrote in summer 1908 to the *Journal
de Mimi Pinson* defending herself and her colleagues in the garment industry
against charges of frivolity. She disputes the assumption that "behind her smiling
and surprised appearance which we chalk up to her youth, [the midinette] had no
serious thoughts." She affirmed her *coquetterie* while also insisting upon a higher
calling: "Who could have supposed that the Parisian workingwoman, this doll
that seemed only to love clothes, had other, less superficial ambitions?...We don't
only take pride in our clothing; we are also eager to win esteem and sympathy.
Certainly, we don't renounce a wardrobe, that, for us, often consists of inexpensive cloth. We bring all of our ingenuity to its production, and after having proved
our *savoir-faire* in the clothing of our rich clients, we continue to bear witness to
our taste for ourselves."[211] Myrtho holds that her interest in fashion is not merely
a colorful accoutrement to her romantic midinette allure. Instead, she speaks to
the importance of an unschooled but superior tastefulness—deployed both in the
workshop and in these women's own *toilettes*. More interesting, Myrtho explains
that grueling daily labor in manufacturing luxury garments engenders a complex
relationship with fashion:

> There are days when we are discouraged. Everyone on earth has days like this,
> but that's when comfort becomes necessary. If we don't manage to overcome our
> sadness, we cry. But if alas the tears sometimes do us good, they also, at other
> times, soften us. Sometimes, they drive us to revolt. And so, [we think] we too

---

[207] Mimi Pinson, "Conseils aux midinettes," *La Bataille syndicaliste*, 14 Dec. 1911.
[208] Ibid.
[209] Mimi Pinson, "Conseils aux Midinettes," *La Bataille syndicaliste*, 5 Oct. 1911.
[210] Mimi Pinson, "Conseils aux Midinettes," *La Bataille syndicaliste*, 9 Nov. 1911.
[211] Letter from "Myrtho," excerpted in Mussette, "Le Carnet de Mussette," *Le Journal de Mimi Pinson*, No. 2, 10 Aug. 1908, 10.

would like to have our share of well-being, our share of luxury. We too would like to wear beautiful gowns that we craft from one end of the year to the next, and get some of the flattery that richly-attired women collect along their way... And these fantastical ideas go along... Until the moment when, ashamed to have spoken our mind and to have inflamed our imagination, we regain a feeling of modesty and find our way back to good sense.[212]

But this return to good behavior includes, for this young workingwoman, an increased interest in self-instruction; she describes sharing books with her colleagues and reading the newspaper as a means of education.

In 1909, when a new magazine for workingwomen, *Midinette: Journal de la femme et de la jeune fille qui travaillent*, attempted to define its readership, it did so by embracing the term "midinette" as a powerful social identity for all workingwomen: "*Midinette* will belong to no one in particular. Rather, it will belong to midinettes, to all midinettes, that is to say, to women and girls who ask that their labor and their talent provide the means for them to meet their needs honestly... the midinette is not only the seamstress, the milliner, or the saleswoman, but she is also the female employee in public and private administrations."[213] Here, the midinette is defined not by her beauty or sexual availability, but by her labor, her skill, and her ability to leverage both to achieve economic stability. All women who work, regardless of age or industry, could draw upon the cultural capital of the designation midinette.

While this was undoubtedly true for many garment workers in this period, it also meant that garment labor was conflated with and at times effaced by an understanding of midinettes as delighted wearers of Parisian fashion and objects of sexual delectation. Romantic frivolity and a heightened interest in fashion thus became both Parisian garment workers gift to the Patrie and its men, and justification for their continued political and economic domination. I explore the national import of this association and the way that it bled into social scientific and philanthropic approaches to the problem of Parisian women's labor in the following chapters.

---

[212] "Myrtho," "Le Carnet de Mussette," *Le Journal de Mimi Pinson*.

[213] "Notre Programme," La Direction, 1–2. *Midinette: Journal de la femme et de la jeune fille qui travaillent*, No. 1, 12 Nov. 1909. BNF JO-50610(5) 1909. The magazine's subtitle was "Sa récréation, son confident, son conseiller, son défenseur, son interprète."

2

"Without Rival"

Workingwomen, Regulation, and Taste in the Belle Époque Garment Industry

In the years leading up to the First World War, France's concern about its industrial competitiveness played out vividly in debates about French, and more particularly, Parisian fashion. Politicians, journalists, and fashion industry leaders demonstrated a keen attachment to the idea of Paris as an unparalleled site of luxury production and taste. While not entirely new, this discourse of superior national taste and skill now bore the marks of heightened nationalist and economic anxiety about French commerce, and deployed concern for and selective admiration of Parisian workingwomen in debates about regulation in the garment trades. This vision of Parisian garment workers as guardians of a French cultural monopoly on luxury taste was deployed by trade industrialists, labor inspectors, philanthropists, and government officials assessing the state of the garment industry at the turn of the century.

Historians have made clear the tremendous rhetorical investment made by French industry and its supporters from the mid-nineteenth century to promote French superiority in handicraft and luxury production as the country's particular genius, setting it above its increasingly powerful industrial competitors, Germany, Britain, and the United States.[1] By the turn of the century, cheaply-made German couture presented a significant challenge to French fashion, and thus was derided for its congenital lack of taste.[2] Nancy Green suggests that French garment trade industrialists employed a "double discourse" at the turn of the century—an internal "self-criticism" about the need for greater productivity, and an external rhetoric for "the outside world," which "proudly placed French elegance first and foremost," and contrasted French "artistry" to the ill-made, mass-produced products of rival nations.[3] I flesh out Green's concept of a "performative" "manufacturers' *imaginaire*" around the garment industry.[4] In examining exhibition reports, ministerial inquiries, and labor reform commissions, it becomes evident that assertions of French fashion genius were threaded throughout debates about

---

[1] Silverman, *Art Nouveau in Fin-de-Siècle France*; Auslander, *Taste and Power*; Walton, *France at the Crystal Palace*; Williams, *Dream Worlds*; Joan DeJean, *The Essence of Style: How the French Invented High Fashion, Fine Food, Chic Cafés, Style, Sophistication and Glamour* (New York, 2005).
[2] Green, *Ready-to-Wear and Ready-to-Work*, 99.   [3] Ibid. 108, 109.   [4] Ibid. 77, 117.

Working Girls: Sex, Taste, and Reform in the Parisian Garment Trades, 1880–1919. Patricia Tilburg, Oxford University Press (2019). © Patricia Tilburg.
DOI: 10.1093/oso/9780198841173.001.0001

industrial trade and regulation for audiences both abroad and at home. This was more than a rhetorical flourish, but actually revealed a peculiarly French investment in fashion and tastefulness.

Furthermore, national taste supremacy combined with fears about the vulnerability of the couture industry to stymie attempts at regulating workplace and environmental hazards in this period. French couture tradesmen doubled down on the special nature of Parisian workingwomen's craft as they resisted reforms aimed at ameliorating those women's labor conditions. Employers found strange bedfellows in this endeavor among labor inspectors charged with assessing unhealthy working conditions and philanthropists devoted to labor uplift. In the case studies examined below, the exigencies of the fashion industry and of French fashion's status as skilled handiwork and "art" muted pressing demands for workplace reform. In each instance, the female Parisian garment worker was front and center, as was a nostalgic vision of her work as pre-industrial, paternalistic, and hand-crafted by her "fairy fingers."

This romanticized vision of the French workplace was at best willfully optimistic given the reality of French labor relations in general and in the Paris garment trades specifically in these years. Gérard Noiriel refers to the period from 1880 to the outbreak of the First World War as one in which "an intense collective mobilization won over the *classes populaires* to the point that, of all the history of the French worker's movement, this era represents, without contest, its apogee."[5] But it is also true that much of the French garment trades maintained small-scale and even familial production well into the twentieth century.[6] Whitney Walton attributes the persistence of traditional hand methods in garment production to a national conviction about the supremacy of French feminine taste.[7]

This chapter begins by exploring rhetoric about the Parisian garment worker around the Franco-British Exhibition of 1908, when French and British commentators alike praised French luxury garment products, and evoked Paris as *the* site of garment trade art and Parisian workingwomen as the preternaturally tasteful if antediluvian instruments of that art. I then interrogate how such encomia to garment worker taste and vulnerability operated in debates about workplace reform during the belle époque. What was the impact of this nationalist discourse of exceptional Parisian taste and distinctly old-fashioned labor on female garment workers in need of protection? This chapter focuses on two loci of labor reform

---

[5] Gérard Noiriel, *Les Ouvriers dans la société française, XIXe–XXe siècle* (Paris, 2002), 99.

[6] The family workshop was imagined as a "solution to the woman question as well as the social question...an antidote to modernity." Marilyn Boxer, "Protective legislation and home industry: the marginalization of women workers in late nineteenth and early twentieth-century France," *Journal of Social History* 20, No. 1 (1986), 45–65, 48–9.

[7] Whitney Walton, "'To triumph before feminine taste': bourgeois women's consumption and hand methods of production in mid-nineteenth-century Paris," *Business History Review* 60, No. 4 (1986), 541–63.

from these years—efforts to eliminate night garment work and those to regulate toxic substances in artificial flowermaking. Ultimately, arguments about the special status of couture as a national industry and cultural patrimony in need of protection were deployed by the couture *patronat* and even by labor ministry officials and inspectors to obstruct these reform campaigns.

The Franco-British Exhibition of 1908

Turn-of-the-century European world's fairs were an ideal screen upon which to project national aspirations and character, and the fashion industry was unsurprisingly central to French self-representation at these events.[8] During 1908's Franco-British Exhibition, held in London to seal the *entente cordiale*, this self-presentation was mirrored back by English industrialists. The Franco-British opened in May 1908 and attracted some 8.4 million visitors.[9] Many English observers used the French dress exhibit as an opportunity to acclaim Paris as a site of matchless luxury production and taste, and Parisian garment workers as inventive and fashionable artists embedded in comfortably traditional labor relations. For their part, French manufacturers used the exhibition to raise up the Parisian garment trade as a special environment engendering tastefulness in its working-class denizens, and to blast attempts to usurp the commercial power of their industry by cut-rate German manufacturers. They did so by focusing on the historic superiority and preternatural artistic sense of the Parisian garment worker.

The French fashion display was indeed striking, and provided visitors with a visual escape in which effect and artfulness reigned. "Nothing to compare with it has ever been seen before," enthused one English visitor, "Dress fabrics and dresses are the greatest of French industries, and they were displayed in bewildering profusion, and with that inimitable sense of effect of which they alone have the secret."[10] The French display featured mannequins in scenes of urbane luxury— a garden party, an opulent salon, a boudoir. Hatmakers displayed their handiwork in a fanciful diorama of Marie-Antoinette and her ladies in the garden of the

---

[8] See Silverman, *Art Nouveau in Fin-de-Siècle France*; Anne Dymond, "Embodying the nation: art, fashion, and allegorical women at the 1900 Exposition Universelle," *RACAR: Revue d'art canadienne/Canadian Art Review* 36, No. 2 (2011), 1–14; Maxime Laprade, "Haute couture et expositions universelles, 1900–1925," *Apparence(s)* 7 (2017), Online.

[9] Alexander Geppert, *Fleeting Cities: Imperial Expositions in Fin-de-Siècle Europe* (New York, 2013), 101–33.

[10] A. Shadwell, "Introduction," in F. G. Dumas, *The Franco-British Exhibition: Illustrated Review, 1908* (London: Chatto & Windus, 1908), 5. For information on the Franco-British, see *The Exhibitions: Great White City, Shepherd's Bush London: 70th Anniversary, 1908–1978* (London, 1978); Debra Kelly and Tom Jackson, "The Franco-British Exhibition of 1908: legacies and memories one hundred years on," *Synergies* 2 (2009), 11–23.

Petit-Trianon. Feather merchants recreated bird life on the Upper Nile. Artificial flowermakers offered their vision of a Japanese chrysanthemum garden.

British and French commentators alike linked the French fashion exhibit to a romantic vision of Paris and its female workers as incomparable sources of garment art and style. Georges Carette, men's wear designer and secretary general of France's couture section at the exposition, boasted that female garment workers in Parisian workshops followed fashion "like the great ladies of high society," and that it was rare to "come across on the street a woman put together *without taste* [*sans goût*]."[11] René Famchon, president of the French hatmaking patronal association, boasted that one of the few English hat displays at the Franco-British was by the London branch of a Parisian hatmaker and accentuated its Parisian source by posing wares on mannequins of French celebrities.[12] Famchon also remarked that artificial flowermaking was "an essentially French industry," and that Parisian flowermaking in particular was "the seat of taste and professional skill"[13] He admitted that Parisian milliners working abroad and in the French provinces were obliged to "come back from time to time and dip themselves into our Capital if they want to conserve the brilliant qualities that they acquired here."[14]

Famchon quoted extensively in his exhibition report from the London County Council's survey of the English garment industry in which British and French manufacturers decry the abilities of English garment workers and applaud the taste and talent of their Parisian counterparts. English hat manufacturers also recommended "regular visits to Paris" for apprentice milliners to learn "artistic sense," given that, "France's superiority when it comes to the clothing industry is due to the long history of Parisian taste in all the artistic professions."[15] An English corset manufacturer with French and English workers insisted that "the young French woman has an artistic sense in her work" and never misses a stitch. He confessed that he had never been able to replicate French handiwork, despite sending French-made corsets to an English factory to be copied.[16] A French corset maker in London held up a piece of embroidered lingerie to interviewers and declared it would have been useless to give such a job to English workingwomen, "It's not so much that they wouldn't be able to do it, but that they wouldn't be able to appreciate and understand its artistic value."[17] According to the survey, English workers lacked the artistic sense and the "creative power" that distinguished French *modistes*.[18] English flower manufacturers grumbled to Famchon that one

[11] Georges Carette, *Exposition Franco-Britannique de Londres, 1908: Section Française, Classe 85: Rapport* (Paris, 1909), 22.

[12] René Famchon, *Exposition Franco-Britannique de Londres, 1908: Section Française, Groupe XIIIB, Classe 86, Industries des Accessoires du Vêtement: Rapport* (Paris, 1910), 584–5, 528.

[13] Ibid. 293, 288. Tiersten mentions Famchon's remarks as part of a broader notion of the environmental influence of Paris as seat of French taste (*Marianne in the Market*, 128–30).

[14] Famchon, *Exposition Franco-Britannique de Londres, 1908*, 225.   [15] Ibid. 255–6.

[16] London County Council, quoted ibid. 156.   [17] Ibid. 156.   [18] Ibid. 255.

simply "could not develop the artistic sense of English workingwomen" and that they lacked "sufficient aptitude and artistic instruction" to compete with French workingwomen.[19] English firms, Famchon boasted, "often employ Parisian milliners," due to their exceptional artistic sense.[20] In a 1909 inquiry into English garment work, French labor investigator Claire Gérard confirmed the "preference" of English hat and corset manufacturers for employing French workingwomen, "because the artistic sense, the originality, the ability to adapt and to copy is lacking in English workingwomen."[21]

The identification of French taste with Paris's female workers was so complete that such references were made interchangeable. Famchon moved effortlessly from acclaiming Paris's "grandes modistes" to praising the "fairy fingers of our milliners" who "instantly create headdresses of such grace, such allure, and such perfect execution that the most elegant ladies around the world fight over them." French workingwomen were "without rival," and were often called to bring "Parisian taste and savoir-faire...to the provinces and abroad."[22] If Paris was the source of style and art, then the French garment trade worker was the delivery mechanism. Famchon quoted Jules Simon's 1861 study of French workingwomen which marked flowermakers as artists of unusual creative capacity:

There is something gay and youthful even in the name flowermaker, and nothing is more charming than the products that come from their fingers...It is the Parisian industry par excellence, and the beautiful women of the Old World and the New purchase flowers for their hats in Paris...Presently, Parisian flora is without rival. Nearly six thousand laborers live in Paris off of its manufacture. The most able among these are veritable artists who study natural flowers with love and reproduce them with more accuracy than the finest painters...[23]

Simon's sunny nineteenth-century vision of the flower industry was replicated in belle époque discussions of this trade. Comparing these women to painters elided negative connotation of sweated garment work, instead imagining these laborers as "gay" artists whose passion, not financial necessity, drives them to the workshop every day. Famchon agreed: "Flowermaking has become, for certain people, not simply a *métier*, but a true art."[24]

Simon was not the only mid-nineteenth-century French commentator quoted in the 1908 report; economist and historian Natalis Rondot's 1854 report on London's Great Exhibition also was cited at length. Rondot observed that the one

---

[19] Ibid. 296, 298.   [20] Ibid. 250.

[21] Claire Gérard, "Les Industries feminines anglaises: la lutte contre la chomage," *Musée Social: Mémoires et Documents: Supplément aux Annales* (June 1909), 133–68, 136.

[22] Famchon, *Exposition Franco-Britannique de Londres, 1908*, 224–5.

[23] Jules Simon, quoted ibid. 287. The quotation is from Simon's *L'Ouvrière* (Paris, 1861), 212.

[24] Famchon, *Exposition Franco-Britannique de Londres, 1908*, 287.

weakness of the burgeoning artificial flowermaking business in London (in the 1850s) was the lack of "Parisian taste and genius": "That which exists in Paris alone is invention; it is that spirit so fertile in ideas, in imagination, which creates fashion and its vagaries; it is that exquisite taste, without which, in the domain of industrial art, there is no elegance, no beauty."[25] The inclusion of Rondot's assessment was not offhanded; Famchon employed mid-nineteenth-century exhibition commentary to provide a sense of the unbroken line of Parisian garment craft tradition. French exhibitors thus promoted their greatest commercial strength as a historical one, an age-old dominance as the global leader in taste.

Far from anomalous, this backward glance at an idealized, pre-industrial commercial landscape corresponded to a general tone in both French and English observations of the 1908 Exhibition.[26] The popularity of the French fashion exhibits is rightly apprehended within an Exhibition-wide deflection of concerns about labor mobilization and industrialization. Descriptions of the French luxury garment exhibits often contained wistful references to the production of *articles de luxe* through a traditional, pre-modern system of female labor. Frequent references to the "fairy fingers" of Parisian workers highlighted the manual, non-mechanized labor of these women and provided an attractive vision of the belle époque working classes. To this end, observers also underscored the antiquated craft methods of the Parisian garment worker. In excerpts of the London County Council's corset industry inquiry provided in Famchon's report, one official cited "the curious tradition" among French *corsetières* of guarding their techniques as "a family secret transmitted from mother to daughter."[27] (Indeed, as Catherine Omnès has shown, the French garment industry did see a "professional heredity" in which trade *savoir-faire* tended to be passed from mother to daughter.[28]) "Famchon ended his report with another sizable quote from Jules Simon praising the harmonious relationship between employers and workers in France. Simon, reporting on the Exposition Universelle of 1878 in Paris, assessed French industry's chances in the global marketplace: "Just as, when a ship is sinking, there is no hope if the captain and the sailors do not get on, one also must consider as lost, from the industrial perspective, a nation in which the bosses and workers, instead of working together for the common good, think only of rendering one another

[25] Natalis Rondot, quoted ibid. 294. The quotation is from Rondot's *Rapport sur les objets de parure, de fantaisie et de goût, fait à la commission française du jury international de l'Exposition universelle de Londres* (Paris, 1854).

[26] Paul Greenhalgh argues that the Franco-British took place amidst political concerns about the British empire, feminism, and labor. The English side of the Exhibition "was attempting to advance with its back to the future, to regress and carry that regression on into the new century." "Art, Politics and Society at the Franco-British Exhibition of 1908," *Art History* 8, No. 4 (Dec. 1985), 434–52, 441. Stephanie Rains notes that British exhibits expressed Edwardian "neo-nostalgia" for "traditional lifestyles and crafts." "The Ideal Home (Rule) Exhibition 1908: Ballymaclinton and the 1908 Franco-British Exhibition," *Field Day Review*, 7 (2011), 4–21, 17.

[27] London County Council, quoted in Famchon, *Exposition Franco-Britannique de Londres, 1908*, 153.

[28] Catherine Omnès, *Ouvrières parisiennes: marchés du travail et trajectoires professionelles au 20e siècle* (Paris, 1997).

miserable and helpless."[29] Famchon assured his readers that Simon's words were as fitting in 1908 as they had been in 1878: "Every bit of this piece, which, after thirty years, still preserves, almost entirely, a marked topicality, deserves to be reflected upon and leads to considerations from which we can take inspiration."[30]

Representations of Paris as an exceptional space of luxury garment production thus relied upon a consoling vision of the industry's paternalistic labor relations. British manufacturers praised Parisian workers' superior skill, yet identified that artistic talent as a symptom of French industrial traditionalism. The London County Council warned that the archaic passing along of corset craft technique from mother to daughter would be a "death blow" to some older houses.[31] For French manufacturers, Parisian garment workers were women who required protection because of their talent and importance to the French economy, and because they were embedded in a charmingly archaic paternalistic workplace. I read these evocations of both the exceptional talent and the political docility of the Parisian working class as a potent and popular fantasy for bourgeois observers on both sides of the Channel as they fended off challenges to their power from both women and labor. Carette, a garment trade *patron* himself, devoted an entire chapter of his Exhibition report to retirement funds in the garment industry, and went into some detail about "the generous feelings for philanthropy" with which the leaders of Parisian couture were imbued. Parisians bosses, according to Carette, had not needed legislative intervention to recognize "that they could not be indifferent to the lot of their workers, who, after having been their collaborators, were obliged by age to take a well-earned rest." Carette noted a "patronal solicitude" in all aspects of a worker's life where "pecuniary assistance could be effective": "for the past twenty-five years, a powerful current of philanthropy has animated the *patrons* [of major couture houses] who have engaged in some lively competition to offer the most considerable benefits to their laborers and employees..."[32] He detailed the various pension and assistance programs provided by Parisian department stores. The Bon Marché was praised for providing dowries for single female employees upon their marriage. La Samarataine had created a nursery for employees' children. Two fashion houses were singled out for offering maternity benefits for expectant mothers in their employ. In striking contrast to these pages of detailed praise for French "patronal solicitude," Carette's comparatively brief section on British employers' pension policies explained tersely that in England, "it is not the custom of industrial or commercial businesses to provide for the retirement of their employees or laborers...The laborer is used to counting on no one but himself."[33]

[29] Jules Simon, quoted in Famchon, *Exposition Franco-Britannique de Londres, 1908*, 586. Quotation from *Exposition universelle de 1878: rapports du jury international* (Paris, 1880).
[30] Famchon, *Exposition Franco-Britannique de Londres, 1908*, 586.   [31] Ibid. 153.
[32] Carette, *Exposition Franco-Britannique de Londres, 1908*, 97.
[33] Ibid. 101.

In his account of the City of Paris Pavilion, French exhibition organizer and journalist Paul Lafage combined a chivalrous fantasy of the city as a fashionable woman ("dressed...in all her best attire...our dear Capital, unique, adorable Paris") with praise of Parisian couture's paternalist care for its workers: "Charity and widespread benefactions attest to the kindness of her heart; education lavished upon her people shows with what zeal and variety the intelligence of her children is cultivated."[34] While the Pavilion principally displayed materials on public works and utilities in Paris, Lafage's essay highlighted professional education opportunities for young girls who would someday become garment trade workers: "Already skillful and clever, these future fairies of the Rue de la Paix can do embroidery work and designs, can work tapestries and crochet, charming naïve attempts like the first artistic efforts of a rude age...[The teachers] are equipping the generations to come with better and more artistic weapons for their own protection."[35] Lafage, like so many observers of the Franco-British, imagined Paris as a nursery for working-class design artists arming themselves for economic survival.

We can read the Exposition's acclaim of harmonious French worker–employer relations not simply as remarks by manufacturers blind to the realities of labor unrest in this period, but rather as defensive protestations against these very realities. I suggest that this vision was a significant component of the French presentation abroad, and one that English manufacturers at the Exhibition found attractive. Back in Paris, reformers and garment labor activists would find this appealing manufacturers' garment imaginary an obstacle to some efforts at regulation within the couture industry.

The *Veillées*

A frequently-condemned aspect of garment work at the turn of the century was the use of *veillées*, overtime nightwork regularly required in Parisian luxury couture shops to meet increased and pressing demands around seasonal society events. As Mary Lynn Stewart and Marilyn Boxer have shown, while women's nightwork was banned in 1892, luxury garment enterprises received exemptions from this law up to sixty days per year, and so-called "family workshops" were completely exempt.[36] Garment industry advocates successfully argued that theirs were special trades with periods of extreme seasonal demand necessitating

---

[34] Paul Lafage, "The City of Paris Pavilion," *The Franco-British Exhibition: Illustrated Review, 1908*, ed. F. G. Dumas (London, 1908), 281–4, 281.

[35] Ibid. 282.

[36] Mary Lynn Stewart traces some of these debates in *Women, Work, and the French State: Labour Protection and Social Patriarchy, 1879–1919* (Kingston, 1989), 126–7; Boxer, "Protective legislation," 47.

nightwork. Many seamstresses were obliged to evade the regulation by taking their work home to complete in time for impatient employers or clients.[37]

In spring 1900, members of the Commission départmental du travail de la Seine met to discuss the question of garment trade nightwork. The Commission included forty-five members: government inspectors, syndical representatives, delegates from the labor dispute board, and at least one luxury fashion house couturier, Gaston Worth. The only two women on the commission were both garment workers and delegates from the Bourse du Travail (the trade union exchange): 22-year-old seamstress Clémence Jusselin and 28-year-old flower-maker Stéphanie Bouvard.[38] In 1908, Jusselin would go on to be one of the leaders of the Syndicat des Couturières, and was elected as the first "prud'femme," a female judge on the Conseil des Prud'hommes, the labor tribunal.[39] She also was one of the founders of a lunch cooperative for Parisian garment workers called Les Midinettes (discussed in Chapter 4). Bouvard, along with her mother Amélie and sister Marguerite, helped found the Syndicat des fleuristes-plumassières in 1896.[40] During her years representing the union and later in organizing her own flowermakers' cooperative, Bouvard advocated for the necessity of reforming structures of apprenticeship and on the skill required in artificial flowermaking.

Throughout the nightwork commission's deliberations in 1900 and 1901, Bouvard and Jusselin attempted to keep the focus on the abuses of overwork, low salaries, and poor hygienic conditions. Time and again, when faced with such criticism, couturier Worth enthused about the special taste and skill of his female workers. In a May 1900 session, he proclaimed that the couture industry, that "essentially Parisian" industry "truly practiced only in Paris," could only "recruit its workingwomen from an elite." Luxury fashion, "a source of tremendous business for our city," necessitated dispensations from certain labor laws because of the rarity and national significance of the industry:

These special works are executed...by personnel necessarily limited to the elite I just spoke of...and whose talent and taste assure the Parisian industry's real and incontestable superiority. It is, moreover, so incontestable that it would

---

[37] Ibid.

[38] *La Question des veillées devant la commission départementale du travail du département de la Seine. Extraits des procès-verbaux des séances, 1900–1901* (Paris, 1901). On Bouvard's campaign against home manufacture, see Lorraine Coons, "'Neglected sisters' of the women's movement: the perception and experience of working mothers in the Parisian garment industry, 1860–1915," *Journal of Women's History* 5, No. 2 (Fall 1993), 50–74.

[39] "Madame Prud'homme," *Le Matin*, 30 Nov. 1908. André de Maday, *Les Femmes et les Tribunaux de Prud'hommes* (Neuchâtel, 1917).

[40] "Syndicat des fleuristes et plumassières," *La Fronde*, 11 Nov. 1898; Marie Videbien, "Bouvard, Stéphanie," *Dictionnaire des féministes: France, XVIIIe–XXIe siècle* (Université d'Angers, 2017) http://blog.univ-angers.fr/dictionnairefeministes/2017/07/04/bouvard-stephanie/ See also the less detailed print version, Charles Sowerwine, "Bouvard, Stéphanie," *Dictionnaire des féministes: France, XVIIIe–XXIe siècle* (Paris, 2017), 202–4.

suffice for you, Sirs, to visit the now open Exposition to bring you to the absolute conviction of this superiority, as evidenced by the complete absence of any foreign competition there.[41]

Worth here referenced the opening of Paris's 1900 Exposition Universelle the previous month. Indeed, the same week that he made this impassioned plea for the renown of French fashion, Worth, who was also serving with Jeanne Paquin as the president of the couture section of the Exposition Universelle and as a member of the jury, toured the Exposition's fashion displays with a Russian prince to whom he remarked "the variety, the richness, and the supreme elegance of the clothing created by our great *couturiers* and *couturières* who dressed the aristocracy of all the European courts."[42] During the May meeting of the nightwork commission, when opponents brought up the overtime needed to produce a court train for the Queen of Spain that year, Worth emphasized the privilege of such labor:

> It is unquestionably an honor to complete such works...Entrusting them to our female compatriots constitutes an homage to their talent, their taste, their aptitude...Is it not evident, in fact, that if an embroiderer in Madrid could have made the *manteau* in question directly, the Queen of Spain would not have ordered it in Paris, but in Madrid, to the detriment of our industry and, consequently, of our workingwomen themselves...[43]

Here Worth fuses concern about national industrial competitiveness and the vulnerability of his female workers with a paean to their exceptional skill.[44]

In a meeting of the commission the following March 1901, Stéphanie Bouvard and Clémence Jusselin presented a report on the conditions leading to a Parisian garment strike that year. They summarized the demands of the female workers: an end to regular *veillées*, and a daily wage rather than being paid by the piece (they asked for 6 francs per eight-hour day for a first hand, 4.50 francs for a second hand):

> Currently the bosses do what they want, that which their interests require, without worrying about the health of their workingwomen...The amount of work demanded of them surpasses their strength...how many become anemic and incapable of continuing in their trade after several years of effort? These long hours of diligent work in cramped workshops where the air quickly becomes

---

[41] "Séance du 25 mai 1900," 16.   [42] "A l'Exposition," *Le Temps*, 30 May 1900, p. 2.
[43] "Séance du 25 mai 1900," 18.
[44] Worth penned an 1895 volume on couture emphasizing the errors of upper-class women's taste. Gaston Worth, *La Couture et la confection des vêtements de femme* (Paris, 1895).

unbreathable can only lead to physical decline, if not moral decline... The bosses will say that their kind of industry is subject to increases of work at the beginning of seasons, moments when their clientele wants to be served promptly. Aren't eleven hours of constant work, tiring the eyes, often in workshops in basements or in rooms into which too many workingwomen are crammed, more than sufficient time?... Can't we assume, with good cause, that workingwomen who are less overworked would complete their tasks with more strength and energy?[45]

Jusselin and Bouvard conceded that many women, especially those with family to support, took on extra work that ruined their health if it meant augmenting their salary. Yet, they asked, "Should we accept the reasoning and sacrifice of these unfortunate women?"

State prosecutor Dagoury responded to the women's report by suggesting that outlawing voluntary nightwork might amount to "a violation of the liberty of workingwomen."[46] A delegate from the local departmental council Duval-Arnould insisted it would be "difficult and even dangerous to do away with all latitude" of the couture industry in this regard, as they might lose clients if they were unable to meet orders for important society events. Stéphanie Bouvard interjected that if nightwork were outlawed, couture houses simply would be obliged to hire more workers, giving jobs to the many unemployed workingwomen in Paris.[47]

Following Jusselin's and Bouvard's report, Worth took the floor once more, saying that he had not intended to speak given the self-interested light in which his opposition to the suppression of nightwork would be seen. Nonetheless, he felt moved to counter "the arguments developed by Mlle Jusselin," and proceeded to do so at length. He demanded, "Isn't it, and excuse me if now I seem to exaggerate the artistic side of our metier, isn't it in Paris and only in Paris that the talented women who are our auxiliaries can be formed?" The level of skill required to create Parisian fashion meant that there was a perpetual shortage of capable workers: "Mlles Jusselin and Bouvard claim that there are enough workingwomen to satisfy needs... Do you believe that you can get a meticulous piece of work, and, I must repeat myself, an artistic one, from just any female laborer, however good a seamstress she might be?"[48] He insisted upon the "impossibility of finding sufficient skilled hands to execute the demanded work... Talent can't be given. I don't even think that, in this instance, it can be acquired."[49] Presaging statements about Parisian garment work during the Franco-British, Worth highlighted the unusual degree of collaboration between these talented laborers, the first hand, and the patron: "Chosen from among all the skilled workingwomen, [the workshop *directrice*] distinguishes herself by a more assured taste... The smooth functioning

---

[45] "Séance du 22 mars 1901," 31.   [46] Ibid. 32.   [47] Ibid. 34.   [48] Ibid. 38.
[49] Ibid. 40.

of the business relies on the constant collaboration between her and the patron on the one hand, and between her and the workingwoman on the other."[50] Thus, working gifted garment laborers overtime was necessary to maintain France's global couture reputation.

Jusselin followed this speech by peppering Worth with brief questions challenging his summary of couture work conditions. How was it, she asked, that during the Exposition the previous year, when couturiers like Worth had requested dispensations for more nightwork than legally allowed, and been refused, orders had still been met? He answered that the Exposition had not been as successful as one had hoped. When Jusselin asked about the low wages resulting from workingwomen being paid by the piece, Worth countered that it was out of the question that workingwomen in couture shops would accept lower wages than they deserved: "...M. Worth affirms that the skilled workingwoman knows her value and will only work for a price that she deserves." Jusselin fired back, "How is it then that workingwomen make only 3 francs a day?" Worth retorted that he employed no workers at that wage.[51]

Another working-class delegate to the commission, piano maker and vice-president of the Conseil des Prud'hommes (labor relations court) Auguste Heppenheimer, joined this tense exchange by likening Worth's argument to that of slaveholders in the American South who suggested they could not conduct lucrative business without slave labor. Yet even this opponent of the *veillées* agreed that the artistic renown of Paris couture was worthy of defense. Opponents of slavery might rightfully demand that if one could not profitably manufacture sugar cane without slave labor, "it would be better for humanity to do without sugar." But, Heppenheimer suggested, the commission must avoid such an extreme solution when it came to couture: "the artful manufacture of women's clothing will long remain one of the glories of the city of Paris, without obliging the workingwomen who produce these marvels with their fairy fingers to kill themselves by deadly nightwork."[52] Heppenheimer rejected Worth's argument that there were not enough highly skilled workingwomen, "those who give the mark of genius, in a word, to Parisian labor," and held that in any case, couture houses should not be permitted to expand "at the expense of the working class."

At the next meeting in April 1901, Heppenheimer acknowledged that Worth had raised considerations regarding the "extreme importance" of the garment industry and its 65,000 workingwomen that had made them all reflect deeply. Nonetheless, he insisted, the industry's national significance was all the more reason to pursue stricter workplace regulation.[53] He expressed frustration about this rhetoric of fashion's national import: "each time that it became necessary

---

[50] Ibid. 41.   [51] Ibid. 42–3.   [52] Ibid. 43.
[53] "Séance du 26 avril 1901," *La Question des veillées...*, 47.

to advance a reform, arguments...were always made with impressive force to maintain the status quo...I contend that the responses made to us do not defend the interests of the industry but of the industrialists."[54] Heppenheimer proposed a rather moderate resolution to reduce the number of legal annual *veillées* from sixty to forty, and to enforce more robustly the existing law.

Responding to Bouvard's contention during that meeting that overwork led to *ouvrières'* anemia and even death, "the depopulation of France,"[55] Worth responded dryly that he would like to see actual statistics on garment worker fatalities, and that he had some workingwomen in his company who had been with the company for forty years.[56] Another opponent of garment nightwork and delegate from the Bourse du Travail, Édouard Besombes retorted that the 10,000 or so workers in the workshops of "grands couturiers" like Worth were only a small percentage of the 55,000 women working in the garment trades.[57] Surely, implored Besombes, one could support the brilliant reputation of Parisian fashion *and* protect its workers: "I will not comment further upon the arguments furnished by our colleague at a previous meeting in which he told us that it was only in Paris that one could find *artistes* (that's the term he used) capable of executing the marvels of taste, of cachet, and of accomplishment that we admired at the Exposition of 1900. Well, I say!...Paris and its clientele will be well obliged to deal with the consequences of worker's protection and submit their orders in a timely manner...And it is certain that in the House of Worth, among the 400 workingwomen employed by him, all are not artists."[58] Besombes's and Heppenheimer's exasperation signals the common deployment of odes to the taste renown of Parisian couture and its workingwomen to check industrial regulation.

During this April 1901 session, Jusselin attempted to refute Worth's and Dagoury's suggestion that garment laborers supported *veillées* by bringing the commission's attention to a petition signed by thousands of workingwomen opposing nightwork.[59] The Ministry of Labor received this petition from the Chambre syndicale ouvrière de la Couture on the occasion of the opening of the 1900 Exposition Universelle. Alfred-Auguste Mallemont, president of a Conseil des Prud'hommes in the Seine region, responded that while admittedly "all workingwomen are against the *veillées*," one had to accept that nightwork was "indispensable in couture. It is an inconvenience inherent to this industry. The industrialists are not responsible for it."[60]

At the May 1901 session, Worth invited members of the Commission to wander the garment district around the Opéra; they would see that all fashion houses were searching for employees capable of producing garments worthy of France's international reputation: "it's not jobs that are lacking for workingwomen but

[54] Ibid. 51.   [55] Ibid. 50.   [56] Ibid. 52.   [57] Ibid. 53.
[58] Ibid. 54.   [59] Ibid. 48.   [60] Ibid. 49.

workingwomen that are lacking [for the jobs]!"[61] Mallemont concurred, and suggested that "All workingwomen are opposed to *veillées*, but good working-women understand the necessities of the industry...She's the one that realizes the importance of the work that we give her and the necessities of the industry."[62] This argument seemingly placed any blame for unemployment or discontent about *veillées* with the workingwomen themselves. The best workers were those artists ready to sacrifice for the national good.

The nightwork commission was only one belle époque space in which garment trade nightwork was lambasted alongside praise of the Parisian garment workers' special tastefulness. Some opponents of the *veillées* deployed the rhetoric of nationally-significant workingwoman's taste to indict nightwork and bourgeois women's excessive appetite for fashion. The Ligue sociale d'acheteurs (LSA), an organization founded in Paris in 1902 to promote humane buying practices on the part of Parisian ladies, targeted "the homicidal *veillée*" as one of the worst abuses of needlework and made its suppression their "primary and principal effort."[63] The organization counseled its members, "Never place an order without asking if it might lead to nightwork or Sunday work." Women should avoid accepting fashion deliveries after 7 p.m. or on Sundays, "so as not to be directly responsible for the prolonged work hours."[64] The LSA also maintained a "Liste blanche" of companies who chose to abide by their demand not to employ workers at night.

The LSA castigated bourgeois women's feminine caprice and bad taste for the subjugation of tasteful and fashion-loving garment workers. In a report exploring the human cost of high fashion, especially *veillées*, in 1905, the Ligue's vice-president Marie-Thérèse Brincard rhapsodized about the fashionable desires and taste of the Parisian workingwoman:

In our day, every Parisienne is elegant, whatever her budget. On the street, her silhouette remains *coquette,* despite the heavy parcels with which she is some-times encumbered. A little bit of nothing—a trimming of scalloped lace, a knot of ribbon, or a tuft of flowers—brightens her bodice. She almost always has a feather in her hat, and when she hitches up her skirt we see a snugly-fitted ankle boot.[65]

In railing against these women's overwork, Brincard echoes the eroticized bour-geois flâneur's ogling of the midinette, seamlessly linking her poverty (her ability

---

[61] "Séance du 24 mai 1901," 57.   [62] Ibid. 59.

[63] "La veillée homicide" was the title of a series of postcards bringing attention to the abuses of garment work. *Statuts revises et adoptes par l'Assemblee generale du 23 decembre 1909.* From *La Ligue Sociale d'Acheteurs de France (Documents).* Publication documentaire de l'Action Populaire, No. 51 (Paris: Victor Lecoffre) See Marie-Emmanuelle Chessel, "Le Genre de la consommation en 1900. Autour de la Ligue Sociale d'acheteurs," *L'Année sociologique* 61, No. 1 (2011), 125–49.

[64] Henriette Brunhes, *La Ligue Sociale d'Acheteurs: rapport présenté par Madame Jean Brunhes, dans la séance du 10 novembre 1903* (Paris, 1903) 11.

[65] Baronne Georges Brincard, "Le Prix des 'bonnes occasions,'" *Bulletin de la Ligue sociale d'acheteurs* (Nov. 1905). Originally in *Le Correspondant,* 25 June 1905, pp. 163–75, 163.

to make fashion out of limited means, "*un petit rien*"), her fashionability, and her labor ("*coquette*, despite the heavy parcels"). Brincard contrasts the midinette's elegance of "a bit of nothing" to the voracious and morally suspect consumption of idle bourgeois women seeking cut-rate prices for their incessant purchases. She applauds the democratization of luxury which has allowed for wise and tasteful purchases by working-class women who "through the dexterity with which they wield a needle, know how to put a touch of original elegance in their homes as much as on their person. These women deserve only praise."[66] By stark contrast, Brincard rebukes non-workingwomen, whose "aptitude" consists of "claiming for themselves, for next to nothing, the work of others." These leisured consumers are "dupes" of department store display: "Often this is simply an occasion for them to buy an object they do not need that seduced them by its trendy appearance and will serve no other use."[67] Here, notions of feminine taste have been inverted, with working-class women armed with a preternatural tastefulness restrained by modest means, whereas bourgeois women's expansive budget leads to improvident, tasteless, and even immoral buying.

While the nightwork commission ultimately voted to affirm a number of resolutions aimed at ending the practice, it passed them along as recommendations only. In fact, it would be another decade before garment nightwork was banned altogether, in 1910–11.[68] This law stipulated that workers could be obliged to work extra hours in moments of seasonal pressure, up to sixty days per year as before, but these supplementary hours would be worked in the early morning as opposed to the evening. That even this minimal (and, in some cases, toothless) reform took more than twenty years despite tremendous opposition to the practice gives a sense, at least in part, of how powerful patronal arguments about Parisian renown were. In March 1911, social investigator Léon Bonneff interviewed a 16-year-old Parisian seamstress as she left work around 10 o'clock in the evening. She confirmed that *veillées* were still the norm for many Parisian garment workers: "Maybe we don't work nights in the workshop itself anymore, but we work in the personal apartment of the boss, or we bring the work home."[69]

Artificial Flowermaking and the *Mauvais Rouge*

One of the Parisian industries most associated with traditional labor practices and national renown was artificial flowermaking.[70] By 1909, Parisian flower

---

[66] Ibid. 163.   [67] Ibid. 164.

[68] See discussions of the *veillées* in the *Petite République* and the *Petit Parisien* in February 1910.

[69] L.-M. Bonneff, "La Misère sous les galons," *L'Humanité*, 3-6-1911. AN F/7/13740.

[70] For a history of the industry, see Marilyn Boxer, "Women in industrial homework: the flowermakers of Paris in the Belle Epoque," *French Historical Studies* 12, No. 3 (Spring 1982), 401–23; Elisabeth Piquet, *Les Fleurs du mal: les maladies professionnelles des ouvriers en fleurs artificielles, France, 1829–1919* (2014); and Claire Lemercier, "Looking for 'industrial confraternity' small-scale industries and institutions in nineteenth-century Paris," *Enterprise & Society* 10, No. 2 (June 2009), 304–34.

manufacture employed some 28,000 workers, 25,000 of them women. 10,000 of those women labored *en atelier*, and the remaining 15,000 at home.[71] Artificial flowers were the product of painstaking, skilled handiwork by laborers who often served a long apprenticeship; even in the 1920s, the bulk of flowerwork was still done by hand.[72] As such, Parisian flowerwork provoked expressive odes to the fairy fingers which gave French taste physical form, especially as traditional apprenticeship structures began to shrink.[73] At the same time, artificial flowers were in declining use in high fashion in these years, while other countries (Germany, Austria, and Italy most notably) had begun to make crippling incursions into the market. Thus, state investigations into the workplace poisoning of artificial flowermakers in this period offer a pronounced example of the way that fears about national competitiveness melded with notions of French taste and with a romantic conception of Parisian garment workers.

Flower manufacturers praised the refined taste of their Parisian workers, and often categorized this sweated work as a labor of love. One flower merchant insisted in 1913 that "The Parisienne succeeds because of her exquisite taste. Taste is the most important requisite of success. Good taste and patience and love of the trade—those are the Parisian tradition."[74] Flower manufacturers stressed the special place of Parisian workingwomen's "chic" in this tradition: "This style is so subtle and is obtained by so light a turn of the finger that it escapes analysis, yet it quadruples the beauty and the price of the flower. We have branch shops in the provinces but none of our first-class work is done outside Paris. You cannot get the style anywhere else."[75] Paris's Chambre syndicale des Fabricants de Fleurs et Feuillages artificiels underscored the particularity of Parisian taste as part of its petition to have customs duties applied on foreign-made artificial flowers around the same time.[76] These flower merchants referred to the influx of artificial flowers from Austria and Germany as an "economic and industrial invasion" and argued that tariffs were "absolutely necessary for our defense; it would be the end of our age-old and beautiful artificial flower industry, whose meticulous production gives it that cachet of finish and good taste which has made its universal reputation."[77] They held up the plight of 50,000 French laborers who worked in their industry and its auxiliary professions, "our collaborators... whose interests are so intimately connected to ours," as one of the primary impacts of foreign

---

[71] Claire Gérard, *Condition de l'Ouvrière parisienne dans l'industrie de la fleur artificielle* (Paris, 1909) 1.

[72] Piquet, *Les Fleurs du mal*, 23.   [73] Boxer, "Women in industrial homework," 409.

[74] Parisian artificial flower employer, quoted in Mary Van Kleeck, *Artificial Flower Makers* (New York, 1913), 189. Van Kleeck conducted interviews with Parisian flowermakers as part of her study.

[75] Parisian artificial flower manufacturer, quoted ibid. 149.

[76] A. Bacquet, président, Chambre syndicale des Fabricants de Fleurs et Feuillages artificiels de Paris, *Mémoire présenté à Messieurs les députés pour l'obtention de droits de douane sur les Fleurs et Feuillages artificiels de fabrication étrangère* (Paris, c.1908–1917). AN F/22/170.

[77] Ibid. 6.

competition.[78] While some flower manufacturers had been obliged to decentralize their shops outside of Paris, "as far as the production of fine flowers and foliage is concerned, Paris will always preserve a monopoly: only a workforce fully possessing the knack of the métier, and production methods transmitted from generation to generation, is capable of every day engendering new creations whose finish is only equaled by the ingenuity that presided over their blooming."[79] To allow this industry to falter would be "like a partial eclipse, diminishing even the radiance of Paris, and possibly redirecting, to the benefit of another capital, the current that every day brings to our beautiful city the most illustrious, wealthiest, and most beautiful women." Flower merchants pleaded with the National Assembly to act, to "defend a part of France's patrimony" and "safeguard...the rights and interests of Industries that contribute to her wealth and her good renown in the world."[80]

Government officials and labor investigators reproduced this rhetoric in their interactions with the flower industry. Claire Gérard (who we met previously singing the praises of the "artistic sense" of French hatmakers and corsetmakers in contrast to their English counterparts) conducted studies on belle époque garment work for the Musée Social, a private, government-supported foundation charged with the scientific study of the social question in France.[81] As part of this work, Gérard published a 1909 report on workingwomen in the Parisian flower industry, to which Stépanie Bouvard contributed.[82] Gérard also profiled Bouvard and her flowerworkers' cooperative "The Flower of Paris," for Le Petit Journal in 1908. Her profile demonstrates once again the way that skill, taste, and national renown colored even the efforts of labor reformers themselves when exposing the abuses of garment work. Gérard titles her article on Bouvard and her cooperative, "The artificial flower: a visit to the fairies that make spring," and proceeds to describe the meticulous and magical craft as these "little fairies" fashion an "enchanted garden" that "one imagines...was created by a magic wand." These workers, Gérard insists, have "fairy fingers" and "the touch of an artist." The work is dangerous, she admits: "Few women know that the female garment worker has fingers deformed by the use of the pincers, eaten away by the acids and the aniline of the dyes. Poor blackened, worn hands that the flowermaker regards and sighs, with her feminine instinct for style..." Nonetheless, the artificial flower craft is "an industry of art" that allows an elite of workingwomen to earn a living: "There are perhaps twenty-five [workingwomen] in the Parisian market who are capable of doing this, and Stéphanie Bouvard has chosen her associates in 'The Flower of Paris' among them." The ingenious flowers they produce voyage around the globe,

---

[78] Ibid.   [79] Ibid. 7.   [80] Ibid. 8.

[81] Janet R. Horne, A Social Laboratory for Modern France: The Musée Social and the Rise of the Welfare State (Durham, NC, 2001). The Musée Social was founded in 1895 by Jules Siegfried and Émile Cheysson.

[82] Gérard, Condition de l'ouvrière parisienne.

and "glorify the skill of the young women of Paris, without rival in the art of the flower." Gérard remarks more than once that Bouvard and her associates bear this difficult work "gaily," and concludes the profile on this note: "A smile on their lips, they tell me about their joy in gazing upon the blooming of an order of *fleurs de Nice*...happy, in spite of it all, to have created beauty."[83]

When the Minister of Industry and Commerce Henry Boucher addressed a charitable association for children working in flowers and feathers in 1896, he expanded on the national role of artificial flower work and the "lovely young girls" who performed it: "They also serve the Fatherland, and while their big brothers carry their bandolier, or maybe a marshal's baton, in their lunch baskets, [these girls] carry a bit of the fortune of France, a part of its good artistic renown, also a part of that moral patrimony to which we hold fundamentally, the good renown of the French woman."[84] Boucher concluded by using the prettiness of the young flowerworkers to dismiss reports of the health dangers of rose work: "I am happy to greet these fresh, pink faces. Your industry is defamed, Mesdames...who told me that the aniline had struck and spread I don't know what ravages across your profession? Well, my God, what can I say? To the contrary, these young girls could find the models for their artificial roses just from looking at the fresh faces of their companions. The good upkeep of the workshops and the attention to cleanliness and hygiene that reign in your profession assure the continuation of this admirable health for which I congratulate you, Mesdemoiselles, and for which I congratulate your future husbands in advance. (*Laughter and applause.*)"[85]

One wonders whether the laughter and applause by the assembled manufacturers was echoed by the young female apprentices in attendance. Boucher praised the apprentices' rosy health to brush aside troubling rumors about the toxicity of the aniline and lead salts used in artificial flowermaking.[86] By 1896, reports of the poisoning of artificial flowerworkers, specifically those fashioning the coveted double-faced red rose, had begun to circulate in the French press and amongst functionaries at the labor ministry. Just the month before Boucher's address, the Parisian flowerworkers' trade association had voted an *ordre du jour* demanding "the removal of harmful materials used in their profession," inspired by a workingwoman who stood at their last meeting to proclaim: "Yes, we make starvation wages. Yes, many of us are, alas, too often forced to choose between

---

[83] Claire Gérard, "La Fleur artificielle: une visite aux fées qui font le printemps," *Le Petit Journal*, 3 Apr. 1908, 1.

[84] Speech by Ministre du Commerce et de l'Industrie (Henry Boucher), *Société pour l'Assistance Paternelle aux enfants employés dans les industries des fleurs et des plumes (Patronage Industriel). 30e annee. Séance solennelle, 31 Mai 1896.* AN F/22/458, 96. On this group, see Boxer, "Women in industrial homework," 411–12.

[85] Speech by Boucher, 31 May 1896, 96–7.

[86] On the discovery of and importance to fashion of synthetic dyes like aniline red see Laura Kalba, *Color in the Age of Impressionism: Commerce, Technology, and Art.* (University Park, PA, 2017). Aniline red was discovered by French dyers Renard frères et Franc in 1859 (p. 28).

dying of hunger or prostituting ourselves. Yes, we are being poisoned by the daily ingestion of toxic materials."[87]

As Mary Lynn Stewart and others have demonstrated, the late nineteenth and early twentieth centuries saw increased attention to the health hazards of French workplaces. Despite numerous studies by social hygienists, governmental labor inspectors, and sociologists, industrial hygiene standards in many cases were slow to take hold. Throughout the nineteenth century, workplace safety and hygiene studies tended to be driven by concerns of industrial efficiency rather than by concerns for workers' health, and tended to examine male workers.[88] Some of the few investigations into predominantly feminine industries in this period were studies of the artificial flower industry. Concern about the so-called *mauvais rouge* (*bad red*) provoked extensive investigation after 1908, and yet, ultimately, no government actions, even as the state moved forward with legislation to ban lead in other industries. In 1898, the French state had passed a law establishing employer liability for workplace hazards. In 1901, labor leaders organized a campaign to protect housepainters from lead which attracted much attention from the press and resulted in a law prohibiting the use of white lead in paint by 1909.[89] The investigation of the *mauvais rouge* took place in these same years, but involved primarily female homeworkers known for their low unionization rates. These factors alone can help explain the differing outcomes of these workplace investigations of lead poisoning. But the debate over the *mauvais rouge* amongst investigators also lay bare the rhetorical power of French tastefulness and a particular vision of the Parisian garment worker herself as a pretty object of delectation. Just as Boucher's speech smoothly combined these visions—the national import of flower work and the innate taste and allure of flowerworkers— so too did ministerial investigations into the *mauvais rouge*. At the same time, the inquiry afforded a rare opportunity for the voices of Parisan flowerworkers to be recorded in significant number.

Rose workers in this period were victims of a double intoxication as the process of creating the *rouge double-face* exposed them to both lead salts and aniline, during dyeing and during assembly. The symptoms of this double poisoning were often conflated by investigators, and included (for aniline) headaches, abdominal pain, vomiting, and sore throats, and (for lead) joint pain, anemia, skin rashes,

---

[87] Sorgue, "Les Bagnes féminins," 18 Apr. 1896, *Petite République*. BMD DOS 331 FLE Fleuriste-Plumassière.

[88] Piquet, *Les Fleurs du mal*, 76–7; Mary Lynn Stewart, *For Health and Beauty: Physical Culture for Frenchwomen, 1880s–1930s* (Baltimore, 2001).

[89] Judith Raithorn, "Le Mouvement ouvrier contre la peinture au plomb. Stratégie syndicale, expérience locale et transgression du discours dominant au début du XXe siècle," *Politix* 3, No. 91 (2010), 7–26; "The banning of white lead: French and American experiences in a comparative perspective (early twentieth century)," *A History of the Workplace: Environment and Health at Stake* (New York, 2015), 27–46.

loss of appetite, vomiting, fatigue, weight loss, and abdominal pain.[90] The toxicity of artificial flowerwork had been widely acknowledged for some time. Léon and Maurice Bonneff warned of the dangers of aniline, lead, and arsenic in flowerwork in their 1900 study, *Professions That Kill: investigation by the workers' unions into work-related illnesses*.[91] It was not until 1908, however, that the *mauvais rouge* was investigated by the French labor ministry, in the wake of a newspaper item alleging the fatal poisoning of two *fleuristes* in Reims (a city about 160 kilometers from Paris and a popular center for outsourcing by Parisian firms).[92] The Minister of Labor sent a clipping about this case to Chief Labor Inspector Grégoire in Reims asking him to investigate.[93] In July 1908, Grégoire reported back to the minister that he could not find any record of such deaths in Reims.[94]

Grégoire did, however, find ample indications that flowerwork was toxic and that the "*mauvais rouge* makes workingwomen sick."[95] He recorded the pervasive ill effects of lead-based rose work on French *fleuristes*, and confirmed the presence of lead in samples provided to the municipal laboratory in Reims by flower manufacturers. Grégoire was told by one manufacturer that some child flowerworkers went through a period of "acclimatization" during which they "begin to suffer from vomiting after a while, and we find ourselves obliged to dismiss them."[96] The noxious effects of rose work were worse for homeworkers: "As for workingwomen working at home everyone recognizes that some of them were sick." One manufacturer admitted that a worker had told him she suffered from "violent stomach aches, lack of appetite, and digestive troubles, and that the doctor had prescribed a milk diet and cessation of double-face flower work."[97] Nonetheless, the degree of ill effects on his workers, the manufacturer averred, "was due to more or less how cleanly they kept themselves." Less hygienic

---

[90] Piquet, *Les Fleurs du mal*, 37, 41.

[91] Léon and Maurice Bonneff, *Les Métiers qui tuent: enquête auprès des syndicats ouvriers sur les maladies professionnelles* (Paris, 1900), 53. In 1901, Delphin Pichardie published a thesis on lead poisoning in the flower industry, *Considérations sur l'intoxication saturnine et en particulier la paralysie chez les ouvrières en fleurs artificielles* (Paris, 1901). That year, Socialist deputy Jules-Louis Breton proposed a labor bill that referenced "professional illnesses" resulting from aniline and lead. Piquet, *Les Fleurs du mal*, 119–20.

[92] "Fleurs empoisonnées," 10 May 1908, *L'Eveil democratique*. AN F/22/571 *Enquêtes sur les conditions du travail dans diverses industries*.

[93] On the history of French labor inspection, see Piquet, *Les Fleurs du mal*, 113–14 and Vincent Viet, *Les Voltigeurs de la République: l'inspection du travail en France jusqu'en 1914*, Vols. 1 and 2 (Paris, 1994).

[94] Inspecteur divisionnaire de la 4e Circonscription (Grégoire) to the Ministre du Travail et de la Prévoyance sociale, 25 July 1908, Nancy. AN F/22/571 *Enquêtes sur les conditions du travail dans diverses industries*. Grégoire indicates that in 1908 Reims had five flower manufacturers, employing 192 workingwomen and 770 female homeworkers.

[95] Inspecteur divisionnaire du travail de la région de Reims, quoted in Caroline Milhaud, *Enquête sur le travail à domicile dans l'industrie de la fleur artificielle*, Office du Travail, Ministère du Travail et de la Prévoyance sociale (Paris, 1913), 407.

[96] Grégoire to Ministre du Travail, 25 July 1908.

[97] Ibid. This milk treatment was refuted by the Office du Travail twenty years before. Piquet, *Les Fleurs du mal*, 112.

homeworkers, it was suggested, who mingled the red dust of the rose work with their families' food and dishes and were already malnourished, were easy victims of "occupational poisoning."[98] (Government investigations into other *maladies professionelles* in this period often blamed workers' illness on their own lack of cleanliness or other perceived moral failings.[99]) Testing on samples of the red aniline indeed revealed quantities of lead.

Grégoire also noted that lead poisoning in the flower industry had been acknowledged for years, and he mentioned several medical treatises on the subject. In fact, he warned, flower manufacturers in Chemnitz, Germany had already outlawed the red dyes used on double-faced roses because of lead poisoning, and, in Austria, the use of lead was forbidden in lacemaking after the "serious lead poisonings" of workers. Grégoire's conclusions were plain: "The result of this analysis is that, contrary to what the manufacturers believe, the red aniline contains lead and, as such, working the double-faced red can very well produce lead poisoning in some weakened subjects."[100] And yet, these findings went unheeded for several more years, as the Ministre du Travail ordered additional inspections and chemical tests.

From 1908 to 1911, two social workers from the Office du Travail, Caroline Milhaud and Sylvain Pitt, conducted an extensive inquiry into conditions in artificial flowermaking, particularly by homeworkers, with special attention to the possible toxicity of red rose work.[101] Milhaud and Pitt spent years interviewing 321 flowerworkers, sixty *entrepreneuses* (subcontractors used to assign piecework to homeworkers), and thirty-five employers—416 interviews in all from 1908 to 1911, primarily in Paris (though some interviews were also conducted in Reims, Lyon, the Loiret, and Orléans). Milhaud conducted the majority of the interviews by way of unannounced visits to workingwomen around Paris (especially in Belleville, Montmartre, Ménilmontant, and Charonne) whose names had been supplied by patronal and syndical associations or by other interviewed workers. Milhaud also authored the final report, published belatedly in 1913.

Before examining Milhaud's investigation into the *mauvais rouge* in some detail, it is worth noting the position of lead investigator Caroline Milhaud. Milhaud was the first prominent female member of the Office du Travail, and the year before she began the flowerwork inquiry, had published a study on *The Workingwoman in France: Her Present Condition and the Necessary Reforms.*[102] Here, she scrutinized the "feminization" of French industry (particularly *travail à*

[98] Grégoire to Ministre du Travail, 25 July 1908.   [99] Piquet, *Les Fleurs du mal*, 121.

[100] Grégoire to Ministre du Travail, 25 July 1908.

[101] Milhaud, *Enquête*. Milhaud published an article urging investigation of women's homework in 1903. Boxer, "Protective legislation," 53. On the history of the Office du Travail, founded in 1891, see Jean Luciani and Robert Salais, "Matériaux pour la naissance d'une institution: l'Office du Travail (1890–1900)," *Genèses* 2 (1990), 83–108.

[102] Caroline Milhaud, *L'Ouvrière en France: sa condition présent, les réformes nécessaires* (Paris, 1907). On Milhaud, see André-Clement Decouflé, "Histoire de l'Office du Travail: une 'administration

domicile), labor laws, wages, and working conditions. (Milhaud lambasted the use of garment industry *veillées* "to satisfy the caprice of the careless women who demand exceptional efforts to have their ball gowns for the horse race or garden party.") She ended the study indicting the ineffectiveness of labor legislation and of the capitalist system in general: "[the workingwoman's] exploitation will only cease with socialism."[103]

Milhaud's work with the Office du Travail, like Claire Gérard's for the Musée Social in this same period, has been examined by historian Hélène Charron as an example of a female cadre of pioneering, non-degree-holding social scientists who quickly disappeared from both the historical record and from the historiography of French social science. As single, childless women without professional degrees at the time of these investigations, Milhaud and Gérard saw their specialized research denied echoes in an "larger intellectual sphere," despite or perhaps because they grounded their investigations of women's work "in concrete feminine experiences and adopt[ed] a point of view that valorized the individuation of women, while their male colleagues persisted in envisioning women only in relation to their interests as fathers and husbands."[104] Milhaud's unusually forceful inquiry on behalf of roseworkers must be read in this light.

The more than 400-page *enquête* provides a thick description of working conditions in the Parisian artificial flower industry during the belle époque, and provides an unusually detailed record of flowerworkers' understanding of their labor. Over the course of this voluminous text, workers and employers alike describe their trade as an artistic craft that called upon working Parisiennes' innate taste and as an industry of national import increasingly threatened from less tasteful foreign competition. Indeed, Milhaud explicitly situates her *enquête* in the context of increased cut-rate foreign competition: "For a long while, France has had the world's monopoly of this industry but this is no longer the case for several years now."[105] In 1870, Austria, Germany, and Belgium could boast not even a single artificial flower manufacturer. By 1905, Austria had thirty, Belgium sixty-five, and Germany 192.[106]

In the midst of this crisis, flower manufacturers who spoke to Milhaud and Pitt reinforced claims of French "supremacy" in the manufacture of "rich designs and for all *articles de choix*."[107] A major Parisian flower manufacturer, Monsieur J, complained that an industry once "essentially French" was now suffering

---

de mission' avant la lettre," *Travail et emploi* 22 (Dec. 1984), 45–54, 51; Karen Offen, *Debating the Woman Question in the French Third Republic, 1870–1920* (Cambridge, 2018) 448–9.

[103] Milhaud, *L'Ouvrière*, 18. This references laceworkers.
[104] Hélène Charron, *Les Formes de l'illégimité intellectuelle: les femmes dans les sciences sociales françaises, 1890–1940* (Paris, 2013), 296–7.
[105] Milhaud, *Enquête*, 16.
[106] Ibid. 17.   [107] Ibid. 18.

competition from Austrian and German manufacturers who in some cases exported their flowers to France, repackaged them, and sold them with a label "French merchandise." Monsieur J also posited that the special nature of the fashion industry made it unwise to regulate: "Regulation should not exist. We cannot regularize labor that is subject to fundamentally mobile and capricious fashion."[108] Monsieur B, another Parisian flower manufacturer, complained about Austrian and German competition as well, but held that "It is by way of the *articles de choix* that France conserves her superiority in the artificial flower industry."[109] For this reason, he argued, better apprenticeship programs were needed. Monsieur M, a Parisian rose manufacturer with some 400 employees, bemoaned cut-rate foreign competition, but noted that, "Even so, *they always come to France to find the design models.*"[110] Monsieur W, the director of an artificial flower concern in Reims, agreed that all French flower work was superior to that of Germany: "as soon as it is a matter of nuances of style, one has to return to France. Flowers bought in Germany are junk. Reims, even if behind [Paris], is a hundred times better than Germany for artificial flowers."[111] Workingwomen in the flower industry also showed an interest in the issue of foreign competition—references to the American stock market crash and "German competition" were common in the workers' interviews included in the report.[112]

The flowerwork investigation, while primarily a description of the grueling conditions of French flowerwork, often remarked the creative abilities and special taste of Parisian flowerworkers. In the introduction to Milhaud and Pitt's investigation, director of the Office du Travail Arthur Fontaine made clear that flower homeworkers were, according to their employers, highly skilled laborers, "who have acquired by way of their endlessly shifting daily tasks an unquestionable aptitude, and who even have the gift of creation."[113] This was a lifelong trade for most flowerworkers, requiring dexterity, technical knowledge, and, especially for luxury flowers like the double-faced rose, superlative ability.[114] Milhaud described those workers who designed and assembled flowers known as *créatrices des modèles*: "They copy from natural flowers, those that seem to have the most character, or they create novelty types inspired from nature and assisted by their imagination." Milhaud clarified that these women "did not form a special category of artisan uniquely occupied with creation. Most of the time, they are ordinary workingwomen." Where once flowermakers could "copy an entire garden," the craft had moved toward increasing specialization so that many workers manufactured only one kind of flower and "thus acquire a very high aptitude."[115] Milhaud's

---

[108] Ibid. 36, 35.   [109] Ibid. 40.
[110] Ibid. 42; emphasis in original.   [111] Ibid. 221.   [112] Ibid. 144, 151.
[113] Arthur Fontaine, Conseiller d'État, Directeur du Travail, "À Monsieur Léon Bourgeois, Sénateur, Ministre du Travail et de la Prévoyance Sociale," 30 Dec. 1912 (pp. v–xi), p. vi, reprinted in Milhaud, *Enquête*. On Fontaine, see Decouflé, "Histoire de l'Office du Travail," 49.
[114] Fontaine, "À Monsieur Léon Bourgeois," p. vi.   [115] Milhaud, *Enquête*, 23.

report included detailed descriptions of the means of fabricating each variety of flower, from the intricate red rose to the simple violet, and underscored the painstaking handicraft of this production. In this trade, she wrote, "rare are those tasks that can be accomplished by unskilled workingwomen"; the work required dexterity, taste, and, for the creation of new designs, "natural gifts."[116]

The investigators frequently mentioned the superior creative abilities and artistry of the Parisian flowermaker, representatives of this "graceful, very feminine, and seemingly completely harmless trade."[117] Paris and its suburbs were virtually the "unique center of artificial flower production" in the belle époque, and several *patrons* and workers made clear that physical presence in Paris was a necessary requirement of tasteful flower creation. Monsieur C, a *petite fleur* merchant with workshops in Paris and in the provinces, asserted that "The flower industry in the provinces is not soaring. For fashion, one must be in the center of creation."[118] Monsieur D, a luxury rose manufacturer in Paris who outsourced foliage to his workshops in the Loiret, actually appreciated provincial *fleuristes'* lack of artistic interest in their work: "The provincial workingwoman doesn't know more than her boss, like the Parisian one, she meticulously executes the work we give her without trying to understand it."[119] The Parisian flowerworker was, according to Parisian manufacturer Monsieur B, "in many cases, an artist: in the workshop and out of it, she creates designs that we reproduce if they are successful."[120] Parisian taste could, in some cases, be learned, if one could go to Paris. Madame M, a 24-year-old homeworker, told investigators that though she had done an apprenticeship in her natal Loiret at the age of 12, she was obliged, when she moved to Paris at 21, to complete a second apprenticeship of eighteen months.[121]

Parisian flowerworkers were lauded throughout the *enquête* as being equipped with superior taste and skill. A female rose manufacturer in Reims contrasted what she knew of Parisian workers to her own workforce: "[A workingwoman in Reims] comes and says, 'I know how to make flowers.' But she doesn't know how to do it. In Reims, there aren't any really good workingwomen... The flowerworkers of Reims only know how to do one design."[122] A subcontractor in Reims who had worked previously in Paris agreed, "The workingwoman of Reims doesn't equal that of Paris. The workingwoman of Paris is a true *fleuriste*."[123] While Parisian flowermakers often learned the trade as young girls, almost half of those in Reims trained as adults.[124] In the Loiret, Milhaud heard similar sentiments from a large manufacturer: "the workingwoman *fleuriste* of the Loiret is much less skilled than her Parisian sister," and was paid accordingly.[125] In Reims and Orléans, apprenticeships were significantly shorter than in Paris, where most flowermakers apprenticed for two to three years. In Reims, the maximum

[116] Ibid. 28.   [117] Ibid. 399.   [118] Ibid. 48.   [119] Ibid. 46–7.
[120] Ibid. 40.   [121] Ibid. 161.   [122] Ibid. 223.   [123] Ibid. 227.
[124] Ibid. 233.   [125] Ibid. 261.

apprenticeship was a year, and Orléans only six months.[126] In Paris, while the general crisis of apprenticeship was bemoaned, Milhaud writes, this crisis "does not seem to have had strong repercussions because the professional value and superiority of the Parisian flowerworker...is uncontested."[127]

Many of the women interviewed by Milhaud declared love for their profession. Mme V, a 32-year-old married worker, "declared that she had much taste for her craft. 'I love my work. It's a passion. To abandon it would cause me pain. As a young girl, I already had the idea of working in flowermaking, and at 12 years old I tormented my mother so she would put me in an apprenticeship.'"[128] Madame L, a Parisian rose maker, enlisted her mother to care for her children so that she could "give herself over [to her métier] with even more ardor than her husband currently is fulfilling his military service."[129] In practice, such beliefs seemed to militate against the reforms in working conditions that flowerworkers plainly desired. Yet throughout Milhaud's study, these workingwomen affirmed their role as creators of fashion, even making their creative ability the basis for labor demands. Mme L, a 51-year-old widowed mother of three daughters in Belleville, designed models, and pronounced in favor of compensating workingwomen for the time spent creating sample models, "the labor of creation."[130]

The *rose rouge* or *rouge double-face* was considered one of the most important luxury flowers and required superior skill and dexterity, with some pieces requiring 200 separate petals.[131] While most French roses were produced in Reims and Orléans,[132] Paris was nonetheless perceived to be *the* site of rose production. While some lesser flowers, so-called *petite fleur* such as violets, daisies, and forget-me-nots, could be produced by less dexterous workers, the rose was the work of only the most able and inventive *fleuristes*. Parisian manufacturer Monsieur B claimed that "The *belle rose* can only be manufactured in Paris. All attempts...to manufacture roses in the provinces have failed. The provincial workingwoman is inferior to the workingwoman of Paris."[133] A manufacturer of *petite fleur* agreed that his workers were paid less "because with even a bit of taste, a person who is not a flowermaker can do it."[134]

Milhaud's description of rose workers, at times, upheld the notion of these women as artists of exceptional taste and skill. Madame B, a 30-year-old home-worker by the Buttes-Chaumont, specialized in *la fleur riche* and was a graduate of a vocational program. Milhaud describes her beautiful apartment and the way that "her grace harmonizes with the fine work that comes from her fingers." Madame B was paid quite well compared to other workers because she "creates designs and copies only her own models, such as the beautiful France rose with

---

[126] Ibid. 375.   [127] Ibid. 373.   [128] Ibid. 157.
[129] Ibid. 159.   [130] Ibid. 151.   [131] Ibid. 40.
[132] Fontaine, "À Monsieur Léon Bourgeois, p. ix.
[133] Milhaud, *Enquête*, 40.   [134] Ibid. 48.

two-toned petals and prominent veins."[135] Madame W, a "young, skilled" married workingwoman in the quartier Voltaire, "who works in the *belle rose fantaisie* and designs models,"[136] is described as having "ingenuity" and "skill," not just in flowers: "[she] knows how to make her own dresses and hats and she decks herself out gracefully with very little."[137]

Most workers in Milhaud and Pitt's inquiry, however, spoke to the frank misery of flower production, particularly by homeworkers: long hours, meager pay, chronic ill health, insalubrious conditions, and malnutrition. Milhaud and Pitt were especially attentive to tracing the incidences of health complaints related to red roses. More than half (52 per cent) of rose workers interviewed in Paris and its suburbs reported health complaints connected to the red dust produced by the *rouge double-face*, including headaches, head colds, sore throat, stomach aches, and vomiting.[138] In the workshops of the Loiret, the percentage was lower (30 per cent), while in Reims, some 79 per cent of rose workers suffered ill effects.[139]

The inquiry also included plentiful testimonies from flowerworkers about the toxicity of red roses. The widow B, a 34-year-old Parisian rosemaker, asserted that the red dye was "unhealthy" and "made her vomit."[140] The O sisters, a trio of young rosemakers in Belleville, declared themselves "happy with their métier," but complained that "the red that comes off of the petals...irritates the nasal mucous membranes."[141] Another *rosière* complained that she had suffered from fever "for several years...she is thirsty all the time and has stomach trouble."[142] The L sisters, two roseworkers in their twenties, each experienced different symptoms: the older, headaches, head colds and sneezing; the younger, a rash on her face the day after working with the *rouge*.[143] Other roseworkers complained that the *rouge* had made them anemic. Madame B, a 30-year-old workingwoman in Orléans, had been making artificial roses since the age of 11, and assured Milhaud of its ill effects: "Mme B...blames the *rouge double face* for giving her a sore throat and for causing white spots in the mouth." But she also admonished her fellow workingwomen for not being more vocal about the *mauvais rouge*. She "reproaches the workingwomen for not knowing how to come out clearly on this subject. According to her, the workingwomen often act against their own good. Once the boss said to some of them, 'Does working with the *rouge* trouble you?' And the workingwomen told him they were able to work just as quickly and that the *rouge* didn't bother them!"[144]

Near the completion of her inquiry, after cataloguing similar health ailments from so many rose workers, Caroline Milhaud declared: "One could not conclude that this was a matter of a collective auto-suggestion phenomenon, as the same complaints were expressed in quite diverse localities and the description of the

---

[135] Ibid. 164.   [136] Ibid. 173.   [137] Ibid. 175.
[138] Ibid. 401.   [139] Ibid.   [140] Ibid. 181.
[141] Ibid. 82.   [142] Ibid. 288.   [143] Ibid. 253.
[144] Ibid. 294. This quotation was repeated in Milhaud's footnote, p. 407.

discomforts suffered were remarkably similar. Moreover, some employers did not deny the damage."[145] But how did officials respond to the material provided in Milhaud's investigation? In his letter to labor minister Léon Bourgeois which prefaces the inquiry, Arthur Fontaine concluded his introductory elegy to artificial flowermaking by acknowledging that women handling red roses were victims of chronic illness. He conceded that though the *rose rouge* had been deemed "harmless" by some, it "in reality contains lead salts: the chemical analysis of the petals of these flowers whose samples were taken by the service of the health and safety inspection at the request of the Office du Travail, leaves no doubt in this regard. Now we know the toxic capacity of lead salts, even when absorbed in small quantities."[146] And yet, Fontaine immediately pivoted, reasoning that the "professional danger" of the red rose did not rise to the level "violent and fatal poisoning." What is more, the dangers of this work "are not permanent, because the workingwomen do not constantly make red roses; the fashion that dictates these bright colors, at certain moments, abandons them according to its vagaries. At any rate, the crisis that artificial flowermaking has undergone since 1909–1910 annuls or momentarily mitigates the source of the danger. Nevertheless, the danger is large enough that the workingwomen's situation calls for the attention of authorities and should motivate an intervention."[147] Fontaine's suggested interventions, however, sidestepped the issue of the toxic roses. He proposed that flowerworkers hit by high rates of unemployment instead learn to work in the feather industry, and that the state might fix a minimum wage for homeworkers as well as higher tariffs to fight "foreign competition."[148] None of these reforms targeted the toxic exposure of flowerwork.

Most employers, unsurprisingly, denied the ill effects of the *mauvais rouge*, or insisted that such effects were a necessary evil in the service of French artistry. Monsieur F, a rose manufacturer in Reims, warned investigators that "if we conduct a campaign against the *rouge double-face*, it will be the end of flowermaking. In Germany, they cannot produce these beautiful nuances." He also claimed that the forewoman of his workshop had made double-faced roses for seventeen years and had never suffered from it.[149] A subcontractor called Madame F admitted that many flowermakers "complain about the *rouge double-face*. But we can't do without it. Fashion demands the use of this red. In Paris and in Reims, it is impossible to do away with it. The workingwomen, thus, incur certain professional risks."[150]

As Milhaud and Pitt were beginning their *enquête*, rumors about the *mauvais rouge* led Paris's Service de l'Inspection du Travail, at the urging of the Office du Travail, to conduct a separate, concurrent chemical investigation of the "suspect petals" in Paris, Orléans, and Reims. Milhaud devotes a substantial portion of the

---

[145] Ibid. 403.   [146] Fontaine, "À Monsieur Léon Bourgeois," p. ix.
[147] Ibid., pp. ix–x.   [148] Ibid., pp. x, xi.
[149] Milhaud, *Enquête*, 222. This quotation was repeated on p. 402.
[150] Ibid. 227. This quotation was repeated on pp. 402–3.

last section of her *enquête* to these separate investigations led by labor inspectors in Reims, Nancy, and Paris. If one compares Milhaud and Pitt's *enquête* to this concurrent investigation (conducted by departmental inspector Mlle Langlois, her superior Boulisset, and the Ministre du Travail), it becomes evident that, in spite of laboratory results and workingwomen's testimony confirming the dangers of the red aniline as early as 1908,[151] any measures to curb these ill effects were either dismissed or postponed time and again. We find buried in this ministerial correspondence a source of this relative inaction: a conception of the artificial flower industry as especially vulnerable and especially important to French national identity.

As we have seen, as early as Grégoire's 1908 report, the Ministère du Travail had been notified by its own inspection about the dangers of the *mauvais rouge*, particularly lead poisoning. Three years would pass before the labor ministry checked in regarding these findings. In March 1911, the Minstère du Travail ordered the chief labor inspector from Paris, Boulisset, to conduct his own investigation into the *mauvais rouge*, given that a recent investigation into homework in the artificial flower industry (the Milhaud/Pitt inquiry presumably) had revealed that many flowerworkers were showing "symptoms of poisoning" linked to the aniline used in red roses. The Ministry asked Boulisset to ascertain whether or not regulations should be put in place banning certain materials or labor practices as a result of these findings. But the ministerial directive ended by suggesting, "We would be well advised not to begin investigations into the artificial flower workshops until, once out of their current crisis, they have resumed normal activity."[152] The next month, the labor minister also asked Chief Inspector Grégoire in Reims to report on any new developments since his July 1908 report, almost three years before. Grégoire responded that while the *rose double-face* was being produced in smaller quantities and that some manufacturers had instituted new assembly procedures that reduced workers' direct contact with toxins, rose production still produced harmful dust inhaled by workingwomen.[153] The director of flower manufacturer Maison Mosbacher, who in 1908 claimed that the presence of lead in his tested aniline must be an exceptional error, was found once again to have barrels of aniline containing lead just days before Grégoire's report.[154]

---

[151] Report from Inspection du Travail dans l'Industrie, Nancy, 25 July 1908 to the Ministre du Travail, indicating the dangers of lead in certain flower dyes, especially red. AN F/22/571 *Enquêtes sur les conditions du travail dans diverses industries.*

[152] Letter from the Ministère du Travail et de la Prévoyance sociale (Direction du Travail) to Boulisset, inspecteur divisionnaire du Travail, 20 Mar. 1911. AN F/22/571 *Enquêtes sur les conditions du travail dans diverses industries.*

[153] Grégoire, inspecteur divisionnaire de la 4e Circonscription à Monsieur le Ministre du Travail et de la Prévoyance sociale, 14 Apr. 1911, Nancy. AN F/22/571 *Enquêtes sur les conditions du travail dans diverses industries.*

[154] On 18 April 1911, Grégoire sent the report of his departmental inspector Pouillot with the results from the laboratory in Reims noting the presence of lead.

By contrast, in June 1911, Paris's chief inspector Boulisset assured the labor ministry that his departmental inspector Mademoiselle Langlois, whose purview comprised almost the entirety of the flower industry in Paris, could find no workers complaining of health effects from the *rose double-face*. Langlois did confirm that rose workers dipped petals into a lead acetate colored with aniline, in order to allow different colors to be applied on the both sides of each petal.[155] In her May 1911 report to Boulisset, she nonetheless dismissed the notion that the *rouge double-face* was particularly harmful or that it should be regulated. She claimed not to have met a single worker who complained of illness related to the roses, "since the demise of the *rouges frottés*," a rose assembled somewhat differently than the *double-face*. Langlois wrote, "As one modest employer told me, work on the *double-face* isn't a rest cure, but what industrial job is favorable to one's health? All that we can ask of the job is that it not be really bad." Langlois intimated that frequent worker complaints about the *rouge* were a feint of sorts covering over workingwomen's disdain for the mess that the red powder produced on their hands, faces, clothing, and (in the case of homeworkers) furniture.[156] In most cases, Langlois claimed, workers disliked making roses because of the mess, and thus, in smaller establishments, the *patrons* themselves did this work "to avoid any difficulty with their staff." Langlois, in the handwritten notes attached to her letter to Boulisset, indicated that while most workers she spoke with "told me that the *double face* was bad, one had to understand that to mean <u>disagreeable</u> and less productive, as they could not tell me of the specific malaises they experienced."[157] This is a curious locution: we must, Langlois insists, understand the women's complaints as being only about the unpleasantness of the *double-face* since they could not explain their maladies to her. Two sentences later, she recalls workers who did indeed describe ill health as a result of rose work, though she claims that they had not experienced these effects since the abandonment of the *rose frotté*.[158]

Langlois categorically opposed banning the aniline in her May 1911 report, and instead embarked upon a lengthy digression about the difficulties suffered by the flower industry at this moment, implying that safety regulations would only add to the industry's woes. She bemoaned that "this industry, far from getting back to its activity of previous years, instead sees the crisis prolong and worsen in the last two years... Almost all of the manufacturers told me that their best months now are inferior to those during even the off-season three or four years ago. America is

---

[155] Milhaud, *Enquête*, 403.
[156] Langlois, inspectrice départementale to Boulisset, inspecteur divisionnaire de la 1ere Circonscription to the Ministre du Travail et de la Prévoyance sociale, 19 May 1911, Paris. AN F/22/571 *Enquêtes sur les conditions du travail dans diverses industries*. This section was also quoted in Milhaud, *Enquête*, 406.
[157] Langlois to Boulisset, 19 May 1911, Paris. This section was also quoted in Milhaud, *Enquête*, 406.
[158] Langlois, quoted in Milhaud, *Enquête*, 406. Milhaud and Pitt did interview some workers who disliked rosework because it was "messy" (ibid. 265, 291, 295).

making some of her own, Germany sends them the rest of their supply <u>directly</u>, and their commissions in France are null." English manufacturers were sending buyers to Paris "<u>to see what was being made</u>, with an explicit order from their companies <u>to buy nothing</u>."[159] Boulisset ended his forwarding letter by praising Langlois's "intelligence and investigative spirit."[160]

In November, Dr Frédéric Heim, an expert in lead poisoning at the Laboratoire d'Hygiène du Travail, alerted the labor ministry to the presence of lead in samples provided by Langlois in May.[161] As a result, Langlois was dispatched to gather the samples and to have them tested at the Laboratoire d'Hygiène du Travail. In March 1912, when at least two of the samples revealed lead, Dr Heim requested further information from Langlois: the name of the workshops from which the samples were taken as well as more observations about the workers in those shops. Heim asked to be able to examine the workers at his laboratory, noting that, "Even in the event that [Langlois] did not notice nor had any knowledge of any lead-poisoning accident, it would be of interest to examine the workingwomen who handled these composites, with a view toward the possible detection of perhaps latent lead-poisoning."[162]

Some eight months passed before the final documents in the dossier were produced: Inspector Langlois refused to turn over the name of the lead-tainted shop in December 1912, and Boulisset agreed with her decision. Her refusal takes the form, once again, of a passionate defense of the artificial flower industry, a letter forwarded to the labor minister by Boulisset. It is an extraordinary document. Langlois references the flower manufacturer from whom the toxic samples were taken, a man who "displayed a very great deference to me" and with whom she had "courteous relations." She doubted that "this industrialist will be very happy to see me handing over his name and address." She also protested that she would be hard pressed to find the *ouvrières* who had worked with this sample a year before (when it was taken) given the "unstable" nature of flowermakers' employment. Even if she could find them, few women could find the time to be examined at the laboratory as the flower business was in its busy season. The majority of Langlois's response was a full-throated "cry of alarm" about the importance of the flower industry. Artificial flowers were in declining use in feminine fashion just as

[159] Langlois to Boulisset, 19 May 1911; emphasis in original.
[160] Boulisset, inspecteur divisionnaire de la 1ere Circonscription to the Ministre du Travail et de la Prévoyance sociale, 2 June 1911, Paris. AN F/22/571 *Enquêtes sur les conditions du travail dans diverses industries.*
[161] Frédéric Heim, Director of the Laboratoire d'Hygiène du Travail, Paris, 23 Nov. 1911 to the Ministère du Travail, Procès-verbal d'analyse. [Lab report included in letter to Despaux, inspecteur divisionnaire du Travail, 23 Dec. 1911, Paris.] AN F/22/571 *Enquêtes sur les conditions du travail dans diverses industries.* Heim co-authored a volume on latent lead poisoning in 1909. Frédéric Heim de Balsac and Édouard Agasse-Lafont, *Le Dépistage du saturnisme latent par l'examen du sang* (Paris, 1909).
[162] Frédéric Heim, Director, Laboratoire d'Hygiène du Travail to Fontaine, Conseiller d'État, Directeur du Travail, 5 Mar. 1912, Paris. AN F/22/571 *Enquêtes sur les conditions du travail dans diverses industries.*

"foreign competition was becoming extremely formidable."[163] Flowermakers in the United States had paid a fortune to lure away the most talented French flower-makers, and they in turn had instructed a new generation of "skilled students." Germany, Italy, and Austria also were invading the market by way of low prices achieved through low salaries. According to Langlois, French flowermaking had "only one weapon" left to battle this competition, "its creative genius and its per-fection of execution. In fine and rich objects, we remain unbeatable... Desiring to fight to the end and not to neglect any chance of resurrection for this attractive part of our industry, several flower manufacturers have just organized a council, with 10,000 francs as capital, with the aim of conducting active propaganda for the revival of *la fleur*."[164]

Langlois explained in detail the effort by certain couturiers and milliners to retain the use of artificial flowers in their creations, as well as the publication of a luxurious album of "the latest creations of the flower industry" for distribution to American and English buyers. She raved in some detail about this patronal meas-ure to publicize the French flower industry, and then apologized to Boulisset for her digression, "but I felt it necessary to insist upon the concern contained in this initiative which one could qualify as desperate, & upon the danger there currently would be in shackling, even the littlest bit, an industry in an economic slump for almost four years now that employs so many people & that is one of the most elegant expressions of Parisian taste."[165] In his letter to the minister, Boulisset endorsed Langlois's refusal to reveal the source of the lead samples or to recom-mend bans of any sort to protect workers' health, suggesting that "the moment is indeed poorly chosen to demand something from the manufacturers and the workingwomen of *la fleur*, so taxed during these last several years."[166] This appears to have been the end of the correspondence.

In her 1913 *compte rendu*, however, Caroline Milhaud made a vigorous, if circumspect, effort to dispute Langlois's and Boulisset's assessment. Milhaud's position was undoubtedly a delicate one as she was countering the claims of not only flower manufacturers but also inspectors in her own office. As Elisabeth Piquet argues, rare were the health and labor investigators in this period who forcefully contested the use of toxic substances on behalf of ill workers and against industrial interests.[167] Milhaud seems to have been an unusually devoted advo-cate of workplace reform. Her 1907 study *The Workingwoman in France* already

---

[163] Mlle D. Langlois, inspectrice départementale du travail to Monsieur l'inspecteur divisionnaire, Paris (Boulisset), 6 Dec. 1912, Paris. AN F/22/571 *Enquêtes sur les conditions du travail dans diverses industries*.

[164] Ibid.   [165] Ibid.

[166] Boulisset, inspecteur divisionnaire de la 1er Circonscription to Monsieur le Ministre du Commerce, de l'Industrie et du Travail, 9 Dec. 1912, Paris. AN F/22/571 *Enquêtes sur les conditions du travail dans diverses industries*.

[167] Piquet, *Les Fleurs du mal*, 76–7, 79–80.

signaled the dangers of lead poisoning amongst workingwomen in certain garment industries.[168]

Milhaud's report and conclusions offer a window into the frustration that could accompany efforts to regulate an industry of perceived national import, particularly when one took seriously the voices of workingwomen. Milhaud is unambiguous in her concluding remarks; the chemical findings had been "indisputable": workers manufacturing the *rouge double-face* had been exposed to lead, and, in a majority of cases, these workers reported illness as a result.[169] When quoting Bacquias, the labor inspector from Orléans, who claimed to have found no workers admitting to negative effects from the *rouge*, Milhaud, as rebuttal, clarifies that he had not yet seen the results of the chemical analysis at that stage. She also appends a pointed footnote in which she copies an earlier quotation from her interview in Orléans with a Madame B (who complained of the ill effects of the *rouge*, and criticized her workingwomen for not speaking up more clearly about this issue).[170] Milhaud also criticized the Parisian inspector Langlois for taking as evidence the commentary of the president of the *syndicat patronal des fleuristes*, and adds some sly italics to Langlois's quoting of this employer (who claimed the lead acetate was gradually being replaced by an aluminum acetate): "We have replaced [the lead acetate] with the aluminum acetate which *possesses in addition to its perfect harmlessness* [emphasis added by Milhaud] the precious advantage of brightening colors." Milhaud is able to reveal the essential lie of patronal objections as to the harmlessness of lead acetate by emphasizing this phrase, which, she writes, "allows a certain doubt to linger as to the totally harmless character of the suspect colors."[171]

Milhaud quoted extensively from the 1908 report of Reims's inspector Grégoire, who "does not share the optimism of his colleagues," including his contention that the *mauvais rouge* was making women and children sick, and his descriptions of the vomiting and digestive troubles suffered by these workers. Milhaud concluded this section with a summary of numerous medical treatises on workplace poisoning involving lead,[172] and with an unequivocal indictment of rose work: "To sum up, it seems beyond doubt that the health of female flowerworkers is threatened by the *mauvais rouge*." She leaves it to public health officials to determine the extent of the danger and, if necessary, "to prohibit the use of reds with a lead base in the dyeing of artificial flowers."[173]

When the *enquête* was finally published in 1913 (after protests from labor reformers that the results were being kept hidden), some deemed the findings

---

[168] Milhaud, *L'Ouvrière*, 39. This references laceworkers.   [169] Milhaud, *Enquête*, 405.
[170] Ibid. 407, 294.   [171] Ibid. 405.
[172] Milhaud cited Jules-Louis Breton's 1910 *Le Plomb*, an 1875 treatise by Alexandre Layet which mentions the lead poisoning of flowerworkers, and Thomas Oliver's 1908 study *Diseases of Occupation*, which specifically noted the dangers of red aniline in English textile work.
[173] Milhaud, *Enquête*, 410.

confirmation of what most labor activists already knew.[174] The advent of the Great War and the radical decline in the flower industry which followed the dramatic shift in fashion in the interwar years meant that the concerns raised in Milhaud's *enquête* went unheeded for some time. A workplace law regarding lead was voted on in 1913, but was not put into effect until 1919. Aniline poisoning was not formally declared a work-related illness (and thus eligible for compensation) until 1931, more than forty years after its effects began to be noted in flowerwork.[175] Many factors account for this lag, powerful patronal control of the industry and the difficulty of regulating an industry dominated by homework chief among them. The rhetoric of national taste was an effective tool for slowing regulation employed both by flower manufacturers and by government officials charged with policing the garment industry.

There is evidence that workers in this period also pressed upon the much-trumpeted national import of Parisian couture to argue for, not against, reform in garment trade working conditions. Throughout these years, labor militants heralded the special tastefulness of the Parisian couture worker as justification for workingwomen's increasingly insistent demands for higher wages and humane labor practices. Stéphanie Bouvard and Anna Blondelu's pioneering all-working-women's union for flower and feather workers made the encouragement and training of "artistic work" one of its primary goals; Bouvard's all-women's flower-work cooperative in part aimed to maintain craftsmanship standards, and established a course in luxury flowermaking at the Bourse du Travail.[176] In practice, proponents of labor reforms often relied upon a similar understanding of garment worker tastefulness as the *patronat*, demonstrating an investment in the garment trade as a space of particular national and cultural importance, and in its workers as both particularly skilled and in need of male protection. Thus, garment trades were defended both for their workers' special puissance as producers of French civilization, *and* for their fragility and vulnerability. These seemingly opposed values appear again and again in debates about the French garment trades, even from working-class militants themselves.

---

[174] Auguste Vallet, "L'Industrie de la fleur et de la plume: le travail à domicile," *La Bataille syndical-iste*, 30 May 1913.

[175] Piquet, *Les Fleurs du mal*, 129, 133.

[176] Boxer, "Women in industrial homework," 420, 421; Auguste Pawloski, *Les Syndicats féminins et les syndicats mixtes en France: leur organisation, leur action professionelle, économique et sociale, leur avenir* (Paris, 1912), 49–50.

3

"Notre Petite Amie"

Charpentier's Oeuvre de Mimi Pinson, 1900–1914

The chief architect of Mimi Pinson's turn-of-the-century resurrection was Gustave Charpentier, a composer and philanthropist who employed the fictional character as a mascot of sorts for his expansive initiative to distract working-class Parisian women from their plight with exposure to the performing arts, the Oeuvre de Mimi Pinson (OMP). Founded in 1900, Charpentier's association provided the workingwomen of Paris with, among other things, free theater tickets, and free music and dance classes. Through the 1930s, hundreds of students from his Conservatoire Populaire de Mimi Pinson learned elementary music, song, and dance, and performed across France at grand Festivals of the People's Muse (*Le Couronnement de la Muse du Peuple*).[1] What began as an effort to provide occasional free entertainment to female workers ultimately became a multifaceted conservatory, charity, and social network. Charpentier, a baker's son from the Nord apprenticed in a mill as a child before winning a scholarship to pursue musical studies, envisioned the OMP as both an aesthetic and political project which harmonized with the interests of numerous leftist factions in belle époque France.[2] Charpentier and his collaborators developed their concept of social art in the heady circles of republican, socialist, and anarchist Bohemia in the 1890s. Many found the Mimi Pinsons a seductive metaphor for a harmonious, solidarist Republic, one in which republican paternalism would regulate the excesses of industrial capitalism while maintaining economic (and gender) order.[3] By scrutinizing the work of this initiative, the social stakes of the midinette ideal come into sharper focus. The men (and some women) who organized and administered the OMP did so by relying on the trope of the gay, seducible, and tasteful young garment worker.

---

[1] On Charpentier's life see *Gustave Charpentier: lettres inédites à ses parents* (Paris, 1984); and Marc Delmas, *Gustave Charpentier et le lyrisme français* (Paris, 1931), a biography completed with Charpentier's cooperation according to Michela Niccolai and Jean-Christophe Branger, *Gustave Charpentier et son temps* (Saint-Etienne, 2013), 23. On the significance of his social initiatives, see musicologist Mary Ellen Poole, "Gustave Charpentier and the Conservatoire Populaire de Mimi Pinson," *19th-Century Music* 20 (1997), 231–52; Pomfret, "'A Muse for the Masses'"; Monjaret et al., *Le Paris des "midinettes,"* 505–18.

[2] Charpentier's "vision of socially responsible art" for workingwomen attested to the "ambivalent rapport" between turn-of-the-century French leftist intellectuals and the workers they sought to liberate. Poole, "Gustave Charpentier," 251–2.

[3] On the gendered aspects of republican solidarism at the turn of the century see Tiersten, *Marianne in the Marketplace.*

Working Girls: Sex, Taste, and Reform in the Parisian Garment Trades, 1880–1919. Patricia Tilburg, Oxford University Press (2019). © Patricia Tilburg.
DOI: 10.1093/oso/9780198841173.001.0001

These assumptions defined not only the work of the OMP and its relationship with its working-class members, but also reinforced the comforting notion of workingwomen's pliability for journalists, politicians, reformers, and countless casual observers. Even as the OMP proffered a vision of emancipated French womanhood as a national renovator, it also deployed a powerful typology of the Parisian garment worker to temper its radical potential. This was not a calculated political ploy, but rather evidence of a broader cultural understanding of Parisian garment workers which ran deep in the mostly male circles of the artistic and intellectual avant garde of this period. For philanthropists and reformers dedicated to her uplift, the working Parisienne was, at once, necessarily frivolous but diligent, dangerous but endangered, seductive but seducible, awash in vulgarity but tasteful. Defined and confined by a nineteenth-century type, the female garment workers of Paris were exemplary targets for a benevolent effort which, at a moment in which feminist action and labor militancy were consolidating,[4] reimagined women's emancipation and working-class uplift as a matter entirely managed by bourgeois male authority and desire.

Charpentier funded the OMP in part through the profits of his successful opera *Louise* (1900), a romance between a Bohemian student and a Parisian dressmaker in which Paris is depicted as a world of overwhelming temptation and potential liberation.[5] *Louise* premiered in February 1900 at the Opéra-Comique in Paris, and was performed in conjunction with the city's Exposition Universelle. The opera was, in fact, part and parcel of the nationalist cultural program of the exposition, a "Republican emblem."[6] With realistic sets evoking garment *ateliers*, working-class apartments, and bustling Montmartois intersections, as well as the use of colloquial language and even the musical imitation of sewing machine noise, *Louise* raised the by-then generic Parisian tale of virtuous seamstress and amorous Bohemian to operatic apotheosis and did so in a style of "new proletarian romanticism."[7]

---

[4] On the "poussée syndicale" of 1904–7, see Rebérioux, *La République radicale?*, 88–9. Rebérioux's timeline omits some impressive strikes in Paris specifically in the garment trades in 1901. See Coffin, *The Politics of Women's Work*, 178–9.

[5] Steven Huebner's "Between anarchism and the box office: Gustave Charpentier's *Louise*," *19th-Century Music* 19 (1995), 136–60, and *French Opera at the Fin de Siècle: Wagner, Nationalism, and Style* (Oxford, 1999).

[6] Jane Fulcher, "Charpentier's operatic 'Roman musical' as read in the wake of the Dreyfus Affair," *19th-Century Music* XVI/2 (Fall 1992), 161–80, 179.

[7] Philippe Blay, "Quand Mimi Pinson croise Ciboulette: Gustave Charpentier et Reynaldo Hahn," in *Gustave Charpentier et son temps*, 89–104, 102. On the realism of the sets in *Louise* see Michela Niccolai, "*Louise* et la mise en scène: de Paris à Moscou," in *Gustave Charpentier et son temps*, 267–86; Kathleen O'Donnell Hoover, "Gustave Charpentier," *The Musical Quarterly* 25, No. 3 (July 1939), 334–50. According to James Ross, Charpentier can be seen as joining in the vision of opera promoted by Alfred Bruneau, "musically and dramatically avant-garde, demonstrably republican, and distinctly French." "Messidor: republican patriotism and the French revolutionary tradition in Third Republic opera," in *French Music, Culture, and National Identity, 1870–1939*, p. 112. Bruneau and Charpentier were, for Ross, part of a "radical cult of the Revolution... central to those left-wing artistic enterprises

The Oeuvre de Mimi Pinson developed from a one-off effort by the director of the Opéra-Comique, Albert Carré, to offer hundreds of complimentary seats to the fiftieth performance of *Louise* in April 1900 "to the workshops of Parisian couture."[8] More than 3,000 requests were received for the 400 places offered.[9] Charpentier went on to solicit free seats for working Parisiennes from a number of theater directors, and asked writers and composers who benefited from *billets d'auteur* to donate them to these women.[10] In soliciting tickets, Charpentier heralded this initiative on behalf of the "humble fairies of Parisian labor," and affirmed "everyone's right to beauty."[11] When appeals to theater directors and authors provided less than satisfactory results, Charpentier famously contacted the "elegant and charitable ladies" of Parisian high society including the Duchesse d'Uzès and Princess Alice of Monaco. One of these society ladies proposed naming the initiative after Mimi Pinson, "delicious, working-class Parisian heroine, Musset's delicate and diligent grisette."[12] By 1901, the Oeuvre de Mimi Pinson was regularly providing theater tickets to working Parisiennes. OMP members were encouraged to invite a family member to join them at the complimentary shows— a detail often emphasized by Charpentier to defend the probity of these outings.

In 1902, Charpentier began holding rehearsals for a workingwomen's chorale group, and, by August of that year, he announced a new Conservatoire Populaire de Mimi Pinson, with evening and weekend classes in song, music, and dance.[13] By 1910, the conservatory had about 500 members, and its students had performed in hundreds of concerts around Paris and France; they would do so through the Popular Front in 1936.[14] Charpentier funded this eventually expansive initiative through subventions from the Ministère de l'Instruction Publique et des Beaux Arts, the Ministre du Commerce, and the Conseil Municipal de Paris, as well as private donations from the "Monde parisien."[15] By 1903, the OMP

---

forming a 'mouvement social'...United in rejecting Théophile Gautier's Parnassian 'l'art pour l'art' ideal, instead they were inspired by a vision of social progress" (p. 115).

[8] Maurice Le Blond, *Histoire de Mimi Pinson* (Paris, 1916), 4. See also Poole, "Gustave Charpentier," 238.
[9] Edmond Stoullig, *Les Annales du théâtre et de la musique: vingt-septième année, 1900* (Paris, 1901), 91. See also Poole, "Gustave Charpentier," 238.
[10] Ibid. 239–40. This initial effort seems to have failed because authors were contractually prevented from disposing of their *billets d'auteurs*.
[11] Quoted in Le Blond, *Histoire*, 6.   [12] Ibid.
[13] Poole, "Gustave Charpentier," 241. "Réglement: Institution du Conservatoire de Mimi Pinson," *Le Conservatoire Populaire de Mimi Pinson—1903*, 6 (Paris, 1903) BHVP, FC, No. 444: *L'Oeuvre Mimi Pinson (Conservatoire Organization and History)*. Charpentier may have been inspired by the conservative singing society L'Oeuvre de la Chanson Française, founded in 1900, where workingwomen took free song classes. Poole, "Gustave Charpentier," 234.
[14] Albert Acrémant, Untitled clipping, *Comoedia*, May 1910. Bibliothèque de l'Opéra, Coupures sur Colette et George Wague, D 412 (3). Acrémant was, at the time, the Secretary General of the OMP. Monjaret et al., *Le Paris des "midinettes,"* 518.
[15] "Réglement: Institution du Conservatoire de Mimi Pinson," 7.

boasted 12,000 members.[16] Two years later, it also had a magazine, a program supplying fine art prints to workingwomen for their homes, a concert series, a book program, vacations and excursions offered at reduced prices, free medical and legal consultations, job placement, and convalescent home.[17]

Historians have rightly situated these efforts within a broad movement toward "social art" at the turn of the century, and of a piece with increased attention by elites on the political left to socialist and anarchist solutions to threats to the Republic from the 1880s.[18] My own examination of the OMP more pointedly interrogates the sexual politics of this philanthropic initiative and links it to a deployment of the midinette type in this period. The OMP wanted to moralize the working-class male by way of the ostensibly more malleable body and mind of the young female laborer. In a speech to OMP members at the Bourse du Travail in 1902, Charpentier declared that together they would build a true "Theater of the People" and that "Paris will no longer envy anything of Athens."[19] That same year, in an essay for *Musica*, Charpentier expressed his conviction that the OMP would "lighten" workingwomen's burden "by procuring some instructive and agreeable distraction for them."[20] This girl, "the guardian angel of the working-class hearth," in turn would beautify her family's home and entertain her father, brother, or husband with wholesome songs and dances.[21]

The Conservatoire Populaire was open to all "female Parisian workers and employees, married or single."[22] Classes were offered two hours every weeknight from 8 to 10 p.m., and on Sunday mornings from 10 to noon, and were held in girls' public schools, municipal spaces, and commercial venues across Paris.[23] Worker-students learned the fundamentals of musical theory, ensemble and choral singing, pantomime, fencing, classical and popular dance, and gained proficiency in any number of instruments: piano, harp, and organ among them.[24] Some courses ran from September to July, and students could progress from elementary to superior classes with prerequisites.[25] The professoriat was drawn from dancers and singers at the Opéra and the Opéra-Comique and the Conservatoire

---

[16] Gustave Charpentier, "L'Oeuvre de Mimi Pinson," *Musica*, 1 Nov. 1902, quoted in *Le Conservatoire Populaire de Mimi Pinson—1903*, 6.

[17] "Declaration de l'Oeuvre de Mimi Pinson," *Journal Officiel*, 2 Feb. 1905, and "Oeuvre de Mimi Pinson: Status," 1931. FC, No. 443: *L'Oeuvre de Mimi Pinson (Status, Subventions, etc....)*. See coverage of countryside excursions for Mimi Pinsons through the 1920s such as "La Grande Balade de Mimi Pinson," *Excelsior*, 24 Aug. 1923; "Quand Mimi Pinson se balade dans la forêt de Sénart," *Le Petit Journal*, 24 Aug. 1923.

[18] Michela Niccolai, *La Dramaturgie de Gustave Charpentier* (Turnhout, 2011), 64; Poole, "Gustave Charpentier," 233.

[19] Charpentier, "L'Oeuvre de Mimi Pinson," 2.   [20] Ibid. 4.

[21] Gustave Charpentier, quoted in Le Blond, *Histoire*, 6.

[22] "Réglement: Institution du Conservatoire de Mimi Pinson," *Le Conservatoire Populaire de Mimi Pinson—1903*, 6.

[23] Ibid.   [24] Ibid.

[25] Ibid. 7. Some classes were limited to students who demonstrated talent.

de Paris, as well as prominent Parisian *artistes*, composers, and performers.[26] The administration of the OMP included numerous workingwomen as "déléguées"; these women managed registration for classes at the Bourse du Travail and maintained attendance records (members were required to attend at least two classes per month).[27]

The Conservatoire's curriculum evinced a marked tension between social uplift and concerns about social control. Mary Ellen Poole's detailed examination of the 1903 curriculum and regulations notes an effort to temper basic musical training with discouragement of "'masculine' instrumental virtuosity or composition studies," to avoid the use of technical terms in instruction, and to highlight Mimi Pinson's role as accompanist rather than *artiste*.[28] Indeed, the Conservatoire Populaire, notably, did not offer educational trips to museums, rudimentary art classes, or opportunities for original compositions by students. Administrators assured instructors and students alike that any professional stage aspirations on the part of the Mimi Pinsons would be discouraged, and the "terrifying destiny" of most performers brought to their attention.[29] They also claimed that OMP classes would teach workingwomen "to know and esteem the benefits of grouping together and of association. There, she will discover the truth that there is happiness only in fraternity…" It would be upon her then "to consider…her duty to her family, to herself, and to prepare, under the smiling and grave auspices of Music, her future emancipation."[30]

Poole effectively illuminates the tensions between the OMP's paternalistic control and administrators' pride in the professional accomplishments of the worker-students. As she demonstrates, Charpentier later came out in support of women's suffrage in 1919, proclaiming himself a "resolute partisan of the emancipation of women," only to be harangued by current and former OMP students who wished he had been more radical in his support (Charpentier held that women should only have access to the franchise at the age of 30).[31] My analysis suggests that OMP administrators and observers of the initiative were ambivalent about the possible "future emancipation" of these worker-students, and that they tempered the initiative's potential radicalism by pressing the notion of garment workers as cheerful, sexually desirable, and adorably dim-witted. OMP students became a familiar reference in belle époque France, as the press wistfully covered many of the association's activities. Charpentier's Mimi Pinsons were imagined as a modernized and moralized version of the early nineteenth-century *grisette*, defined according to a winning formula repeated throughout press coverage about these women and even in the OMP's own institutional literature.

---

[26] Acrémant, Untitled clipping. See also Tristan Rémy, *Georges Wague: le mime de la Belle Époque* (Paris, 1964), 105.

[27] "Réglement: Institution du Conservatoire de Mimi Pinson," 6.

[28] Poole, "Gustave Charpentier," 246.

[29] "Observations générales," *Le Conservatoire Populaire de Mimi Pinson—1903*, 9.　　[30] Ibid.

[31] Poole, "Gustave Charpentier," 236.

First in this formula, women who took part in the OMP were seldom referred to by name, but were almost always called "Mimi Pinson," thereby subsuming all working-class Parisian women under this fictional identity, whatever their age, profession, or marital status. The worker-students of the Conservatoire Populaire are identified regularly as "young girls," adolescents safely ensconced in the family home (and perhaps less physically fearsome than adult women). Yet women who registered for the Oeuvre's services ranged from teenagers to women in their thirties and forties (some using the married title "Madame").[32] The new Mimi Pinson, like her nineteenth-century predecessor, was also associated almost exclusively with the luxury garment trades, even though OMP members practiced all sorts of professions. Though fictive, the public face of Mimi Pinson as a young, single garment worker nevertheless was significant, another means of defusing the menace of contemporary labor activism.

The perceived inborn gaiety of the midinette was omnipresent in popular discussions of the Mimi Pinsons. Charpentier made midinette cheerfulness one of the founding ideals of the OMP, telling the assembled workingwomen at the inaugural meeting of 31 August 1902, "I dreamed..... of building with you a theater that was as gay as your smile, as sunny as your regard, as dramatic as your destiny."[33] Whereas many benevolent societies aimed at workers made melodramatic hay of the poverty and misery of working life, the OMP instead was grounded in an understanding of its members as already perfectly content, in spite of their sweated labor. In a piece on the Conservatoire Populaire's pantomime class in 1910, *Fantasio* imagined that workingwomen's performance would be more cheerful than that of professionals: "You, Mimi Pinson...you who offer us each day the bouquet of your laughter...while others learn to plumb the depths of their complicated souls, you, Mimi, you learn to smile."[34] Another piece on the pantomime course underscored the childlike gaiety of the worker-students: "Always laughing, always ready to run or sing, the Mimi-Pinsons listen to the mime's lessons...They smile, then they cry, they seduce, then they pout; and the slightest emotion slides across these pretty faces like sunbeams."[35] What is vertiginous about discussions of the OMP is the omnipresent assertion of midinette gaiety on one hand, and the fundamental assertion that garment workers were in need of more gaiety on the other.

Midinette gaiety had as its corollary in popular representations a certain childish ingenuousness on the part of OMP workers. The Conservatoire Populaire's 1903

---

[32] See stacks of membership cards in the Fonds Charpentier. FC, No. 447. David Pomfret argues for age as an undervalued but crucial category of historical analysis. Pomfret, "'A muse for the masses," 1474.

[33] Le Blond, *Histoire*, 8.

[34] "Pierrot, professeur de Mimi Pinson," *Fantasio*, Jan. 1910. Bibliothèque de l'Opéra, Coupures sur Colette et George Wague, D 412 (3), 173.

[35] "Pierrot Professeur au Conservatoire de Mimi-Pinson," *Petit Journal*, 11 Apr. 1910. Bibliothèque de l'Opéra, Coupures sur Colette et George Wague, D 412 (3), 191.

manual concluded with a music theory class in the form of an imaginary dialogue between a teacher and a Mimi Pinson. Even in this lesson plan, Mimi Pinson is imagined as a young featherbrain who must be led by the male professor to even basic knowledge of her own abilities. Here, the cultural trope of the beautiful, inherently tasteful, but pliable garment worker is used as a catechism of sorts. When asked if she will have the patience to learn musical theory, Mimi responds that while in her school days such classes seemed like a punishment, "Today, after my hard day, Mimi-Pinson classes are my only recreation. I think about them in the workshop, and the memory makes my work less painful, and in the evening, when I return home, my little room takes on the mood of a party." This Mimi Pinson dreams of attending the theater, where she promises not to yawn or chatter like the wealthy *habituées* of those spaces. She worries, however, that one must have white, bejeweled hands to go to the theater. The instructor concedes that Mimi Pinson has only "little pink hands," but asks her to submit to the OMP's paternal confidence in her talents: "We know you better than you know yourself. Let us direct you toward the magnificent and charming goal where your impulsive genius and natural charm will flourish.... Our goal: to glean from you the fragments of beauty that lie dormant in you, to bring them out and reveal them to the world in the light of day."[36] The OMP, then, was understood not to inculcate anything new in its students, but rather to allow native gaiety and good taste to flourish, while at the same time tempering the horrors of garment trade labor.

This secular catechism ends with the professor teasing the dim-witted worker-student, and disallowing any reaction to his teasing other than laughter:

MIMI-PINSON. It must be difficult to learn all these instruments! Really difficult! Since nobody ever dared teach them to me.
PROFESSOR. Less difficult than your work as a little fairy, assuredly.
MIMI-PINSON. You're making fun of me.
PROFESSOR. Mockery for you will always come with an indulgent smile. The cruelest intention wouldn't dare cause Mimi Pinson pain! We will laugh![37]

To prove to this student her own indomitable cheerfulness, the teacher follows this proclamation with a Musset verse about Mimi Pinson wearing flowers and being gay. This dialogue encapsulates the OMP's approach to workingwomen, employing nostalgic notions of garment trade gaiety, native taste, and feather-brainedness to renovate French society and bring "a renaissance of working-class art."[38] Mimi's talents exist outside of her own capacities; she contains within her a "impulsive genius" that requires the patience and attention of her mostly

---

[36] "Spécimen du programme d'enseignement du Conservatoire Populaire de Mimi-Pinson," *Le Conservatoire Populaire de Mimi Pinson—1903*, 10.
[37] Ibid.   [38] Ibid.

bourgeois instructors in order to flower. At the same time, lessons at the OMP drive away the agonies of sweated garment labor (while effectively erasing any other variety of female work). Any insults rebound off of this ideal working-woman who, incredibly, cannot be wounded, so impenetrable is her naïve adorableness.

Alongside repeated references to their youthful, empty-headed gaiety, the worker-students of the OMP were held up as purveyors of a purified French national taste. Because of their association in the popular imagination with the Parisian garment trades, OMP workers were also considered naturally chic and were invested with an inborn decorative style. Indeed, central to the cultural usefulness of the OMP's students for observers was that they allowed an easy merging of the body of the female worker with particularly French notions of the national responsibility of feminine taste. All other kinds of Parisian female labor were effaced in popular descriptions of the group's members, and rarely was the hardship of daily work mentioned.

As Lisa Tiersten demonstrates, bourgeois Frenchwomen in this period were taught to cultivate personal style as both "individualized artistic practice" and as the duty of a new kind of "consumer-citizen."[39] Workingwomen were a peripheral presence in such initiatives. Tiersten points out that numerous republican pedagogical and political figures made decorative arts instruction a plank in their reforming platforms, sometimes "including the Parisian textile worker and even the lowly female sweated laborer alongside the male artisan in the pantheon of French artists."[40] Scholars generally have not been sufficiently attentive to the symbolic role played by workingwomen in the culture wars of this period. Anxieties about bourgeois wives' unbridled consumption and the intendant threats to the *foyer* made room for a novel politics of workingwomen as exemplars of French taste—women who produced (and moderately consumed) works of French fancy and creativity.

In the decade before the Great War, the OMP and those who remarked on its efforts found the Mimi Pinsons a convenient occasion to commend the innate taste of the Parisienne—but a Parisienne who labored *for* the consumer economy rather than one who seemed to lose herself in its excesses. These were women who managed to exemplify French national taste and luxury consumption, paradoxically, without artifice or extravagant expense. In an article for *La Fronde* in 1900, novelist Marcelle Tinayre recounted "the joyful sight" of several OMP seamstresses taking advantage of free tickets at the opera. While the working-women's clothing, Tinayre wrote, was "a bit modest, a bit somber amidst the brand-new décor of the theater," the Mimi Pinsons nevertheless charmed her

---

[39] Tiersten, *Marianne in the Market*, 123, 227.
[40] Ibid. 214. For a discussion of debates over decorative arts reform and mass consumer culture, see Williams, *Dream Worlds*.

with "the whimsy of their hats, the beauty of hair waved with that special taste of Parisiennes..."[41] Reporting on an OMP event in 1914, Maurice d'Arcus remarked that each midinette, had "her charm and her chic" and "that Parisian spirit that one cannot acquire...an innate taste, the art of the rag, that consists of dressing oneself with nothing and fashioning a hat with the same."[42] Later that same year, poet, novelist, and reformer Camille Mauclair praised the "artistic sense of these 'little hands,' these flowermakers, these milliners" who had "a taste, a knowledge, a pep" that was enchanting.[43]

Some elevated the working Parisienne's supposed innate taste to an art, and characterized the women of the OMP as artists participating in the august tradition of French craft. Indeed, Charpentier's initiative grew out of reformers' indignation that the workingwomen who created French fashion were excluded from realms of high art like concert halls and theaters. Maurice Le Blond, an OMP administrator, explained:

> Humble seamstresses created the luxurious cloaks of the lovely ladies seen entering those magnificent portals. Modest flowermakers adorned the boxes where the ladies soon will take their seats. Burly masons erected these temples of art. Yet all of these workers are forbidden to enter these places. Such sanctuaries are reserved for a privileged caste only.[44]

Though Le Blond linked upper-class consumption and the sweated trades, he assigned Mimi Pinson's labor a vital and exalted national function: maintaining the international reputation of French taste through the creation of fine goods. In Le Blond's estimation, luxury trade workers were active producers of art deserving of admission to high cultural spheres. The male masons mentioned in Le Blond's list of artisans presumably would gain admission to the "temples of art" only as a guest of Mimi Pinson.

At times, it seemed that the OMP's primary goal was the revitalization of the working class as a whole by way of young workingwomen's taste. Writing to the Prefect of Paris in 1905 to formalize the OMP's constitution, Charpentier claimed to seek "the moral and intellectual improvement" of Paris's workers by art lessons that would refine "their taste and show them the Beautiful, thereby diverting them from so much vulgarity and drabness..."[45] Le Blond recalled that the OMP

---

[41] Marcelle Tinayre, quoted in Le Blond, *Histoire*, 4. FC, No. 444. This article originally appeared as "Les 'cousettes' à l'Opéra-Comique," *La Fronde*, 1 May 1900.

[42] Maurice d'Arcus, "Le règne du Midinettisme," c.February 1914. FC, No. 449: Mimi-Pinson: Remise de l'épée d'Academicien à Gustave Charpentier.

[43] Camille Mauclair, "Une belle volonté," *La Muse*, 29 June 1914. FC, No. 449. On Mauclair and decorative arts reform, see Williams, *Dream Worlds*.

[44] Le Blond, *Histoire*, 3. Le Blond was one of the leaders of the Naturiste movement, republican politician, and Emile Zola's son-in-law and editor.

[45] Letter from Gustave Charpentier to Monsieur le Préfet, Paris, 30 Jan. 1905. FC, No. 443.

was intended to raise the level of crude working-class music.[46] Such initiatives at once relied on the notion of the working Parisienne as innately tasteful and targeted the inferior state of her day-to-day aesthetics.

At the same time, the OMP called upon the native abilities of working-class Parisiennes to counter the excesses of bourgeois taste. The 1903 OMP Instructional Methods handbook noted that all classes would take bourgeois music as a negative model: "These lacy concoctions of bad taste that the whims of a great bourgeois century imposed on the splendid bareness of proud Music have always shocked the people, who remained attached to simple songs."[47] The OMP's dance program similarly sought to free popular festivals from hiring "professional female dancers, used to the lies of the stage, with their artificial and frivolous science." "Why," asked Le Blond, "call upon our theaters' ballerinas, when there is so much natural grace to use amongst the People?"[48]

The handbook assured students and the public that Mimi Pinson would learn "popular songs and classic tunes, songs of the people..." After completing her studies at the OMP, she would retain her naturalness: "Mimi Pinsons will learn to sing, certainly, but...her voice will still have the freshness and emotion of her first songs. Her taste will have developed, but she will have preserved her innocence..."[49] OMP dance instructors were warned that the first year of dance study should not attempt any "real dancing" but simply teach "innocent, grave, religious gestures...some popular dance reduced to its primitive expression." This restraint in instruction would permit "the native grace of the charming Parisiennes to show itself fully, without resulting in fatigue, boredom, humiliation, or ridicule for her."[50] Concert programs for the OMP gave prominence to "French works from the Romantic and post-Romantic era," particularly Berlioz, Bizet, and Massenet. Musset's poetry was also included.[51]

This call to protect and purify the working Parisienne's native taste considered Mimi Pinson a woman out of time—a nostalgic vessel for the expression of the artistic spirit of her race. In the epigraph which topped the music theory course in the Conservatoire Populaire's handbook, Charpentier insisted: "I neither hoped for nor desired to compete with the [national] Conservatoire, still less with the National Academy of Music and Dance: simple songs, slow dances, accompaniment on primitive harps...the first songs of Humanity."[52] The Conservatoire Populaire's handbook told the worker-student that she would sing "the songs of your race, preserved for you by the memory of centuries, chosen by your

[46] Le Blond, *Histoire*, 16.
[47] "Méthodes d'Enseignement, Institution du Conservatoire de Mimi Pinson," 8.
[48] Le Blond, *Histoire*, 18.
[49] "Méthodes d'Enseignement, Institution du Conservatoire de Mimi Pinson," 8.   [50] Ibid. 9.
[51] Françoise Andrieux, "Les ouvrières parisiennes chantent et dansent dans les banlieues," in *La Banlieue en fête: de la marginalité urbaine à l'identité culturelle*, ed. Noëlle Gérome et al. (Saint-Denis, 1988), 233–43, 237.
[52] "Spécimen du programme d'enseignement du Conservatoire Populaire de Mimi-Pinson," 10.

ancestors because they bore perfect witness to their sensibilities. By way of these simple songs, naïve and profound, we will renew your poetic soul, we will purify your taste in art, and we will make of you a new ideal."[53] Workingwomen will acquire no new talents, but will have their native artistic taste revealed.

While ostensibly concerned with teaching performing arts to workers, the OMP regularly addressed questions of the female laborer's decorative taste. Charpentier and his associates created a new branch of the OMP in 1905, L'Image de Mimi Pinson, which solicited donated prints and other *objets d'art* from artists and merchants to brighten female workers' domiciles. The OMP awarded lucky members works of art like lithographs by Auguste Rodin to "adorn the little room of the Parisian Workingwoman."[54] In a form letter to prospective donor artists, Charpentier explained that this new branch of the Oeuvre was created "with an eye toward the further diffusion of the taste for beauty among Parisian workers" and asked artists to "contribute to the elevation of the working-class ideal."[55]

In March 1905, *La Fronde's* Marie-Louise Néron wrote approvingly of the program's effort to correct the "aesthetic lack" in workers' homes, but expressed concern about the debasing influence of bourgeois style. She wondered if it might not be wiser to "leave the Mimi Pinsons their naïve miniatures, their gaudy lithographs, which suffice them" rather than introducing their "simple souls" to "our needs for luxury, which can only deaden their heart if not completely corrode [*gangrènent*] it…"[56] Similarly contemptuous of bourgeois taste, the editors of the OMP's magazine *Mimi Pinson: Journal des ouvrières parisiennes* fired back at Néron that they had never sought to introduce female workers to the "detestable taste" of "bourgeois luxury": "Beauty does not need to be gilded, intricate, or opulent to be moving. And really, is it art that corrodes the People? No, rather it is dishonest luxury, that glossy and hideous rubbish, which does so."[57] Thus, the decorative and social goal of the OMP was the purging of the false and overly sumptuous luxury of the bourgeoisie rather than the wholesale elimination of luxury. Working Parisiennes' simple, tasteful clothing and homes might even serve as remedial models for their upper- and middle-class sisters.

This concern clearly struck a chord with the French press; the next issue of *Mimi Pinson* excerpted a number of articles from around France responding to Néron's critique. Jean d'Albignac lauded the OMP's "noble endeavor" to replace the pictures "devoid of all artistic value… which can only distort taste" now sullying the walls of the working-class home, and instead to offer workers pieces that "would elevate their taste and their minds…"[58] A journalist in Alsace remarked

---

[53] Ibid. 11.
[54] *Programme, Réunion-Concert, Oeuvre de Mimi Pinson, Conservatoire populaire de Musique, de Comedie, et de Danse*, Feb. 1907. FC, No. 444.
[55] Letter from Gustave Charpentier, 25 Jan. 1905. FC, No. 444.
[56] Marie-Louise Néron, quoted in "Echos de la presse," *Mimi Pinson* 2 (10 Mar. 1905), 7. FC, No. 444.
[57] Ibid.
[58] D'Albignac, "Des images pour Mimi Pinson," *Mimi Pinson* 3 (10 Apr. 1905), 12.

that in teaching "these tidy little fairies" to "distinguish the ugly from the beautiful," the industrial workplace would also be beautified.[59] A reader in Liège defended Charpentier's program in passionate terms: "Because they spend long hours in workshops deprived of air, bent over exhausting and futile works of fashion, is it fair that these humble midinettes should renounce the joys of art? Yet it is typical of our overheated utilitarianism to consider Beauty as superfluous, a luxury reserved for a privileged caste. Thus, Life and Art are divorced. And Art, isolated, deprived of nourishing roots, is emasculated and shrinks to the size of an agreeable and pretty pastime."[60] Charpentier's program successfully reunited Art and Life, but also could restore gender stability—at once feminizing female workers and preventing the emasculation of Art itself.

Mimi Pinson's aestheticized femininity was brought to its logical conclusion in frequent descriptions of Mimi Pinson herself as a decorative object, an Art Nouveau flower in human form.[61] In describing a summer chorale and ballet performance in the Tuileries Gardens by women from the OMP, Le Blond rhapsodized: "Garbed in crinoline dresses, the skirts and bodices made fairy-like by the orange, violet, green and pink lights of the electric projectors, they come forward like ghostly figures from the past...the clusters of dancers knot together and unknot, making mobile garlands of flowered forms. An emotional silence hangs over the immense crowd, the entire park meditates...Oh, the delicious enchantment!"[62] By way of electric projectors, the Mimi Pinson appear as apparitions out of time, and their performance bewitches and calms the crowd. Charpentier himself, in the libretto for the Couronnement de la Muse, has the poets acclaim the working Muse of Paris in one of the first performances of the show in 1898:

> O lovely one,
> this dancer
> is a flower of life
> made up of a bit of each of us all.
> It is our soul
> in the form of a flower
> that would be a woman,
> flower-woman,
> whose grace and perfume
> are transformed into dance rhythms.[63]

[59] *Journal d'Alsace*, quoted in "Echos de la presse," *Mimi Pinson* 3 (10 Apr. 1905), 9.

[60] Fuss Amoré, *La Meuse* (Liège), quoted ibid. The author was possibly Henri Fuss-Amoré, a Belgian anarchist and union organizer in Liège.

[61] On the Art Nouveau motif of the *femme-fleur*, see Silverman, *Art Nouveau*, 206.

[62] Le Blond, *Histoire*, 21.

[63] "Fête Municipale du Centenaire de Michelet, Place de l'Hôtel-de-Ville, le dimanche 24 Juillet 1898, à 5 heures. Programme Officiel du Couronnement de la Muse de Paris," FC, No. 423.

Even socialist commentator Gustave Téry, in criticizing the presentation of a Parisian workingwoman as Charpentier's "Muse of the People" at a *fête* honoring Victor Hugo in March 1902, was enchanted by the notion of the proletarian flower-woman. The People of Paris had "plucked from the corner of a working-class neighborhood, this living flower and, in a superb and charming gesture, were going to offer it to the poet."[64] This transmutation of the female labor force into a Flower-Woman served not only to transform labor into a graceful decorative object, but also to make her stand for all of France; this flower who is made, in Charpentier's words, "of a bit of each of us all."

The sensuality of the previous passages speaks to the way that the Mimi Pinsons' physical attractiveness functioned as a crucial pillar of this philanthropic endeavor. The OMP relied on a popular understanding of Parisian garment workers as at once sweated laborers in need of distraction and as fashion-conscious love-lies ready for seduction. In describing the mission of the Conservatoire Populaire, Charpentier underscored the enjoyment of watching these women in class: "What a pleasure it is to see them, how charming... How spruce most of them are, and pretty, without affectation, the blondes as much as the brunettes, always gay, always smiling!"[65] Charpentier here made space in what amounts to his conservatory's mission statement for a description of the physical allure of its students. Indeed, he goes on to stress the worker-students' innate desire to please, and suggests that the classes of the OMP appeal to these women as a means of improving their skills of *coquettrie*: "In watching them, we see that they are content, happy to be agreeable and to make themselves more beautiful by learning beautiful things, thrilled to add to their ingenuous charms the seductive power of a limpid voice... They work! They work!"[66] The refrain about his students' diligence is part and parcel of the dreamy vision they provide: women who please, who embellish with beauty and fashion, but who also labor. Indeed, Mimi Pinson was chosen as the namesake for the initiative because she seemed to harmonize these possibly discordant qualities, as "Musset's delicate and laborious grisette."[67]

As a cultural type, this ideal working-class woman indeed was defined by her role as a source of male inspiration and erotic stimulation. Male artists, poets, and politicians, in referencing the OMP, conjured up a female body that they figuratively, and sometimes literally, possessed, a single workingwoman who was at once a subordinate sexual object and a vessel of artistic inspiration. In his study of late nineteenth-century London social efforts, Seth Koven articulates the essential interconnectedness of Victorian philanthropic initiatives aimed at the poor,

[64] Gustave Téry, "Fête bourgeoise," *La Petite République socialiste*, 7 Mar. 1902. FC, No. 423. Téry describes his disappointment at finding that this is actually a bourgeois celebration.
[65] Charpentier, "L'Oeuvre de Mimi Pinson," *Musica*, 1 Nov. 1902, quoted in *Le Conservatoire Populaire de Mimi Pinson—1903*, 2–5, 4. FC, No. 444.
[66] Ibid.   [67] Le Blond, *Histoire*, 6.

Victorian sexual politics, and the "extent to which politics and erotics, social and sexual categories, overflowed their boundaries, affecting one another in profoundly consequential ways for our understanding of poverty and its representations, social politics, and emerging sexual and gender identities…"[68] A close analysis of the OMP extends Koven's "genealogy of benevolence and social welfare" at the turn of the century to the French context.[69]

It was a well-worn part of Charpentier's legend that *Louise* had been based on an affair from the composer's own student days in Montmartre.[70] His friend, the playwright Saint-Georges de Bouhélier, related the genesis of the opera: "I knew, at that time, his fondest dreams. It was to go amongst the people and renovate them… This idea of a people's theater, above all, captivated him."[71] Two sentences later, he shifts to Charpentier's romantic confessions: "Once we were passing by the boulevard de Clichy, and he pointed to a large, gloomy building… 'Louise's House!', he told me. And he spoke of his heroine. He had known her when he was a very young man, before his departure for Rome… For Charpentier, composing a piece was to recall the past. He confessed that he had expanded upon one of his affairs of the heart."[72] Charpentier himself admitted in his unpublished *Mémoires* that *Louise* developed out of his idea "to put into music the love affair that lit up my twenties."[73]

In 1900, art critic Arsène Alexandre recalled that, in his younger days, he would watch Charpentier take a "walkabout" every day at noon at a busy intersection in Montmartre "just as the workshops let out… amongst the laborers, the stylish workingwomen, the poor, the flâneurs…"[74] This, writes Alexandre, was his method of composing. Charpentier was more specific about the source of his noontime inspiration in his *Mémoires*:

I like to roam around the Delta roundabout… From 13h to 14h after my lunch at Ramponneau, I pass by the review of the happy workers and smiling girls who come down from Clignancourt often arm in arm, as if they were going to a party. Seamstresses, boxsellers, laundresses, *confectionneuses*, in groups of three or four advance like conquerors into the square, bright-eyed, lips ready for retort, with a steady step striking the pavement and tightening skirts along the length of their ardent thighs. My figure makes them laugh. They know me well.

---

[68] Seth Koven, *Slumming: Sexual and Social Politics in Victorian London* (Princeton, 2006), 6.
[69] Ibid. 15. [70] Huebner, "Between anarchism and the box office," 141.
[71] Saint-Georges de Bouhélier, quoted in Delmas, *Gustave Charpentier et le lyrisme français*, 32.
[72] Ibid. 32–3. Charpentier made a habit of recalling his youthful affair with "Louise." See the recollections of composer Emmanuel Bondeville in Louis Aubert, *Notice sur la vie et les travaux de Gustave Charpentier* (Paris, 1956), 8.
[73] Gustave Charpentier, *Mémoires*, quoted in Niccolai, *La Dramaturgie de Gustave Charpentier*, 150.
[74] Arsène Alexandre, *Mémorial*, 16 Feb. 1900, quoted in Delmas, *Gustave Charpentier et le lyrisme français*, 33.

"It's the photographer" they say, amused by the camera with which I ogle them in every direction.[75]

Unlike Alexandre, Charpentier makes plain that his *bain de foule* is focused exclusively on female workers. And he is not merely an observer; his ogling and photographing of the women is obvious enough that he has become well known to them. We, of course, only have Charpentier's word that his daily intrusion amused these women.

According to musicologist Philippe Blay, Charpentier lived until his death in a *union libre* with a woman, possibly a worker, some seventeen years his junior named Camille Willay—and carried on numerous liaisons outside of that union, including with students from his Conservatoire Populaire.[76] Of interest here is not simply that Charpentier had romantic relationships with working-class Parisiennes, but rather, that he and so many of his friends and colleagues in the elite cultural and political circles of turn-of-the-century France celebrated this identity between his personal affairs and his philanthropic efforts. A widespread perception of the midinette as a source of light-hearted sexual dalliance facilitated and even was fundamental to reform efforts of this kind.

Charpentier apotheosized this romantic union between the working Frenchwoman and bohemian artiste in his opera *Louise*. While excellent studies by Steven Huebner, Jane Fulcher, and others have situated *Louise* in the context of fin-de-siècle opera, Wagnerism, and anarchism,[77] scant scholarly attention has been paid to the way that *Louise* confirmed and reified a powerful trope of the female garment worker in Paris as a site of erotic pleasure and national communion. In the opera, the seamstress Louise and poet Julien meet as neighbors; his poet studio in Montmartre overlooks the apartment Louise shares with her parents. He pursues her and tries to convince her parents to let them marry. When these efforts fail, Louise leaves the workshop to live in a *union libre* with Julien on the Butte. In one scene, the seamstresses sing of their overwhelming attraction toward the men who pursue them; in the words of the seamstress Irma, "when I am in the street. All my being catches fire! | Under the ardent rays (eyes) that desire me...| The grazing, the appeals, the flatteries inflame me and intoxicate me!"[78] Here, Charpentier, himself a proud ogler of garment workers, has a

---

[75] Charpentier, *Mémoires*, quoted in Niccolai, *La Dramaturgie de Gustave Charpentier*, 76.

[76] Philippe Blay, "Quand Mimi Pinson croise Ciboulette: Gustave Charpentier et Reynaldo Hahn," in *Gustave Charpentier et son temps*, 103. Willay (1877–1957) was not discussed in biographies or reporting about Charpentier, but the correspondence in the Fonds Charpentier show that many OMP students knew of her, often including salutations for "Camille" in their letters. Willay is buried alongside Charpentier in Père-Lachaise. She served as Charpentier's personal secretary and secretary for the OMP after World War I. See Niccolai, *La Dramaturgie de Gustave Charpentier*, 290–2. Le Blond was married to Émile Zola's daughter Denise, born to his mistress Jeanne Rozerot (who had been the seamstress for Zola's wife Alexandrine, herself a former Parisian garment worker).

[77] Huebner, "Between anarchism and the box office."

[78] Gustave Charpentier, *Louise* (libretto), *French Opera Libretti*, Vol. III (New York, 2005), 264–5.

fictional seamstress confirm the delight and excitation such ogling provokes. To be sure, Charpentier creates in Louise a young workingwoman who pushes against social and parental control for her own pleasure—and is not, within the story of the Opera, punished for it. Louise, writes Michela Niccolai, is "an autonomous character" whose love for Julien is, for the composer, a pretext of sorts which allows her to reject constraint in favor of liberation.[79] David Pomfret agrees that intellectuals and artists like Charpentier "celebrated these girls' spirited and youthful contravention of stuffy bourgeois norms as a regenerative force" and saw in characters like Louise an appealing version of the "modern girl."[80] Nonetheless, in such renderings, young workingwomen's autonomy is grounded in their desiring and desired bodies.[81]

The sexual relationship between Louise and Julien is elevated as a progressive personal liberation ("Let us be free according to our conscience!"), and an engine of Julien's artistic success. Following the consummation of their love, the couple is fêted by a band of bohemian men, several grisettes, and other working Montmartois. Louise is crowned the Muse of Montmartre, reaffirming her important and inextricable roles as quencher of male desire and inspirer of male artistic creation.

The opera, a box office smash, was tremendously popular with the well-heeled audience of the Opéra-Comique, but also became associated with public festivals organized by Charpentier which brought the monumental mythos of the working Parisienne to cities around France: the Couronnement de la Muse du Peuple.[82] This massive undertaking involved a parade, pantomime, ballet, orchestra, and chorus—composed by Charpentier and often accompanied by singers and dancers from the OMP.[83] The Muse, a young workingwoman elected by the city's female workers and often wearing a gown donated by local merchants, presided over a scene representing the "reconciliation" of the artist and the working classes. The female worker and the Poet are drawn toward one another in the midst of a joyous festival crowd. After begging the workingwoman for a kiss, the artist explains the purpose of the fête that surrounds them and tells her: "the art of the Dance, like the art of the Song, like all art, was created by the People...Let us

---

[79] Niccolai, *La Dramaturgie de Gustave Charpentier*, 167.

[80] Pomfret, "'A muse for the masses'," 1455.

[81] Anarchists were supportive of liberated sexual relations and paid "lip service to the equality of both sexes," but "underlying that liberated attitude was a profound distrust of women." Richard Sonn, *Sex, Violence and the Avant-Garde: Anarchism in Interwar France* (University Park, 2010), 30.

[82] The opera also was followed by a less successful sequel, *Julien*, in 1913.

[83] There were at least twenty-six festivals of the Couronnement de la Muse du Peuple from 1897 to 1916, including Paris, St-Étienne, Nancy, Lille, Lens, Enghien, Amiens, Limoges, Niort, and Riom. The show was performed occasionally into the 1950s. See Pomfret, "A muse for the masses," as well as Andrieux, "Les ouvrières parisiennes chantent et dansent dans les banlieues." Charpentier dedicated the composition to Georges Montorgueil, "enthusiastic apostle of the Muses." Quoted in Delmas, *Gustave Charpentier et le lyrisme français*, 146. For the broader context of Third Republican music, see Jann Pasler, *Composing the Citizen* (Berkeley, 2009).

proudly unite the instinct for Beauty with which our souls are blooming." At last, the artist and the workingwoman dance together.[84]

In accepting his election to the Académie des Beaux-Arts at the Sorbonne in 1914, Charpentier spelled out Mimi Pinson's important role as a Muse for the male artist—a role that fused sexual and artistic satisfaction. In front of a crowd of thousands, including the president's wife, Henriette Poincaré, Charpentier told the assembled workingwomen that when they walked home from work in the evening, they stimulated in the "slightly mad minds" of men not only "desires for love affairs" but also "novels of which you will not be aware."[85] He imagined a male poet who, fired by the sight of a female garment worker, took "the image of an august and fragile goddess" back to his lonely room. Having thus mentally absconded with Mimi Pinson, the poet takes possession of her through writing, in a scene that subtly mirrored a sexual encounter:

> Close the door. Quick, some light, unless the moon and the lamppost outside are enough... Paper. Pencil. And we write, we rush, we have so many things to get down, things that seem so beauteous! The pages pile up. After one, we throw off our hat; after another, our coat. At the detour of an idea, we light our pipe. And all of a sudden, we stop. It's finished... With the fever broken, it seems that everything has vanished... The room is dark. The extinguished pipe rests near the blackened paper. And here in the dark a dot twinkles, a glimmer, that look from before, that lovely and gay look, the look that does not die... Be proud, little Parisiennes. Think how many works of art are born thanks to you, works which are, in part, yours, without you even noticing that passerby who gazes at you, the artist whom you inspired...[86]

Thus, a fevered tussle in the artist's room between his pencil and the captured sight of the workingwoman on the street results in the birth of a work of art. Following Charpentier on stage at the Sorbonne was a young poet named Paul Verlet who offered an amorous homage to Mimi Pinson as well, thanking Mimi on behalf of twenty-something men, "We throw the flowers of our youthful kisses at you, | And we cry: Thank you for preserving | Your fervent lover's heart under your embroidered outfit."[87] *Gil Blas's* Jean Baruy noted that when a young workingwoman dressed as Mimi Pinson presented Charpentier with his academician's sword, she first kissed it: "Fortunate the academician who has their sword

---

[84] *Fête de la Muse du Peuple: Programme officiel, Ville de Nancy, Dimanche 15 août 1909.* FC, No. 423 bis.

[85] Charpentier, quoted in Le Blond, *Histoire*, 26.

[86] Charpentier, quoted ibid. The speech was reprinted in "Une fête à la Sorbonne," *Journal des débats politiques et littéraires* (11 Feb. 1914), 3–4.

[87] Ibid.

baptized by the lips of Mimi Pinson...I am sure that all night he had dreams of cape and sword in which Mimi Pinson was the heroine..."[88]

The association of Charpentier's Mimi Pinsons with male sexual adventure characterized responses to most aspects of the OMP initiative. Jean d'Albignac lauded the Image de Mimi Pinson, writing that through its aesthetic instruction, Charpentier and the other men leading the program "will have really deserved our girlfriend, Mimi Pinson" ("...notre petie [sic] amie...").[89] Other male commentators combined this figurative sexual relationship with memories of actual romantic contacts with working-class women. When the republican Minister of Public Instruction and Fine Arts Joseph Chaumié paid a visit to the Conservatoire Populaire in 1902, he greeted the five hundred or so female students by reminiscing about his own youthful dalliance with a working-class woman:

> With charming good-nature and paternal candor, [Chaumié] recounted that, back in the day, when he was a university student, he had known a Mimi Pinson who had many shortcomings, and that he was happy to see that today's Mimi Pinson inherited only the virtues of her predecessor: the exquisite grace and charm of the Parisienne.[90]

Though Chaumié's address is referred to as "paternal" and "charming"—and allegedly is met with "outbursts of joy" from the gathered student-workers—it nonetheless seems a surprising anecdote for a government minister to relate to a group of female workers—and to be recorded in the OMP's magazine and, a decade later, in the group's official history.[91] The journalist Brécy, relating the speech in Le Figaro, also described Chaumié's address as that of a "bon papa," and yet began the article by assuming that sexual dalliance was his readers' primary knowledge of garment workers: "Mimi Pinson...you know her well. She is the one whose lovely laughter and girlish grace adorned our fathers' twenties."[92] Reporting on the minister's visit for Le Petit Parisien, Paul Lagardère offered a slightly expanded version of the above anecdote. In Lagardère's retelling, Chaumié prefaced his remark by talking about his wife and grandchildren, assuring the collected Mimis that they should not fear him, and then offered the reminiscence about the Mimi Pinsons he had "known" when he was a university student, "pretty, like you, and graceful, but their character was quite frivolous! I knew their song, and I hummed it sometimes, daydreaming, those pretty verses by

---

[88] Jean Baruy, "Mimi Pinson remet une épée à Gustave Charpentier," Gil Blas, 10 Feb. 1914. The woman was named Marie or Marguerite Magnier.

[89] Jean d'Albignac, "Des images pour Mimi Pinson," Mimi Pinson: Journal des ouvrières parisiennes 3 (10 Apr. 1905), 11–12, 12. Reprinted from l'Actualité. FC, No. 444.

[90] Le Blond, Histoire, 11. This same story was reprinted in Mimi Pinson: Journal des ouvrières parisiennes 3 (10 Apr. 1905). FC, No. 444.

[91] Le Blond, Histoire, 12.

[92] Brécy, "La vie de Paris: M. Chaumié chez Mimi Pinson," Le Figaro (11 Nov. 1902), 2.

Musset…If the song is pretty, in fiction, it is not always so in life and I am grateful that you have repudiated the frivolity of the beautiful girl celebrated by the poet…"[93] Here, the minister's remembered youth is meant as an amiable warning to today's Mimi Pinsons to avoid the improprieties that nevertheless had been such a pleasure to him in his student days. Chaumié suggests that garment workers are indeed burdened with a preternatural looseness of morals. During this gathering, a seamstress named Émilie Gaty (remarked by Lagardère as "elegant and pretty in her blonde beauty") read a poem to Chaumié. In this poem, composed by Charpentier's friend Saint-Georges de Bouhélier, Gaty admits the reputation of female garment workers, but thanks the minister for seeing past it.[94] It was this recitation which provoked Chaumié's anecdote about the dissolute Mimi Pinsons of his youth. The use of this early nineteenth-century trope of the working-class woman as a sexual rite of passage for bourgeois men was one of the ways that the organizers and officials involved with the OMP managed the uncomfortable potential of a program that provided new opportunities and public exposure for female workers. Thus, defined by her (imagined) youth, sexual submission, and joyful labor, Mimi Pinson became a means by which middle-class observers in particular eroticized the working class. Yet this eroticization was somewhat sanitized by the rhetoric of social uplift.

Charpentier's worker-students also were praised and sometimes lampooned in belle époque popular entertainment. In 1903, music-hall star Félix Mayol performed and recorded Paul Marinier and Harry Fragson's "Le Conservatoire de Mimi Pinson." 1908's "La Musique de Mimi Pinson" raved about the "coquette allure" of Charpentier's "sweet workingwomen."[95] Some songs approached the OMP as an opportunity for bawdy innuendo. The lewd flâneur narrator of 1907's "Pinçons Mimi Pinson!" ("Let's pinch Mimi Pinson!") lures a singing hatmaker back to his apartment to "advance [her] studies" by playing "the lil flute…while I plug the holes."[96]

The pervading cultural association of Charpentier's Mimi Pinsons with sexual allure, compliant labor, and feminine distraction also served to neutralize and prettify working-class demands. The Parisian press in these years commonly featured anecdotes in which a cheerful, well-dressed Mimi Pinson serves as a pleasing interlocutor between bourgeois consumers and their downtrodden workers, romanticized images with political import. OMP students were enlisted to perform at festivals and concerts around Paris and France aimed at the uplift of

[93] Paul Lagardère, "M. Chaumié chez Mimi Pinson," Le Petit Parisien (11 Nov. 1902), 1–2, 2.

[94] Ibid. 1. Saint-Georges de Bouhélier's poem was reprinted in Le Blond, Histoire, 11, and in the OMP's magazine, Le Blond, "L'Histoire de 'Mimi Pinson' (Suite)," 2–4; Mimi Pinson: Journal des ouvrières parisiennes 3 (10 Apr. 1905).

[95] Jean Daris, "La Musique de 'Mimi Pinson,'" music by Ad. Gauwin (Paris, 1908). BNF-L VM7-134711.

[96] Raoul Le Peltier, "Pinçons Mimi Pinson!" Music by George Krier (Paris, 1907). BNF-L VM7-130234.

the working classes, and thus became an attractive public ornament to such initiatives. In December 1902, worker-students from the OMP performed at a benefit for *Les Midinettes*, an organization devoted to the creation of *restaurants coopératifs* for Parisian workingwomen only. A journalist for *Gil Blas* enthused about the event: "A charming meeting brightened the Bourse du Travail yesterday. In the large hall pretty, smiling faces crowded around the young composer Gustave Charpentier."[97] The Mimi Pinsons performed at a *soirée* organized in April 1905 to benefit La Mutualité Maternelle, an initiative to aid working mothers in Paris by funding several weeks of maternity leave pay following childbirth.[98] A writer for the OMP newsletter described their role in spreading word of this group's work: "Mimi-Pinson is a messenger, the prettiest, but also the most useful of messengers. In familiarizing working-class communities with the Mutualité Maternelle...Mimi-Pinson will have accomplished a good deed."[99] Throughout these years, students of the Conservatoire Populaire seem to have been in high demand to perform at *soirées* and *matinées* devoted to raising funds for philanthropic efforts aimed at workers.[100] In such venues, they became an appealing cipher for the working class as a whole, with their cheery songs and non-threatening desirability palatable packaging for social uplift.

Describing the first general meeting of the OMP at Paris's Bourse du Travail in August 1902, Maurice Le Blond wrote, "This immense locale, where at times so many massive, cruel strikes have been declared, has never hosted such a gathering, one dominated by clear laughter and pretty little faces."[101] Working-class demands for a living wage became, in Charpentier's inaugural speech at this meeting, the far less politically volatile "Right to Beauty for all."[102] Indeed, the Bourse du Travail had been the scene of a powerful thirty-five-day strike by Parisian garment workers just the year before, a strike which included hundreds of women.[103] A cartoon in *Charivari* from 1902 titled "À la Bourse du Travail" welcomed this new use of the building by depicting a Mimi Pinson in a trim skirt, blouse, and feathered hat making a speech to a group of equally smart women in feathered hats (Figure 3.1).[104] The caption reads: "Sister colleagues, let us demand from our bosses a six-hour day so that we can attend Monsieur Charpentier's dance and

---

[97] "Les 'Midinette,'" *Gil Blas*, 15 Dec. 1902.

[98] The initiative was open to all French female workers at least 16 years old living in the *département* of the Seine, and cost three francs per year. Marcel, "Causerie," 2, in *Mimi Pinson: Journal des ouvrières parisiennes* 3 (10 Apr. 1905).

[99] Ibid.

[100] Léon Dieuze, "Causerie," in *Mimi Pinson: Journal des ouvrières parisiennes* 1 (10 Feb. 1905).

[101] Le Blond, *Histoire*, 8.   [102] Ibid.

[103] See Coffin, *The Politics of Women's Work*, 178–9.

[104] Helen Harden Chenut notes that feathered hats were associated with bourgeois refinement. One trade unionist newspaper from 1916 called upon women to reject such hats as the "false elegance" of the bourgeois. *The Fabric of Gender: Working-Class Culture in Third Republic France* (University Park, 2005), 230–1, 247.

r, et merveilleusement approprie a ces circonstances c
es !

A LA BOURSE DU TRAVAIL

— Mes chères collègues, réclamons à nos patronnes la journée
de six heures, pour pouvoir suivre les cours de danse et de
musique de M. Charpentier.

(Le Charivari, 1902)

Figure 3.1. "A la Bourse du Travail," *Le Charivari*, 1902, reprinted in Le Blond, *Histoire de Mimi Pinson*, p. 18.

Source: Bibliothèque Historique de la Ville de Paris, Fonds Charpentier, Dossier 444.

music classes."[105] Instead of angry men in workers' smocks or, worse yet, angry laboring women, the trade union hall now hosts stylish young women demanding only lessons in *arts d'agrément*.

A similar use of Mimi Pinson came in a 1902 cartoon from the *Journal Amusant* depicting an attractively dressed woman (in a dapper skirt, frilly blouse, short cape and hat), singing as she walks down the street carrying a hat box (Figure 3.2).

[105] *Le Charivari*, 1902, reprinted in Le Blond, *Histoire*, 18.

Figure 3.2. *Journal Amusant* (1902), reprinted in Le Blond, *Histoire de Mimi Pinson*, p. 9.
Source: Bibliothèque Historique de la Ville de Paris, Fonds Charpentier, Dossier 444.

The caption, playing on the double meaning of the French word *note* as both a musical sound and a bill, reads: "That which we now call seamstresses' notes, ever since Monsieur Charpentier established the Oeuvre de Mimi Pinson."[106] An elegant couple pictured walking behind the Mimi Pinson, like the bourgeois readers of the *Journal Amusant*, are given the mollifying image of a fashionable, contented, and entertaining working class. The Mimi Pinsons' charming musical training thus tidily supplants both their political demands and their power as commercial agents, a particularly seductive bourgeois fantasy in the context of the heightened labor agitation of the belle époque. The *Journal Amusant* printed a similar cartoon the same year, this time an image of two finely dressed ladies in a salon discussing a seamstress:

—It's that my dressmaker makes pretty notes … extremely high notes.
—She's expensive?
—Oh no, she sings with the oeuvre de Mimi Pinson.[107]

---

[106] *Journal Amusant*, 1902, reprinted in Le Blond, *Histoire*, 9.   [107] Ibid. 15.

Once again, the OMP is an occasion for bourgeois amusement—and the possibly tense economic relationship between fashionable lady and wage-earning seamstress is effaced or at least mitigated by the seamstress's charming artistic distraction. It should also be noted that both cartoons from the *Journal Amusant*, and that from *Charivari*, were reprinted in the OMP's official history without comment.

Some of the Conservatoire Populaire's classes were held in spaces provided by Parisian companies such as the piano merchant Pleyel. Like the scene at the Bourse du Travail, descriptions of the Mimi Pinsons' first meeting at the Maison Pleyel suggested an appealing counterimage to the rampaging radical worker:

> You had to have seen the crowd of young workingwomen, descending upon the Maison Pleyel, to have seen them running from one room to another, laughing as they hurtled down the austere stairways. Some stopped to bang on a piano with jumbled chords; others stood in amazement before the velvets and gold, circling the gilt harps as if they were saintly statues. Clear laughter mingling with rapturous cries from every corner like a fanfare of youth, it was a veritable assault—an assault that will be remembered for a long time at Pleyel's.[108]

This scene—workers chaotically roaming the gilded halls of a commercial space ordinarily closed to them—could easily evoke fears of revolutionary disorder and labor militancy. But here, the rioting hordes are replaced by young women who demonstrate respect for the ornate décor and who are supervised by older bourgeois men. By repeating several themes at least twice—youth, laughter, and reverential wonder at luxury objects—Le Blond blunted the potentially threatening political import of this working-class female invasion of the bourgeois public sphere.[109] The OMP as an institution mediated the possibly troubling liberation of the working Parisenne through Charpentier. As Maurice d'Arcus put it: "For an autocrat that reigns with absolute power, there is not one more popular than M. Gustave Charpentier. He achieved the difficult and delicate problem of getting elected by suffragettes. He is the emperor and king of the land of midinettism."[110] Here, like the midinette in general in this period, Charpentier's Mimi Pinsons are something of an antidote to the *femme nouvelle*—emancipated to a degree, but pleasingly obedient to male authority.

When dealing with philanthropic or social institutions aimed at working-women in this period, a lively one for women's political rights and workers' rights, many commentators employed an effective rhetorical trio—combining assurances of workingwomen's aesthetic charms and desire to please with the

---

[108] Ibid. 9.
[109] Maurice d'Arcus, "Le règne du Midinettisme," *c.*February 1914. FC, No. 449: *Mimi-Pinson: Remise de l'épée d'Academicien à Gustave Charpentier.*
[110] Ibid.

supervisory presence of kindly male authority and a nostalgic glance backwards to the nineteenth-century grisette. Commentators on the OMP wove together these three rhetorical flourishes to promote a more emancipated French woman while at the same time defusing anxieties around women's emancipation. A nostalgic look backward toward the 1840s was a key component of this effect. Indeed, verses from Musset's *Mimi Pinson* appeared regularly in OMP institutional literature, speeches, and reportage about the initiative. As we shall see, this repetition served a clear purpose when applied to the work of the OMP. In what follows, I present several close readings of polemic around the OMP, with particular attention to the way that nostalgia was employed to curb the initiative's more radical implications.

In June 1902, the pages of *Le Figaro* hosted a war of words between Charpentier and some of the OMP's critics. The Comte d'Haussonville, a prominent philanthropist and social investigator of Parisian workingwomen, publicly excoriated the OMP and Charpentier. He reasoned that workingwomen were incapable of resisting the seductions of the theater and that their modest savings would quickly be depleted once the temptation was introduced. He quoted a garment trade employer who claimed to have witnessed a female worker returning to work, after a free night at the theater, having lost her taste for labor: "She no longer has the heart for her tasks."[111] That same month, literary critic Gaston Deschamps expressed concern that bourgeois theater subjects were inappropriate for the (presumably) young, impressionable students of the OMP: "Is it good to offer these recreations to these young girls?... Poor little things, a fairy tale would have achieved the same thing."[112]

Charpentier and his collaborators responded with a vigorous defense of the OMP that at once resisted the image of working-class decadence conjured by critics, and championed the initiative's social usefulness. Nostalgia was crucial to this rhetorical tightrope act. Charpentier began his defense by noting that Deschamps had evidently not read Musset, as he mistakes Mimi Pinson for the Mimi of Henry Murger's *Scènes de la vie de bohème* (1851).[113] In part to scold Deschamps for this error, in part to counter his arguments about the immoral potential of the OMP, Charpentier interspersed his response to Deschamps with verses from Musset's mid-nineteenth-century story. These quotations seem, at first blush, strange non-sequiturs. But on closer analysis, he employs these older verses strategically.

After quoting the most famous line from Musset ("Mimi Pinson est une blonde, | Une blonde que l'on connaît | Elle n'a qu'une robe au monde | Landerirette! | Et qu'un bonnet"), Charpentier insists that the OMP is not a

[111] Comte d'Haussonville, "A propos de Mimi Pinson," *Le Figaro*, 11 June 1902.
[112] Gaston Deschamps, "Les ouvrières au théâtre," *Le Figaro*, 3 June 1902.
[113] Gustave Charpentier, "Mimi Pinson," *Le Figaro*, 9 June 1902.

"virtue class" for workingwomen, but rather simply provides "evenings of relaxation" to "adorable beings who work all day." Charpentier exposes Deschamps's hypocrisy in deploring an evening out for workingwomen, but also finding it "entirely natural that we make them work from eight in the morning to ten at night with just time to swallow a couple of radishes as break…" Garment worker morality is, if not pure, at least the equal of bourgeois and aristocratic women:

> Are there among these young women those with a dull or depraved soul? Perhaps. But assuredly no more than in the bourgeoisie or the aristocracy of title, politics, or money; I would dare say there are fewer.
>
> > *It is the shell of a fine pearl*
> > *The dress of Mimi Pinson.*

Here, the line from Musset underscores Charpentier's defense of workingwomen's morality—a rare pearl enclosed in a homemade dress. In his conclusion, Charpentier again pivots from a critique of bourgeois (feminine) morality to a verse by Musset. He suggests that Deschamps

> turn his gaze away from the society demi-vierges with whom he dines, these university flirts…and deign to observe for a moment our people. He will see modest souls, a bit frivolous, a bit flighty, a bit sensual, full of cheerful courage, patient devotion, frank honesty, and real virtue…He will then know the Parisian workingwoman, that admirable creature! But he should beware:
>
> > *To undertake these conquests,*
> > *It is not enough to just be a handsome guy;*
> > *One must be honest.*
> > *Because it is not far from her head*
> > *The bonnet of Mimi Pinson.*[114]

Charpentier derides the loose morals of *tout Paris* and the New Woman (those university flirts), and commends the comparatively "real" virtue of industrious workingwomen. Yet he also affirms workingwomen's "futile" and "sensual" nature, and imagines that she can be romantically conquered. The half-century-old Musset verse here efficiently counteracts the vison of promiscuous elite women and precocious bluestockings, and reminds readers that Mimi Pinson is, at heart, a source of relatively wholesome romance *and* uncomplaining labor.

My second case study is a report on the pantomime class at the Conservatoire Populaire in *Gil Blas* in 1910 by journalist and aviatrix Louise Faure-Favier.

---

[114] Charpentier, "Mimi Pinson," *Le Figaro*, 9 June 1906.

Faure-Favier begins by quoting from Musset's Mimi Pinson and contrasts her to the twentieth-century midinette: "She has certainly changed, Mimi Pinson…she is no longer the grisette of yesteryear."[115] The new Mimi Pinson improves on her predecessor while preserving her most salient characteristics: "She is still charming, but more intelligent, more mature. She is still sentimental and cheerful." Indeed, the new Mimi Pinson is also more "respectable and well-behaved" than her predecessor. In part, this is due to the benevolence of Charpentier, whose OMP is a "school of good sense and virtue" for the workingwomen of Paris: "He has brought more elegance, more art, more poetry, into their lives. It is a beneficial charity because it is charming." The social value of the OMP as a philanthropic initiative *is* its charm.

Faure-Favier is pleasantly surprised by the elegance of the women in the mime class; they sit attentively on the school benches listening to remarks on classical and modern pantomime by their professor, the celebrated mime Georges Wague.[116] The students are each asked to mime a scene in which a woman enters a room, and removes her hat and veil in front of a mirror: "This one enters smiling slightly, walks gracefully, takes off the veil and pins with a pretty, very feminine motion and sits down coquettishly. This is the Woman who wants to please and who pleases."[117] These worker-students exemplify the unthreatening feminine grace and coquetry of Musset's nineteenth-century heroine, all smiling, blonde youth and desire to please. Faure-Favier further frames the students as a useful corrective to the troubling artifice of the middle-class woman *and* the vulgarity of the working-class woman:

> With what candor they compliment one another!…Nothing here of the socialite's grimaces and false smiles; nothing of that dark, hard look of the jealous friend that tells the society lady assuredly her outfit is harmonious and that she looks beautiful.
>
> Nothing either of the somewhat loud exuberance, let's say it, a bit *of the people*, that one might suppose. I was struck by the elegant bearing, by the good taste, by the simplicity, and by the sweetness of the voices of these graceful young girls.[118]

Mimi Pinson's genealogy with a fictional nineteenth-century romantic pin-up girl and her modest elegance are critical ingredients in the ultimately comforting vision of femininity she provided.

---

[115] Louise Faure-Favier, "Autour de la vie féminine," Gil Blas (2 Jan. 1910), 2.

[116] On Wague and his pantomime class at the OMP, see Rémy, Georges Wague, and Tilburg, Colette's Republic. Wague's class produced numerous music-hall professionals: Fabienne Lysis, Madje Lipton, Mlle Hertzka, and Régine Flory. See Rémy, Georges Wague, 105.

[117] Faure-Favier, "Autour de la vie féminine."   [118] Ibid.

Faure-Favier's description of the OMP class was part of a longer column on "la vie féminine" which concluded with a lengthy description of the recent work of the Conseil national des Femmes françaises and the question of women's suffrage.[119] Faure-Favier takes as a given that her readers generally accept the necessity of women's suffrage, but suggests that the well-connected society ladies of the Conseil are presenting their case in venues in which they risk nothing—the offices of Republican politicians (President Fallières, Prime Minister Aristide Briand, and Député de la Seine Ferdinand Buisson) who find the women's "apostolate" both "charming" and "inoffensive."

The two halves of the article on the surface seem to hang together uncomfortably— from an airy pantomime class to women's suffrage. But in fact, the rhetorical shift is seamless— from modern working girls who are, despite appearances, well-behaved and charming, to modern feminists who are, despite appearances, well-behaved and charming. In both sections, women's- emancipation-in-progress is managed by paternal figures of republican authority. Indeed, in both sections, Faure-Favier leans upon the way that both initiatives temper female emancipation with feminine charm. In addition, the entire piece is introduced by a callback to an attractive, unthreatening literary character from the 1840s.

A writer for *Nos Loisirs* employed a similar rhetorical gambit in a piece about the Conservatoire Populaire in April 1910. The young women, "those who labor every day, bring to their poses and their voice a spring of always lively sensations and the grace of their joy," all made possible through the "solicitude and devotion of M. Gustave Charpentier..." The conservatory includes, the author notes, summer and off-season "excursions in the provinces or around Paris." Here the author is pulled backward in time to a lengthy digression about Musset's Mimi Pinson, which begins as a reverie at the site of Charpentier's students:

> These gangs bring us back to the time of big omnibuses crowded with grisettes bouncing along to Ranelagh or Belleville. Having stitched, basted, hemmed, sewn, and darned all week long, they would go on Sunday to frolic around Paris in the arbours of the countryside. That is the good poet Musset's Mimi Pinson...who wore a little bonnet with flowers, a gingham dress, a silk apron, and grey ankle boots. When it rained, she would go watch a melodramatic play while eating oranges, because she cries very willingly, Mimi Pinson, which proves that she is good.
>
> *Mimi Pinson has only one dress in the world*
> *And one bonnet...*[120]

---

[119] The Conseil national des Femmes françaises was founded on 18 April 1901. Christine Bard, *Les Filles de Marianne: histoires des féminismes, 1914–1940* (Paris, 1995), 28.

[120] "Le Conservatoire de Mimi Pinson," *Nos Loisirs*, 3 April 1910. Bibliothèque de l'Opéra, Coupures sur Colette et George Wague, D 412 (3), 190.

This last line, by Musset, one of the most commonly quoted in writing on the OMP and the midinette in general, offers a compact summary of the grisette's aesthetically pleasing poverty. The grisettes of yesteryear appear to the author as he watches the OMP students. He imagines their labor, but passes quickly from that to Sunday outings in the countryside, appealing nineteenth-century fashions, and the workingwomen's sentimental enjoyment of Parisian melodramas. The passage above is followed by a long rumination on the plight of the fictional Mimi Pinson after pawning her dress for a hungry friend. The reader is cast backward with the author to reflect on this fictional character's generosity. Then, without transition, the author returns to Parisian workingwomen's present condition, decrying the lack of solidarity of bourgeois women with their working-class sisters. The author marvels that bourgeois ladies have nothing but disdain for the poor *ouvrière*'s fate, so envious are they of her prettiness and taste.

The ceremony at the Sorbonne in February 1914, at which Charpentier was presented his academician's sword by a company of Mimi Pinsons in front of a crowd which included government officials, students from the École des Beaux-Arts, and the French President's wife, serves as a final case study. Charpentier had been elected to the Académie des Beaux-Arts in 1912, and his election was seen by some as a sea change in academic artistic circles, a victory for a new generation of artists.[121] The 1914 ceremony brought together writers, artists, and politicians devoted to a notion of social reform through art: Georges Bourdon, Fernand Lefranc, Jean Ernest-Charles, Jean Boucher, Camille Mauclair, Albert Acrémant, and J. M. Gros.[122] The ceremony was hosted by Radical deputy Joseph Paul-Boncour, who in 1910 had celebrated the OMP in a report to the Beaux-Arts budget commission.[123]

The ceremony flawlessly staged the midinette's social value as nostalgic consolation, inborn aesthetic grace, and obedient, if picturesque, labor—all under the careful supervision of male cultural and political power. In his acceptance speech, Charpentier likened workingwomen's manual labor to other forms of patriotic art: "The sword, the quill, and the paintbrush have won unparalleled glory for the Fatherland. Can [Mimi Pinson's] needle not lay claim to such glory as well? A dress from Paris, worn by a Parisienne, is that not also art, marvelous art... [?]"[124] This comparison not only raised fashion to high art, but also effected a sly slippage between the production of the dress and the wearing of the dress by a Parisienne of indeterminate class. Both Mimi Pinson's labor and her aesthetic sensibility were required by the nation—a workingwoman's equivalent to both soldiering and fine art.

[121] Le Blond, *Histoire*, 22.
[122] Ibid. 23.   [123] Delmas, *Gustave Charpentier et le lyrisme français*, 141.
[124] Gustave Charpentier, quoted in Le Blond, *Histoire*, 25.

But even as the ceremony represented a moment in which workingwomen's labor was brought visibly into the circles of the artistic elite—both figuratively in Charpentier's speech and literally in the Sorbonne's amphitheater that evening— the emancipatory potential of such a presence was controlled and confined by those who attended and wrote about the event. The ceremony was described on the front page of *Le Figaro* by literary critic and theater director Georges Bourdon.[125] Only in Paris, Bourdon wrote, could one stage such an event and not be ridiculed (just the idea of garment workers at the Sorbonne is amusing.) But the workingwomen of the OMP are gently surveyed "under the paternal regard" of Louis Liard, the vice-chancellor of the Académie. In his account, Maurice Le Blond also remarked Liard, "watching with a kindly and paternal eye the jubilant crowd of Parisian workingwomen bedecking the seats of the immense hall."[126] Camille Mauclair rhapsodized about the performance of Eugénie Brunlet of the Opéra-Comique, a gifted soprano and, he noted, a former OMP student.[127] But he also made plain that it is Charpentier who has "organized everything, seen to everything" in this "theater of Athens where the people are actor and spectator." Charpentier was "the man of the crowd, gifted with an exceptional, magnetic talent, always gentle and courteous, but always obeyed." Charpentier's male authority is commanding, and it is his artistic vision and grandeur which organizes this event. As a result, Mauclair concludes, the ceremony became "a spectacle of intelligent democracy" that he watched with "great reassurance."[128] The incursion of workingwomen into the hallowed halls of the university is also bounded in the ceremony by the use of nostalgia. The one garment worker to speak that evening, Marie Magnier, presented the sword to Charpentier dressed as Musset's Mimi Pinson.[129] Bourdon offers a lengthy description of Magnier, though he does not name her, "Musset's Mimi Pinson, in a flowered muslin dress and lace bonnet, a rose in her bodice and a fichu draped around her neck, Mimi Pinson with blonde curls, with her smiling mouth and blue eyes, that is to say the true Mimi Pinson, and not a theater actress."[130]

---

[125] Georges Bourdon (1868–1938) was editor at *Le Figaro* and a theater director who worked at one time at the Odéon. He also served as president of the Syndicat national des Journalistes. Georges Bourdon, "La Vie de Paris: Mimi Pinson à la Sorbonne," 10 Feb. 1914, *Le Figaro*, p. 1.

[126] Le Blond, *Histoire*, 24.

[127] Camille Mauclair, "Une belle Volonté," *La Muse*, 29 June 1914. FC, No. 449. The archives note this article was published in June 1914, but it was likely published closer to the February event. Eugénie Brunlet (1895–1965) debuted in 1913 as Céleste in *Céleste*, and performed as the title character in *Louise* multiple times during her career.

[128] Ibid.

[129] Magnier appears in a filmed reconstitution of the event, *Gustave Charpentier reçoit son épee d'academicien* (Paris: Gaumont Pathé, 1914), 1:22 mins. www.gaumontpathearchives.com, Ref. No. 1409GJ 00008. It also includes scenes of Mimi Pinsons creating cocardes for soldiers, an initiative detailed in Chapter 6.

[130] Bourdon, "La Vie de Paris."

Le Bulletin de l'Oeuvre de Mimi Pinson

Though the Mimi Pinsons appeared frequently as decorative entertainment in OMP festivals, concerts, and charitable events from 1900 through the 1930s, if they spoke at all, it was most frequently, like Marie Magnier, to recite words written by male organizers. There were few echoes of the voices of the OMP's worker-students in reporting on the *oeuvre*. A perusal of the OMP's short-lived magazine, *Mimi Pinson*, however, illustrates the push and pull that characterized women's relationship with the initiative and its organizers. Administrators crafted a pleasing and mildly emancipating philanthropic product, and responded with scolding if working-class members pushed beyond the bounds of the emancipation as they defined it. Mary Ellen Poole rightly notes that the magazine "encouraged its subscribers to inform themselves about new labor legislation…and to stand up for their rights, to the point of striking if necessary."[131] But the newsletter's editors were demonstrably uncomfortable with working-class readers directing their own liberation. Indeed, we can read the *Mimi Pinson* magazine as a contested terrain upon which a struggle was waged between OMP administrators' vision of their organization and that of its members.[132]

The magazine contained poetry, puzzles, horoscopes, edifying articles, as well as chatty reports about members' concerts and trips. The majority of the content was produced by male OMP administrators and other male writers, artists, poets, and politicians. Members could admire ruminations on democratic art by painter and politician Henri Dujardin-Beaumetz, an essay on popular theater and national education by Jules Michelet, poems by Saint-Georges de Bouhélier, and sketches of "Mimi Pinson" by Théophile Steinlen. Yet the magazine also provided information about job announcements, new conservatory courses, and a forum for subscribers to communicate with each other and with OMP organizers.

Through this forum, we can detect a group of workingwomen who are less compliant than popular representations suggested—a defiance editors took pains to curb. In response to protests from members that the magazine was not arriving regularly in the summer of 1902, the editors counseled calm: "But we never said that the Bulletin would come out on fixed dates. We will try to publish it monthly. That is all we can promise." When several members demanded that the newspaper appear every Sunday, the editors cautioned that Mimi Pinson "is not rich enough" to buy the paper every week. The same issue admonished certain workingwomen for their behavior at free theatrical performances: "we still regret

---

[131] Poole, "Gustave Charpentier," 236.
[132] The Fonds Charpentier contain an issue from August 1902 of *Mimi Pinson: Bulletin de l'Oeuvre de Mimi Pinson (mensuel)* and several issues of a revamped *Mimi Pinson: Journal des ouvrières parisiennes* from 1905. FC, No. 444.

the comportment of several workingwomen in the theaters where they were *guests...*"[133] The Théâtre des Nouveautés had discontinued its complimentary tickets for Mimi Pinsons because of the "excessive noise made by some inconsiderate 'Mimi Pinsons'.... We hope that M. Micheau, the very kind and very popular Director, will consider the privation of this season as sufficient punishment" for all of the "penitent." As a lesson, the editors reprinted a remorseful letter to Micheau ostensibly from one of the "delinquents" in question: "I was so very joyful to go to this beautiful theater! How many times had I passed by it, read the posters, and watched the beautiful ladies who were arriving! How many times did I tell myself: that's not for the likes of me!"[134]

A section of each issue called "Correspondence" allowed the editors to respond to individual readers. Women sent questions and requests, signed with their membership number, and the editors responded by printing the number and the response (never the original question from the workingwoman). The editors offered Member #16168 detailed instructions about how to become an OMP delegate (a preferred member who received benefits after having brought twenty new recruits to the Oeuvre). Member #283 was encouraged to tell her voice instructor that she was interested in learning a solo: "stop being a shrinking violet..."[135] Often, the responses took a tone of mild paternal condescension. Member #13513 was told that she had not yet received one of the Art Nouveau engravings by Paul Berthon to which she was entitled because she likely had missed a meeting.[136] In one of the rare instances in which a workingwoman is quoted extensively in the pages of *Mimi Pinson*, Gustave Charpentier himself asked the editors to reprint a letter of thanks from an OMP member to demonstrate the gratitude of members for his initiative:

> I am alone on this earth, and while I am young, life had seemed really sad to me; the future seemed terribly gloomy...now, I have a family, I have a bunch of very nice little sisters; my heart once so sad is filled with cheer; with what pleasure, I hurry to my singing class or mandolin class after my workday is done...But I don't forget that I owe all of my happiness to a big heart, to our good and noble director, Gustave Charpentier.
>
> This is the most beautiful oeuvre you could have chosen. How many young girls, with no idea how to entertain themselves, allow themselves to be led toward nasty entertainments. Your oeuvre has as its goal not simply to ease the workingwoman's life, but to bring her back to an honest life.[137]

[133] Marcel, "Causerie," in *Mimi Pinson: Bulletin de l'Oeuvre de Mimi Pinson*, Aug. 1902. FC, No. 444.
[134] Ibid.
[135] "Correspondance," *Mimi Pinson: Journal des ouvrières parisiennes* 1 (10 Feb. 1905). FC, No. 444.
[136] Ibid.
[137] Letter from Member No. 14532, 31 Dec. 1904, reprinted in *Mimi Pinson: Journal des ouvrières parisiennes* 1 (10 Feb. 1905). FC, No. 444.

This Mimi Pinson's letter, unsurprisingly as it was published by the editors at Charpentier's insistence, perfectly summarizes the initiative's conception of its mission and of its targets.

The magazine did take seriously the necessary enlightenment and (controlled) emancipation of garment workers. Some pieces critiqued working conditions and employer malfeasance in the garment industry. An April 1905 article applauded certain Parisian department stores for offering pensions to their female employees, and ended the list with a call to those fashion houses not yet providing such a benefit: "Let's go, MM. Paquin, Worth, Doucet, Raudnitz, Rouff, Doeillet, Beer, etc., join the movement!"[138] The OMP bulletin confirmed a sense of female garment trade workers as uninterested in syndical activity and in their proper rights as workers. OMP administrator Léon Dieuze expanded on this idea in a March 1905 article titled "The Workshop."[139] Dieuze begins by insisting that, despite her gay appearances, Mimi Pinson suffers. Because of the "tradition and legend that falsely gives her graceful figure a frivolity with a smile on her lips that belies the ardor in her eyes and the valour in her heart," it would be easy to imagine that her "painful days" please her, as we see her going about her life "cheerful... satisfied with a bird's diet, and the most meager salary for thankless and difficult work." In fact, in her workshop, "Mimi Pinson endures crueler tortures than Dante could have imagined for his hell." He goes on to describe the health hazards of the average work day in couture and places the blame for these conditions, in part, on "the bosses and inhuman subcontractors who abuse the power of their money" (though Dieuze admitted that employers needed to remain competitive). He also places some blame for her condition squarely on the workingwoman: "One has to confess, aren't the ones most guilty of all of this misery those who accept it with insouciance and resignation? If one must accuse someone and make them responsible for the miserable condition of the workingwoman, she should lay into herself, reproach herself for not knowing her most elementary rights." The OMP is envisaged as a mechanism for enlightening these ignorant workingwomen at long last, and as a space for educating Mimi Pinson on labor boards and legislation regarding workplace sanitation and injuries.[140] This might seem a somewhat curious vision of social reform—exonerating employers for workplace conditions likened to Dante's inferno, but reproaching the sufferers of these tortures. Yet such an approach is made more legible if one considers the pervasive cultural stereotype of Parisian workingwomen in the garment trades as carefree flirts. Dieuze concluded that while it was "of course necessary that Mimi Pinson instructs herself on the laws that can ameliorate her lot... She might strike, that's her right, but she will never ignite any riot than that of love in our hearts."[141]

---

[138] "Les Retraites pour les ouvrières," *Mimi Pinson* 3 (10 Apr. 1905), 8. FC, No. 444.
[139] Léon Dieuze, "L'atelier," in *Mimi Pinson* 2 (10 Mar. 1905), 6. FC No. 444.
[140] Ibid.   [141] Ibid.

When members attempted to use the magazine and the OMP for matters deemed extraneous or controversial by editors, they were told so in no uncertain terms:

10.124.—Your letter dealt with questions which are too personal.

9.109.—Pointless to go on. It's not interesting.[142]

We can glean from these tantalizing fragments that garment workers solicited diverse kinds of assistance and counsel from the OMP, not all of which were deemed appropriate by administrators. While editors responded enthusiastically to inquiries from readers asking to write for the paper, they also made clear that their interest in these workers related only to how they might illuminate the problems of French labor: "Of course, Mesdemoiselles! Make haste in communicating your thoughts and reflections to us! But only tell us about your workshop or office; nothing except that which concerns your labor." The editors were bewildered in March 1905 when Member #2414 asked to submit her poetry: "Verses? Why?...Instead, tell us workshop stories."[143]

Editors were quick to remind readers that the ultimate goal of the Mimi Pinsons' artistic exposure was the brightening of the working-class home. A March 1905 editorial insisted that "Mimi Pinson is only the messenger of these benefits, intended for her family, her people..." Her musical training will fill her "humble lodging" with "the soothing songs of forgetting." The fine art prints she carries home from OMP meetings will be "a sunbeam of art that will brighten the gloomy abode..." The editor admits, "We give Mimi Pinson all the joy of art we can muster, it's true! But where does this gift go, if not to working families, to the home of the people beloved by the artist, her older brothers."[144] This defense of the true goal of the OMP—the workingwoman as conduit of working-class uplift—is here being made directly to workingwomen readers of the magazine.

In the same issue, the editors asked readers to nominate the Parisian garment workshops with the best ventilation, comfort, and facilities. More than three thousand members responded and the results were published in April 1905.[145] A number of Mimi Pinsons criticized the magazine for not having "posed the inverse question," allowing workingwomen to opine on the least comfortable workshops in Paris. One workingwoman, for example, included a devastating indictment of her workplace: "Our workshop is so insalubrious that every month one or two of us end up in the hospital, and don't come back. They use gas to

[142] "Correspondance," *Mimi Pinson* 2 (10 Mar. 1905).   [143] Ibid.

[144] "Une rémarque," *Mimi Pinson* 2 (10 Mar. 1905), 6.

[145] Podo, "Notre Enquête," *Mimi Pinson* 3 (10 Apr. 1905), 13. FC, No. 444. The Maison Beer received the most votes (87), because its workshops were bright, comfortable, well-ventilated, and clean. Workers "very much appreciated the kitchens and lunchrooms."

illuminate the shop all day, and our première prefers not to have the windows opened. By the end of the day we could cut the air with a knife." The editors, however, were incredulous that their readers would be so reckless as to share "unpleasant confidences." They insisted that such revelations would be "danger-ous for us, and for you, dear little irrational ones who haven't thought about the aftermath of the resentment of the humiliated bosses."[146] They chide the Mimi Pinsons for their lack of forethought and recommend silencing of patronal criti-cism. Even as administrators encouraged a vision of a revitalized working class by way of more humane labor practices, they also reflected back to garment trade workers a puissant vision of their own picturesque diligence and obedience. The tantalizing moments in the bulletin when these women push back against editorial condescension or simply attempt to use the organization for their own needs indicate that this vision was not accepted wholesale by its targeted audience.

Conclusion

Charpentier's archive contains numerous letters from OMP students and former students to "le Maître," expressing gratitude for the organization, and fondly rec-ollecting the joys of their days as members. After the ceremony at the Sorbonne in 1914, former Mimi Pinsons wrote Charpentier expressing regret that they could not attend, pride in his accomplishment, and fond memories of their own time at the OMP.[147] Many evinced a strong personal affection for Charpentier and his partner "Madame Camille," updating him on their professional accomplishments and sending photographs of their children even decades later. Several former students (Eugénie Brunlet, Aimée Lecouvreur, Jeanne Ségala) became successful performers at the Opéra-Comique, while others made a living in lesser concert halls. Some continued in garment work, while still others became nurses, music teachers, chicken farmers, or housewives.[148]

The demands and complaints of many other letters suggest that many worker-students took Charpentier and the administrators at their word—that this was an oeuvre *for* workingwomen. In February 1902, eight garment workers including Stéphanie Bouvard and Clémence Jusselin (on behalf of their flowermaker and needleworker unions, respectively), made a public announcement in *Le Figaro* that they had delivered a bouquet of violets to Charpentier's house on the anni-versary of the premiere of *Louise.* They encouraged other garment workers to follow suit by leaving a "simple 2-sous bouquet" on his doorstep with their OMP membership number attached, "to tell [M. Gustave Charpentier] how grateful we

---

[146] Ibid. 13.   [147] FC, No. 444.
[148] See Charpentier's notes on "Mimi Pinson: ce que sont devenues mes meilleures MIMI-PINSONS." FC, No. 444.

are to him for founding the Oeuvre de Mimi Pinson."[149] Thirty-year-old Nelly Roques wrote Charpentier in 1914 and recalled being one of the first students of the OMP as a teenager: "I lived for Mimi Pinson; it absorbed me, one day in Montmartre, another at the Bourse du Travail, where I signed up…all the new members." She recalled singing at concerts at the Bourse du Travail and at the Trocadéro, and OMP-sponsored trips out of Paris, "we [were] happier and happier still…"[150]

The OMP, however, also educed a revealing social discomfort, and bore witness to the evolution of the traditional image of the Parisian workingwoman from the belle époque through the interwar years. The Mimi Pinsons were lauded for maintaining traditional notions of French femininity even as they stepped outside of feminine norms. The repeated emphasis on "special" native taste, rather than on any physical signs of their labor, indicates the aggressively optimistic view of the working class which observers grafted upon these women. The OMP, by creating a philanthropic initiative that affirmed and reveled in contemporary notions of midinette sexual availability, gaiety, and taste, dovetailed with a pervasive cultural understanding of Parisian garment workers in this period. In the chapters which follow, we will see in what diverse political, social, and philanthropic contexts this pliable, delectable body was also deployed.

---

[149] *Le Figaro* (4 Feb. 1902), 5.
[150] Letter from Nelly Roques to Gustave Charpentier after his ceremony at the Sorbonne, 1914. FC, No. 444.

4

"An Appetite to Be Pretty"

Garment Workers, Lunch Reform, and the Parisian Picturesque in the Belle Époque

In a lavishly illustrated 1899 study of the Parisian lunch hour, Georges Montorgueil, a journalist and practiced connoisseur of "Parisian mores," noted wistfully:

> [The Parisienne] only has an appetite to be pretty. To be appealing is the yoke under which all other needs of her nature are bent. Her vanity dominates her stomach; her interest in her appearance kills her hunger [*sa coquetterie tue sa faim*], or at least staves it off and allays it...her gourmandise recedes before the desire to be noticed.[1]

A reader familiar with turn-of-the-century French femininity might well presume that Montorgueil here alluded to the efforts by chic bourgeois ladies to maintain a fashionably slender form. In fact, this quotation appeared in a volume entirely devoted to the workingwoman's lunch hour, and the sacrifice of food described above is made in the service of consumer purchases, not dieting; the laboring Parisienne "has cut back on roast beef for ribbons."[2] Montorgueil's lyrical reimagining of sweated garment workers' privation as girlish vanity, far from idiosyncratic, was a common assessment of Parisian workingwomen in the first decades of the twentieth century.

This chapter considers a defining moment of the working Parisienne's day to which early twentieth-century French observers returned again and again: *midi*. The noon lunch break afforded Parisian artists, writers, and tourists alike a daily glimpse of the "fairies" of the city's luxury garment workshops as they took to the boulevards and parks for an hour in the sun—an hour imagined to consist of flirtation, window-shopping, laughter, and, I will establish, conspicuous under-eating. Indeed, crucial to the picturesque allure of the lunchtime seductions that filled popular midinette literature was the notion of the female garment worker as

---

[1] Georges Montorgueil, *Midi: le déjeuner des petites ouvrières (les minutes Parisiennes)* (Paris, 1899), 39. Montorgueil (1857–1933) was the pseudonym of journalist, *homme des lettres*, and native Parisian Octave Lebesgue.
[2] Ibid.

Working Girls: Sex, Taste, and Reform in the Parisian Garment Trades, 1880–1919. Patricia Tilburg, Oxford University Press (2019). © Patricia Tilburg.
DOI: 10.1093/oso/9780198841173.001.0001

a frivolous under-eater cheerfully forfeiting food for fashion and pleasure. No longer the tragically starving workingwoman of nineteenth-century fiction and art, nor her virtuous, anorectic middle-class sister, whose physical wasting increased their moral fortitude,[3] the under-eating midinette of the early twentieth century was envisioned doing so as a means of engaging more fully in the capitalist marketplace, making her body a more appealing advertisement for and object of urban consumption. This cultural fantasy of the midinette's lunch hour, which fetishized the supposed moral precariousness of her lifestyle as well as the sparseness of her diet, was echoed by social reformers, who, in this same period, sought to carve out spaces for workingwomen's lunches that kept them from the cafés and parks where they were believed to flirt much and eat little. By focusing in on the social imaginary of and debates around workingwomen's lunches, this analysis joins studies by scholars like Anne Lhuissier and Martin Bruegel that seek to move the history of French workers' food reform out from the historiographical margins.[4]

The Lunching Midinette in Popular Culture

Lunch breaks during which workingwomen in Paris's luxury garment trades spread out across the city were the setting of numerous films, novels, songs, and plays from the early twentieth century. The charms of the midinette lunch hour existed within a certain urban geography—the rue de la Paix, the boulevard de l'Opéra, the streets around the Madeleine, and the Tuileries gardens. As Anaïs Albert argues, the fact that the offices of the Parisian mass press abutted those of the couture industry meant that lunching garment workers shared a daily space with many of the city's journalists and writers, who devoted substantial space in their writing to the workingwomen of haute couture. The narrative possibilities opened up by this setting were evident: removing the midinettes from their less picturesque workshops and placing them in an unregulated public space in which they could see and, more crucially, be seen.

In these texts, the midinettes are commonly depicted in joyous groupings—laughter, song, and bird-like flocking draw the narrators' attention to these young women as they leave their workshops and take to the boulevards on their lunch hour. The opening vignette of critic Arsène Alexandre's lyrical non-fiction *Les Reines de l'aiguille* (*The Queens of the Needle*) (1902) (a self-described

---

[3] See Patricia McEachern, *Deprivation and Power: The Emergence of Anorexia Nervosa in Nineteenth-Century French Literature* (Westport, 1998); Bram Dijkstra, *Idols of Perversity: Fantasies of Feminine Evil in Fin-de-Siècle Culture* (New York, 1986); Helena Michie, *Flesh Made Word: Female Figures and Women's Bodies* (New York, 1990).

[4] Anne Lhuissier, *Alimentation populaire et réforme social: les consommations ouvrières dans le second XIXe siècle* (Paris, 2007), 31–3, 70; Martin Bruegel, "Le Genre du déjeuner: alimentation et travail dans le Paris de la Belle Époque," *Food & History*, 14, nos. 2–3 (2016), 21–50.

"Parisian" study illustrated with etchings of attractive workingwomen) emphasizes the jubilant cacophony of the midinettes' invasion of central Paris with a scene oft-repeated in pop cultural products in this period:

> From noon to one o'clock, in the neighborhoods of the Opéra and the Madeleine, an unbelievable activity resumes, a frenetic swarm...The seamstresses, exiting the workshops in waves at the strike of noon, scatter noisily in search of food. They overflow with gaiety, the result of a first relaxation of their overexcited nerves, though not yet to the extreme. The street is, this time, a little like their home; they feel at ease there and so fine, that, for the most part, they come out-side without jackets and hats...[5]

A joyful swarming, a headlong rush, an excess of gaiety—these workingwomen transform the boulevard into their home. They are at ease and appealingly under-dressed—a Parisian attraction that leavens capitalist productivity with girlish animation.

George Montorgueil, a writer who made a career out of describing the Parisian picturesque, included a similar scene in his collection of vignettes *La Vie des boulevards, Madeleine-Bastille* (*The Life of the Boulevards, Madeleine-Bastille*) (1896). After quoting an obligatory line from Musset's *Mimi Pinson*, Montorgueil describes the workingwomen of the Rue de la Paix at lunchtime:

> between noon and one o'clock, a humming like a swarming beehive. The industrious bees with their slender corselets spread out around the neighborhood and forage for the nectar of their noon meal. These are the collaborators with whom Caprice associates to produce marvelous jewel boxes; the diligent work-ingwomen, daughters of Parisian taste, volunteers in the battalion of Fashion. In small groups, they strut through the crowd with their playful youth and the impertinent laugh of their white teeth, untroubled by the glances they receive.[6]

Montorgueil here joins together several components of the midinette ideal: diligence, taste, laughter, and youthful allure. The young women are also slender-waisted creatures who delicately collect bits of "nectar" rather than consuming a substantial meal. Alexandre insisted that these women favored eating in boisterous groups, "a need to stay in groups, like the sparrows of Paris...Such is the necessity of collective labor and the effect of habit, as much with seamstresses as

---

[5] Arsène Alexandre, *Les Reines de l'aiguille: modistes et couturières (Études parisiennes)* (Paris, 1902), 17. Tiersten uses Alexandre as an example of critics who drew attention to garment workers to critique the bourgeois Parisienne's consumer rapaciousness. See *Marianne in the Market*.

[6] Georges Montorgueil, *La Vie des boulevards, Madeleine-Bastille*, 21–2.

with bees."[7] A 1903 vignette about a lusty midinette told from the perspective of one of her bourgeois lovers begins with a similar image: "What flâneur at noon between the Opéra and the place Vendôme has not felt proud to be French, or Parisian at least, not looking at the Column, but at the letting out of the couture workshops, like that of a humming hive, at these exquisite bees, slim, flighty, swishing, piquant…We catch them on the fly between the couturier and the thirty-sous restaurant, and they let themselves be led, happy to nip on something other than the daily pittance."[8] These few examples stand in here for countless comparisons in belle époque pop culture of midinettes to sparrows, bees, and fairies, analogies which present workingwomen as interchangeable, diminutive, and possessed of undersized appetites.

Most writers who took the lunching midinette as their subject emphasized the women's airy joyfulness. André Vernières' didactic novel *Camille Frison: ouvrière de la couture* (*Camille Frison: Workingwoman in Couture*) (1908), while intended as a brutally realistic exposé of the "sweating system," and devoting many pages to the moral temptations of the midinette's noon pause, also viewed the lunch hour through the insistently rosy lens of a connoisseur. The male narrator explores the rue de la Paix at noon with a friend:

> All is gaiety around us. Before going back up to the workshop, the female laborer likes to get some air…Their complexions are glowing, their gestures exuberant, and their gait unrestrained. At one window, we see some disheveled models who blow kisses to their comrades who pass by below. From one end of the street to the other, it's like a great burst of laughter under the balmy April sun, a celebration where hearts warm and wills soften.[9]

Here, the trope of the gay working Parisienne attains hyperbolic heights. Written at a time when labor disputes gripped public attention, it is politically telling that observers insisted upon recording workingwomen's work day as "a great burst of laughter" and a "celebration." Sweatshops are transformed into bordellos—with half-dressed lovelies leaning out the window blowing kisses, others in the street softening wills and warming hearts with their flushed faces and uninhibited gaits. Alexandre's *Reines de l'aiguille* devotes pages to the lunch hour in the Tuileries, noting the picnicking workers' "delirious laughter" as they jump rope, read, and chat: "The spectacle, then, of these low-cost feasts is exquisite. The garden is delightfully warm."[10]

---

[7] Alexandre, *Les Reines de l'aiguille*, 22.
[8] Gay-Gael, "Notre Soeur," *Le Frou-Frou*, 26 Dec. 1903.
[9] André Vernières, *Camille Frison, ouvrière de la couture* (Paris, 1908), 49.
[10] Alexandre, *Les Reines de l'aiguille*, 20–1.

Urban chroniclers and fiction writers accentuated the childlike playfulness of the garment trade workers on their lunch break. Alexandre claimed to have witnessed lunching midinettes regularly playing schoolyard games:

The last crumbs shaken from their skirts, they begin spontaneous foot races and games of tag. Some, and not the youngest among them, suddenly pull jump ropes out of their pockets, to the applause of the others. And the soldiers are drafted to turn the handles for them and whistle at them, around the flying dresses and rhythmic jumps.[11]

Playing tag and jumping rope while their skirts fly merrily about them, these women seem anything but degraded cogs in the industrial machine. What is more, they are joined in their game by soldiers—an attractive vision of female labor and the forces of order sharing public space just a year after female garment trade workers had taken to the streets of Paris in a thirty-five-day strike during which government troops were used against strikers.[12]

The primary narrative interest of these scenes and reportage was to posit the lunch hour as a liminal moment in the midinette's day in which she was vulnerable to sexual dissipation by way of working-class and (more often) middle-class men. Lighter midinette fiction and entertainment often featured male admirers who exploit the lunch pause to flirt with attractive young garment workers. Maurice Ordonneau and Arthur Verneil set the opening act of their vaudeville operetta *Mimi Pinson* (1882) during a lunch hour when university students and aristocrats gather around groups of lunching Parisian workingwomen.[13] In Montorgueil's 1897 study *La Parisienne*, he specified the varieties of lunchtime midinette seduction: "It's Don Juan's hour. We can lock down the milliner with a bouquet of violets, but we conquer the laundress only with a *gloria* [a sugared coffee with brandy]."[14] Alexandre described the amorous "intruders" who could usually be found circling the lunching midinettes in the Tuileries: "From time to time, administrative *sous-officiers* escaped from the offices of the Ministry of War come to prowl around the groups [of midinettes]."[15]

The male narrator of Vernières' novel *Camille Frison* (1908) is introduced to the pleasures of the midinettes' noontime display by a colleague—the husband of a seamstress he had met at a restaurant: "You will see all of the couture industry parade before you, and it is a true spectacle, you know!" Part sex tourism, part ethnographic observation, the two men lunch in the environs of couture

---

[11] Ibid. 21.   [12] Coffin, *The Politics of Women's Work*, 178–83.

[13] Maurice Ordonneau and Arthur Verneuil, *Mimi Pinson: vaudeville-opérette en trois actes*. Music by Michiels (Paris, 1882).

[14] Georges Montorgueil, *La Parisienne peinte par elle-même* (Paris, 1897), 87. On *gloria*, see William Walton, *Paris from the Earliest Period to the Present Day*, Vol. 4 (Philadelphia, 1899), 187–8.

[15] Alexandre, *Les Reines de l'aiguille*, 21.

workshops and then stroll the rue de la Paix. Seated at the restaurant before noon to await the midinettes, the colleague serving as "guide" explains that "the workingwomen of couture...have a certain number of common traits, and when you have observed one, you will know them all."[16] Thus, in this dehumanizing pseudo-scientific aside, the midinettes are again presented as interchangeable and alluringly knowable. The two men are charmed as the lunching midinettes discuss fashion and love letters. They notice that, "At one nearby table, some men have saved a place for a young female guest, who soon arrives, and sits across from their faces beaming with satisfaction...A *rendez-vous* which will be followed by an absence from the workshop..."[17] Another workingwoman is drawn into a tête-à-tête with male diners when they notice her eyeing their dish of mussels and offer her a taste:

> And the workingwoman, without being asked twice, puts her fingers into the dish. They find this an excuse for some banter, an occasion to engage in conversation. Now they are speaking quickly. They laugh readily. They are at their best. Then, invitations—to go to the country on Sunday, or the theater, depending on the weather—are proffered, on the off chance, and timidly refused, which only leads to them being accepted. Then, when the time comes to pay the bill, the young men cry:
>
> —Leave that alone, mesdemoiselles![18]

The narrator's guide indicates that this is simply "how things happen at the restaurant" for Parisian garment workers and their admirers.[19] A visceral desire for food, over the course of the meal, weakens this young woman's moral resolve (unlike her immediate acceptance of the food, she needs to be asked multiple times to agree to an outing).

As Rebecca Spang demonstrates, the image of the restaurant as an "urban reference point" and a site of "erotic gastronomy" in popular literature dated back to the early nineteenth century and the invention of the modern restaurant itself. The belle époque seems to have attached the midinette to this literary genealogy with gusto.[20] One finds countless scenes of this ilk throughout midinette literature, in which the lunch hour—the park, the restaurant-bar, or, most dangerous, the unsavory *gargote* (cheap restaurant or dive)—is a site of predatory courtship. Louis Artus's 1911 play *Les Midinettes* (whose entire second act was set in a Paris park during lunch, and starred music-hall icon Mistinguett) constructs an amusing subplot in the person of Monsieur Lherminier, an elegant older gentleman who moves between the high society salons of his peers, and the Jardin des Tuileries,

---

[16] Vernières, *Camille Frison*, 29.   [17] Ibid. 33.   [18] Ibid. 34.   [19] Ibid.
[20] Rebecca L. Spang, *The Invention of the Restaurant: Paris and Modern Gastronomic Culture* (Cambridge, MA, 2000), 215.

where he courts lunching midinettes: "They thrill me. You cannot imagine the pleasure the 'little twentysomethings' that come there cause me, the pleasure for my eyes, my heart…and the rest. I think of them constantly…I dream of them. I write of them."[21] He illustrates this lyrical inspiration one afternoon by serenading the picnicking midinettes. In this lascivious (but ostensibly charming) number, Lherminier defends a chic older gentleman who follows the midinettes "from the workshop to the restaurant…with a perseverant step":

> Walking behind your boots
> That have been recently resoled,
> He is only a little indecent
> Seeing your childish figure
> And shivers only a little in thinking about them.

Here, the lunch hour is a time for female workers to present themselves for amorous encounters ("When you show him your nimble legs, | Raising your thin petticoat | With a slightly cheeky gesture"). The midinettes' pursuer covets their youth and energy, and includes their poverty in the erotic catalogue of their attributes (with their recently resoled boots). The last stanzas of the song make plain that their pursuers' intentions are not platonic: "At night, after caresses, | He will speak gently" (before leaving "furtively" at dawn). The midinette, in her now empty bed, is told, "You will be gay!"[22]

The stage directions describe the lunching midinettes as "very interested" in Lherminier's song, and so beguiled that they join him in singing the refrain, becoming, Lherminier says, his very own "Conservatoire de Mimi Pinson." The good-natured tone offers a sense of just how familiar such a scene would have been; Lherminier, the fictive milliners, and presumably the audience seem to take for granted that young garment workers are cheerful and ready sexual prey, as interested in liaisons with wealthy older men as in matrimony with their humble peers. As confirmation of this assumption, Lherminier's object of desire, Julie the milliner (played by Mistinguett, herself the daughter of a garment worker), spends the play equivocating between two men she meets on her lunch hour—an honest laborer named Grabure, who hopes to marry her, and Pierre, a bourgeois writer and the husband of one of her clients. The denouement of the play finds Julie and Pierre kissing in the park, having decided to begin an "amourette"—a casual love affair—even as Pierre assures her that he will never leave his wife.[23]

Sometimes, for the fictional midinette, what begins as a lunchtime flirt ends in conjugal respectability. In *Oscar et Kiki la Midinette*, a silent film from 1913, Oscar,

---

[21] Louis Artus, *Les Midinettes: comédie en quatre actes* (Paris, 1912), 84. First performed at the Théâtre des Variétés, 31 Jan. 1911.
[22] Artus, *Les Midinettes*, 85–6.   [23] Ibid. 121.

a chic gentleman who makes a habit of watching midinettes at lunchtime in the Tuileries, is well known to the garment workers as "gallant." He buys raspberry ice cream for the hatmaker Kiki and her co-workers one afternoon, and takes that opportunity to slip Kiki a love letter. When he later arrives at the workshop to pick her up, he finds that their flirtation has led to her firing. He chivalrously takes her arm and leads her out of the workshop, saying, "Come with me, my Kiki. Henceforth you will be Mme Oscar."[24]

Yet even when marriage is the conclusion of the lunching midinette's seduction, it often is preceded by a fall from virtue and/or many trials. *Couturière sans aiguilles* (*Seamstress without Needles*) (a vaudeville operetta from 1905) closes with the engagement of its protagonists, the teenage seamstress Juliette and her suitor Agénor (a café-concert musician). The couple reminisce about their first, lustful lunchtime encounter: "And this is how | In a restaurant | Between the *saucisson* and the cream dessert | We become lovers | It's the start | Of tender moments where we say to each other: 'I love you!'"[25] Agénor recalls that he first loved Juliette because "you are not like the other women; you didn't give yourself right away. I had to court you for at least two days."[26] Though the affair leads to a marriage proposal, much of the operetta celebrates the sexual promiscuity of the atelier—where young garment workers candidly discuss their lovers. The dress-makers hail the lunch hour as a time for "Lovers that makes us blush."[27] The chaste seamstress heroine Denise of de Lannoy's 1919 novel *Modiste et grande dame* (*Milliner and Lady*) tries valiantly to avoid a restaurant seduction by taking the metro home during the lunch hour to eat with her family.[28] Fate intervenes, however, when she is injured crossing the street during a gas explosion and is taken to a nearby café to be resuscitated. The restaurant is so perilous a place for the virtue of young workingwomen that even when brought there semi-conscious, Denise promptly meets (and eventually makes a miserable marriage with) a dashing count. In Gustave Le Rouge's popular 1917 melodramatic thriller *Le Crime d'une midinette* (*The Crime of a Midinette*), 16-year-old milliner Florette is first approached by her abductor while she window-shops for jewelry and dines in a *crémerie* with a fellow midinette. As a skilled garment worker, the author notes, Florette reapplies her make-up and mends her ripped bodice while imprisoned by her would-be rapist.[29]

In midinette literature, substantial or luxurious meals were often a marker of moral corruption or sexual engagement: the young woman in *Camille Frison*

---

[24] *Oscar et Kiki la midinette* (1913). Film Scénarios, 1909–15. BNF-R. 4-COL-3(3051). Léonce Perret, dir., *Oscar et Kiki la midinette* (Paris, 1913), Gaumont Pathé Archives.

[25] Georges Sibre and Albert Verse, *Couturière sans aiguilles: vaudeville-opérette en un acte* (Paris, 1905), 13. Premiered at the Bobino, directed by Eugène Dambreville, music by J. Deschaux.

[26] Ibid.   [27] Ibid. 6–7.

[28] Pierre de Lannoy, *Modiste et grande dame, roman inédit* (Paris, 1919).

[29] Le Rouge, *Le Crime d'une midinette*, 39.

dipping her fingers into the plate of mussels, the consummation of Juliette and Agénor's love over *saucisson* and dessert. Broadly speaking, however, the chroniclers of the Parisian midinette in many cases went to great lengths to convince readers that their attractive subjects were ordinarily willful under-eaters—and not especially hungry. Under-eating is referenced repeatedly in these essays, novels, songs, and plays as part and parcel of the appealing, feather-brained frivolity of Parisian garment workers.

Delicate appetites and disordered eating were, by the early twentieth century, (mis)understood even by many physicians as signs of "coquettishness" and as part of a trend toward a slenderer silhouette for middle- and upper-class women.[30] As we shall see, this conception of under-eating as a sacrifice for style was also used in representations of the midinettes, though here the image was slightly altered. Though the midinette likewise was idealized for her small stature and thin waist, her under-eating in favor of fashion was understood to result from a lack of appetite and a desire to economize for fashionable things (rather than the drive for modish thinness which preoccupied some middle-class women). These related but distinct images reveal how much is missed when scholars focus almost exclusively on middle-class women in histories of the body.

Susan Bordo has demonstrated that Victorian fiction tended to use female hunger as a "code for female desire," just one more voracious and threatening appetite of female sexuality.[31] Thus, for the midinette to be under-eating and yet not particularly hungry, provided an ideal, desirable (but not excessively desiring) body for consumption by the bourgeois viewer/reader/lover. What is more, this vision of the midinette blurred the generic conventions of nineteenth-century literature in which delicate appetites were the purview of virtuous upper-class ladies. By mapping slight appetites onto working bodies, pop cultural narratives erased the privation of actual workers, and did so at a time when this privation was itself the subject of government inquiries, reform efforts, and labor campaigns. In such narratives, the well-documented hunger of workingwomen was transfigured, as if by enchantment, into coquettish under-eating.

Georges Montorgueil enthused about the working Parisienne's non-eating in *Midi: le déjeuner des petites ouvrières* (*Noon: The Lunch of Humble Workingwomen*) (a book with remarkably few references to actual eating). He reproached "moralists" who agonized over the hunger of these women and who claimed that

---

[30] See Edward Shorter, "The first great increase in anorexia nervosa," *Journal of Social History*, Vol. 21, Issue 1 (Fall 1987), 69–96. Shorter notes that at the turn of the century, "references to anorexia in aid of modish thinness and romantic acceptance begin to proliferate" (p. 82). Mary Lynn Stewart and Nancy Janovicek trace the fashion industry's particular investment in promoting a slender frame in the decades straddling World War I, though they are skeptical how often this led to extensive dieting by significant numbers of Frenchwomen. Mary Lynn Stewart and Nancy Janovicek, "Slimming the female body? Re-evaluating dress, corsets, and physical culture in France, 1890s–1930s," *Fashion Theory: The Journal of Dress, Body & Culture* 5, No. 2 (June 2001).

[31] Susan Bordo, *Unbearable Weight: Feminism, Western Culture, and the Body* (Los Angeles, 1993), 206.

the joyous comportment of the midinettes was a "ruse" masking the misery of an underfed life:[32]

> the laughter of the workingwomen rings true. And their joy is not an act. The mediocrity of their meals causes them neither sadness nor embarrassment. "One should not live to eat, said Harpagon, but rather eat to live." [These women] are not so sure of that: they live, or believe they do, and do not eat…Their appetite is so frail that the most fragile emotion can cut it. Propose some pleasure to them unexpectedly and their appetite, as if by magic, disappears.[33]

Here was the common refrain of the midinette's enthusiasts: that these were workingwomen who lived for and *on* pleasure, not food. As an example of this, Montorgeuil recounted his time spent with Ernestine Curot, the 17-year-old worker elected as the "Muse of Paris" in 1898. As one of the competition's judges, Montorgueil escorted Curot and two of her female companions to the famed couturier Worth to be dressed for a *fête* at the Hotel de Ville, and then to the *fête* itself. At the end of this busy day, during which Montorgeuil never saw the young women eat, he suggested that they should have dinner:

> The Muse looked at me with an almost ironic face: "Eat? But, monsieur, she said, we don't eat when we go to the theater!" I insisted, I invoked the physical necessities, the fatigue of this long day, the depleted strength that they needed to replenish. I preached in vain:
> —When we go to the theater, we do not eat.
> They did not eat. They went to the theater.[34]

Casting aside the counsel of their bourgeois escort, these young workers happily forgo meals for entertainment; Montorgueil is amused by their flippancy. Alfred Desfossez's 1904 play *Les Midinettes*, whose entire first act is set in a "midinette restaurant," features an equally blithe midinette who, when given money by a male admirer to eat a steak for lunch rather than just fried potatoes, announces she will instead use the funds to go to the theater.[35] Here, as is often the case in cultural products featuring midinettes, benevolent bourgeois paternalism confronts the worrisome if adorable lifestyle of the garment worker—with malnourishment in the garment trades neatly transformed into a girlish lifestyle choice.

When midinettes are portrayed eating at all, it is often to highlight the charming lightness of their meals. Desfossez's band of lunching midinettes eat sparingly

---

[32] Montorgueil, *Midi*, 68.   [33] Ibid. 68–9.   [34] Ibid. 74–5.

[35] Alfred Desfossez, *Les Midinettes: drame en 5 actes et 7 tableaux* (Paris, 1904), 5, 7. First performed at the Théâtre des Fantaisies Saint-Martin, 1 Jan. 1904, Théâtre de Belleville, 31 Jan. 1904, and Théâtre Montparnasse, 14 May 1904.

and frivolously: fries, pickles, pastries, *crèmes au chocolat*. In *Midi*, Montorgueil referred to workingwomen's lunch as "a bird's meal," and in *La Vie des boulevards* (1896) as light fare: "fries or artichoke" and "some cherries."[36] A lengthy scene in *Camille Frison* likewise represents midinettes as impractical eaters and capricious consumers:

> Some bought oranges from a street cart, others candy from the grocer, brightly colored cards, or complimentary theater tickets from the tobacco shop. Still others crowded around the ambulant pastry salesman. Further along, some waited, bowls in hand, in front of a shop where fries bubbled in the frying pan...There were some who entered the dairy shop, the baker's, the delicatessen, to lay in hasty provisions before launching themselves into the commotion of a bar where they ordered only a white wine or a coffee...[37]

Oranges, fries, candy, wine, and coffee—hardly the makings of a nourishing meal, but a list perfectly calibrated to evoke the gay impulses of the ideal midinette. A song from this era titled "March of the Workingwomen" celebrates an equally insubstantial lunch:

> Do you hear noon ringing?
> It's time for your lunch;
> The fried potato's bubblin'
> And the brie's runnin' at the dairy.
> Go get your beakful
> In a nice paper cone.
> And drink a dewdrop
> At the neighborhood Wallace.[38]

Some fries, a bit of cheese, and a drop of water from a public fountain—another sparse midinette lunch, no more than a "beakful," but one that evokes pleasure rather than pathos. The 1903 song "The Joyous Midinettes" was typical of the genre in that undereating was seamlessly linked to girlish, bird-like caprice and gaiety: "Lunching, | Often enough, | For two sous worth of fries only, | They are, unpretentious, | Always as happy as larks [*pinsons*], | Ignoring sorrow, they have fun with nothing, without any worry for tomorrow."[39] Midinette lunches were depicted in this way consistently—meals of small quantity, and often composed of snacks or sugary treats.

---

[36] Montorgueil, *Midi*, 38; *La Vie des boulevards*, 21–2.   [37] Vernières, *Camille Frison*, 38–9.

[38] A. Poupay, "La Marche des ouvrières," quoted in Vernières, *Camille Frison*, 48. "Wallace du quartier" refers to cast-iron drinking fountains installed around late nineteenth-century Paris.

[39] P. Bades and V. Mignon, "Les Joyeuses Midinettes," Music by P. Bades and H. Tarrelli (Saint-Denis, 1903). BNF-L, VM7-112393.

Alexandre's extended chapter on the midinette lunch hour veers between romanticizing the lightness of the women's consumption, and playing up the tragic insufficiency of their collations— two closely related responses. He depicts the plaintive under-eaters ("huddled in their cloaks, they melancholically eat the humble and austere nourishment they hold in the fold of a newspaper spread open over their knees"[40]) and later refers to the "mouse-sized stomachs of the little Parisiennes." He admits that, "It is incontestable that in Paris, the working-woman at four francs a day finds nowhere to feed herself adequately." Yet, on the very next page, he concludes, "this life is essentially pleasant and emits a potent perfume of kindness, of affectionate temperament, and instinctive delicacy."[41] He approves of the "pensive or cheerful young women" who descend from their workshops to buy a pleasantly insubstantial lunch from a seasonal fruit and vegetable cart: "delicious fruits and crudités... cherries, apples, pink radishes."[42] The workingwomen eat quickly so that they can reserve more time for games.[43]

Montorgueil similarly notes in one breath the misery of these women's diets ("the 'petite main' makes a sum so modest that we ask ourselves by what miracle she is able to live. To this question one workingwoman responded: 'Why, we do not eat to our appeasement'") and on the very next page assures readers that nonetheless, "this distress" is hidden by a "mask of insouciance and gaiety" provided by youth and taste. These women, rest assured, "remain piquant and, so desirable, that they would make some conquests of old men along their way if they did not all have horror of banal vice." Montorgueil adds that the "frugal meal" of fries, artichokes, and cherries was seasoned with "the salt of playful remarks" and "more laughter than the copious feasts of modish cabarets." Thus, the "lugubrious" portrait painted by reformers is banished by images of alluring women and quaint picnics.[44] Some workingwomen, Montorgueil continued, even found spare change for an occasional coffee or vanilla ice cream. Under-eating is thus both denounced and eroticized.

Furthering this eroticization of the underfed garment worker, the midinette's under-eating was explained as a choice made in the service of an instinctive attachment to fashion and coquetry. As an example of his thesis that working-women's "*coquetterie*" (concern for one's appearance) deadened their hunger, Montorgueil pointed again to the Muse of Paris (Ernestine Curot) and her friends:

Did they eat during these blissful days[?]... Eat! Sure, they were considering it. Considering their beautiful gowns, yes, which they saw were lined with silk, and so, they confided to one another, later they could unstitch the lining and make two dresses out of one.[45]

[40] Alexandre, *Les Reines de l'aiguille*, 19–20.   [41] Ibid. 24, 25.   [42] Ibid. 18.
[43] Ibid. 21.   [44] Montorgueil, *La Vie des boulevards*, 186–8.
[45] Montorgueil, *Midi*, 71.

Indeed, not eating, Montorgueil revealed, was "the secret to not jeopardizing either the delicate gracefulness of her body or the return on her earnings."[46] Once again, the Parisian garment worker is seen to prioritize that which observers like Montorgueil wished she would—fashion. As a result, the reality of the malnourished, sweated laborer is neatly elided in favor of a chic coquette who chooses not to eat her fill in order to revel in the pleasures of Parisian couture (rather than being deprived of adequate nourishment because of a meager salary).

Vernières' *Camille Frison* features a garment worker who spends her lunch hour at a restaurant describing the "ravishing little embroidered collar" at Galeries Lafayette that she will soon buy: "She had gone without meat for eight days in order to have the money."[47] Like many renderings of Mimi Pinson, midinette concern for appearance and fashion is an instinctive drive—far more urgent than a steady diet. In this way, novelists assuaged fears about the wretchedness of sweated labor (by depicting workers' under-eating as a coquettish sacrifice for apparel and make-up) and reaffirmed cultural expectations about the impeccable tastefulness of Paris's workingwomen.

Indeed, many scenes of the midinette lunch hour involve no eating whatsoever, and instead depict garment workers covetously touring the boulevards' shop windows. The (purported) midinette columnist "Gaby" from *Le Journal de Mimi Pinson* described her own lunch hours thus: "I love to *flâner*... My nose is pressed up against the shop windows of the boutiques in the neighborhood... It amuses me so just to look—without even really seeing at times—the loads of things that are in there!"[48] These young women are not fomenting revolution as they examine the luxury goods produced by their labor but which lie beyond their reach. Rather, they are lighthearted *flâneuses* whose consumerist desires affirm the capitalist economy of which they are the bottom rung. As Rita Felski and others have observed, workingwomen's taste for luxury was often portrayed as the first step in a descent toward sexual promiscuity.[49] And to be sure, many of these stories understood appetites (for fashion, for food, for sex) as interrelated and corrupting.

The under-eating midinette differed significantly from her predecessor the Romantic grisette, who, while also devoted to sweets, was depicted consuming large amounts of food as part of her lusty gaiety. Louis Huart's *Physiologie de la grisette* (1841) mentions the persistent ravenousness of the grisettes, despite their near-constant eating. He describes the average grisette transforming her work bag into "a pantry" stuffed with kilos of roasted chestnuts and pralines, *fromage d'Italie* [liver cheese], oranges, cake, and crayfish legs. Grisettes consumed such an "immense quantity" of *galettes* during their workday that "these merchants are making a fortune." Huart claimed that grisettes digested these cakes even better

---

[46] Ibid. 76.   [47] Vernières, *Camille Frison*, 35.
[48] Gaby, "Babil de trottin," *Le Journal de Mimi Pinson, à l'atelier et dans la famille* 2 (10 Aug. 1908), 2.
[49] Rita Felski, *The Gender of Modernity* (Cambridge, 1995), 72.

than male workers because of their "*estomac d'autruche*," a stomach that can digest anything easily.[50]

Thus, the delightedly under-eating midinette represented an evolution of the grisette, from a workingwoman who indulges in gourmand pleasures to one who forgoes food for non-comestible consumer pleasures. This would prove to be an image of astonishing resilience in the decades to come. Pulp novels, stories, and songs from the 1920s and 1930s continually restaged the image of the under-eating midinette choosing fashion over food. In Jean Béarnais's novel *Nouvelle Mimi Pinson* (1929), the entire staff of a Parisian couture workshop curbs their eating to allow for fashion expenditures: "They had the habit of meeting up at a little café on the rue Camartin where they would lunch frugally on charcuterie and a *café-crème*. These meager meals allowed them to save up to buy powder, rouge and, on occasion, a little, elegant outfit." Béarnais's heroine seamstress Mimi, before agreeing to a meal with her soon-to-be-lover Jean, considers her co-worker Mado, who, thanks to a wealthy lover, is always fashionably dressed ("du dernier chic") and eats her lunch "in restaurants, *à la carte*."[51] Stéphane Manier's 1933 novel *Midinettes* features Yvette, a 26-year-old *second main* in a Parisian couture house who sacrifices eating for her love of fashion: "To stay *coquette*, to save money, Yvette only eats once a day, at lunch, at an inexpensive restaurant."[52]

One also cannot underestimate the power of this pervasive stereotype in belle époque reform efforts. The novel *Camille Frison*, for example, was actually summarized as evidence of the real plight of working Parisiennes in Claire de Patz's *France from Within* (1912), and de Patz included detailed descriptions of the midinette's lunch hour from this book.[53] One review of *Camille Frison* insisted that unlike romantic tales of "Jenny l'Ouvrière...from yesteryear," this story was "an investigation...of the real condition of workingwomen in the needle trades..."[54] As we shall see, many philanthropists and reformers readily parroted the pop cultural contention that the midinette's frivolous and under-developed appetite for food complemented other more highly-developed (and morally treacherous) appetites.

Lunch Reform and the Midinette

Alongside these picturesque representations, the female worker's noon pause drew increasing attention in the belle époque as a target of reform. Workingwomen

---

[50] Huart, *Physiologie de la grisette*, 33–5, 38, 91.

[51] Jean Béarnais, *Nouvelle Mimi Pinson: roman d'amour inédit* (Montrouge, 1929), 2–3. On 1930s French pulp fiction see Joelle Neulander, "Model detectives: modernity, femininity, and work in interwar romance comic strips," *Proceedings of the Western Society for French History* 37 (2009) 283–303.

[52] Stéphane Manier, *Midinettes* (Paris, 1933), 38.

[53] Claire de Pratz, *France from Within* (London, 1912), 212.

[54] "Andrés Vernières, *Camille Frison, ouvrière de la couture*," *La Justice*, 24 June 1908.

in the needle trades made demands in this period for longer lunch hours (primarily to allow them to return home to eat instead of spending money on a restaurant),[55] for a half-day off on Saturdays for errands they were now obliged to complete at lunch,[56] for government-subsidized cooperative restaurants where they could eat a meal for a reasonable price,[57] and for free access to municipal park chairs at lunch.[58] Turn-of-the-century reformers generally concurred with garment workers that the lunch break needed improvement, and so proposed initiatives to create lunchrooms, both secular and confessional, where midinettes could safely enjoy a wholesome, modestly-priced meal. Such initiatives, however, while engendered in part by concern for the insufficient salaries and diet of the Parisian female workforce, were also motivated by interlaced fantasies and concerns about the moral susceptibility of the garment trade worker.[59]

One of the first workingwomen's lunchrooms was established in the 1890s at the place du Marché Saint-Honoré by the Union Chrétienne des Ateliers de Femmes, a group composed of garment trade *patronnes* and society ladies. This first effort faced difficulties finding an affordable location close to garment trade workplaces, attracting clients, and developing an appealing and affordable menu. A short-lived Catholic restaurant on the rue Jean-Jacques Rousseau, and another, the Restaurant de Dames seules, on the rue de Richelieu followed. This latter space included a reading room and library, a restaurant *à prix fixe*, and a second restaurant *à la carte*.[60] In 1893, a group of Protestant society ladies opened the Foyer de l'Ouvrière, a kitchen on rue d'Aboukir amidst the most poorly paid of the needle trades—military caps and hat manufacture.[61] Given the popularity of this endeavor, other locales opened in subsequent years: on the rue Réaumur, rue de la Victoire, faubourg Saint-Denis, and rue de Richelieu, which drew its clientele from the hatmakers and seamstresses working along the rue de la Paix.[62] The rue du Bac saw the establishment of a multi-confessional restaurant run by Jewish, Catholic, and Protestant society ladies. In his social investigation *Les Ouvrières de l'aiguille à Paris* (*The Workingwomen of the Paris Needle Trades*) (1895), Charles

---

[55] "Un meeting à la Bourse du Travail," *L'Action*, 17 Jan. 1910.

[56] Marcelle Capy, "La Midinette et la semaine anglaise," *La Bataille syndicaliste* (26 May 1914), 3.

[57] "Grève dans l'industrie du vêtement," 23 Sept. 1918, APPP BA 1376: Grèves de l'habillement, 1917 à 1918.

[58] "Résolution relative à la gratuité des sièges dans les promenades intérieures de la Ville de Paris et prorogation de la concession," *Bulletin municipal officiel de la Ville de Paris*, 24 June 1922, pp. 2752–3.

[59] Albert mentions the linkage made between restaurant reform and fears about sexual dissipation in "Les Midinettes parisiennes à la Belle Époque," 64.

[60] Comte d'Haussonville, *Salaires et misères de femmes* (Paris, 1900), 48. Charles Benoist refers to the lending library at this establishment in *Les Ouvrières de l'aiguille à Paris* (Paris, 1895), 233–4.

[61] The Comte d'Haussonville noted that the directrice was too forceful in pushing a "certaine influence religieuse." *Salaires et misères de femmes*, 52. One article puts the founding of the rue d'Aboukir site as 1893. Maurice Bonneff, "Fin de saison—fin de travail," *L'Action* 18 (July 1908).

[62] Ibid.; Milhaud, *L'Ouvrière en France*, 109.

Benoist estimated that, in the high season, 1,200 to 1,500 lunches were served weekly in restaurants for women in the needle trades.[63]

In 1902, an assortment of public school teachers, feminists, accountants, and labor representatives (including Clemence Jusselin, who served as secretary general of the group and as the secretary of the Chambre syndicale des Ouvrières-Lingères in Paris), founded a workingwomen's restaurant cooperative called "Les Midinettes."[64] This project, which sought over time to make workingwomen the primary stakeholders in the cooperative, modeled itself after successful networks of workers' restaurants in Geneva and in Lyon (established in 1890 and 1892 respectively).[65] This organization sought to keep Parisian workingwomen from the "dangers" of both "insufficient diet" and "the unhealthy promiscuities of the street," and did so as a matter of solidarist duty: "The restaurants of 'Les Midinettes' constitute then not only a work of solidarity but even more a means of education and feminine emancipation which merits the encouragement of all of the friends of social progress."[66] In December 1902, a fundraiser for this initiative at the Bourse du Travail featured singers and harpists from the Oeuvre de Mimi Pinson, with their "laughing" and "pretty little sweet faces," according to a journalist for *Gil Blas*.[67] (This writer seemed unaware that the initiative's leadership included a number of professional women: "Some generous men...have resolved to give a bit of comfort to the poor workingwoman...")

Another Parisian establishment opened on the rue Béranger offering a "pension complet," meals and lodging for workingwomen at a weekly cost of between 7 and 12 francs.[68] The Cercle du Travail féminin on the boulevard Capucines promoted itself as a "center of entertainment and friendship" for workingwomen without any confessional or political association. Its services included a restaurant, as well as affordable seaside vacations for subscribers. By 1908, the Cercle boasted 900 members, and provided "carefully prepared" lunches in its restaurant for around 250 women for less than 80 centimes each.[69] In 1906, the rue Saint-Honoré saw the opening of the Réchaud de midi, where, for about 10 centimes, workingwomen could cook their own meals. The organizers provided supplements of vegetables, salad, and wine for a small price. By 1908, some 120 female garment workers from the neighborhoods of the rue de la Paix and the Place Vendôme ate

---

[63] Benoist, *Les Ouvrières de l'aiguille*, 234.

[64] *"Les Midinettes": Restaurants coopératifs d'ouvrières. Société anonyme à Capital et à Personnel variables, Siège Social: 98, Boulevard de Sebastopol* (Paris, 1905). In *La Femme dans les organisations ouvrières* (1910), Compain refers to a soon-to-be-opened *restaurant de midinettes* which has raised 10,000 francs. Whether this is the same initiative is difficult to say, though Jusselin is mentioned in both places.

[65] Ibid. 6.

[66] *Programme: Les Midinettes, Théâtre de l'Ambigu, Matinée du Jeudi 1er Juin* (1905), back cover. Fonds Jeanne Bouvier, Boîte XIX: Travail à domicile, Papiers divers, Fonds Marie-Louise Bouglé, BHVP.

[67] "Les 'Midinettes,'" *Gil Blas*, 15 Dec. 1902.   [68] Bonneff, "Fin de saison—fin de travail."

[69] Ibid.

there every day.[70] As social investigator Caroline Milhaud pointed out in 1907, however, these various endeavors were still insufficient to feed the more than 40,000 workingwomen in the Parisian garment trades alone who worked outside of the home.[71] By 1912, the number of lunchrooms, soup kitchens, and "réchauds" expressly serving workingwomen in Paris swelled to thirty-five—with names like the "Repas de Midinette" and "Restaurant du Syndicat de l'Aiguille."[72]

In addition to lunchrooms, some reformers focused on supporting businesses that provided employees with adequate lunching facilities on site—principally kitchens where workers could prepare and heat their own meals. The Ligue social d'Acheteurs, founded in 1902, gave high marks to workshops that provided stoves and lunching spaces.[73] Charles Benoist, in describing the clientele of the *restaurants d'ouvrières*, observed that most of the diners were young women, as older and married women preferred to economize further by remaining at the workshop to eat: "Fortunately, there are employers who provide the necessary utensils for them to heat their food."[74]

The menus of workingwomen's lunchrooms offered a corrective to the widespread association of midinettes and frivolous eating. While the popular imagination envisioned midinettes lunching on a "beakful" of sweets and snacks, diners at the Foyer de l'Ouvrière enjoyed complete meals consisting of a meat dish, vegetable, and bread for only 11 sous.[75] The Restaurant de Dames seules offered a 90-centimes *menu fixe* (bread; wine, beer, or milk; a meat dish; a vegetable dish; and a dessert), as well as an *à la carte* selection which included meat, fish, soups, salad, and vegetables.[76]

For some reformers, the economically-driven malnourishment of the garment worker was the principal impetus for the lunchroom initiatives. A schoolteacher who helped found the Société des Midinettes (a restaurant cooperative) wrote of a former student, a leather worker "reduced to nibbling a couple of fries or bits of charcuterie, while walking, showered by rain or wind. Isn't this a fortifying nourishment and consumed in conditions which promise a happy effect!...After this, you can go ahead and call all the congresses you want to combat the ravages of tuberculosis and to halt the white slave trade!"[77] Maurice Bonneff, a working-class activist who co-authored several inquiries into the lives of French workers with his brother Léon, offered a similarly frank appraisal of the workingwomen's lunch. He agreed with more romantic portrayals that many of the workingwomen preferred eating their "frugal" and "modest" meals outside, but not because of

---

[70] Milhaud, *L'Ouvrière en France*, 109–10; Bonneff, "Fin de saison—fin de travail."
[71] Milhaud, *L'Ouvrière en France*, 110.
[72] Office central des Oeuvres de bienfaisance, *Paris Charitable et Bienfaisant* (Paris, 1912).
[73] *Bulletin de la Ligue social d'acheteurs* (Novembre 1904, 1er trimestre 1905), 7–8.
[74] Benoist, *Les Ouvrières de l'aiguille*, 234.   [75] Bonneff, "Fin de saison—fin de travail."
[76] Haussonville, *Salaires et misères de femmes*, 48. The prices in this menu approximate those found in sample menus provided in Benoist, *Les Ouvrières de l'aiguille*, 232.
[77] *"Les Midinettes": Restaurants coopératifs d'ouvrières*, 5.

picturesque playfulness on their part. Instead, he quoted a workingwoman herself (rare in most of these sources):

> First off, the bistros are not much interested in our patronage. We do not order apéritifs. Even so, lunch rarely amounts to less than 25 sous. That's fine for rich people. To cut costs, sometimes, we order smaller portions. Often, we drink only water. This time, the bistro gets angry, and hit us with a fine. Yes indeed! When we ask for the bill, they have us paying ten centimes extra, to punish us for contributing, by way of our sobriety, to the slump in wine sales! They charge us for the silverware too. So much that, despite our rigorous calculations, our desire for economizing, we end up spending wildly: 23 sous![78]

Bonneff remarks that this "economy of the little *sou*" is "infinitely distressing...it gives us a glimpse of an entire life of privation and labor, and the anemia and the tuberculosis that decimates so many workingwomen."[79] Unusual among many descriptions of the midinette lunch, Bonneff's article defines these women's under-eating as a painful economic necessity—rather than as a sacrifice for fashion or a preference for insubstantial meals. In their enquête "The Tragic Life of Workers" (1911), the Bonneff brothers demonstrated that even a modest daily midday meal exceeded the salary of many women in the flower industry.[80] They also noted that added money for food could not be gleaned from other parts of the workingwoman's budget—minimal heating and laundry costs, and "the already limited costs of clothes." Rather than blaming excessive coquetry and taste for fashion, the Bonneffs highlighted the inequitable salaries of women compared to men as the root of their pecuniary misery.[81]

Historian Martin Bruegel has analyzed belle époque scientific studies of working-class Parisian nutrition, and found that lunchtime menus targeting a female clientele (the lighter fare of the new *crémeries* as opposed to the heavier meals at the *marchands de vin* preferred by male workers) provided about 80 per cent of the calories of male meals. What is more, female lunchers paid a heavier cost for such meals. A so-called "real meal" cost 29.7 per cent of the daily mean salary for workingwomen whereas men in this period spent only 18.9 per cent of their mean salaray on a full lunchtime meal (with more calories than the average feminine full meal).[82] Bruegel also establishes that while workingwomen consistently were

---

[78] Quoted in Bonneff, "Fin de saison—fin de travail."

[79] Ibid.

[80] Léon Bonneff and Maurice Bonneff, *La Vie tragique des travailleurs, enquêtes sur la condition économique et morale des ouvriers et ouvrières d'industrie* (Paris, 1911), 315–16. (Orig. 1908) 26–7, 330–1. Both brothers were killed in World War I. See the preface to the 1984 edition by Michelle Perrot (Paris, 1984).

[81] Bonneff and Bonneff, *La Vie tragique*, 315–16.

[82] Bruegel, "Le Genre du déjeuner," 21–50, 28. Bruegel analyzes a number of belle époque studies, especially Louis Landouzy, Henri et Marcel Labbé, *Enquête sur l'alimentation d'une centaine d'ouvriers et d'employés parisiens* (Paris, 1905), Jean Laumonier, "Bouillons ouvriers et restaurants populaires,"

criticized for eating too quickly, this was often due to the household errands they were obliged to run during their lunch break. He demonstrates that while workingmen tended to eat during their entire lunch break, workingwomen often devoted only about fifteen minutes of the lunchtime pause to eating.[83]

Yet despite available contemporary data and the pleas of investigators like Milhaud and the Bonneffs, many reformers, even those decrying abusive labor practices, reaffirmed the prevalent notion of female garment workers as frivolous and willful under-eaters. In his 1900 *enquête*, the Comte d'Haussonville admitted that it was difficult to construct a menu for a workingwomen's restaurant, as "Generally, [these girls] have little appetite, despite their twenty years, and this is understandable given the sedentary existence they lead, deprived of fresh air and exercise. Big pieces of meat do not tempt them. They only like small dishes. Some demand dessert and coffee."[84] Novelist (and former workingwoman) Simone Bodève concurred in her study *Celles qui travaillent* (1913), declaring that it was a mistake to establish restaurants for workingwomen alone: "our young women eat little and drink even less... In places where a restaurateur is assured of a male clientele, the food will be both more varied and fresher, simply because its consumption is certain... [To the young workingwoman] eating seems to be an irksome operation; eating a lot is, in her eyes, shameful and indelicate."[85] The men of the Académie Goncourt remarked that the "young working-girl will always prefer the creamery" to the new women's only lunchrooms, because in the creamery she could eat "side by side with the clerk or employee, who notices her, admires her, amuses her, and gives rise in her mind and heart to dreams and sentiments which do not always deceive."[86]

During the First World War, Catholic churches near the major garment work-shops began offering "Missions de Midi," half-hour lunchtime services designed specifically for midinettes to pray for France's victory and for her soldiers.[87] In May 1916, Abbé Poulin addressed thousands of these lunchtime pilgrims at Notre Dame in a service presided over by the archbishop of Paris, Cardinal Amette. In Poulin's sermon, which reportedly managed to "interest, to charm, and finally to raise superb feelings of patriotism and piety" in the assembled workingwomen, the priest posed the question, "Who are the young women who come, on this day, to honor and pray to Mary?" In response, he sketched a portrait of capricious

---

Bulletin générale de thérapeutique, 141 (1901), and numerous studies and articles from Parisian dailies during the 1900s.

[83] Bruegel, "Le Genre du déjeuner," 38.

[84] Haussonville, *Salaires et misères de femmes*, 47.

[85] Bodève, *Celles qui travaillent* (Paris, 1913), 128–9.

[86] Lucien Descaves et al., *The Colour of Paris: Historical, Personal & Local* (London, 1908), 67. The authors collaborating on this text were Léon Hennique, Octave Mirbeau, Gustave Geffroy, J. H. Rosny, Paul Margueritte, Léon Daudet, Justin Rosny, Jules Renard, and Elémir Bourges.

[87] G. Latouche, "Notre Dame envahie par les midinettes," *Dieu et patrie: l'héroïsme du clergé français devant l'ennemi (publication hebdomaire)*, 80 (4 June 1916), 437.

midinette under-eaters more interested in pleasure than nutrition—even while addressing a crowd of workingwomen sacrificing their lunch hour to church-going. He described the working Parisienne: "a being of grace, delicate and temperamental... like the sweet birds who make their nests 'under the arches of Notre Dame'...lover of sour candies, of fries and vinegar...preferring a ribbon or a flower on a hat to three lunches..."[88]

A certain Dr Parfait, writing in a magazine aimed at midinettes in 1909, alerted readers to the deleterious health effects of workingwomen's insufficient meals: "The mealtime of the workingwoman—yours, charming lady readers—is perhaps the most interesting and most alarming aspect of her situation, as much from the point of view of the stomach as that of the crowded closeness of the restaurant." Tuberculosis and stomach ailments were a certain result of such under-eating, the physician warned. He suggested, however, that these inadequate meals were in no small part the result of workers' aesthetic vanity: "some workingwomen, rather than trying to feed themselves well, prefer to lunch on a ten-centime black coffee and a croissant...so that they can buy themselves a bit of ribbon, a cravat, or a bouquet of violets."[89] In order to convince his working-class readers to heed his advice, Parfait patronizingly framed his admonition as beauty tips:

> Remark—and this argument will have more value in your eyes than all the best ones in the world—remark, I say, that frequent congestion of the face often leads to eczema...Eczema which disfigures, which makes the most beautiful woman ugly, and which resists even the most energetic treatments.[90]

Tuberculosis and any of the other serious health ailments Parfait enumerates in this article evidently would not concern the gay midinette in the way that threats to her beauty might. Here, another middle-class male reformer relies on a potent cultural fantasy of midinette frivolity even as he tries to combat systemic mal-nourishment in the garment trades. Simone Bodève similarly explained the under-eating of Parisian workingwomen in part as a result of their devotion to fashion. Bodève refers to the lunch hour as the best time to see the *ouvrière parisiennes* "lively and happy": "those privileged ones that can 'treat themselves' to restaurants lunch on four mouthfuls and a thousand words, then rush off to the department store to try on hat styles."[91] Other workingwomen, led astray by their "vanity," agree to accompany a seducer to a meal simply for "the joy of entering a

[88] "Pèlerinage des missions de midi à Notre Dame de Paris," *Bulletin Mensuel du Syndicat de l'Aiguille, association professionnelle mixte de patronnes, employées et ouvrières en habillement, métiers similaires et professions connexes*, 220 (June 1916), 4.

[89] Dr Parfait, "Midinette et l'hygiène: vous mangez trop vite," *Midinette: Journal de la femme et de la jeune fille qui travaillent* (12 Nov. 1909), 10.

[90] Ibid.

[91] Bodève, *Celles qui travaillent*, 14.

beautiful restaurant," and later, kill themselves with night work and privations in order to have a wardrobe without asking for anything from their lover."[92] A fantasy of intentional and frivolous under-eating in the service of fashion and beauty worked as only one important element in a prevalent vision of the midinette as sexually available, sexually desirable, and politically neutered.

We also seem to be witnessing in this popular literature a novel representation of under-eating and non-eating. Instead of the fasting, devout bourgeois anorectics of nineteenth-century fiction, whose physical wasting enhanced their vulnerability and distance from the concupiscence of the material world,[93] the imaginary working-class female under-eaters of the early twentieth century did so as a sacrifice for consumer choice and pleasure. This image also benefited from an extraordinary consistency over the decades, from the turn of the century through the 1930s. Despite years of reform efforts around workingwomen's nourishment (examined below), L'Intransigeant's Chamine (pseudonym of the journalist Geneviève Dunais) could still refer in 1931 to the midinettes' lunch as a "not properly speaking a meal" but "a bit of air and café-crème." The lunching midinettes are "dressed like dolls...each one, imperceptibly, trying to be the most beautiful." While men eat at restaurants where they can be well fed for a good price, the young workingwomen prefer cafés: "It is hardly that [the young men] earn more. Even with equivalent earnings, the young women prefer to dispose of their money to clothe themselves with care."[94]

The midinette's lunchtime corruption, a scene reiterated across popular literature in this period, bled into government investigations of conditions in the garment trades. Indeed, turn-of-the-century lunchroom initiatives were driven not only by perceptions of workingwomen's under-eating, but by alarm about the lunch hour as a site of temptation, seduction, and moral peril—a fall from virtue which was itself a staple of romantic representations of these women. A Catholic commentator in La Croix applauded the recent philanthropic effort to establish workingwomen's restaurants as a social duty to protect "these children" who found themselves threatened by "terrible dangers of moral and physical order" in Paris's mixed-sex cafés and restaurants at lunchtime: "The result is a liaison begun during lunch, pursued into the street, and which almost always ends badly." Garment workers and their "light, insouciant souls" needed to be protected from the "temptations...that multiply around [them.]"[95] During the 1901 government commission on veillées, flowerworker Stéphanie Bouvard, leader of the fleuristes-plumassières' union, advocated requiring all employers to provide refectories.[96]

---

[92] Ibid. 67–8.   [93] See McEachern, Deprivation and Power.
[94] Chamine, "'Un peu d'air et de café-crème...': déjeuner des midinettes," L'Intransigeant 27 (Aug. 1931), Fonds Jeanne Bouvier, Boîte XIX.
[95] M.E., "Les Restaurants féminins à Paris," La Croix, 27 Sept. 1912.
[96] "Séance du 22 février 1901," La Question des veillées devant la commission départementale du travail du département de la Seine, 25.

Workingwomen, she argued, often lived too far from their workplace to return home for lunch, and earned too little to dine at restaurants. More important, having the garment laborer lunch in a designated space at the workshop would "safeguard her morality and remove her from the influences of the street."[97] Bouvard asserted the critical need for this reform: "We must demand that employers have specially-designated lunchrooms. If not, we will see a great number of workingwomen, who do not earn enough to go to a restaurant, eating instead in the street in all weather and to the detriment of their health and their morality."[98] M. Walckenaer, a mining engineer and member of the Commission, was sympathetic to Bouvard's argument: "it is the fear that young women, obliged to go out into the street and to take shelter in cheap cabarets for their meals, find themselves exposed to moral or material dangers more frightful than the inconvenience of their current way of life."[99]

Fear of these unspecified but doubtlessly well-understood "moral dangers" even seems to have helped shape reform initiatives. The founding documents of the Société des Midinettes' restaurant cooperative included as justification of its work a vision of the moral dangers of the lunch hour: "And here, then, is my workingwoman, obliged to go eat outside, in the street, in the square, on a bench on the boulevard, exposed to bad weather, to glacial temperatures, to rain, to wind; exposed also to all the repugnant and dangerous promiscuities, so much so that her moral health is as threatened as her physical health."[100] Inclement weather and moral danger are placed side by side as threats to the lunching midinette. Paul Deschanel's 1909 initiative, Réfectoire, afforded married and unmarried seamstresses, laundresses, milliners, and embroiderers during the off season "a wholesome and fortifying meal, as well as a shelter from bad weather and the temptations of the street."[101] The Ligue social d'Acheteurs paid special attention to the lunch environment of needle-trade *ateliers*. In compiling their Liste Blanche, the Ligue specified which fashion houses provided their workers with facilities to prepare and consume midday meals. The explicit benefit of such facilities was to shield female workers from the insalubrious moral and physical atmosphere of lunch outside the *atelier*. The Maison Lelong, for example, was praised for offering a stove where employees could heat up their lunch, "so as to have them avoid a meal at the corner restaurant where one is always badly fed and exposed to often dangerous encounters."[102]

---

[97] Ibid. 26.   [98] Ibid. 27.

[99] Ibid. 28. The Commission could not agree on the proposition, and it was withdrawn.

[100] Madame Barthélemy, school principal, quoted in *"Les Midinettes": restaurants coopératifs d'ouvrières*, 4.

[101] "Pour les ouvrières parisiennes: une oeuvre utile," *Midinette: Journal de la femme et de la jeune fille qui travaillent* (12 Nov. 1909), 4.

[102] Baronne Georges Brincard, "La Ligue social d'acheteurs et les Maisons de la Liste Blanche," presented to the Assemblée générale of the Ligue, 23 April 1904. *Bulletin de la Ligue social d'acheteurs* (Nov. 1904), 5–12, 7.

In his 1900 report, the Comte d'Haussonville described in detail the scenario to be forestalled by the creation of workingwomen's lunchrooms:

> while they mull over an economical meal, menu in hand, a gallant from the dairy shop arrives and proposes adding something to their lunch or even paying for the whole thing. If they refuse on account of pride, the gallant does not surrender. He returns the next day and offers some object for their toilette, a silk ribbon or a plated brooch? After all, there's nothing wrong with this. So, each young woman that consents to have something paid for, whether a lunch or a ribbon, is on the path that will lead to her ruin.[103]

Echoing popular midinette fiction, Haussonville's sociological study neatly joins fashion, food, and moral ruin—and does so with the narrative suspense of a pulp novel. In his 1895 study of the needleworkers of Paris, journalist, historian, and later politician Charles Benoist composed a comparably lurid scene in which a workingwoman, driven by dreams of copious restaurant lunches and fashion purchases, falls for her seducer:

> She who hardly earns enough to feed herself, who lunches sparingly and hurriedly at noon, and is bent in two over her work, she has a dream: to be able to eat, like this girl or that girl, at a restaurant…which she imagines as a place of delights. As soon as she has a couple of sous, she will go. As soon as she has gone, she will be unable to go without it, by vanity and pleasure.
>
>   One day not too far off, she will meet a gallant from her class there…She will resist as best she can, but for all sorts of reasons her best is not good enough. First off, she is poor, and second, she is *coquette*…She has the curiosity to know and the desire to have: a bagatelle, a bauble, a ribbon…The modest workingwoman gives in one night. In a dark alley, she slips through a half-open door into a disreputable house…She will not come out again.[104]

Restaurant dining again figures as a gateway temptation leading inexorably to desires for fine things, a seduction, and, in short order, moral ruin. Like many fiction writers and midinette enthusiasts, Benoist's inquiry knits together this imaginary workingwoman's meager diet and her supposed *coquetterie*—and conflates hunger and acquisitiveness as the cause of her fall. The very tone of the passage echoes the melodramatic narrative of much midinette fiction—a virtuous but dreamy working-class girl, a gallant encounter, a dark alleyway.

Benoist returns to the restaurant later in his study, reiterating the inevitability of workingwomen's fall after exposure to its temptations. Once these women have

[103] Haussonville, *Salaires et misères de femmes*, 21.
[104] Benoist, *Les Ouvrières de l'aiguille*, 118–20.

the occasion "to lose themselves, they are lost: and such an occasion is offered them at least once a day. Where then? They tell you themselves: at the dive restaurant [*la gargote*]!"[105] Benoist investigates a *gargote* on his own one afternoon, employing the lurid tones of a *feuilleton* [serial fiction]: "In the Paris of elegance, one hundred feet from the Madeleine, a boutique painted bright red. First, we see a room where a fat man with a hoarse voice and an apoplectic expression reigns over the gleaming zinc counter. At the back, a second room, from which curls acrid smoke, part grease and part pipe, a thick bluish vapor that clings to you as soon as you enter."[106] Benoist climbs to the second floor where he finds workingwomen ordering their "semblance of a lunch," all with the "same monotone and weary tone": "if they eat, it is either nothing or less than nothing. The worst poison at the *gargote* does not affect the stomach. Here, in this kind of private dining room, there were no masons or carpenters, as there were downstairs. There were only gentlemen, and what gentlemen!"[107] On the very next page, Benoist conjures an imagined milliner: "Hunger does not move her and she waits. While waiting, she calculates...three hundred francs per month, an apartment and furnishings. Neither perversity nor passion. Business and, in a manner of speaking, an 'installation.' She adds a liaison to the daily routine of her life, without missing a step, like a flower or a feather on a hat..."[108] The fall of this fictive hatmaker is not brought on by "material misery," but by an attachment to fine things. Benoist quotes an unnamed male expert on the subject: "It is not the insufficiency of salary that leads the workingwomen astray, but the taste for fashion [*le goût de la toilette*], the reading of *feuilletons*, the close quarters of the workshop, bad behavior, and the relaxation of family control. She is corrupted by the very air she breathes. If she earned 6 francs instead of 1 fr. 50, she wouldn't become corrupted any less quickly."[109] Later, Benoist places hunger and moral frivolity on a comparable plane of social priority when examining the degradation of the garment trade worker: "one must first combat hunger, then vanity [*la coquetterie*], vanquishing in the workingwoman both the human animal and the woman. One must drive Paris out of Paris, deprive the street of all its temptations."[110] The Parisian street was the site and origin of these women's seemingly inescapable moral ruin, and the lunch hour the critical space in which their (very literary) fall began: "There, in the street, the novel opens that will draw to a close at the wine bar."[111] Workingwomen's lunchrooms appear in Benoist's study, then, as a weapon against sexual and moral temptation, not simply or even primarily as a space for affordable meals: "'Ah! The gargote!' as they told us! Against it, at least, we are not disarmed! From now on, we can set the Restaurants d'ouvrières against it... Workingwomen find there wholesome, nicely prepared food at a modest price,

---

[105] Ibid. 123. [106] Ibid. 123–4. [107] Ibid. 124. [108] Ibid. 125. [109] Ibid. 127.
[110] Ibid. 143. [111] Ibid. 143–4.

an undoctored drink; there they are sheltered from disagreeable encounters..."[112] Thus, reform-oriented social scientific inquiries, like their pop cultural contemporaries, seemed unable to avoid imagining garment workers' lives in melodramatic and romantic literary terms.

Seamstress and labor activist Jeanne Bouvier confirmed the stereotype of the midinette who cut food costs in favor of fashion: "Lunch was often reduced to its simplest expression...in order to achieve the necessary sum for the purchase of this or that fashion accessory...They impose a severe diet on themselves in order to be beautiful." The result was anemia, tuberculosis, and a high mortality rate in the garment industry. But rather than moralizing judgment, Bouvier explained the acculturation from which this situation arose, placing garment workers from their childhood in the heart of a nationally-significant craft. Because midinettes had handled and made "luxury objects" from a young age as apprentices, it was natural that they would be invested in French fashionability: "They grow up in this speciality of the clothing industry, one of the glories of our national industry. How could they not love finery, beautiful gowns, good-looking hats, and everything that makes up a woman's wardrobe, when these children become young women while spending all day making dresses to adorn other women!" Rather than pathologizing this interest, Bouvier suggests, "If midinettes had a better salary, they could dress themselves without cutting down on their food."[113] She did, however, make a point of informing readers that, unlike the average midinette, she had sensibly saved for a small house in the country upon her retirement, not dresses or hats.

Syndicalist Marcelle Capy provided a pragmatic explanation for garment workers' under-eating in favor of fashion which was nonetheless nearly absent from most discussions: the importance of being well-dressed to one's employment in a fashion house. A "badly dressed" midinette "is not accepted by the bosses." Midinettes were also, Capy pointed out, the seamstress and hatmaker for their families. Capy interviewed a young woman in a major Parisian couture house who explained that she meticulously planned her clothing purchases around end of season sales. But because she left work each day once stores were already closed, and stores were also closed on Sundays, she had no choice but to sacrifice most of her lunch hour to shopping: "Instead of eating enough...she snacked on some fruits and charcuterie and ran to the sales."[114]

---

[112] Ibid. 144. As W. Scott Haine demonstrates, many workingwomen met their future spouses at Paris cafés. Haine suggests that bourgeois and working-class attitudes about women's presence in spaces like cafés diverged; workers generally did not view the café as a place of moral danger for respectable workingwomen. W. Scott Haine, *The World of the Parisian Café: Sociability among the French Working Class, 1789–1914* (Baltimore, 1996); and "Privacy in public: comportment of working-class women in late nineteenth-century Parisian proletarian cafés," *Proceedings of the Annual Meeting of the Western Society of French History* 14 (1987).

[113] Bouvier, *Mes Mémoires*, 97.

[114] Marcelle Capy, "La Midinette et la semaine anglaise," *La Bataille syndicaliste* (26 May 1914), 3.

Some union organizers suggested a different danger for lunching midinettes. In a March 1901 meeting of the Commission départementale du travail de la Seine, Clémence Jusselin reported that a recent garment strike had failed, in part, because certain employers had forced their workers to eat in their workshops (some even providing lunch and a small daily raise for those women who remained), in order to "prevent workingwomen from coming into contact with strikers."[115] Indeed, police reports throughout this period indicated that the lunch hour was a key moment for agents' surveillance of workingwomen and their possible contacts with labor agitators.[116] During garment trade strikes in 1917, the Préfecture de Police conducted surveillance of restaurants frequented by midi-nettes, using police spies to assess the influence of syndicalizing "young men" on the lunching workingwomen.[117]

By the last years of World War I, despite a profusion of reportage and fiction denying hunger in the garment trades, female garment workers demanded increased lunch allowances and lunch facilities throughout the various strikes in their trade from 1901 to 1917. The organ of the hatmakers' union, *L'Ouvrier Chapelier*, published a letter from a milliner at the Maison Lewis in 1914 recount-ing the appalling lunch conditions at her workshop, and the way that lunch reform was often more concerned with controlling midinettes during their breaks than providing a sustaining meal:

> The house provides lunch, but in such a deplorable and insufficient fashion that everyone is obliged to buy themselves something else with their own money and at exorbitant prices...Lunch is obligatory for everyone and no one can leave during those hours...The salaries are pathetically low; a very good *ouvrière* can earn 60 to 75 francs a month."[118]

This garment worker counters visions of a gaily under-eating midinette, placing the blame for deficient meals squarely on workers' meager salaries, rather than girlish lack of appetite or fashionable outlay. Workingwomen's solutions to their

---

[115] "Séance du 22 mars 1901," *La Question des veillées*, 28. Worth took exception to Jusselin's report, insisting that workingwomen could meet union representatives at other times than lunch, and boasted that his workers had "non seulement des réfectoires, mais encore des femmes, payées par la maison, et le materiel spécial pour faire cuire les aliments qu'elles apportent avec elle" (pp. 36–7).

[116] Report from the Chef du Service des Renseignements Généraux to the Préfet de Police, 29 Sept. 1917, "Au sujet de lettres anonymes adressées à des ouvrières des Maisons 'LAROCHE' et 'MORIN.'" APPP BA 1376 Grèves de l'habillement, 1917 à 1918.

[117] Report from the Ministre de l'Intérieur (Direction de la Sûreté Générale) to Préfet de Police, Paris, 11 Sept. 1917, No. 2432. BA 1376. One report referenced a 16-year-old female embroiderer who witnessed young men trying to convince workingwomen at restaurants to strike. Report from the Chef du Service des Renseignements Généraux to the Préfet de Police, "Au sujet d'une certaine effer-vescence qui se serait manifestée parmi les midinettes: modistes, brodeuses, couturières, travaillant dans le quartier de l'Opéra," 28 Sept. 1917. BA 1376.

[118] "Chez les modistes," *L'Ouvrier Chapelier*, 1 May 1914. The letter was penned, according to edi-tors, by "une de nos actives camarades du Syndicat" at the Maison Lewis.

lunchtime difficulties also could differ from those envisioned by philanthropists. In 1920, garment workers in the city's center sent numerous petitions to the municipal council asking that chairs in Paris's public gardens and parks be made free for workingwomen during the lunch hour, so that they could enjoy fresh air and rest their legs while eating lunch.[119] Two years later, when the municipal council at last voted to make this change, songwriter and playwright Hugue Delorme could not resist memorializing the decision in a sentimental poem, "Le Repas des Midinettes," employing now decades-old clichés about garment worker under-eating, tastefulness, and flirtation.[120]

When workingwomen in the Parisian garment trades took to the streets in these years (events explored in the next chapter), even the socialist press leavened these women's militancy by recycling the image of the cheerily lunching midinette. During the "grève des midinettes" of September 1910, several newspapers described the striking women as carefree lunchers, even though one of the garment workers' primary demands that year was a longer lunch break, "an hour being too short a time for those who could not go to a restaurant."[121] During a significant garment trade strike in May 1917, *L'Humanité* tagged the popular trope of the lunching midinette:

Noon.

A long cortege advances along the *grands boulevards*. It is the midinettes of Paris, with their blouses adorned with lilacs and lilies of the valley. They run, they jump, they sing, they laugh. And yet, this is neither the feast of Sainte-Catherine nor the Mi-Carême: it is the strike.[122]

Thus, this socialist newspaper views female labor militancy in the Parisian garment trades through an unmistakably nostalgic lens.

Other socialist journalists played up the allegedly novel activism of female garment trade workers by suggesting that the romantic image of the under-eating *midinette* was outdated. In May 1917, one left-leaning journalist, remarked the successful strikes in the garment trades that spring:

This is no longer the time when Jenny l'Ouvrière and Mimi Pinson contented themselves with a lunch comprised of a cone of fries and a dinner of a cutlet of

---

[119] "Renvoi à la 3e Commission et à l'Administration, avec avis favorable, d'une proposition de M. Luquet tendant à assurer au public à certaines heures la disposition gratuite des chaises des squares et promenades," *Bulletin municipal officiel de la Ville de Paris*, 27 Dec. 1921, pp. 5341–2.
[120] "Résolution relative à la gratuité des sieges...," *Bulletin municipal officiel de la Ville de Paris*, 24 June 1922, pp. 2752–3; Hugues Delorme, "Le Repas des midinettes," *Les annales politiques et littéraires: revue populaire*, 9 July 1922, p. 35.
[121] "Un meeting à la Bourse du Travail," *L'Action*, 17 Jan. 1910.
[122] "La Grève des midinettes parisiennes," *L'Humanité*, 16 May 1917.

brie seasoned with a couple of sentimental refrains from the "masterpieces" of
Paul Delmet or some other equally mushy novelist.

The war, which has changed many things, modified all of that.

And it is not a pity.[123]

This passage seems to do several things at once. It applauds the newfound activism of workingwomen in the garment trades, but also does so by reaffirming a romantic vision of these women as formerly frivolous (reading popular romantic literature, singing, not striking, under-eating). The author uses the literary archetypes of Jenny l'Ouvrière and Mimi Pinson as a useful reference for readers to place the current labor unrest in its proper historical context—midinettes once were flippant and unengaged; since the war, they no longer accept their exploitation. This is a pointed example of the way that the midinette archetype could bolster and obscure political action—here, the striking garment workers are depicted as heroically overcoming their historic lethargy, giving the 1917 actions increased weight while eclipsing the very real contributions of female labor activists in the decade before and ignoring the role that such images might indeed have played in suppressing garment trade activism in years past.

The lunching midinette was an especially potent and commercially attractive version of the *femme nouvelle*: a young woman who bolstered the consumer economy with both her labor and her acquisitiveness, and who did so by a seemingly effortless denial of troubling female hunger and desire. The preceding analysis suggests the way that the ubiquitous appearance of an adorably under-eating young workingwoman might have somewhat neutered the perceived threat of working (female) bodies across the political spectrum at precisely a time when visions of proletarian misery were poised to bring significant change in France. Focus on the moral perils of the lunch hour, while grounded in a picturesque fantasy of the midinette, also may have made female labor militancy more palatable. By 1917, many employers had begun providing midday meals for their employees, indicating some progress in this regard since the first significant midinette strikes in 1901.[124] Nonetheless, garment strikes that May saw Parisian workingwomen demanding a longer lunch hour as well as salary supplements for workers who chose to eat outside of the workshop.[125] In the fall of 1918, striking midinettes successfully militated for the establishment of government-sponsored cooperative restaurants—justified not as moral protection for midinettes, but as a consequence of rising food prices. Pierre Dumas, secretary of the Fédération de

---

[123] "Les Grèves féminines parisiennes: et on s'en fout...On f'ra la s'maine anglaise," *La Bataille syndicaliste*, 24 May 1917. AN F/22/170. Lunch and lunch allowances were raised during these strikes. Paul Delmet (1862–1904) was a turn-of-the-century composer of popular Parisian songs.
[124] Ibid., press clipping.   [125] "Les Grèves," *Le Temps*, 24 May 1917.

l'Habillement, told the assembled garment workers that this success emanated from the "action you have led," as well as that "Public opinion will no longer have before its eyes the distressing sight of workingwomen eating their noon meal on a bench with a sandwich."[126] The next chapter takes the increased midinette labor militancy of these years as its focus.

---

[126] "Grève dans l'industrie du vêtement," 23 Sept. 1918; "Réunion des ouvriers grévistes de la grande couture et de la broderie, Salle Ferrer à la Bourse du Travail, le 12 Octobre matin," 12 Oct. 1918. BA 1376.

5

"They are nothing but birdbrains!"

The Midinette on Strike, 1901–1919

In August 1923, *Le Quotidien*'s Jean Perrigault remarked a startling transformation in the Parisian workingwoman:

> Mademoiselle Pinson is no longer the *grisette* of 1845...Mademoiselle Mimi no longer wants to die "unknown on the fifth floor, between a flower pot and a hem, after having pawned her dress for four francs and having made a shawl out of a curtain"...Mademoiselle Mimi-Pinson has joined a union and has gotten organized: Musset would not recognize her...[1]

Perrigault presents an appealing image. In the midst of stark social change following World War I, the garment workers of Paris have, after almost eighty years, shaken off melodramatic romance to attend to their plight as laborers. And yet by 1923, in reality, the workingwomen of Parisian couture had been striking, spectacularly and successfully, for more than two decades. From 1901, the Parisian clothing trades had seen a remarkable escalation of labor activism and subsequent legislative reform driven by and on behalf of the more than 80,000 women working in the capital's couture industry. Time and again (in 1901, 1908, 1910, 1911, 1916, 1917, 1918, and 1919), the midinettes of Paris walked out of their shops and took to the boulevards in work stoppages that captured unprecedented media attention and garnered meaningful gains for garment workers across the city. Perrigault's belated recognition of midinette militancy was typical of much of the public reaction to garment labor campaigns in these years, which took in the strikes as an amusing urban spectacle emptied of political meaning. Indeed, French journalists, government officials, and labor leaders alike promoted a romantic and infantilizing vision of the female garment *grévistes* as insouciant girls in need of paternal care (whether of the state, *syndicat*, or reforming bourgeoisie), and replicated the pervasive belle époque type of the midinette. In the face of debilitating and at times violent strikes in the heavily feminine garment trades, an image of the female Parisian fashion worker as charmingly capricious and pleasure-loving persisted.

---

[1] Jean Perrigault, "Un Voyage de Mimi Pinson," *Le Quotidien*, 27 Aug. 1923. FC, No. 458. *Le Quotidien* was an interwar leftist newspaper. See François Dubasque, "*Le Quotidien* (1923–1936), instrument de conquête électorale et relais d'influence," *Le Temps des médias* 1, No. 12 (2009), 187–202.

Working Girls: Sex, Taste, and Reform in the Parisian Garment Trades, 1880–1919. Patricia Tilburg, Oxford University Press (2019). © Patricia Tilburg.
DOI: 10.1093/oso/9780198841173.001.0001

This chapter assesses the symbolic work performed by such a persistence, and also attends to the voices of workingwomen who lamented the condescension of strike coverage and stressed their own demands and experience. In tracing the discursive work of the midinette as type, this chapter draws upon archival material from the Préfecture de Police de Paris, trade union journals, cartoons, workers' memoirs, labor reform inquiries, songs, novels, and newspapers. The aestheticization of workingwomen by way of the midinette was a rhetorical flourish that had real consequences for the handling of garment trade militancy by the press, politicians, police, labor leaders, and couture workers themselves. It also framed the evolution of a new brand of militant midinette over the course of these strikes, workingwomen who at once defied and deployed popular perceptions of the midinette to win unprecedented workplace reforms.

Workers in the Parisian needle trades began to unionize in the 1860s, and by the 1890s female couture workers were creating their own organizations and were pushing to become a more significant presence in male-dominated unions.[2] Women made up a small percentage of unionized workers in France in the early twentieth century, varying between 4 and 21 per cent in any year (despite making up about 36 per cent of the working population).[3] Despite consistently low rates of women's syndicalization, the number of unionized female workers tripled from 1900 to 1911; union participation in general only doubled in those same years.[4] These same years saw the creation of 131 women-only unions, bringing the total to 162, and membership in these groups quintupled.[5] As Madeleine Guilbert has shown, female strikers were more vulnerable to firing during strikes, and had fewer resources to sustain themselves during work stoppages than their male counterparts.[6] Nonetheless, the belle époque saw notable women-only strikes which drew special interest from the press and from syndical leaders.[7]

The first widely-publicized and significant strike in Parisian couture occurred in 1901, when thousands of tailors and seamstresses left their workshops for more than a month to protest abusive piecework practices. The strike meetings held at the Bourse du Travail were regularly attended by 1,800–2,000 female

[2] Crowston, *Fabricating Women*, 394–5. Also Marie-Hélène Zylberberg-Hocquard, *Féminisme et syndicalisme en France* (Paris, 1978) and *Femmes et féminisme dans le mouvement ouvrier français* (Paris, 1981); Patricia Hilden "Women and the labour movement in France, 1869–1914," *The Historical Journal* 29, No. 4 (1986), 809–32; Coffin, *The Politics of Women's Work*. During the July Monarchy, striking garment workers were greeted with references to their youth and prettiness. DeGroat, "The public nature of women's work"; DeGroat, "Women in the Paris manufacturing trades."

[3] Zylberberg-Hocquard, *Femmes et féminisme*, 108–12. A consistent strike movement only came with the legalization of syndical activity in 1884.

[4] Madeleine Guilbert, *Les Femmes et l'organisation syndicale avant 1914* (Paris, 1966), 28.

[5] Zylberberg-Hocquard, *Féminisme et syndicalisme*, 207.

[6] Guilbert, *Les Femmes et l'organisation* syndicale, 225–8. See also Michelle Perrot, *Les Femmes, ou les silences de l'Histoire*, 127.

[7] Guilbert, *Les Femmes et l'organisation syndicale*, 231.

needleworkers, including a number who took to the tribune as orators.[8] Judith Coffin mentions that during this strike, a generally sympathetic press focused on the romantic figure of the seamstress as a pretty guardian of French artistry against "foreign" influences. The anti-Semitic press particularly emphasized the insidious role of Jewish manufacturers and immigrant contractors and piece-workers in exploiting the midinette.[9] By the end of the strike in 1901, Nancy Green has shown, several hundred immigrant tailors either left France or remained unemployed; the government applauded this outcome as an opportunity to replace immigrant men with Frenchwomen.[10] Nonetheless, as Coffin points out, the 1901 strike was something of a failure for female workers, whose grievances overall lost out to those of striking tailors; however, it was still a "benchmark of a shifting politics of protest in the clothing trades."[11] The next watershed in midi-nette militancy came in 1910. That July, several hundred women walked off the job at the men's clothier Maison Esders and were followed in the months to come by thousands in a strike lasting into October. That action launched a series of rolling strikes in the Parisian clothing trades throughout 1910 and 1911, and women made up a majority of the strikers (as opposed to 1901).[12]

In the last years of World War I, Parisian garment workers once again took to the streets in considerable numbers; wartime labor strikes in 1916, 1917, and 1918, according to Yves Pourcher, seemed to crack "the lovely social edifice" of the *union sacrée*.[13] In May 1917, seamstresses at the Maison Jenny seeking the *semaine anglaise* (mandating Saturday afternoons off) and a raise sparked a strike that spread rapidly to some 20,000 workingwomen across the garment industry, including hosiery, embroidery, hatmaking, fur, leather, artificial flowers, and feather work. The midinettes were victorious in relatively short order, returning to work by the end of May with the concession of the English week. In the month that followed, tens of thousands more male and female workers struck across numerous industries, including impressive and violent strikes of female munitions workers, the so-called "munitionettes." The spring 1917 strikes were notable for their "spontaneity"; the majority of actions were not launched by the *syndicats*.[14] In March 1918, Parisian *confectionneuses*, women working in mass-produced ready-to-wear operations across the city, walked out once again, demanding a minimum wage and a cost-of-living allowance. That September and October, Parisian midinettes took to the streets once more to demand the eight-hour day. All told, 1918 saw 42,000 workers on strike in and around Paris, 90 per cent of

---

[8]   Ibid. 239.

[9]   Coffin, *The Politics of Women's Work*, 178–81. See also, Green, *Ready-to-Wear*, 86.

[10]   Green, *The Pletzl of Paris*, 130.   [11]   Coffin, *The Politics of Women's Work*, 181.

[12]   See press clippings in AN F-7-13740. Coffin, *The Politics of Women's Work*, 182.

[13]   Yves Pourcher, *Les Jours de guerre: la vie des Français au jour le jour entre 1914 et 1918* (Paris, 1994) 225.

[14]   Jean-Louis Robert, *Les Ouvriers*, 137.

them women.[15] The following spring, in 1919, midinettes joined 500,000 striking workers in May and June, almost half of them in the department of the Seine.[16]

Belle époque and wartime strikes in Parisian couture often took place simultaneously with strikes in other French industries, though these strikes did not elicit the same nostalgia-tinged lyricism as the *grèves des midinettes*. A major strike by miners in Montceau-les-Mines made front-page headlines the same week as the seamstresses' strike of February 1901. Strikes by railway workers in 1910 led to the imprisonment of hundreds of union leaders, and the firing of thousands more.[17] This was a moment of extraordinarily intense labor activism across French industry, and women played significant roles in many mixed-sex strike actions.[18] Yet, as Guilbert shows, the belle époque socialist and syndicalist press often failed to even mention the female presence in strikes like those in the textile industry in 1902 and 1904 in which women represented more than half of the strikers.[19] Delighted representations of the midinette strikes in those same years must be read against this backdrop.

Paris's midinette strikes were consistently treated as a thing apart, by labor partisans and by law enforcement. Reporting on midinette strikes in the major Parisian dailies tended to be grouped alongside *chroniques théâtrales* and *fait divers*, rather than with front-page coverage of strikes in other industries and sober political analysis. The midinette strikes of 1901 and 1910 appeared later in each edition of *Le Temps* than reporting on other "syndicalist agitation," often on the front page.[20] Thus, while there were numerous plainly defined unions across Parisian couture who were in concert and competition with other male-dominated unions, the socialist and mainstream press created the category of the midinette strike, setting coverage of Parisian garment workers apart from other strike reporting in this period.

This chapter reads the midinette strike fantasy as a case study of discourse in action. The midinette type was maintained and even flourished in the face of disparate working conditions and demands, unprecedented women's labor action, and the feminization of French industry during the war. The astonishing continuity of strike imagery from the modest if highly publicized seamstress strike of 1901 to the turbulent mass strikes of the war years is worth interrogating. This is not merely a study of representations, but of the interaction between this type and the workings of power on the ground in crucial moments of labor activism. The persistence of this symbolic system in the face of the tremendous changes in French industry in these years offers a measure of its cultural import as a mechanism for

---

[15] Gérard Noiriel, *Workers in French Society in the 19th and 20th Centuries* (New York, 1990), 143.
[16] Stovall, *Paris and the Spirit of 1919*, 257.
[17] Magraw, *A History of the French Working Class*, 50, 52.
[18] Noiriel, *Workers in French Society*, 73.
[19] Guilbert, *Les Femmes et l'organisation syndicale*, 396–7.
[20] See, for example, *Le Temps*, 30 Aug. 1910.

apprehending social change. This chapter also reveals that many midinettes were active in both promoting and resisting this cultural code.

The midinette strikes appear frequently in histories of the belle époque and of the French working class as atmospheric sidenotes, but no sustained cultural history of the *grèves des midinettes* exists. The profits of such a study are twofold. On one hand, my analysis posits the midinette ideal as an effective balm to the growing pains of French industrial capitalism. Women in the garment trades were, after all, in Lenard Berlanstein's words, on the "unenviable cutting edge of sweated conditions," and "among the first to experience competition from factory methods."[21] My investigation also furthers excellent scholarship unpacking the long and tumultuous history of workingwomen's place in male-led French syndical organizations, which tended to see low-paid female workers as a threat to male labor. Patricia Hilden and others have traced the deep hostility, "antifeminism," and, at best, paternalism, which dominated male labor leaders' attitudes toward workingwomen throughout the late nineteenth and early twentieth century, and the silencing of activist women in these circles.[22]

Decades of agitation in the clothing trades did finally bring concrete reforms, with the passing of a minimum wage law for homework in 1915, the establishment of the *semaine anglaise* in 1917, and the institution of an eight-hour work day in 1919.[23] More recent scholarship suggests that the midinette strikes were fundamental in transforming modern French labor relations. For Claude Didry, Parisian midinettes were a "forgotten avant-garde of the proletariat," and their wartime strikes a turning point, "in which the midinette movement led to laws that inaugurated the fundamental mechanism of collective bargaining in France."[24] As such, it is all the more pressing that historians take seriously the cultural phenomenon of the *midinette en grève*.

"The Beautiful Strike"

The major Parisian dailies of these years greeted protests by striking Parisian garment workers with amusement, and as a captivating and mostly innocuous urban spectacle.[25] Garment workers in Paris tended to strike in their best clothes, and many of them (though certainly not all) were young and unmarried. According

---

[21] Lenard Berlanstein, *The Working People of Paris, 1871–1914* (Baltimore, 1984), 90.

[22] Rebérioux, *La République radicale?*, 171. Hilden, "Women and the labour movement in France," and *Working Women and Socialist Politics in France, 1880–914* (Oxford, 1986); Guilbert, *Les Femmes et l'organisation syndicale*; Zylberberg-Hocquard, *Féminisme et syndicalisme* and *Femmes et feminisme*.

[23] Green, *Ready-to-Wear*, 83–4.

[24] Didry, "Les Midinettes, avant-garde oubliée du prolétariat," 79. Guilbert also suggests that women's participation in belle époque strikes shifted the relationship between syndicalist organizations and women (*Les Femmes et l'organisation syndicale*, 243–4).

[25] Stovall points out that Haussmannization made the Parisian streets a compelling stage for spectacular protest (*Paris and the Spirit of 1919*, 155).

to Crowston, this "paradoxical combination of intrinsic femininity with organized militancy" had been a feature of seamstress activism since the late seventeenth century, though belle époque observers did not make this connection.[26] The Parisian garment strikes of these years were often visually distinctive from labor protests in other industries. This chapter assesses how this distinctiveness was read and understood by those who commented upon the strikes.

Across the political spectrum, commentators remarked the attractiveness, youth, and charm of striking midinettes. *Le Temps*'s drama critic Adolphe Brisson visited a strike meeting at the Bourse du Travail in February 1901 to observe the "demoiselles en grève," after having been convinced to attend by a seamstress.[27] He witnessed a vote: "800 little hands are raised. Oh! The surprising spectacle! 800 quivering hands, some gloved...hands of ingenious Cinderellas, little Parisian fairies."[28] The strike meeting was, above all, a scene of gaiety: "They laugh, they chat. These demoiselles have come here in little groups, like a pleasure outing. It amuses them, to occupy the audience with themselves and to wave the flag of social revolution."[29] Marie-Louise Néron for *La Fronde* remarked that Parisians saluted a group of striking seamstresses on the boulevard, "heading off arm in arm, laughing, prattling away" like "a flight of startled sparrows," with sympathetic cries of "Vivent les couturières!"[30]

Coverage of the "beautiful strike"[31] of summer 1910 made reference to the "valiant female strikers,"[32] to their "beautiful bravado,"[33] "our midinettes...a lovely racket,"[34] "little girls...our sweet female strikers,"[35] "our amiable strikers,"[36] "these young girls so dignified, so graceful, so firm, so courageous...these brave, valiant little sisters."[37] The republican-socialist newspaper *L'Aurore* described the strike (in an ironically-titled article "Midinettes révolutionnaires") as bringing together about a hundred "chatty and amused young women" at the Bourse du Travail. Far from an unnerving proletariat menace, the garment workers are, as usual, the object of urban *flânerie*: "The curious and the gawkers laugh at this feminist action that we don't even know how to take seriously."[38] *Le Petit Parisien* related an amusing anecdote in which "a young and charming *blondinette* with an alert

---

[26] Crowston, *Fabricating Women*, 395.

[27] Adolphe Brisson, "Promenades et visites: ces demoiselles en grève," *Le Temps* (13 Feb. 1901), 2.

[28] Ibid.   [29] Ibid.

[30] Marie-Louise Néron, "Physionomie de la grève," *La Fronde* (13 Feb. 1901), 1–2. Néron repeated an almost identical scene in "Physionomie de la grève," *La Fronde* (15 Feb. 1901), 1–2.

[31] *L'Humanité*, 28 July 1910.

[32] "Victoire de femmes: la grève de la Maison Esders," *Voix du Peuple*, 7 Aug. 1910.

[33] J. Morin, "La Grève des confectionneuses," *L'Action*, 18 Aug. 1910.

[34] "Les 'Midinettes' continuent à manifester," *Le Petit Parisien*, 3 Sept. 1910.

[35] "La Grève des confectionneuses: le public protège les femmes contre la police," *L'Humanité*, 4 Sept. 1910.

[36] "Grève de la Maison Reaumur: pas des défaillances à enregistrer," *L'Humanité*, 6 Sept. 1910.

[37] Elisabeth Fuss-Amoré, "La Grève des confectionneuses: un bon exemple à suivre," *L'Humanité*, 21 Sept. 1910.

[38] "Midinettes révolutionnaires," *L'Aurore* (19 Aug. 1910), 3.

expression" stood on a table at the Bourse du Travail and gave an impromptu concert for the strike committee. The "fillette" regaled her listeners with pleasant popular songs—"*Petit Panier, Et autre chose aussi,* and *la Valse brune*"—and was joined by other "Mimi Pinsons." A striking pipe fitter in the crowd applauded and sang out, "You are so pretty!"[39] The decorative prettiness and joviality of the midinettes lighten the somber mood of the strike (at least for the *Petit Parisien*'s readers) and transform the union hall into a site of feminine song and flirtation rather than proletarian anger.

During the couture strikes of May 1917, journalists referred to protesting work-ingwomen as a "joyous troupe," "amiable strikers,"[40] and "our midinettes...the bataillon of 'lady combatants' with the bodices bedecked with innocent *muguet* or fresh lilacs...our fairies of the needle."[41] *Le Petit Parisien* saluted "the courage and tenacity of the little 'revoltées'" and noted that passers-by "amusedly watched the lovely *tapageuses*."[42] *Le Figaro*'s Alfred Capus deemed the striking midinettes "these little Parisiennes who remain so friendly to us and to whom one must at all costs restore their smiles and confidence in life."[43] Repeatedly specified as young, beautiful, and joyous in the press, the strikers also were more often labeled with diminutive, general, and plural terms—*midinettes, cousettes, fées de l'aiguille* (fairies of the needle)—than with a precise profession (hatmaker, fur worker, flowerworker, seamstress).

Coverage of midinette strikes consistently played off the reputation of midinettes as objects of erotic delectation rather than determined militants. The cover image of *Le Rire* from 2 March 1901, "La Grève des couturières," shows an exasperated male union leader trying to hold a vote. Before him, a sea of upstretched, disembod-ied female legs wave in colorful stockings and boots amidst a sea of frilly petticoats, while he shouts, "I asked you for a vote by raised hands..."[44] (Figure 5.1). The image provides its presumably mostly male bourgeois readership with a group of striking workers who are nothing but shapely body parts, quite incapable of coordinated syndical action. While feminist Marie Bonnevial reported the same week that the needleworkers new to syndical action conducted themselves "like old militants," this cartoon is more representative of reporting on the seamstress strike.

Brisson's chronicle of a visit to the Bourse du Travail during the same strike vividly detailed one *gréviste*'s physical appeal and fashionability:

> Mlle Louison doesn't seem to have suffered too much from patronal tyranny. She wears a dress of blue serge that tightly clings to her waist, a bolero jacket that makes the promise of her bust jut out in the friendliest fashion. She has jewelry,

[39] "Grève de Midinettes: Mimi-Pinson chante...le 'Petit Panier' et l'"Internationale'," *Le Petit Parisien*, 30 Aug. 1910.
[40] "La Grève des midinettes parisiennes," *L'Humanité*, 16 May 1917.
[41] "La Grève des midinettes," *Le Petit Parisien*, 17 May 1917.   [42] Ibid.
[43] Alfred Capus, "Le Gouvernement et les grèves," *Le Figaro* (27 May 1917), 1.
[44] Willette, "La Grève des couturières," *Le Rire*, 2 Mar. 1901 (cover).

Figure 5.1. Willette, "La Grève des couturières," *Le Rire*, 2 March 1901.

furs, wavy strawberry blond hair—adorned by this warm color in which art plays more of a role than nature. Her eyes are caressing and bright, her lips painted. Mlle Louison is ravishing.[45]

Louison's attractiveness is a put-on, consumer purchases of hair dye, make-up, and clothing designed to beguile men like Brisson; it also diminishes any claim

---

[45] Brisson, "Promenades et visites," 2.

she might have to patronal abuse. Later, Brisson observes that Louison is "extremely amused" by a female orator's speech entreating that "woman must unite with man": "[Louison's] mouth opens like a flowering pomegranate revealing appetizing teeth, snow-white teeth. She evidently shares the same convictions on the union of the sexes as the honorable previous speaker."[46] Brisson neuters the political intent of the orator's speech, reducing her rhetoric to sexual innuendo, and focuses attention back on the enticing sexuality (and political vapidity) of the midinette.

Cartoons from the 1910 strikes almost a decade later similarly eroticized striking garment workers. In September 1910, the satirical magazine *L'Assiette au Beurre* dedicated an issue to "Les Midinettes Révolutionnaires," and the majority of cartoons, all by Maurice Radiguet, derided the strikers as promiscuous flirts. The cover image depicted a female garment worker mounting a staircase, waving a red flag (Figure 5.2). She begins to speak, but is interrupted by a burly laborer standing below:

—And when the Great Evening [*Grand Soir*][47] comes...

—Shut up, Mimi! When the Great Evening comes, I know you... you'll go sleep with a grand bourgeois!

L'Assiette au Beurre was a leftist satirical magazine, critical of the government, and supportive of anarcho-syndical causes, workers' rights, and, in principle, sexual liberation (though generally anti-feminist).[48] Radiguet depicts the Parisian midinette as entirely incapable of serious militancy, so susceptible was she to sexual dissolution (with bourgeois men and with police) and to the temptations of fashion and urban pleasure. In "L'Agent est bon enfant," several smiling midinettes hang off of two policemen, presumably monitoring the protest (Figure 5.3).

The mustachioed officer in the foreground seems to laugh as he tells the midinettes, "Ladies, if you keep this up, you're going to see some hard ones."[49] The police and the midinettes are shown enjoying this turn of affairs, from possible political violence to flirtatious physical contact. While these very strikes saw violent altercations between garment workers and police, this cartoon reimagines such

[46] Ibid.

[47] The "Grand Soir" was a syndical term referring to the moment when a general strike would signal the dawning of a new society. See Zylberberg-Hocquard, *Femmes et féminisme*, 110.

[48] Patricia Leighten, "The world turned upside down: Modernism and anarchist strategies of inversion in *L'Assiette au beurre*," *Journal of Modern Periodical Studies* 4, No. 2 (2013), 133–70, 142. See also Élisabeth and Michel Dixmier, *L'Assiette au beurre: revue satirique illustrée, 1901–1912* (Paris, 1974); Anne-Marie Bouchard, "'Les Midinettes révolutionnaires': prostitution et Grand Soir dans la presse subversive (1890–1910)," *Médias 19* [online], (2013). The Dixmiers make clear that Radiguet moved toward anti-union imagery in this period, and that the magazine in 1910–12 was interested in depicting the exploitation of workers, while also hostile toward the *syndicats* (pp. 117, 131–3).

[49] Maurice Radiguet, "L'Agent est bon enfant," *L'Assiette au beurre* (17 Sept. 1910), 402.

Figure 5.2. Maurice Radiguet, "Les Midinettes Révolutionnaires," *L'Assiette au Beurre*, 17 September 1910.

scenes as an excess of working-class feminine desire. Some strike reporting mirrored this fantasy. In a May 1917 strike, *Le Temps* featured an interview with a twenty-something garment worker, whose dress "if somewhat worn...did not lack for elegance and showed off her well-shaped and harmonious body." While trying to enter a fashion house to incite more workers to strike, the young woman

Figure 5.3. "L'Agent est bon enfant," *L'Assiette au Beurre*, 17 September 1910.

was detained: "A cop grabbed me by the arm; he had recognized me. We've been going out for some time."[50] As the only striker given a voice in this article, the young woman leaves an impression of midinette militants as pretty coquettes who date rather than battle the police.

[50] J. G., "Les Midinettes à l'assaut," *Le Temps*, 24 May 1917.

Radiguet's 1910 cartoons represented striking midinettes as capricious coquettes more interested in sexual liaisons with upper-class men than with the humble laborers of their own class. In "After the Battle," an elegant midinette leaves a pair of workingmen for a bourgeois dandy, as she tells him, "Just because [the pipe fitters] marched with us during the strike, now they expect us to act like we know them afterwards..."[51] (Figure 5.4). With her ornate feathered hat and stylish hobble skirt, this midinette could easily be mistaken for a bourgeois *dame*, her fashionable garb as much a sign of her lack of commitment to labor's battles as her choice of companion. While other scholars have noted left-leaning observers' suspicion of female labor activism, the actual mechanisms by which this suspicion was deployed have been less well explored. The image of the midinette was one such mechanism—a nostalgic, erotic, and comforting version of working-class female sexuality that could also be used to detach women's labor concerns from the principal agenda of socialist and syndicalist action.[52]

As tensions rose in the 1910 strike, Parisian mass dailies were perplexed by the move from light-hearted singing and flirtation to militancy. They dismissed garment workers' newfound combativeness as feminine emotionalism. On 2 September, *Le Temps* complained that while the Bourse du Travail had been "brightened up... by the songs and speeches" of the midinettes early in the strike, the women now had become "overexcited... like Furies."[53] In an article that same day titled "The Midinettes lose patience," *La Petite République* reminisced fondly about the first days of strike just weeks before when "the young girls had contented themselves with invading the Bourse du Travail each morning and cutting the somewhat arid speech of M. Dumas, secretary of the Fédération de l'Habillement, with joyous songs... Their exit was merry and after a semblance of demonstrations along the boulevards, the young striking women dispersed like a flock of sparrows to return to their maternal abodes."[54] Now, regrettably, the once "so gay" workers were increasingly "nervy"—surely because of their parents' "long faces" when the strikers returned home in the evening. The women are insouciant, childlike, and charmingly inexpert in the ways of syndicalist action ("a semblance of demonstrations"). When they abandon singing gaiety for nervous irritation, this is taken as aberrant but not terribly concerning, and is blamed on parental disapproval, not reasoned political dissent.

Le Matin reported the events of 2 September 1910 with a comparable tone of amused consternation, noting with mock alarm: "The midinettes yesterday

---

[51] Maurice Radiguet, "Après la bataille," *L'Assiette au beurre* (17 Sept. 1910), 415.
[52] See also Bouchard, "'Les Midinettes révolutionnaires,'" 2.
[53] "Les 'Midinettes,'" *Le Temps*, 2 Sept. 1910.
[54] "Les Midinettes perdent patience," *La Petite Republique*, 2 Sept. 1910. The next day, the *Pétite République* saw striking confectionneuses as "de plus en plus suréxcitées." "Les Midinettes s'agitent," *La Pétite République*, 3 Sept. 1910.

Figure 5.4. Maurice Radiguet, "Après la bataille," *L'Assiette au Beurre*, 17 September 1910.

transformed themselves into Amazons. Adieu gaiety! Adieu smiles!" Up to this point, the *confectionneuses* from the Maison Réaumur were happily attending morning meetings at the Bourse du Travail, "notwithstanding the worry that creased their pretty foreheads."[55] But on this day, "the young voices used to cooing 'Caroline! Caroline!'" were instead shrilly chanting the name of their employer. After some brief excitement, five "belligerent midinettes" were taken into custody by the police: "Faced with the fat mustache of the brigadier, their anger cooled; their nerves calmed."[56] The main Parisian dailies portrayed striking couture workers as (mostly) obedient followers of male syndicalists and docile in the face of state authority.

Journalists tended to represent midinette strikers as equipped with little understanding of the stakes or political nuance of their actions. They were carefree "girls" out for a lark, chatting, singing, oblivious to anything approaching syndical solidarity and strategy. In February 1901, *Le Matin* watched several thousand young workingwomen take to the street at lunchtime in an unsuccessful attempt to call out their non-striking sisters: "all the time babbling...they came and went, wandered around, in groups of two, three, five, or six, called to each other, came together, and chatted mostly about anything but the strike."[57] During the wartime May 1917 walk-out, *Le Figaro*'s fashion critic Camille Duguet derided the midinette strike as insufficiently attentive to the dire national context, and blamed the movement on "a number of foreign laborers, either Czech or Polish." She added that "the midinettes might have reflected on the sacrifices heroically made each day by their employers. But did these pretty little birdbrains go to the trouble of even thinking about that? Two drops of protest intoxicate them like champagne."[58]

The 1910 midinette strike made the front page of *Le Temps* only once, and only then as an extraordinary editorial admonishment of the workingwomen's increasing militancy. This front-page piece from 6 September offered no reporting on the strike itself. Instead, it took the strikers to task: "today the same groups of errand girls will trot, little blindly-following sheep, crossing the same streets of the capital; the same boos will be launched under the windows of the recalcitrant employers, the same gibes thrown at their workshop colleagues who have remained loyal producers. And we will record another inefficient and useless demonstration, no longer amusing and curious like on the first day..." While the editors admitted that the midinettes' demands were "perhaps just, even legitimate," the form in which they were presented was "suspect":

The "midinettes" are not made for the street. That they ask for a raise in their salaries, that they exercise their right to strike like other laborers, no one contests that. But they must find a manner of their own to publicize and assert their demands...More than other women, midinettes, in this terrain, lose their charm and their seduction. When their joyful cortege meanders, on Saint Catherine's day, around the streets and intersections of Paris, Parisians applaud, happy to see this promenade "of heart-shaped mouths and pretty smiles"; but when these same mischievous and impish faces become nasty and ill-tempered, when the little

---

[56] Ibid.   [57] "La Journée de la grève," *Le Matin*, 15 Feb. 1901.
[58] Camille Duguet, "Propos féminins," *Le Figaro* (22 May 1917), 3.

hands usually kindly and loyally open close in menacing fists, *voilà*, this is what spoils the landscape and ruins our memories. The "midinettes" should not have the bearing of those ferocious rioters from Germinal; they have nothing in common, moreover, with those women who in Paris, have made the boulevard their home and who vice has made "the bad soul" of the street. The "midinettes" are, on the contrary, the charming soul of the street. They should plead their cause while remaining on the terrain which is properly theirs...[59]

Puckish good fun, banter, charm, and seduction—these are the signs under which the working-class woman is permitted to enter the spectacle of the street. The striking garment workers threaten this urban idyll and their place in it with their untoward political assertiveness—and risk by way of this assertion transforming into rioting viragos or prostitutes.

The reference in the passage above to St Catherine's day was not offhand. Strike reporting often evoked the *fête* of St Catherine (patron saint of hatmakers) when discussing the midinettes *en grève*. A tradition that hailed from the nineteenth century, the St Catherine *fête* was celebrated throughout Paris's couture workshops every 25 November, festive *goûters* during which milliners danced, snacked, and concocted fantastic hats for the unmarried of their group.[60] This tradition, itself the focus of delighted annual press coverage, combined all of the most salient aspects of the midinette type—couture skill, unmarried young women, and workplace gaiety. Journalists, when faced with bands of female garment workers marching about the city, unsurprisingly conjured the Catherinettes, repackaging dissatisfied laborers as reveling bachelorettes.[61]

Le Temps's J.G. rhapsodized at some length about the transformation of the traditional romantic midinette during May 1917 strikes. His whimsical description conveys at once the cultural familiarity of the midinette, and the way this ideal made tolerable garment worker demands. He wrote that he did not recognize the "mobilized midinette...Of course, this name, a familiar diminutive, evokes the bawdy flocks of young girls who, at the strike of noon noisily burst into the streets...like schoolgirls at recess." He pronounces these women a scenic element of the Parisian landscape and a national treasure: "From their skilled hands come the marvels which have assured the good renown of Parisian taste. They are themselves living examples of this supreme taste...They are a part of the physiognomy of Paris, and one of its most original and picturesque features." Disregarding garment strikes in the decade before the war, J.G. reflects, "We used

---

[59] "Aux 'Midinettes,' " *Le Temps*, 6 Sept. 1910.

[60] See Monjaret, "La Sainte-Catherine dans la couture: une fête féminin," *Ethnologie française* 16, No. 4 (Oct.–Dec. 1986), 361–78.

[61] See, for example, references in "Une Grève de couturières," *Petit Parisien*, 26 Nov. 1911; "La Grève des midinettes parisiennes," *L'Humanité*, 16 May 1917.

to say that if they ever went on strike, it could only be a *grève en dentelles*." But after a week of strike, Parisians "now know what a hardy and combative spirit the midinette has when she is ready for battle."[62] Public sympathy for couture workers' demands had been "seduced by the amiable legends, and finally and especially moved at the thought that such beauty had such minimal reward..."[63]

The continuity of clothing trade strike imagery is particularly remarkable during the war, amidst the upheaval of mobilization, the bombardment of the capital, and hundreds of strikes across France (including some by *munitionettes* in 1916 and 1917). The garment industry itself even collapsed for a time. Most small and mid-sized Parisian couture shops laid off all of their workers and closed within days of the declaration of hostilities in August 1914; that month couture and hat-making employed only 16–17 per cent of the previous year's average number of workingwomen.[64] The large couture houses kept their doors open by having the midinettes accept half-pay, "war wages" that continued even after business picked back up in 1915.[65] By the beginning of 1915, many couture houses reopened, but unemployment and under-employment remained high for many garment workers throughout the war.[66] Some found jobs in hospitals, bandage-making, or in weapons manufacturing industries; in the department of the Seine alone, 100,000 women got jobs in metalworking, compared to 8,000–9,000 before the war.[67] The war years overall saw a 100 per cent increase in women's work in Paris, a contrast to other areas of France where women's labor even declined in this same period.[68]

Observers reacted to threats to the *union sacrée* from diverse sectors of the economy, including strikes amongst the relatively well-paid *munitionettes* (some 30,000 female armament workers in the Paris region struck in 1917 alone),[69] by burnishing, rather than reassessing, a nostalgic vision of the Parisian garment worker. Recent scholarship by Tyler Stovall, Laura Lee Downs, and Maude Bass-Krueger reappraises women's wartime strikes, noting, among other things, the way in which the garment strikes were read as "a festive assembly of pretty young women who sang their way into the Ministers'—and the public's—hearts."[70] Both

---

[62] J.G., "Les midinettes à l'assaut," *Le Temps*, 24 May 1917.

[63] "L'Ordre public," *Le Temps*, 29 May 1917. Conversely, popular fiction rarely showed midinettes striking. See Marie-Hélène Zylberberg-Hocquard, "L'Ouvrière dans les romans populaires du XIXe siècle," *Revue du Nord* 63, No. 250 (July–Sept. 1981), 603–36, 632.

[64] Omnès, *Ouvrières parisiennes*, 97.

[65] Maude Bass-Krueger, "From the '*union parfaite*' to the '*union brisée*': the French couture industry and the *midinettes* during the Great War," *Costume* 47, No. 1 (2013), 28–44.

[66] Thébaud, *La Femme au temps de la guerre de 14–18*, 229.

[67] Omnès, *Ouvrières parisiennes*, 97–8.

[68] Jean-Louis Robert, "Women and work in France during the First World War," 257.

[69] Zylberberg-Hocquard, *Femmes et Féminisme*, 140.

[70] Bass-Krueger, "From the '*union parfaite*' to the '*union brisée*'," 30. Stovall, *Paris and the Spirit of 1919*; Downs, "Women's strikes and the politics of popular egalitarianism in France, 1916–1918," in *Rethinking Labor History* (Urbana, 1993), and *Manufacturing Inequality*.

Downs and Stovall observe that the female and more traditionally feminine nature of the garment strikes made them more sympathetic than munitions strikes, including *munitionettes*; Stovall argues for these strikes as a "reshaping" of women's work and of working-class identity in this period.[71] War industry strikes also were covered differently by the press than those in the garment trades because of wartime censorship.[72] Still, the relatively sympathetic treatment of Parisian garment worker protest was embedded in a symbolic system of the midinette that pre-dated the war.

Proof of the national import of this ideal came in the days following the May 1917 garment strike, as the mainstream Parisian dailies hailed the reintegration of the formerly striking midinettes into the Parisian picturesque. As the strike was poised to end on 20 May, *Le Figaro* described "picturesque scenes" at the union hall of the rue Grange-aux-Belles: "*Poilus* on leave found it amusing to mingle with groups of female protesters, singing with them *La Chanson de la Semaine Anglaise* set to the tune of a famous song from the Latin Quarter."[73] A peacefully concluded strike thus hits perfectly complementary notes of national unity and Parisian gaiety. On 4 June, the same week that tens of thousands of metalworkers (the majority of them women) walked out of factories across Paris,[74] *Le Figaro* allotted front-page space to a report by Julien de Narfon on a patriotic prayer service for midinettes at Notre Dame in honor of "France and our armies": "Thus their first 'English week' ended with a very French day, in the highest sense of the word."[75] The cardinal's sermon made oblique reference to the recent strikes in praising the midinettes' youth and "very keen feeling for justice—so keen...that when you believe yourselves victim of some injustice, you sometimes allow yourselves to be carried away in rowdy and foolhardy protests."[76] As strikes proceeded across the country, the midinettes were seen to have recovered from their rash (but successful) moment of militancy and to gather in the city's cathedral to pray for the nation.

Labor and the Striking Midinette

We should not underestimate the power of such images to color and even derail women's labor demands, even within socialist circles. To be sure, some labor

---

[71] Stovall, *Paris and the Spirit of 1919*, 59, 132; Downs, "Women's strikes," 128. Downs touches on contrasting press descriptions of the midinettes and the munitionettes, with garment worker gaiety and femininity opposing munitionettes' violence. See also Michelle Zancarini-Fournel, "Femmes, genre et syndicalisme pendant la Grande Guerre," in *Combats des femmes, 1914–1918: les françaises, pillier de l'effort de guerre* (Paris, 2004), 98–110.

[72] Dubesset et al., "The female munitions workers of the Seine," 203.

[73] "Fin de la grève des midinettes," *Le Figaro*, 20 May 1917.

[74] Downs, "Women's strikes," 130–1.

[75] Julien de Narfon, "Les Midinettes à Notre Dame," *Le Figaro* (4 June 1917), 1.   [76] Ibid.

activists pushed back against the image of the Parisian workingwoman as lacking in the flinty resolve and calculation required in labor negotiations. During the strikes of summer 1910, labor supporters noted that "certain bourgeois newspapers, whose unique role is to denigrate the strike movement and the militants, do not dare to come down against a strike this popular. They find it simpler to instead treat the strike as a simple *amusette* [idle pleasure]." This socialist writer continued with a biting condemnation of the sexual exploitation of midinettes by bourgeois men: "We believed that these hacks might have found funnier subjects than the revolt of unfortunate female slaves who demand a meager salary to support their little families. It's true that this wouldn't serve the needs of well-to-do boys, the little dandies of the bourgeoisie who count on the workingwoman's poverty to make them their playthings."[77] The following week, the garment workers' union issued a frustrated statement: "We are not 'midinettes' simply looking to amuse ourselves, but serious workingwomen who want to earn our living, and earn it by working…"[78]

An editorial from the communist *L'Humanité* that same month took the bourgeois press to task for its coverage of midinette strikes, specifically criticizing *Le Temps* (and quoting from its extraordinary front-page reprimand of garment workers in September 1910). *L'Humanité* reproached *Le Temps's* editors for "only [wishing] to see midinettes in merry little groups—followed no doubt by old *messieurs*":

> This newspaper, ordinarily so serious, allows tasteless jokes at the expense of the *confectionneuses*. [The editor of *Le Temps*] has the good grace to call the midinettes "the charming soul of the street"; but he imagines that this insipid compliment gives him every right, notably that of confounding our *camarades* with street-walkers…and at the very least denying them the opportunity to demand a less brutal existence. He happily consents to see the smile of these women, but refuses to see their suffering.[79]

The corrosive objectification of workingwomen by bourgeois men at once envisages these women as sexually available (even purchasable) and nullifies their political voice. That same week, the Syndicat général de l'Habillement de la Seine placed posters around Paris to counter the denigrating tone of press coverage of the strike:

> For women, mothers, to have left their jobs, they must have had very powerful motives, and we find the jokes of those who represent the strike as an *amusette*

---

[77] "Dans la confection: grève de la Maison Reaumur," *L'Humanité*, 31 Aug. 1910.
[78] "La C.G.T. va 'appuyer' les confectionneuses en greve," *Le Journal*, 6 Sept. 1910. This statement came from the CGT's male secretary Dumas.
[79] "Grève de la Maison Réaumur," *L'Humanité*, 6 Sept. 1910.

at the very least inappropriate. If the workingwomen of the Maison Réaumur have walked off the job, demonstrated in the street, and suffered police brutality, it is because the Maison Réaumur exploits its female laborers in especially atrocious conditions.[80]

This journalist challenges the bourgeois narrative of the strike by affirming the oppressive working conditions of the *confectionneuses*, their brutal treatment by the police, and, not incidentally, their positions as mothers. Indeed, it was a common refrain of strike partisans that higher wages and reduced working hours would be beneficial to women as laborers, but also as mothers and wives.

La Bataille syndicaliste recounted a meeting at the Bourse du Travail during the garment strikes of November 1911 in which the reporter debunked the commonly held wisdom about these strikers: "These women, these mothers, that certain journalists claim not to take seriously, discussed their professional interest for more than two hours, with an ease and sureness of expression that many militants would envy." Women's maternal role was invoked, but in the service of a broader notion of the strikers as reasoned agents of labor reform. One woman spoke at the meeting of a warning by her employer that she personally would gain nothing from negotiations on behalf of less skilled workers in her *atelier*: "She responded with dignity: 'Monsieur, I am not here to discuss my competence or my personal interests, but to represent and defend the interests of the entire workshop. We are all in solidarity and the cause that I defend is everyone's cause.' "[81]

Despite sharp critiques of the bourgeois press, left-leaning journalists nonetheless often reproduced images of the midinettes as pretty ingénues. But they foregrounded midinette femininity as evidence of their position as sympathetic victims of state authority. The youth and frailty of the striking midinettes were contrasted to the brutality of the forces of order, a brutality often framed as a deficit of masculine chivalry. Labor partisans pressed the midinette's much-romanticized diminutiveness into the service of a new model of working-class female political action—no longer fearsome *pétroleuses*, but women of admirable pluck rising up in righteous indignation against the loutish Parisian police. A journalist for the republican-socialist Parisian daily *L'Action* caustically related a scene in which police agents beat and pushed to the ground "young midinettes" during a December 1911 strike:

The young midinettes would not allow themselves to be mistreated in this way without defending themselves. Their umbrellas beat over the backs of the policemen, their nails even made several cuts on the faces of their adversaries... The moral of this story is that if M. Lépine is teaching his officers English,

[80] "La Grève de Réaumur," *L'Humanité*, 8 Sept. 1910.   [81] *La Bataille syndicaliste*, 30 Nov. 1911.

German, even jiu-jitsu, he never taught them that a Frenchmen—even if he is a police officer—must always feel a certain repugnance about hitting women.[82]

The author depicts this use of force as a clear transgression of norms of French masculinity. The gendering of the encounter—young midinettes resisting a cowardly masculine assault with umbrellas and fingernails—reimagines the violent encounter of capital with labor as at least insufficient chivalry, at most a sexual violation.

La Bataille syndicaliste expounded on the meaning of this police violence, "a manifestation of a very particular sadism," the following day: "without a doubt, Lépine's brutes follow the example of their boss and get drunk on ether! But we can hope that the Parisian population, so chivalrous, will not allow acts of brutality perpetrated with such coldness... The *confectionneuses*, so brave, so resolute, know that they can do nothing without the financial and moral support of the organized working class. Yet their cause is so just that they have confidence and feel certain of success."[83] While this scene roots the defense of the workers in the "just" cause of the strike, it also foregrounds the gender violation of the encounter and makes plain that the *confectionneuses* are entirely dependent on (male) organized labor.

One description of the final days of the garment trade strike of May 1917 included a section on a "Brutal Boss" who was "said to have grabbed the neck of one young *manifestante* who still bears, at the current hour, the marks of this very special manifestation of the *Union sacrée*... If these facts are true, this oaf deserves to have the father, brother, or fiancé of the brutalized workingwoman put their foot somewhere or their fist in his face."[84] Here, the broken promise of the *union sacrée* appears as bruises around the neck of a young female striker—a worker who will be avenged not by her own actions but by those of her male relatives.

At the heart of labor responses to the midinette strikes of the 1900s and 1910s was a conviction that, in the words of Pierre Dumas, the Secretary General of the Fédération de l'Habillement, the Parisian garment trades constituted "an immense unorganized (and, for a long time in certain specialties, unorganizable) feminine proletariat."[85] The reasons for low unionization rates among female Parisian garment workers were multiple. Several congresses of the Fédération de l'Habillement in these years highlighted the issue, and explained it as in part coming from the high number of women working from home. The census of 1906 listed 1.2 million

---

[82] M.D., "Une bagarre entre midinettes et agents," *L'Action*, 1 Dec. 1911. *L'Action* was a "quotidienne, anticléricale, républicaine, socialiste," which ran from 1903 to 1924.
[83] P.D., "La Grève Esders: rupture des pourparlers; les ouvrières accalment la grève," *La Bataille syndicaliste*, 2 Dec. 1911.
[84] Unknown newspaper clipping, "Pour les cousettes, cette fois, c'est la Victoire," 23 May 1917.
[85] Pierre Dumas, "Le Congrès de l'Habillement," *La Bataille syndicaliste*, 17 Aug. 1912.

ouvrières a domicile, with 850,000 of those working in the garment industry.[86] Feminist organizers pointed to the tremendous resistance and hostility to women's unions in certain trades on the part of male union members. French historians have explored and in some cases hotly debated the "supposed 'docility' of women workers."[87] While some early women's historians somewhat accepted the notion of female workers as "touchingly naïve," Patricia Hilden and Roger Magraw contest explanations of weak female labor militancy as "some alleged instinctive female 'docility' or conservatism" and instead trace "specific impediments to such involvement, including those created by male union leaders."[88] Marilyn Boxer admits that, in some cases, garment workers did actively resist certain reforms (maximum hours, night work), but as a way of maintaining a living wage, not naivety.[89] Women's participation in the CGT grew considerably in the first decade of the twentieth century, with more than 100,000 female members by 1911, or 10 per cent of the total membership (it had been 6.3 per cent in 1900).[90] Yet, as Hilden puts it, patronizing references to the novelty of midinette militancy in strike after strike "effectively cloaked women's existence as subjects of their own struggles, which were achieved out of their own consciousness."[91] My study argues that the notion of "instinctive female 'docility'" was particularly pronounced in the Parisian garment trades and was linked to a powerful cultural ideal of the Parisian midinette as young, cheerful, and featherbrained.

Because of women's low unionization rates, midinette strikes were heralded consistently by labor partisans as turning points, with once hopelessly exploited workingwomen finally standing up. The CGT's official organ, *La Voix du peuple*, reflected on the successful strike at Maison Esders in 1910 that "This seamstresses' strike will be a beautiful example. It will show women that their destiny too is in their hands, provided that they unite by syndical action."[92] *L'Humanité* similarly remarked that month, following a strike meeting at the Bourse du Travail, "Next to us, a comrade cried, 'If women are getting involved, the revolution is near!' Indeed, comrade, that's our opinion as well. Women, who have taken such an important place in modern industry, are beginning to free themselves..."[93] While the 1910 strikes were unsuccessful—couture workers returned to work in October without gaining their demands—some socialist papers held up the female strikers as a new brand of feminine activism: "we hope that their movement, whatever the

---

[86] Thébaud, *La Femme au temps de la guerre de 14–18*, 120.
[87] Magraw, *A History of the French Working Class*, 65.
[88] Ibid. 63, 65; Hilden, "Women and the labour movement," 818.
[89] Boxer, "Protective legislation and home industry," 52.
[90] Magraw, *A History of the French Working Class*, 65; Hilden, "Women and the labour movement," 827. The only woman included in the 164 delegates to the CGT's congress in 1900 was *fleuriste* Stéphanie Bouvard. Zylberberg-Hocquard, *Féminisme et syndicalisme*, 163.
[91] Hilden, "Women and the labour movement," 822.
[92] "Victoire de femmes: la grève de la Maison Esders," *La Voix du Peuple*, 7 Aug. 1910.
[93] "Dans la confection: un mouvement qui s'étend; de succès en succès," *L'Humanité* (27 Aug. 1910), 2.

other results, will at least have served to enlighten the consciousness of all of the feminine proletariat."[94] During the strikes launched at the Maison Esders in 1911, *La Bataille syndicaliste* was astonished by the seamstresses' activism (despite the fact that there had been a massive garment strike just the year before): "They sometimes are slow to perceive the abuses of which they are victim: but when they realize it, no obstacle will stop them from breaking the yoke…"[95] A year later, at the Congrès de la Fédération d'Industrie des Travailleurs de l'Habillement, Pierre Dumas lauded the "beautiful struggles" of midinettes in 1910 and 1911.[96] Yet he made his statement about the "unorganizable" nature of the female proletariat in his very next paragraph.

As a result of this powerful perception of midinettes as apolitical, even fierce proponents of women's unionization evinced a curious amnesia about working-women's activism in the decades straddling the Great War.[97] In September 1910, *L'Humanité* could say that "this revolt of women is, in some way, a new thing."[98] Seven years later, the same newspaper again envisioned the growing unrest in the garment industry that month as a sudden explosion after decades of quiescence: "like a trail of gunpowder, the demand for the English week and for the cost of living allowance has made its way among the women of the various branches of the clothing industry, who until now had been so exploited and so docile."[99] A journalist for the *Pétite République* contrasted the increasingly militant *grévistes* in 1910 to passive nineteenth-century literary precedents, suggesting that the public was "more or less sympathetic to the young midinettes who, unlike Jenny l'Ouvrière, no longer are 'content with little, content with nothing.'"[100] This last phrase ("contentes de peu, contentes de rien") was the oft-quoted line from Janin's 1840 typology of the *grisette*.[101] "Jenny l'Ouvrière" was the popular heroine of an 1850 five-act play by Adrien Decourcelle and Jules Barbier, and an 1847 song by Émile Barataeu.[102] This offhand allusion to a literary type speaks to the way that the nineteenth-century Parisian imaginary of the *grisette* saturated early twentieth-century popular representations of workers in the fashion trade. Labor

---

[94] "Fin de la grève des confectionneuses," *L'Humanité*, 9 Oct. 1910. AN F/7/13740.
[95] "Une grève de couturières," *La Bataille syndicaliste*, 8 Nov. 1911. AN F/7/13740.
[96] Pierre Dumas, "Le Congrès de l'Habillement," *La Bataille syndicaliste*, 17 Aug. 1912.
[97] Hilden notes the phenomenon by which workingwomen's strikes in general were often read as "a surprising anomaly or a 'sudden awakening'" (*Working Women*, 137).
[98] A.S., "La Grève de Reaumur: le commissaire était nerveux, il fait frapper des Femmes," *L'Humanité*, 27 Sept. 1910. AN F/7/13740.
[99] "Les Grèves dans l'habillement," *L'Humanité*, 22 May 1917. AN F/22/170.
[100] "Les Midinettes prennent des décisions secrètes," *La Pétite République*, 8 Sept. 1910.
[101] Jules Janin, "La Grisette," 10, 12.
[102] "Jenny l'ouvrière" appeared in an 1847 song by Étienne Arnaud and Émile Barateau, followed by Decourcelles and Barbier's play *Jenny l'ouvrière*, which premiered in Paris in November 1850 at the Théâtre de la Porte-Saint-Martin. Jenny is a 20-year-old Parisian embroiderer. See also "Jenny l'ouvrière," in *Chansons nationales et populaires de France*, ed. Théophile Dumersan, and Noël Ségur (Paris, 1866), 165. Striking workers were referred to as "Jenny l'ouvrière" throughout strike reporting. See "La Grève s'étend dans la couture," *L'Humanité*, 15 May 1917.

activism among these women had been on the rise and highly publicized during the preceding decade, and yet observers still imagined this activism as something novel and entertaining. Reactivating this older literary type cloaked garment strikes in the 1910s in a reassuringly romantic, pre-industrial nostalgia, presenting readers anxious about labor unrest, political division, and international geopolitical tensions with a digestible modernity. Two years later, in his 1912 study of women in French unions, Auguste Pawloski could still affirm, "[The French working-woman] remains ignorant of her rights and her interests. She is eternally Jenny l'Ouvrière, and syndicalism has had little hold over her until the day that men, persuaded of the necessity of women's unions, facilitated their creation."[103]

The war saw repeated expressions by labor leaders of garment workers' activism as a long-awaited transformation. When skirt makers at the Maison Courtisien walked out of their workshop in September 1916, Vignaud, the male treasurer of the Syndicat général de l'Habillement de la Seine noted that in this case the *patronne*, "thinking to find an exploitable workforce at her mercy in this milieu, *for once* was wrong."[104] The CGT's *Bataille syndicaliste* set the midinette strike of 1917 against a backdrop of supposed female garment workers' historic inaction. Rather than dismissing the frivolous needle worker as a convenient fiction of bourgeois consumers, the editors insisted instead that this older type of insouci-ant *ouvrière parisienne* had disappeared: "Surely, they never dreamed of this, Messieurs les Grands Couturiers Parisiens, when they set off this movement which, coming from their houses, seemed to win over all the workshops where the fairies of the needle have so long toiled without demanding anything."[105] Disregarding years of intense midinette activism leading up to 1914, the war was seen as dragging garment workers out of their age-old political docility and daft girlishness.

Thus, it is perhaps unsurprising that even union delegates, labor agitators, and the leftist press represented workingwomen in the needle trades as young and attractive tools of syndicalist action, rather than as peers. In 1917, police agents intercepted an anonymous letter written in August from a union agitator to a garment worker at the Maison Laroche, a Mademoiselle Crouzy, inviting her to meet to discuss the unionization of her shop. The letter scolded Crouzy for not responding to an earlier letter, and asked that she respond as quickly as possible on behalf of her fellow workingwomen. The second paragraph informed "Mlle Crouzy, the most beautiful redhead of the Maison Laroche" that she had been named syndical delegate for her shop, and that her "second" would be "a *mécanic-ienne*, the little one with the scars on one side of her face." One might imagine that physical references were merely a way of assuring that the roles and

---

[103] Auguste Pawlowski, *Les Syndicats féminins et les syndicats mixtes en France* (Paris, 1912), 11.
[104] Vignaud, "Dans la couture," *La Bataille syndicaliste*, 3 Sept. 1916; emphasis added.
[105] "Et on s'en fout…On f'ra la s'maine anglaise," *La Bataille syndicaliste*, 24 May 1917.

personalities involved were clear—a necessary tool in an illicit correspondence. But this physical objectification was accompanied by increasing threats aimed at women that the authors take for ignorant and docile subjects to be bullied: "You would prefer to starve to death than to demand a raise, you pile of stuck-up ladies." The anonymous author warned Crouzy and her comrade that if they were not both in attendance at the meeting, the male authors would arrive in number to demolish "the boutique as well as the *ouvrières*. We'll do damage...And you the *déléguées*, you will be responsible if your comrades don't march." After this threat, the letter proceeded to lay out in detail what demands Crouzy was to make, and ended with a final admonition: "We need a response right away, you will sign your name as well as that of your comrade...We count on you, beautiful ginger."[106] It seems unlikely that secret labor agitation correspondence between male workers included similar physical observations and attention to both the beauty and the mindlessness of their addressees. These compliments were part and parcel of the way many labor leaders understood workingwomen—pretty and possibly useful, if obedient. The police investigated and discovered that Crouzy was a 41-year-old bandage and stocking maker. Despite the patronizing tone of the anonymous letter, the police observed that Crouzy was, in fact, an experienced striker, having been a delegate to the Comité de Grève the previous June.[107]

Some labor partisans disputed the narrative of female workers' empty-headedness. Feminist Louise Compain used much of her assiduously researched 1910 work *La Femme dans les organisations ouvrières* (1910) to demonstrate that the low unionization rate of female needleworkers was due in large part to male workers' hostility. She quoted a dismissive exclamation from the male secretary of the Syndicat des Bijoutiers as an example of this rhetoric: "[Female workers] don't regularly pay their dues, and they don't have the *esprit syndical*. They are nothing but birdbrains."[108] While Compain dismissed this criticism as "vituperousness," she herself leaned upon the trope of the frivolous Parisian garment worker when assessing the syndical potential of female textile workers in Lille:

> In these smoky *cités*, embroiled in the economic free-for-all, the workingwoman is not distracted by a thousand attractions, like the milliner or the Parisian *petite main*. She is truly the companion of her worker comrade and has not learned to scorn his smock or his coarse hands in favor of dreams of a student or a clerk whose fleeting love will make of her a "lady."[109]

---

[106] Anonymous letter contained in report from the Chef du Service des Renseignements Généraux to the Préfet de Police, 29 Sept. 1917, "Au suject de lettres anonymes adressées à des ouvrières des Maisons 'LAROCHE' et 'MORIN.'" APP *BA 1376 Grèves de l'habillement, 1917 à 1918*.

[107] Rapport from Chef du Service des Renseignements Généraux to the Préfet de Police, 29 Sept. 1917, "Au suject de lettres anonymes adressées à des ouvrières des Maisons 'LAROCHE' et 'MORIN.'"

[108] Quoted in Louise Compain, *La Femme dans les organisations ouvrières* (Paris, 1910), 27.

[109] Ibid. 64.

Compain affirms the traditional image of the couture worker as distracted coquette seeking pleasure and romance outside of her class. In describing the tireless effort of Clémence Jusselin to organize Paris's seamstresses, Compain again laments that so many workers still fit this older type: "The dexterous 'petites mains' are airheads; they do not understand what a vital interest lies for them in union organization, so many other solicitations pursue them!"[110] Like many of the journalists reporting on the couture strikes, Compain proposes female activism as a process of overcoming, a maturation from frivolous romantic prey to serious partner for her male counterpart. Unionization is thus associated with sexual propriety; the unaffiliated seamstress foolishly dreams of romantic entanglements with a Latin Quarter student, more attentive to "solicitations" on the street than to her rights. Thus, the sluggish pace of workingwomen's unionization is explained by even feminist partisans as a natural consequence of the loose morals and foolishness of some young workingwomen.

Mimi Pinson Speaks

What if we turn the kaleidoscope by a click and attempt to view the strikes from the perspective of the women who conducted them? The available sources for such an attempt are meager compared to the chorus of documented male voices, but we can hear striking midinettes from time to time—in police reports on union hall meetings, in the rare writings of midinette militants, and in the distinctive strategies of their strike actions. Following Hilden, who argues that "working women's self-perceptions diverged markedly at once from the *positions expressed* by male unionists and from more general societal attitudes about women in this period,"[111] like Nan Enstad in her study of New York City garment strikes in the same period, I am interested in the way that female workers "fashion[ed] a subjectivity out of the very language and tropes that had been marshalled to control them."[112] In Paris, militant female workers contested and appropriated the midinette type during garment strikes.

First, while midinette strikes were depicted by the press and many labor leaders as spontaneous responses to some perceived slight, midinette unions had been organizing with purpose throughout the belle époque, and evinced a keen attention to the importance of public perceptions of their struggle. During the February 1901 needleworkers' strike, female *grévistes* were approached by male university students eager to show their solidarity by joining the manifestations on the rue de la Paix. The strikers responded, however, that they "did not want people to say that the women needleworkers only went on strike to have a pretext for flirting

[110] Ibid. 52.   [111] Hilden, "Women and the labour movement," 810.
[112] Enstad, *Ladies of Labor*, 110.

with young men" and so declined the offer. The students readily understood this reasoning, and instead offered the seamstresses "moral and financial support."[113] Some seamstresses made a point of bringing their children and husbands to Sunday strike meetings, though this fact seems to have only been reported by the feminist paper *La Fronde*.[114]

Months before the strikes of summer 1910, the Syndicat des Couturières, led by seamstress Clémence Jusselin, set out to "direct an ardent propaganda campaign to succeed, and to move public opinion by way of lectures and posters."[115] Jusselin's group was referred to by one leftist journalist that winter as the "the largest and most active" of the women's unions.[116] Jusselin's election to the Conseil de Prud'hommes in 1908 as the first ever woman to hold such a position was considered an "unhoped for success" for Parisian garment workers.[117] The same month, a group of garment workers from the rue de la Paix sent a letter to *La Guerre sociale* detailing their exploitation and asking "Is there a newspaper in the Parisian press capable of taking an interest in us? ... We have had enough and we would like someone in the press to shout it loudly."[118] These women argued that, far from quiescent, midinettes had been struggling to hold their workshops accountable to recent labor reform legislation: "We complain, we write to the labor inspector, no one budges." In exposing the inadequacies of current legislation and the dire stakes for women who protested the continuing practice of night work, these women challenged commentators who suggested that they only need rise up: "We simply have to stop accepting it, they will tell us, but we are obliged to take it, under pain of firing."[119] Throughout this letter, the women conveyed a group identity, referring to garment workers in various contexts as "us" and "ours," and displayed a shrewd concern with the usefulness of the press as arbiter of public opinion. By February, labor minister René Viviani decreed the end of *veillées* in couture workshops.

In May 1917, six female garment workers representing a Catholic women's *syndicat* in Paris addressed a letter to the labor ministry presenting their thoughts on the English week. Led by their seamstress president Eugénie Beeckmans and all self-identifying as "Mademoiselle," the women claimed to speak for their nearly 3,000 members in supporting the reduction of work hours on Saturday.

---

[113] Maria Vérone, "A la Bourse du Travail," *La Fronde*, 16 Feb. 1901, 1–2. Days later, a group of university students raised funds for the seamstresses by singing their composition, "La Camargnole des Couturières," *La Fronde* (20 Feb. 1901), 1–2.

[114] Marie-Louise Néron, "La Physionomie de la grève," *La Fronde* (25 Feb. 1901), 1–2.

[115] T., "Les Misères de la couture," *L'Action*, 17 Jan. 1910.   [116] Ibid.

[117] "Le Syndicalisme féminin," *Le Petit Parisien*, 17 Jan. 1910.

[118] Letter from "un groupe d'ouvrières de la rue de la Paix," reprinted in "Les Midinettes en ont assez d'être exploitées," *La Guerre sociale*, 19–25 Jan. 1910.

[119] Ibid. They referenced a "little riot" at Maison Lanvin the week before that led to the firing of forty seamstresses, reported in "Une Insurrection de midinettes," *Le Matin*, 11 Jan. 1910. Jusselin acted as intermediary between the fired workers and the *patronne*.

They argued that, given the workingwoman's obligations in her household, free Saturday afternoons were the only way to assure that she could "devote herself to family life for all of Sunday, and thus help the reconstitution of the family hearth compromised by women's work outside the home." They further insisted that it was a "great social and national interest to guarantee women total freedom on Saturday afternoons," without reducing wages. This letter reveals a group of "midinettes" who are informed newspaper readers and organized union members, equipped with a keen sense of the uses of publicity.[120]

That same month, Marguerite Debray, president of the Syndicat des Ouvrières en Atelier, a Christian women's union, wrote to the Chambre syndicale patronale de la couture and to interior minister Louis Malvy to articulate the concerns of Parisian needlewomen. She began her letter expressing it a "duty" to raise their voices in light of couture strikes that month. While she insisted, "we are neither revolutionaries nor partisans of violence theory," it was impossible to deny that couture workers were in an "extremely difficult" position. Insufficient salaries and the rising cost of living during the war made one ask, "How...can an honest workingwoman live?" Debray maintains multiple times that these demands are not new (contradicting the press's seeming amnesia): "As to the English week, we have on many occasions demanded its application in our profession."[121]

Militant garment workers also demonstrated an acute sense of the significance of and irreplaceable nature of their labor as fashion producers. At a meeting at the Grange-aux-Belles on 18 May 1917, one "young" union delegate stood up to assert both the necessity of the strike and the importance of her labor: "Let's stick it out to the end...I will not let myself be impressed by the beautiful words of the bosses. The ones who dared to say that they would always love their working-women if it meant spending their last *sou* for them! They are talking about closing their companies. Well, if they do, we will divvy up the clients. In truth...orders are pouring in and our employers await our return with impatience. Let's stay firm, and we'll get the English week and the twenty sous!"[122] Debray also articulated the national importance of her *métier* as a lever in favor of workingwomen's demands: "If the working conditions of the *ouvrière* are not modified, the recruitment of *ouvrières* will become impossible and the future of French Couture will be compromised. Every day we notice how many young women leave our métier

---

[120] Letter from the Chambre syndicale des ouvrières de l'habillement (5, rue de l'Abbaye) reprinted in "La Semaine anglaise," *La Libre Parole*, 22 May 1917. The letter was signed by Mlle Beeckmans, présidente; Mlle Lecomte, vice-présidente; Mlle Chatelet, vice-présidente; Mlle Deiss, secrétaire; Mlle Mathieu, trésorière; Mlle Tissot, vice-trésorière. APPP BA 1423, BA 1423 *Chambre syndicale de l'habillement, 1909 à 1918*.

[121] Letter from Marguerite Debray to the président of the Chambre syndicale patronale, Paris, 17 May 1917, copied to the Ministre du Travail, Paris, 18 May 1917. AN F/22/170. On Debray and Christian women's syndicalism see Joceline Chabot, *Les Débuts du syndicalisme féminin chrétien en France, 1899–1944* (Lyon, 1998).

[122] "La Grève des ouvrières de la couture et de la mode," *L'Humanité*, 19 May 1917.

to find a more lucrative profession." Debray proclaims that she and her colleagues are "profoundly attached to our métier," and that "this is a cry of alarm that we are emitting."[123] In addressing herself directly to the minister and to couture employers, Debray counters some facets of the midinette ideal—emphasizing the history of garment trade grievances and affirming the virtue of the average couture worker—while also making efficient rhetorical use of the national value placed on midinette skill and labor.

Militant garment workers also developed strike strategies that played off of the midinette type. It was common practice for midinettes to dress elegantly in their marches, a detail that, as we have seen, observers found charming evidence of their coquetry. Tyler Stovall suggests that this was in fact a tactic, by which striking workers presented themselves not as "a horde of dangerous revolutionaries" but as "stylish young women whose elegance symbolized all that Paris was supposed to stand for," while also offering "a concrete advertisement of their craftsmanship."[124] Closer scrutiny of garment strikes reveals a number of such tactics, all taking advantage of the midinette type.

On 28 September 1910, when protesting garment workers were hemmed in by police near the city limits in the 18th arrondissement, several newspapers described the women abandoning the protest to picnic, becoming carefree diners like those populating midinette lunch hour fiction. As reported by *La Petite République*, when the women were blocked by the police, they decided instead to purchase fried potatoes and mussels, and to "picnic gaily on the faded grass of the embankment."[125] *L'Humanité*, however, revealed that this light-hearted picnic was, in actuality, an evasive tactic. While the protesters left the Bourse du Travail in the morning intent on "débauchage" in a garment shop on rue du Baigneur, they found themselves pursued closely by police agents, restricting their ability to act. Therefore, "the midinettes then headed out of Paris, and, organized, in small, smiling groups, light tea parties on the grass of the city walls." The police were bemused: "Was this a country party or a manifestation? The police did not know what to think really. Thus, they decided to abandon a surveillance that seemed as ridiculous as it was useless." *L'Humanité* revealed that this "tactical maneuver" worked: "Freed in their movements, [the strikers] made their way to rue du Baigneur in small groups."[126] Profiting from their reputation as pleasure-seeking and unserious, the midinettes are able to momentarily evade police scrutiny. It is difficult to imagine a group of male pipe fitters successfully convincing the forces of order that their surveillance was "ridiculous" and "useless."

[123]   Debray to the président of the Chambre syndicale patronale, Paris, 17 May 1917.
[124]   Stovall, *Paris and the Spirit of 1919*, 63.
[125]   "Les Midinettes," *La Petite République*, 28 Sept. 1910.
[126]   "La Grève de Reaumur: dinette sur les fortifs, bagarres à Montmartre," *L'Humanité*, 28 Sept. 1910.

That same month, September 1910, a group of striking *confectionneuses* exploited their position as liminal figures within the world of Parisian fashion to infiltrate couture houses disguised as upper-class shoppers. Police spies alerted the authorities that the strikers planned to enter "targeted shops." "Coiffed, wearing hats, and nicely dressed, the strikers would enter as lady shoppers, and once a number of them were inside the shop, they would upend merchandise."[127] One might dismiss this as hysterical fantasy on the part of the police, so common was the literary trope of the midinette who transforms into or is mistaken for a *grande dame*. Two days later, however, *Le Journal* reported such an action had been attempted. Journalists noticed that afternoon that the midinettes were less numerous in protesting outside of the Magasins Réaumur: "What had happened? Were the *confectionneuses* starting to weaken...[?]" In fact, following a secret meeting, "[the strikers] had agreed 'to dress up as lady clients,' to put on hats in order to arouse less suspicion, and to arrive individually around seven in the evening." The maneuver was discovered, however, and the women found reinforced security at the entrance to the store.[128]

The notes of police spies at strike meetings allow us to glean some sense of the role of midinette militants in these events. While women orators were generally outnumbered by male union leaders at the lectern, a number of midinettes addressed hundreds and sometimes thousands of female garment workers at these meetings. Jeanne Bouvier, Bouillot of the embroiderers' union, Hélène Arend were all garment workers or former garment workers turned militants who figured prominently in strike organization in these years.

Labor leader and former garment worker Monette Thomas was one militant midinette whose speeches were well documented by police spies and by the socialist press, and who herself contributed frequently to a socialist newspaper. Thomas was a married seamstress who gave birth to a child during these years of union and suffrage activity, a girl she and her husband named Louise-Michel after the famed Communarde.[129] Thomas was a key orator during garment strikes in 1918 and 1919, held meetings of leftist groups such as the Ligue des Droits de l'Homme and the Comité d'Action suffragiste at her home in Paris's 1st arrondissement, and proudly joined what she called the "midinettes' movement."[130]

---

[127] Préfecture de Police de Paris, typed report, 6 Sept. 1910. AN F/7/13740.

[128] "Les Confectionneuses manifestent avec les employés rue Réaumur," *Le Journal* (8 Sept. 1910), 2.

[129] Thomas and her husband Gabriel Thomas announced the birth in *Le Populaire*, to which she was a regular contributor, 10 Jan. 1919. She wrote an admiring article about Michel in *La Sentinelle*, 31 Mar. 1919.

[130] Police spies reported on a meeting of the Ligue des Droits des Hommes, at Thomas's home on 25 Sept. 1918. Thomas said that the "mouvement des midinettes reussira, car le patronat a peur." APPP BA 1376. Thanks to Annie Metz at the Bibliothèque Marguerite Durand for information on Thomas. Thomas and her husband Gabriel joined the Ligue as it became increasingly pacifist around 1917. See Emmanuel Naquet, "La Société d'études documentaires et critiques sur la guerre. Ou la naissance d'une minorité pacifiste au sein de la Ligue des Droits de l'Homme," *Matériaux pour l'histoire de notre*

She spoke to the thousands of midinettes who came to listen to her speeches, and spoke *as* a Parisian "midinette." In 1918, for instance, Thomas expressed frustration that "employers represent the midinette as a *coquette*, [a woman] who is not serious and who relies on the generosity of her lovers despite the fact that we are honest women who have hearts and minds and needs to satisfy just as much as the daughters of the bourgeoisie."[131] After the war, as the eight-hour workday became law, Thomas explained that this legislation would oblige female workers either to relinquish the English week ("obtained by the workingwomen of couture"), or to work longer hours, still burdened by the "double job" of household tasks. Such a choice meant, wrote Thomas, that "the midinettes cannot be satisfied." She detailed the many tasks that occupied workingwomen in their non-work hours: preparation of meals, laundry, and piecework to augment insufficient salaries. She wrote movingly of providing women with true leisure hours in which they could "dispose of their time in a useful or agreeable fashion…in this way, mamas could have the joy of taking their babes-in-arms for a walk, wives could spend a bit more time at home, have more time to dress themselves better, and, by this means, hold on to their mates, too often losing their way at the cabaret." Younger women, "still exempt from worries," would "have the possibility, by educating themselves, of liberating their mind of the prejudices of current society."[132] Thomas recognizes that workingwomen will use their hard-won leisure hours in diverse ways, both in socially beneficial roles as more attentive mothers and help-meets, and in individually rewarding "pleasurable" pastimes. Thomas's is a world of workingwomen with complex and distinct needs and desires, united by a successful campaign for the English week.

When Thomas joined the memorial march to the Mur des Fédérés honoring the Commune in 1919, the first time this traditional socialist *fête* had been held since the war, radical republican daily *Le Rappel* used her as an example of the obligatory "femme au corsage rouge" at such events:

there is never a demonstration at Père-Lachaise without a *citoyenne* in a scarlet bodice.

Mme Monette Thomas, wearing the red flag of the 3rd arrondissement, really stood out. We admired the mouth of Mme Thomas singing *l'Internationale*.[133]

---

temps 30, No. 1 (1993), 6–10, 9, and *Pour l'humanité: La Ligue des droits de l'homme de l'affaire Dreyfus à la défaite de 1940* (Rennes, 2014). Thomas also collaborated with feminists in Guadeloupe. Clara Palmiste, "L'Utilisation de la mémoire de l'esclavage dans les revendications des feminists guadeloupéennes (1918–1921)," *Sextant* 25 (2008), 43–54, 45.

[131] Quoted from the Paris police archives in September 1918 by Bass-Krueger, "From the 'union parfaite' to the 'union brisée'," 40. Trans. by Bass-Krueger.
[132] "Les Femmes et les huit heures," *Le Populaire*, 1 May 1919, 2.
[133] "Manifestation au Mur des Fédérés," *Le Rappel*, 26 May 1919, 1.

Needless to say, this was the only body part admired by the author in a piece that included references to numerous male partisans. A month earlier, *Le Rappel* reported on a speech given by Thomas at a conference in which she insisted that the Socialist party should be represented by ideological "purists." The journalist editorialized, "Mme Monette Thomas is a 'purist.' Didn't we learn that she named her little girl Louise-Michel (with an *e*)? But let's put Mme Monette Thomas's personality aside, and comment a bit on the content of her proposition."[134]

Thomas and her comrades at socialist daily *Le Populaire* employed the term "midinette" as a useful identity for female militants, rather than a marker of political docility or naivety. *Le Populaire* described Thomas's speech at a union meeting in September 1918 in which she deftly explained the principal demands of the movement (the eight-hour day and cost-of-living allowances) as animated by her "esprit de midinette."[135] Hers was the only speech by a female delegate to be summarized in this detailed report on the meeting, and it emphasized the compatibility of "midinette sense" and lucid political argumentation. When Thomas herself took issue with the labor ministry's statement during these same strikes that the cost-of-living allowance of 3 francs should not raise a worker's daily salary above 15 francs, she did so in the voice of a midinette. She was outraged that the public might be led to believe that most garment workers made anywhere near 15 francs a day. She used the image of politically-engaged midinettes to challenge the ministry: "15 francs! This rate made thousands of midinettes assembled at the Grange-aux-Belles jump up with indignant surprise." She also objected to the idea that garment salaries should be capped in this way: "Should the midinettes be restricted in this way to a mediocre wage and have their exploiters alone the right to lucrative profits? The *cousettes* aim to prevail in winning 1. The right to a material existence, with the three francs cost-of-living allowance; 2. The right to an intellectual existence, the eight-hour day."[136] As a former seamstress and as a labor militant, Thomas herself identified with the term "midinette," and associated it with clear political purpose and organization, not empty-headed frivolity.

Directly below Thomas's statement, *Le Populaire* described two union meetings the previous day at the Bourse du Travail and the Maison des Syndicats (rue Grange-aux-Belles) at which she had spoken. "*Monette Thomas*," the article read, "with that penetrating knowledge of the psychology of the Parisian midinette, gave an extremely picturesque speech, sprinkled with anecdotes that was very well received."[137] During these same strikes, seamstress Hélène Arend was described

---

[134] "Les Censeurs des Elus," *Le Rappel*, 17 April 1919, 1.

[135] "Communications: Le meeting de l'Habillement," *Le Populaire*, 17 September 1918. *Le Populaire de Paris* was founded during the war by socialist (and Karl Marx's grandson) Jean Longuet, and became the *organe* of the SFIO in 1921. Bellanger et al, 442.

[136] Monette Thomas, "L'Habillement revendique," *Le Populaire*, 25 September 1918, 2.

[137] "Les Meetings d'hier," *Le Populaire*, 25 September 1918, 2.

as a similarly exceptional voice of reason and authority. She was reported to have presided over a union meeting at the Grange-aux-Belles "with much authority and suppleness,"[138] and the next day, "It is always Hélène Arend who leads the discussions. Always listened to by the large audience, she rarely relies on her male advocates, who are, by the way, numerous and perched on every corner of the stage."[139] These descriptions were typical of references to Thomas and Arend, but were absolutely exceptional compared to other strike leaders mentioned in such articles—mostly men, referred to by their last name only and with very little in the way of descriptors. "Our friend" Millerat, for example, was introduced with his union title, and a suggestion that he delivered his speech "with vigor," but otherwise only the topic of his speech was reported.[140]

Thomas played an unusual role in strike meetings in 1918 and 1919 by managing the public image of the strikes from within midinette culture. She interacted with and advised the midinettes on their militancy as one of their own. In the fall of 1918, she met with female strike delegates before union meetings to collect their individual assessments of movement in their shops. On the afternoon of 23 September, Thomas encouraged the 2,000 female couture strikers at the Maison des Syndicats to maintain a calm demeanor and "proper conduct" on the street, "as to not indispose public opinion and to not provoke incidents by forcing the police to intervene…"[141] She also suggested that the midinettes "not sing any songs with a patriotic or anti-patriotic leaning" during their marches, "to avoid giving the movement a political character." (Previous strikes had seen midinettes consistently singing L'Internationale.) Thomas instead recommended that strikers learn the song that would appear in Le Populaire the following day, written by a midinette explicitly for the strike, "a song concerned uniquely with the seamstresses' movement and underscoring their demands."[142] The next day, at the Maison des Syndicats, Thomas again gave striking midinettes "excellent advice of a practical nature. She reminded them that malevolent eyes were trained upon them and that good conduct in the street was indispensable."[143] According to a police report, she also encouraged the strikers "to avoid any altercations with the police"[144] and called for calm bearing in the street. She again announced the song about to appear in Le Populaire, "created especially for the workingwomen of

---

[138] Ibid.

[139] "A la Maison des Syndicats," Le Populaire, 26 September 1918, 2. Arend was likely visibly pregnant during these speeches, as the following May, her seven-month-old son Robert with her partner (and fellow union member) Voldia Tchigiek, died. L'Humanité, 30 May 1919.

[140] "Les Meetings d'hier," Le Populaire, 25 September 1918, 2.

[141] Police report, "Meeting des ouvrières grévistes de la couture," Paris, 23 September 1918, Maison des syndicats, 33, rue Grange-aux-belles. APPP BA 1376.

[142] Ibid.   [143] "Les Meetings d'hier," Le Populaire, 25 September 1918, 2.

[144] Police report on meeting at the Maison des syndicats, afternoon of 24 September 1918, APPP BA 1376.

the clothing industry, 'which will be the rallying chant of the workingwomen on strike."[145] In both meetings, Thomas insisted that, despite the seeming success of the demand for the cost-of-living allowance, the midinettes should not to go back to work until the eight-hour day also had been won. Garment militants took Thomas's advice about the choice of song, as a police report from 25 September noted that the strikers "let us hear at several moments rather inoffensive songs, such as that published in Le Populaire specially for the midinettes.'"[146] Two days later, at a meeting of some 3,000 militants at the Salle de la CGT, the working-women sang "their strike song titled 'La Grange aux belles'..."

The song, which appeared in Le Populaire on 25 September, was described as an "unpretentious song by a midinette" written for the strike of 1918, and was meant to be sung to the tune of "Auprès de ma blonde," a jaunty, romantic folk song dating back to the seventeenth century. The new lyrics melded attractive and nostalgic signs of the traditional midinette with confident activism. In the early verses of the song, the midinettes sing of their scenic arrival at the union hall, a "pretty gaggle" of "Mimi-Pinsons."[147] Their auditors are assured that the midinettes are "loyal workingwomen" and that their female clients will be "satisfied," but this satisfaction is dependent upon the garment workers' economic viability: "The clients are satisfied, | My purse too." The last verses become more insistent in their economic demands: "To hell with your promises, | We need something in writing. | Three francs cost of living | And eight hours too... Rest for mothers, | Bread for the kids."[148] The seamstresses march under the sign of a pretty nineteenth-century literary heroine and assert their devotion to labor and even customer satisfaction. Yet they also assert precise economic demands with a healthy skepticism for patronal duplicity. As in Thomas's writing on the strike, the import-ance of leisure time for workingwomen as mothers is given prominent place. By coordinating action and behavior during the strike protests, Thomas and other union leaders exhibited a keen understanding of the public representation of the striking midinette. They decried the image of the midinette strikes in the "bourgeois" press and carefully planned the aesthetic presentation of the marches themselves.

Militant garment workers like Thomas were also aware of the power of deroga-tory elements of the midinette type. In her speech at the Maison des Syndicats on 23 September, Thomas stoked the indignation of the assembled workingwomen by recounting the words of a garment patronne from the rue d'Antin who had told her female workers, "Yes, if we grant you the eight-hour day, you will have more time to go shut yourselves up in those houses where the blinds are always closed."

[145] Police report on meeting at the Salle des Grèves, Bourse Centrale du Travail, on the afternoon of 23 September 1918, APPP BA 1376.

[146] Police report, "Grève dans l'industrie du vêtement." 25 September 1918, APPP BA 1376.

[147] "La Grange-aux-Belles," Le Populaire, 25 September 1918, 2.   [148] Ibid, 2.

The audience reacted with "astonishment and indignation."[149] Couturier Jeanne Paquin was pilloried throughout these proceedings as an example of a midinette who had betrayed her sisters, and who had not risen to power by "honest means" (a claim which often met with "hearty applause" by garment workers). Another speaker even accused Paquin of killing an apprentice forced to hide in an airless closet during an inspection.[150] An orator at a later meeting accused Paquin of having a collaborator tell an audience of foreign ladies in Zurich, "Look, Mesdames, at the splendid output of Parisian fashion, accomplished by our brave workingwomen and able to be brought to you at such a price because we let them starve to death."[151] Outlandish flourishes of this sort affirmed the midinettes' collective identity as industrious, nationally significant, and respectable, in stark contrast to the image of Paquin, a *midinette manquée*. Police spies noted that this speech played nicely off of Paquin's "marked unpopularity in the world of seamstresses."[152]

In more than one instance, Monette Thomas herself was invoked as a feminine corrective to bourgeois propaganda about midinette immorality. In October 1918, novelist and pop culture journalist Max Viterbo suggested that the midinettes were using the strike as a vacation: "he had joked rather crudely about the so-called holidays of 'Mimi Pinson' (and by that he meant the seamstresses' strike)." Thomas was saluted by her comrades at *Le Populaire* for refuting Viterbo's characterization: "Bravo, Monette Thomas!...Monette Thomas, charming apostle, has just rapped the fingers of M. Max Viterbo." In fact, Viterbo, who was obliged to apologize, declared he had "never had a malevolent intention as regards these courageous women." The editors at *Le Populaire* acknowledged that Viterbo's remark was part of a broader dismissal of the midinette strikes, but also imagined Thomas's rebuttal as in keeping with a generally sympathetic public response: "The public is quite disposed to be so gobsmacked by such poppycock that they will not allow this nonsense of the 'very amusing' strike of the frolicking midinette."[153] The next month, in response to an editorial by literary critic Fernand Vandérem in *Le Figaro* comparing non-striking midinettes to demi-monde prostitutes, Brotteaux of *Le Populaire* gleefully agreed, "All the tarts of Paris to the rescue of the bourgeois order! All the honest workingwomen stand with Bolshevism! I was sure of it, but I had never seen the admission made so guilelessly. I dedicate this passage, for its propaganda, to my valiant little

---

[149] Police report, "Meeting des ouvrières grévistes de la couture," Paris, 23 September 1918, Maison des syndicats, 33, rue de la Grange-aux-belles. APPP BA 1376.

[150] "Meeting des ouvrières grévistes de la couture," 23 September 1918. On Paquin and the strikers see Bass-Krueger, "From the '*union parfaite*' to the '*union brisée*'," 39–42.

[151] Police report, "Réunion de la grande couture, de la confection, et de la fourrure," Paris, 27 Sep. 1918, Salle de la C.G.T., 33, rue de la Grange-aux-belles. APPP BA 1376.

[152] Ibid.   [153] "Bravo, Monette Thomas!" *Le Populaire* (9 Oct. 1918), 2.

comrade, Monette Thomas."[154] Worker and socialist leader Maurice Maurin found Thomas's speech at the Maison des Syndicats on 25 September a captivating example of the militant garment worker: "*Monette Thomas* maintains more than ever the heart and the attention of her audience. She gives us a course in the extremely picturesque, always courageous, and sometimes powerfully inspiring morality of the workingwoman... It is truly effective to have Monette Thomas train students for action. Only a completely liberated woman can tell other women the things [Thomas] told them yesterday."[155]

Thomas's advice was all the more pertinent as the strike (and the war) became increasingly tense. In a meeting on 24 September, just days before the launching of the Meuse-Argonne offensive, Prime Minister Georges Clemenceau raged at his ministers that the continuing "grève des midinettes" in Paris was a threat to the war effort.[156] That same day, more than twenty protesting Parisian strikers were arrested; almost all were unmarried female garment workers between the ages of 15 and 25, detained for attempting to lure non-striking workers away from their workshops.[157] Six more young female garment workers were detained that day for loitering.[158] On 26 September, eighteen midinettes (aged 15 to 28) were arrested for loitering, and another three for assaulting a police officer.[159] Yet, in the face of these arrests, as well as government and male syndical opposition, the midinettes pushed to continue the work stoppage in the first weeks of October 1918, repeatedly refusing male labor leaders' counsel that they accept the compromise offered by the *patrons*.

The events of the fall 1918 strike, in which Thomas was a key player, reveal the periodic clashes between a predominantly male labor leadership and the will of the rank-and-file garment workers who drove the strike. On the morning of 4 October, Marschouk and Jouhaux of the CGT took to the podium at the Grange-aux-Belles to convince the midinettes they had already gained "appreciable" results. But they were continually shouted down by cries by the assembled garment workers of "And what about the eight-hour day?" and "The eight-hour day or the continuation of the strike!" Jouhaux became perceptibly frustrated as he argued that the eight-hour day could not be won as easily as the English week.

---

[154] Brotteaux, "Les Femmes voteront," *Le Populaire* (23 Dec. 1918), 2.

[155] Maurice Maurin, "A la Maison des syndicats" (26 Sept. 1918), 2.

[156] Raymond Poincaré, *Au service de la France: neuf années de souvenirs. Tome 10, Victoire et armistice, 1918* (Paris, 1958), 356.

[157] "État Nominatif des Arrestations opérées depuis le commencement de la grève des ouvrières couturières." APP BA 1376. Three of the arrested female workers were older than 25: 32-year-old Jeanne Lavaud, 26-year-old Isabelle Vital, and 44-year-old "Mme Labarthie." All arrested were released once their domicile was verified.

[158] Gérard, Cre. Bonne Nouvelle à Préfet de Police et Procureur, 24 Sept. 1918, APPP BA 1376. The women arrested were aged 20–23.

[159] Ibid. Those arrested were almost all seamstresses.

He warned the assembled workingwomen, "Don't come running crying to your militant brothers in a couple of days if, by an impulsive move, you decide to continue this strike today."[160] Thomas rose to say that while the gains of the strike were not "negligible," they should be wary of ending the strike before anything was signed on paper with their employers. Several male orators followed her at the lectern, generally in support of the absolute autonomy of the workingwomen to decide on the continuation of the strike. Victor Lefèvre (metalsmith, secretary of the Union des Syndicats de la Seine, and the so-called "darling" of the midinettes) reproached male militants for playing the role of either "makers or breakers of the strike," and assured the strikers, "you alone are mistresses of this situation."[161]

In that meeting of the afternoon of 5 October, tensions from the day before were soothed.[162] Marechal, treasurer of the Fédération nationale des Travailleurs de l'Habillement, guaranteed the strikers that they would be supported by the socialist militants whatever they decided. Thomas rose once more to argue that the strike should not end before the resolution of the eight-hour day. Her argument, unlike those of many of the male orators, spoke to the realities of midinette labor. She pointed out that should the midinettes return to work without a signed agreement on the eight-hour day, their employers would insist upon ten-hour days for a time to make up for the backlog of orders made during the fifteen-day strike. Several female delegates from various shops also urged the continuation of the strike; "Mme Ellène (?) from the maison Bromet" sharply criticized male militants who spoke against prolonging the strike. Lefèvre and Millerat then made passionate pronouncements in support of the workingwomen. During the vote, female strike leaders moved about the hall "lobbying in favor of the strike" and "argued with workingwomen from the Maison LANVIN who wanted to return to work." All the while, a midinette played refrains from popular songs like Madelon on a piano while others sang along. The final vote was 957 to 715 in favor of continuing the strike.[163] Le Populaire wrote of this Friday night vote that "this considerably larger majority spoke in total knowledge of the cause, and with total awareness."[164]

Five days later, as the strike dragged on, Millerat, so vocal in his public support of the midinettes at the Grange-aux-Belles, privately expressed frustration with their unwillingness to return to work. While he believed that the patronal concessions were adequate, the midinettes continued to insist on the eight-hour day.

---

[160] Police report, "Réunion des grévistes de la grande couture et de la broderie," Paris, 4 Oct. 1918, 11h. APPP BA 1376.

[161] Police report, "Réunion des ouvrières grévistes de la grande couture et de la broderie," Paris, 4 Oct. 1918, 17h, 33 rue de la Grange-aux-Belles. APPP BA 1376.

[162] Police report, "Réunion des ouvrières grévistes de la grande couture et de la broderie," Paris, 5 October 1918, 15h30, 33 rue de la Grange-aux-Belles. APPP BA 1376.

[163] Ibid.   [164] "Les Midinettes lutteront jusqu'au bout," Le Populaire (7 Oct. 1918), 2.

According to a police spy, "Poor MILLERAT is in despair. 'I don't know what they've got in their heads or what they want to happen,' he said, 'If tomorrow we bring them the eight-hour day, they will ask for something else. I don't know who is pushing them, but surely someone is working them from behind the scenes.'" He suspected renegade male union members were "agitating the workingwomen."[165] The female strikers' resistance to male union leaders' advice is incomprehensible to Millerat without male agency at its root.

By 12 October, the couture workers finally signed an agreement to end the strike, without a clear concession on the eight-hour day.[166] Nonetheless, the deliberations of this week in October open a window onto the particular activism of the *midinettes en grève*. First, some male syndical leaders like Millerat and Jouhaux saw these women as exasperating if well-intentioned, and framed their activism as feminine caprice and recklessness when not in harmony with the leadership's objectives. Second, the October 1918 strike meetings bear witness to the autonomous if fractured political voice of the midinettes during this strike. Undoubtedly, garment workers were not unanimous in their approach to the strike. They spoke, often discordantly, to each other and to the syndical leadership about their demands, and bristled at the imposition of political direction from militants they deemed disloyal to their goals. But they also appeared, by 1918, to be well-versed in Parisian strike culture, and clear, as a group, about both the stakes of labor militancy and their considerable role in Parisian labor politics.

Tyler Stovall has cautioned scholars against imagining something like a coherent or cohesive working-class identity in the period of the war and directly after. And indeed, many Parisian couture workers did not strike in these years and even evinced indifference or antagonism toward midinette strikes. Louise Délétang's wartime diary is famously hostile toward striking female munitions and garment workers.[167] As Stovall points out, while Délétang writes with a well-defined sense of class as an exploited worker, she was incensed that striking laborers might threaten the nation at war in such a way. Indeed, some "midinettes" resisted unionization and strikes not out of an inherent docility but out of a fierce loyalty to the French war effort. In January 1918, a group of seamstresses from the Maison Premet denounced Russian tailors in the same establishment whom they accused of "defeatism" and of being the "instigators of the latest strikes" who "who want once again to incite us to strike."[168] In investigating this claim, the police learned

[165]   Police correspondence, Paris, 10 Oct. 1918. APPP BA 1376.

[166]   Police report, "Réunion des ouvrières grévistes de la grande couture et de la broderie," Paris, 12 Oct. 1918, 11h, Salle Ferrer, Bourse du Travail. APPP BA 1376.

[167]   Louise Délétang, *Journal d'une ouvrière parisienne pendant la guerre* (Paris, 1936).

[168]   Letter from "Une groupe d'ouvrières de la Maison Premet" dated 18 Jan. 1918, Paris. Included with letter from the Chef du Service of the Préfecture de Police to the Préfet de Police, "Rapport: Au sujet d'une dénonciation anonyme concernant le personnel étranger de la maison PREMET, 8, place Vendôme," 8 Feb. 1918. APPP BA 1423, *Chambre syndicale de l'habillement, 1909 à 1918*.

that a number of the women working at Maison Premet had husbands serving on the front, and thus "accepted with difficulty the presence, among the tailors, of five Russians old enough to bear arms."[169]

The Legacy of the *Midinette en Grève*

The consequences of these strikes during the interwar years were mixed. On one hand, the midinette continued to resonate in the Parisian imaginary through the 1920s and 1930s. I began this chapter with the 1923 declaration by journalist Jean Perrigault that "Mademoiselle Mimi Pinson has joined a union." Two months later, Parisian milliners, famously resistant to unionization, organized an ultimately successful campaign for a wage increase, and the hatmakers' union newspaper devoted virtually all of its front page to this action. Here, too, the past was invoked as a foil to a new brand of feminine activism: "Single women, 'trottins,' 'midinettes,' Hatmakers on strike! This would have made one smile once. Today, it's a fact. A painful fact that, one fears, will repeat itself. Because the conditions of existence of the working-class woman have worsened considerably since the war."[170]

Interwar popular writers persisted in conceiving of female garment activism as capricious and flippant. René Saint-Ursanne's 1925 one-act play *La Grève des midinettes* (designed to be performed at so-called "honest *soirées*" for young audiences) described a workshop of Parisian hatmakers: "A wind of strike has blown through the milliner workshops of the rue de la Paix. In the Maison Triboulet, the brains are overexcited and they decide to take part in the demonstration."[171] The young hatmakers move effortlessly from chatting about theater to discussing strikes in nearby workshops. They watch those first strikers clash with police from the windows of the workshop, and deem the clash "entertaining."[172] Ultimately, the young milliners learn that their out-of-town *patronne*, ignorant of the strike, has nonetheless raised all of their salaries. The milliners realize the error of the strike, and conclude that they are indeed the good-hearted but silly featherbrains imagined by the public: "We get compared to the sparrows of Paris...they might have faults...but they have a good heart."[173]

Stéphane Manier's 1933 pulp novel *Midinettes* included a similar vision of Parisian garment workers' strikes. The narrator, a bourgeois writer, recounts the

---

[169] Chef du Service of the Préfecture de Police to the Préfet de Police, "Rapport: Au sujet d'une dénonciation anonyme concernant le personnel étranger de la maison PREMET, 8, place Vendôme," 8 Feb. 1918.

[170] P.M., "Le Mouvement des modistes," *Le Couvre-Chef: Fédération Ouvrière de la Chapellerie, Modistes, Chapeliers, Casquettiers* 37 (Oct. 1923), 1. AN F/7/13741 Chapellerie 1905–29. Confection Militaire, 1905–12.

[171] René Saint-Ursanne, *La Grève des midinettes, comédie en un acte pour jeunes filles* (Paris, 1925).

[172] Ibid. 32.   [173] Ibid. 43.

first time he met his midinette neighbor Mathilde: "There was at this time in Paris a picturesque strike of midinettes. It was the First of May, and the strikers with their fresh laughter formed a cortege to roam the streets of Paris. So, Mathilde was singing, along with her companions, not the *Internationale*, which she didn't know, but some sentimental refrains that were in style. Like the others, she wore, pinned to her bodice, not the red eglantine rose, but a little bouquet of good-luck *muguets*."[174] The midinettes on strike resemble pop cultural visions of the midinettes *tout court*—singing, laughing, romantic. They are clearly marked as distinct from traditional socialist agitation—ignorant of *L'Internationale* but well versed in sentimental popular song.

Some labor partisans' memoirs of this same period consistently recalled midinette strikes as joyous affairs, made up of exceptionally improvident if winsome workingwomen. In 1938, Parisian laborer and union member Gaston Guiraud reminisced about wartime strikes, and made special mention of the light character of the midinette strike.[175] Across the city, "the corteges of young and friendly rebels that came together en masse at the Bourse du Travail, all with their popular song on their lips... In the fever of this moment, this multitude of 'Pierettes,' insouciant and indifferent to the dangers of the future, had suddenly become fanatical union members."[176] Guiraud describes the union hall as "embellished" by the 2,000 midinettes, who make up "a charming audience" and who react with good humor and tenderness when a male union leader, "the beloved" and "chou-chou" of the midinettes, scolds them for their plight.[177] The midinettes maintain their inborn gaiety and carefreeness, but are unnaturally attentive to their rights, one imagines for the first time. Guiraud notes that the strikers won their demand—a 20 sous cost-of-living allowance—but he bemoans that "A quickly acquired triumph, a too easy success will not test the endurance of the 'cousettes' and soon their insouciance will make them forget the effort of union organization." Just a couple of paragraphs later he again combines a lament about the "state of mind" of most "cousettes" with a suggestion that "thanks to the cohesion of the campaigns and the action led by the unions of private industry, the *semaine anglaise* is finally being enforced as originally conceived."[178] Thus, even in the face of considerable labor militancy in the garment trades and multiple successes, this labor leader persists in imagining the midinette as too careless for serious syndicalism.

On the other hand, some workers' labor militancy was modeled on that of the striking midinettes. René Michaud, a teenager during the wartime strikes of 1917, recalled his own military equipment factory striking only *after* the midinettes

---

[174] Manier, *Midinettes*, 14.
[175] Gaston Guiraud, *P'tite Gueule* (Paris, 1938). Guiraud was secretary of l'Union des Syndicats confédérés de la région parisienne.
[176] Ibid. 227.   [177] Ibid. 228.   [178] Ibid. 231.

began their strike: "The movement set off by the *cousettes* spread like an oil stain."[179] For Michaud, it was workingwomen, along with more radical young male workers like himself, who made wartime strikes so powerful. He recalled marching along the boulevards singing the midinette strike song, ("Et on s'en fout | On veut la s'maine anglaise") which he and his comrades were "proud to claim," and to which they added their own verse threatening their bosses with castration.[180] Indeed, the successful campaign for the English week by Parisian couture workers was succeeded not only by strikes across French industry but also actions by so-called "midinettes" in other cities around France, including Marseille and Bordeaux, who "demand the same advantages as their comrades in Paris."[181] At the triumphant conclusion of the 1917 strike, Pierre Dumas told a crowd at the Grange-aux-Belles, "when the women workers of France will have obtained the English week, they must remember that it was to a strike of midinettes that they will owe this benefit."[182] The next week, encouraged by the unusually rapid success of the midinette campaign, a Catholic employees' union pleaded with the labor ministry to approve long-dormant legislation aimed at salaried *employés*.[183] Unlike Parisian midinettes, these workers, they complained, "do not have unions that ably and promptly demand for them a raise in wages. They don't have a local hall on the rue Grange-aux-Belles where they can express their demands; they don't roam the boulevards proclaiming that 'we don't give a d...! we want the English week!'" The *employés appointés* juxtaposed their quiet, obedient labor to the raucous demands of the midinettes: "The midinettes having broken windows here and there the other day around 2 p.m., the [labor] minister, by 4 p.m., had drafted a law on the English Week..."[184] This letter, while plainly discounting a decade of garment trade militancy on behalf of the English week, nonetheless uses the midinettes, grudgingly, as justification for repositioning its own demands.

Historian Claude Didry suggests that the interwar years saw the socialist press taking Parisian midinettes seriously as labor activists at long last. The successful garment trades strikes of May 1935, and those of the following May presaging the rise of the Front Populaire, confirmed the position of the midinette, writes Didry, in the "laboring avant-garde...one of the major figures of the working class," and no longer simply "a sentimental woman in the masculine imaginary."[185] The preceding study suggests that the resistance to this transformation in the French imagination was forceful, and it gives some sense of the tremendous power of pervasive cultural typologies to divert and manage efforts at social change

---

[179] René Michaud, *J'avais vingt ans: un jeune ouvrier au début du siècle* (Paris, 1967), 74.
[180] Ibid. 75.   [181] "Les Grèves," *Le Figaro* (2 June 1917), 3; "Les Grèves," *Le Figaro*, 4 June 1917.
[182] "Pour les cousettes, cette fois, c'est la victoire," *L'Humanité*, 23 May 1917.
[183] Louis Marsolleau, "La Peau de chagrin," *Le Figaro* (28 May 1917), 1.   [184] Ibid.
[185] Didry, "Les Midinettes, avant-garde oubliée du prolétariat," 85. Didry sees in the midinettes a potentially effective genealogy for workers today, in the face of the failure of socialist parties to grapple with the global sweating system now dominating fashion production.

from below. But it also suggests the process by which a century-old image of Parisian couture workers did transform, from the gradual evolution of syndical investments in garment trade campaigns (especially in the face of important successes by these campaigns), and from the seasoning of a generation of militant garment workers who adopted aspects of the midinette ideal and turned it to their political advantage.

6

Mimi Pinson Goes to War

Sex, Taste, and the Patrie, 1914–1918

During the First World War, the psychic and physical distance between the *poilus* of the trenches and the women of the homefront became a primary way for Europeans to understand the social dislocation of the war. In France, where the border between front and homefront was blurred considerably by the proximity of the battlefield to non-combatant areas and by the bombardment of Paris itself, this separation was nonetheless, or perhaps even more significant.[1] This chapter explores how and why the workingwomen of the Parisian fashion industry became an appealing way for observers to make sense of the war. The midinettes of Paris suffered unemployment and drastically cut wages during the war; at the same time, they were elevated in wartime ephemera as a nostalgic and erotic image of a France made whole. They were embraced by the press, by government agencies, and by trench soldiers as a soothing counterimage to more troubling female types on the homefront—the lady of leisure, the gender-bending *munitionette*, or the unfaithful wife. As a cheerful and desirable national girlfriend, the Parisian garment worker was imagined offering her body, her gaiety, and her inimitable taste to the war effort. Physical intimacy between these women and trench soldiers emerged, particularly in the early years of the war, as a potent fantasy of prewar wholeness—with the midinette's body serving as a talisman to ward off violence, defeat, and death.

One patriotic initiative was particularly popular: the Cocarde de Mimi Pinson, a campaign by female Parisian needle workers to manufacture tricolor cockades (*cocardes*) for front soldiers. What began as the spontaneous production of morale-boosting mementos by a group of unemployed garment workers soon expanded to include a government-funded exposition, a shop, an operetta, poems, and several songs. The cocarde campaign was born of the frustrated jingoism of unemployed garment workers in Paris who felt excluded from the national war effort. In response, Charpentier added two patriotic service efforts to his OMP—an association to fund and train workingwomen as nurses, and the cocarde campaign. After decades of cultural representations championing the agile "fairy fingers" of working Parisiennes, a wartime role that hinged on garment workers'

---

[1] Susan Grayzel, " 'The souls of soldiers': civilians under fire in First World War France," *The Journal of Modern History* 78 (Sept. 2006), 588–622.

Working Girls: Sex, Taste, and Reform in the Parisian Garment Trades, 1880–1919. Patricia Tilburg, Oxford University Press (2019). © Patricia Tilburg.
DOI: 10.1093/oso/9780198841173.001.0001

status as tasteful ingenues and as romantic consolers of men was readily intelligible to both the participants and the wider public. Government officials, journalists, and even soldiers applauded garment workers' patriotic participation under the sign of Mimi Pinson, gay guardian of French taste and as the loving and (safely) eroticized national Girlfriend.

Historians have traced the French public's fascination with and ambivalence about upper-class women's wartime participation. Contemporaries lauded the healing social benefits of contact between upper-class ladies of the Red Cross and the often lower-class *poilus* (the colloquial name for front-line French soldiers in World War I), a conception of "national reconciliation based upon an acceptance of the status quo in terms of both class and gender subordination."[2] But both Red Cross nurses and leisured *marraines de guerre* could also be read as idle society ladies looking for a bit of distraction or increased social status.[3] Working-class women's patriotic volunteerism, however, has been nearly absent from the secondary literature on World War I.[4] Historians instead have been attentive to workingwomen's wartime labor, with the figure of the female munitions worker garnering particular consideration from both contemporaries and scholars.[5] Yet just as important as debates about new kinds of female work during the war was the deployment of pre-war tropes of female labor to mitigate anxieties about gender upheaval.[6] While the Mimi Pinsons entered the war effort as workers, volunteer nurses, and fundraisers, they were acclaimed by the public for their service as tasteful (and sexually consoling) creators of patriotic decorative objects, and as an ideal symbolic figure for managing anxieties about the social dissolution that came with the war.

The War on Taste

The cocarde campaign must be understood within a broader wartime discourse entreating Parisian garment workers to defend the Nation with their taste and labor. The war years saw an elevation of both Paris and its garment workers as emblems of the cultural *patrimoine* for which the *poilus* were fighting. Mary Davis traces the "stylish patriotism" of haute couture during the war years, including the

---

[2] Margaret H. Darrow, "French volunteer nursing and the myth of war experience in World War I," *American Historical Review* 101:1 (1996), 80–106, 94.

[3] Ibid. 79–85.

[4] Susan Grayzel, *Women's Identities at War: Gender, Motherhood, and Politics in Britain and France during the First World War* (Chapel Hill, 1999), 206.

[5] See Mathilde Dubesset et al., "The female munitions workers of the Seine," in *The French Homefront, 1914–1918*, ed. Patrick Fridenson (Oxford, 1992).

[6] Mary Louise Roberts demonstrates that gender, particularly the image of the single woman, was "central to how the war experience was understood by those who lived through it." *Civilization Without Sexes* (Chicago, 1994), 7.

extensive and popular luxury fashion exhibits at the world's fair in San Francisco in 1915. While other belligernt nations like Germany and Great Britain refrained from even participating, France "seized the opportunity to demonstrate the nation's cultural resilience" by "convey[ing] the importance of fashions as uniquely French, and more importantly, as one of the nation's signal contributions to global culture."[7] Jeanne Paquin travelled to New York in 1915 to continue her fight against the copying of French dress models and to demonstrate the continued supremacy of Parisian couture.[8]

During the bombardment of Paris in 1918, several French writers, provoked by a German editorial alleging that the destruction of Paris would be no loss for civilization, countered with a slim volume of essays on the capital's wonders. Following chapters such as "Paris and the Churches" and "The Museums of Paris," the editors concluded with an essay on the Parisian woman, by Daniel Lesueur (the *nom de plume* of Parisian poet and novelist Jeanne Lapauze). Lesueur equated the stylishness of Parisian women with the grace of Paris as a whole and insistsed upon the "supreme taste" of Parisiennes of all castes: "The most immense fortune would not procure for a woman far from the Parisian type that which the midinette possesses in equal parts with the great lady that she dresses on the rue de la Paix."[9] The truly representative Parisienne, argues Lesueur, is Mimi Pinson, with her simple elegance and gentle soul. This ideal working Parisienne is "quite young, very pretty, with elegant dimensions, coiffed with a charming hat (since she made it herself), dressed with that simple 'chic' which is our secret."[10] Undiscerning foreigners will take Mimi for an idle woman of means, but Lesueur follows this fictive *coquette* home to discover that she tends to a happy child and hardworking husband.

Like many during the war years, Lesueur moves beyond simply remarking the metropolitan tastefulness of Paris's workingwomen to elevating this tastefulness to an essential element of French national character. The average Berlin matron, she writes, uses more coquetry (and money) to dress herself "grotesquely" than the charming midinette who trots to work every day "at once proper and delicious." The midinette is exemplary of a meaningful national difference: an innate grace and style which places the French nation above its German enemies. The pre-war trope of the midinette as a pleasing image of labor is here transformed into a model for French wartime solidarity and perseverance: "That is their particular virtue: adorning the hardest effort with smiling grace." Lesueur then addresses the midinettes of Paris, and frames their legendary grace and cheerfulness as a precious national inheritance: "Admirable daughters of your old father, our sublime

---

[7] Davis, *Classic Chic*, 134–5.

[8] Dominique Sirop, *Paquin. Suivi du catalogue de l'Exposition 'Paquin—Une Retrospective de 60 ans de Haute Couture' organisée par le Musée Historique des Tissus de Lyon, Decembre 1989–Mars 1990* (Paris, 1989), 42.

[9] Daniel Lesueur, "La Parisienne," in *La Beauté de Paris* (Paris, 1919), 289–92, 290.

[10] Ibid. 291.

Paris, you are the soul of his soul. You have his strength and his smile, his heroism and his grace. You dress well, that's understood... But those who would consider only your incomparable taste, do not know that this taste is made out of an extremely vast, delicate, and profound spiritual heritage."[11] Such encomia to the inimitable taste of working Parisiennes was nothing new in 1918. But the specific aim of this volume—a counter polemic to stir patriotic defense of a city and a nation under attack—indicates the extent to which fashionable working Parisiennes had become imbricated with the rhetoric of national defense.

When Catholic writer Berthe-Marie Bontoux devoted a hefty tome in 1917 to applauding the national service efforts of Frenchwomen during the war, *Les Françaises et la grande guerre*, she also underscored the national stakes of Frenchwomen's tastefulness. Bontoux urged Frenchwomen to put aside the more outrageous styles of the war years, and to avoid the bad taste which characterized their German and Austrian enemies. She likened the appearance of vulgar clothing styles in France during the war to an enemy invasion. Since German soldiers were unable "to steal our capital's couturiers and milliners," female Berliners have been reduced to copying old French styles from a century before, "but deforming them with their habitual heaviness."[12] Parisiennes' wartime adoption of "jupes trotteuses" and plunging necklines were, writes Bontoux, "a direct violation of patriotic dignity."[13] While Bontoux scolds upper-class Parisiennes dressed in garish colors, she applauds Paris's workingwomen who bring together wartime solemnity and taste: "Black, or at least neutral shades, and simple, unpretentious *tailleurs* with nonetheless harmonious lines, these are true wartime fashion. And this is the style adopted by our Frenchwomen, and quite especially these midinettes who with a quick step head to their couture workshops to continue their daily labor."[14] Here the midinette's persistent labor and demure chic are models of national strength. Bontoux's volume was devoted to soaring defenses of the Christian charity and fidelity of Frenchwomen, and this section on French fashion is written with the same tone of solemn jingoism.

La Cocarde de Mimi Pinson

Facing severe unemployment or half-pay, Parisian garment workers were at once anxious to find ways to make a living, and to serve the war effort. Parisian philanthropic societies opened more than 500 wartime *ouvroirs* (workrooms) where unemployed garment workers could find some temporary employment sewing

---

[11] Ibid. 291–2.
[12] Berthem-Bontoux, *Les Françaises et la grande guerre* (Paris, 1917), 93. Berthem-Bontoux was the *nom de plume* of Berthe-Marie Bontoux.
[13] Ibid. 96.   [14] Ibid. 97.

clothing for the troops.[15] Needleworker Louise Délétang recounts searching for piecework jobs in these years, from pillowcases to soldiers' shirts, making as little as 20 sous for ten hours' work.[16] Délétang swings between gratitude for work and disgust at the elegant *bourgeoises* who indulge an unseemly taste for luxury while soldiers die: "serious women, worthy of the name Woman, dress up rarely" while "those who only have a powder compact as a brain and a powder puff in place of a heart" indulge in fashion purchases: "and we...who live off of fashion and luxury...we live by way of those women there."[17]

In September 1915, several unemployed garment workers approached Charpentier with their plan to raise the morale of soldiers on the front by creating patriotic cocardes. By December, the organization had received more than 100,000 cocarde requests from soliders.[18] To celebrate the women's inititative, Charpentier and the OMP opened a boutique where cocardes could be purchased to benefit wounded soldiers, and had cocardes exhibited in the windows of some Parisian newspaper offices. The OMP also organized the Exposition de la Cocarde de Mimi Pinson in November 1915 at Paris's Petit Palais—a spectacular display of thousands of cocardes, good-luck charms, badges, and trophies arranged in scenes of patriotic whimsy, "a gift from the Workingwomen of Paris to the *Poilus* at the Front."[19] The exhibition also involved a city-wide competition between the seam-stresses of Parisian couture houses and department stores, and several lifesize wax figure dioramas honoring the mythology of Mimi Pinson. The program for the Concours des Cocardes reads as a perfect embodiment of the *union sacrée*: a group of workingwomen (almost all "Mademoiselles") are listed as the organizers of the campaign,[20] but the competition is overseen by Charpentier, "Parisian Business," "The Parisian Press," and a smattering of government officials. Labor, capital, and political power came together to help workingwomen boost the morale of the troops. Postcards were produced depicting the wonders of the exhibit as well as visits to the exposition by soldiers on leave.

Employees from La Belle Jardinière, Maison Jenny, Lanvin, and the Magasins du Louvre decorated massive panels with cocardes arranged in nationalistic designs which were, in the words of one journalist, an affirmation of "the immortality of the Parisian workingwomen's genius."[21] The panel for the Magasins du Louvre depicted two Mimi Pinsons, one stitching cocardes and the other showering a

[15] Thébaud, *La Femme au temps de la guerre*, 114–18.

[16] Délétang, *Journal d'une Ouvrière Parisienne.*   [17] Ibid. 255.

[18] Sterny, "Au Palais des Beaux-Arts (Petit-Palais)," *Les Amis de Paris* (Dec. 1915), 289.

[19] *Concours des Cocardes de Mimi Pinson: Catalogue, Novembre 1915* (Paris: Palais des Beaux-Arts de la Ville de Paris), 9.

[20] The worker-organizers are listed inside the catalogue cover: Andrée Gatineau, (Sécrétaire); Louise Mauranne, Marguerite and Georgette Georgen, Yvonne Augé, Henriette Lebourg, Béatrice Cochin, Antoinette Cucuel, Marthe LeBlanc, Germaine Ramier.

[21] "La Cocarde de Mimi Pinson," [11 Nov. 1915]. FC, No. 466, *Mimi Pinson (Guerre, 1914–1918) La Cocarde de Mimi Pinson: organisation, magasin.*

Figure 6.1. "Exposition des Cocardes de 'Mimi Pinson,' 6, Une Salle de l'Exposition des Cocardes," postcard, 1915.
Source: Bibliothèque de la Ville de Paris, Fonds Charpentier, Dossier 469.

line of soldiers and military vehicles with cocardes. La Belle Jardinière's panel was a towering Marianne in a Phrygian cap sowing a field with cocardes, all framed by the rays of a brilliant rising sun (Figure 6.1).

In this image, the future of a nation at war lies in small pieces of Parisian taste sown by an allegorical woman representing both a department store, republican France, and workingwomen. In this way, fashion and taste became one weapon in the defense of not only the nation but also traditional gender and class roles. The central hall of the exposition featured a massive "Altar of the Nation," assembled by students at the Beaux-Arts and decorated by "Mimi Pinson." Fasces draped in a tricolor flag were surrounded by laurel leaves, ethereal female muses, and the names of key military campaigns. Rifles were propped against the "altar." According to the exhibition catalogue, the Altar originated as an "innocent gesture of the Workingwoman, who was the first to have the tender thought of sending to 'her *Poilu*' a cocarde, a keepsake," but had been elevated here, with the help of bourgeois art students, into "an apotheosis."[22]

The exhibition's somewhat dissonant assemblage of patriotism, working-class labor, and bourgeois consumption was epitomized in the "Stand de la Mode"—a lifesize (and eerily lifelike) wax figure display (Figure 6.2). Here, there are no visual references to the war or to women's labor, only feminine fashion; two stylish ladies and two equally stylish young girls in gowns by Jeanne Paquin stand in an

---

[22] *Concours des Cocardes de Mimi Pinson: Catalogue*, 10.

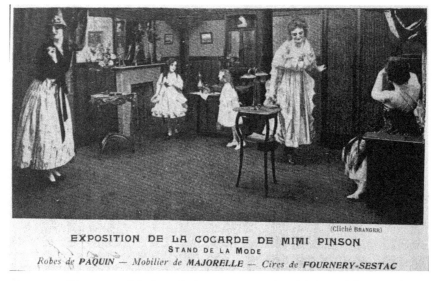

Figure 6.2. "Exposition de la Cocarde de Mimi Pinson: Stand de la Mode," postcard, 1915.
Source: Bibliothèque de la Ville de Paris, Fonds Charpentier, Dossier 469.

interior nicely appointed with furnishings by Majorelle. Somewhat awkwardly to
the side of this grouping was a third wax figure labeled "Mimi Pinson dressed by
Paquin" (Figure 6.3).

This last figure is the perfect union of Mimi Pinson's multiple roles as erotic
object to be consumed, as consumer and producer of fashion, and as guardian of
a tasteful Republic. The wax Mimi wears make-up, a full ankle-length skirt, heeled
shoes, and a cinched jacket bearing a cocarde. Here was a new version of the
Parisienne who had held court over the Exposition Universelle of 1900.[23] Like her
bourgeois predecessor, this working-class Parisienne wears a couture Paquin
dress, a so-called "war crinoline" which was on fashion's cutting edge in 1915 and
graced haute couture magazines that year.[24] Unlike 1900's Parisienne, 1915's model
wears a Phrygian cap and cocarde instead of a crown, and she is identified specifically as Mimi Pinson. Despite the Phrygian cap, she cannot be mistaken for a
fearsome *sans-culottes*, as she smiles and poses daintily alongside fine furnishings,
with the caption: "Mimi Pinson, dressed by Paquin."[25] This is a rather astonishing
fantasy—a vision of a working class that is female, decorous, and that has the
financial resources to dress in couture. While the 1900 Parisienne topped a frieze
depicting artisans at work, 1915's working Parisienne carries in her own person

[23] Silverman, *Art Nouveau in Fin-de-Siècle France*, 288–93; Ruth Iskin, *Modern Women and
Parisian Consumer Culture in Impressionist Painting* (Cambridge, 2007).
[24] Valerie Steele, *Paris Fashion: A Cultural History* (Oxford, 1988), 237–41; Bass-Krueger, "From the
'union parfaite' to the 'union brisée'," 33.
[25] FC, No. 469. *Mimi Pinson (Guerre, 1914-1918) Exposition des Cocardes; Photos et Cartes Postales*.

Figure 6.3. "Exposition de la Cocarde de Mimi Pinson: Stand de la Mode, Mimi Pinson habillée par Paquin," postcard, 1916.

Source: Le Musée national de l'Éducation.

decorative femininity, luxury consumption, and labor—yet without the troubling physical signs of such exertions. The pre-war equation of Mimi Pinson and French taste came to bear increased weight in the context of patriotic mobilization.

This reappropriation of Mimi Pinson served partially as a reproach of the bourgeois Parisienne, the dizzy socialite who revels and primps while her man fights in the trenches. This criticism was evident when Charpentier and government officials opened a wartime boutique in which Mimi Pinsons sold their cocardes and other handicraft to an upper-class clientele to benefit wounded soldiers.[26] In December 1916, *L'Action* described a wealthy lady's visit to this boutique, and her egoistic attempt to haggle over the price of a hat with the Mimi Pinson saleswoman. As the saleswoman refused to reduce the price, the "haughty" lady insisted upon speaking to the store manager. When she is introduced to Charpentier himself, she blushes with shame and begs for the privilege of paying four times the hat's listed price.[27]

The cocarde campaign also offered a welcome example of a loyal and obedient homefront. For Georges Montorgueil, the cocarde exposition brought to mind the heady first days of the mobilization when female workers marched down Parisian boulevards linking arms, waving flags, and singing: "And what was admirable was their order and discipline, the unanimity of all these young souls suddenly feeling the grand inspiration of the Nation coursing through them."[28] A journalist for *Le Radical* approvingly reported one Mimi Pinson opened the cocarde exposition in November 1915 by thanking the Prefect of the Seine and the President of the Municipal Council for wartime unemployment assistance.[29] Encomia to the Mimi Pinsons' orderliness and gratitude tempered fierce anxieties about national unity and financial crisis that came with war—conjuring a fictive submissive working class (and female population) at a moment when the nation's very survival seemed to depend on the industrious morale of those behind the lines.

More than simply an example of obedient homefront femininity, the charitable efforts of the women of the OMP became a primary way of defending French taste—and, by way of taste, a profound cultural inheritance that validated the carnage of the trenches. This symbolic role took on increased national weight in the war years due to a catastrophic drop in the luxury garment trades. As Margaret Darrow explains, when the fashion trade picked up again in 1916, many questioned whether this was a positive show of French economic power or a blatant example of the frivolity of the homefront.[30] Fashionable women became a target of these wartime anxieties. And yet the fashion industry was foundational to French national identity—an exemplar of all that was superior about French

---

[26] Michel Georges-Michel, "Mimi-Pinson," *L'Excelsior*, 19 Nov. [1916].

[27] "Marchandage," *L'Action*, 5 Dec. 1916.

[28] Georges Montorgueil, "La Cocarde de Mimi Pinson," *L'Éclair*. FC, No. 467.

[29] "Les Cocardes de Mimi Pinson," *Le Radical*, 12 Nov. 1915. FC, No. 467.

[30] Darrow, "French volunteer nursing," 69.

culture. Mimi Pinson was, Darrow notes, a similar "embodiment of what was uniquely French about French civilization—its gaiety, insouciance, sophistication, style, and wit—and the exemplar of French femininity."[31] In this context, the women of the OMP became a convenient means of reconciling competing wartime concerns. By lauding Charpentier's worker-students and their cocardes, French society in distress could take comfort in an ideal woman who knew "how to work," who maintained French luxury craft supremacy, and yet who also presented a vulnerable and attractive version of French womanhood.

In opening the exhibit, actress and former OMP student Simone Steyer read a speech (written for her by Camille Mauclair) explicitly linking superior French chic and military might. Addressing her fellow Mimi Pinsons, Steyer proclaimed: "Those that you love are at the front? Well, daughter of the Republic, you must put a cocarde on that front! The Boches have besmirched and dishonored the battle: we have to show them that the French have not forgotten the 'war in laces' [la guerre en dentelles]."[32] This last phrase, referring to the tradition of gentlemanly warfare in the seventeenth and eighteenth centuries, connected Mimi Pinson's confections to a more gracious style of combat. Maurice Le Blond similarly rhapsodized about Mimi's Cocarde as a sign of the "invincible taste of a people": "Ah! the Boches can mobilize their designers to try to dethrone the supremacy of French fashion! But you wouldn't have found this in Berlin!"[33]

The cocarde project allowed participants and observers alike to affirm the reassuring pre-war version of Mimi Pinson as an innately tasteful Parisienne and an exemplar of French fashion's supremacy. Charpentier himself said as much to Pierre Laguionie, director of the Printemps department store, in a letter thanking him for the cocardes contributed by his workers: "No doubt these little marvels will be noticed at our next contest. Everyone will appreciate their enticing originality and affectionate intention. The perfect taste [of your young artists] and their unrivaled inspiration bear witness once more to the immortal genius of the Parsienne."[34] Seamstress Geneviève Paulais from the Maison Jenny was delighted that she and her co-workers could take part in the cocarde initiative, a "truly French ouevre," she wrote, "which reunites all the treasures of French taste, the charm of the Parisienne, and a reminder of our beloved Poilus."[35] Le Figaro commented that the Mimi Pinsons had "applied themselves to this project in which ingenuity and taste duel with one another... The artistic sense of our Parisian

[31] Ibid.

[32] "Compliment de Mimi Pinson aux Autorités de la Ville de Paris, Dit par Mlle Simone Steyer de l'Oeuvre de Mimi Pinson, Écrit par M. Camille Mauclair," Discours prononcés à l'Inauguration de l'Exposition de la 'Cocarde de Mimi Pinson'..., 11 Nov. 1915. FC, No. 466. "Boche" is a derogatory slang word for a German person.

[33] Le Blond, Histoire, 31.

[34] Lettre from Gustave Charpentier to Pierre Laguionie, Aug. 1915. BNF, IFN-53030518.

[35] Letter from Geneviève Paulais (Maison Jenny) to Gustave Charpentier, 1 Aug. 1916, Paris. FC, No. 471.

workingwomen displayed itself in a million ways, each more graceful than the last."[36] *Le Petit Journal* praised the "exceptionally delicate taste" of these "midinettes from several Parisian couture houses."[37] *Le Gaulois* declared that Mimi Pinson's Cocarde "once again reveals the good taste of our fairies of the needle."[38] In 1916, a journalist for *J'accuse*, charmed by the cocarde initiative, exclaimed "Bravo! Mimi Pinson! Work your lovely fingers. Remind the world that behind the France that fights, there is the France that labors, the France of Paris, the France of Mimi Pinson, that is doing all it can and is dreaming."[39] At once hard-working and starry-eyed, Mimi Pinson represented French labor and the capital city itself. Berthe Bontoux praised the cocarde initiative as an exemplar of the "ingenious patriotism" of Frenchwomen: "On the double, with that taste without rival which is their custom, they manufacture cocardes destined for our '*poilus*', cocardes so pretty that they are exhibited at the Petit-Palais."[40]

The continued production of Parisian taste in the form of Mimi Pinson's Cocarde soothed concerns about the loss of a certain essential national character and a certain notion of French femininity, even if or perhaps because this labor was now unremunerated. In this way, Paris's workingwomen were made guardians not of the home fires or the nation's future sons (as might appear in descriptions of middle-class women in wartime), but rather of French labor *and* nationally-significant Parisian chic that would be crucial when the war finally ended. A journalist from *J'accuse* reporting on the cocarde initiative imagined the role of garment workers at the end of the war: "Little workingwoman, humble daughter of the People, make us enchanting gowns with which we can dress the beautiful ladies at the hour of victory, at the hour when you will throw aside your scissors and your needles so that you can kiss our soldiers on their fine faces drooping from the war, and so that with them, you can sing the prettiest of your songs!"[41] Again, we see a skillful collapsing of the workingwoman's cultural functions— erotic object, worker, producer of beauty for the upper classes. Mimi is required simultaneously to labor in the sweated luxury trades, kiss returning soldiers, and preserve the airy character of pre-war France with her fanciful designs and songs—a weighty cluster of roles for an unemployed laborer.

Perhaps most surprising, the recipients of Mimi Pinson's cocardes—soldiers on the front—also made this association between national pride and the tasteful midinette. In a letter of thanks to the OMP in February 1917, one cannoneer at the front addressed Mimi Pinson as the "graceful and gay symbol" of France's

[36] "Cocardes," *Le Figaro* [undated], Nov. 1915. FC, No. 466.
[37] "La Cocarde de Mimi-Pinson," unsigned, *Le Petit Journal*, the day after Petit-Palais exposition opening [12 Nov. 1915]. FC, No. 466.
[38] *Le Gaulois*, 12 Nov. 1915.
[39] "La Cocarde de Mimi Pinson," *J'accuse*, 17 Aug. 1916. FC, No. 466.
[40] Berthem-Bontoux, *Les Françaises et la grande guerre*, 72.
[41] "La Cocarde de Mimi Pinson," *J'accuse*.

"ingenuity, beauty, liberty... The country is sacred, but you are its charm and its expression."[42] Two self-proclaimed "troglodytes" serving in the trenches in Champagne wrote to Charpentier in 1915 asking for "these charming cocardes as only Mimi Pinson's little fingers know how to make," whose "good taste" would "make their Boche neighbors green with envy."[43] Having read about the project in the *Bulletin des Armées*, an artillery soldier wrote requesting a cocarde, this "charming symbol" of "all the elegance and all the heroism of our France... Little Mimi Pinson, if we are no longer waging the 'war in laces,' we are nonetheless battling for an Ideal—Art, Beauty, Elegance, and Charm. And you and your cocardes personify all of that in our eyes."[44]

Soldiers, particularly but not exclusively those from Paris, shared the conflation of Parisian garment workers with the supremacy of French taste and the importance of the capital city as emblem of French civilization. Charles Rearick has argued that the trenches saw the national dissemination of the Parisian picturesque by way of working-class Parisian *poilus* and time spent in Paris on furloughs.[45] Charles Cognault received his cocarde in May 1916 and enthused that it helped "to remind me of my Paris, in all her grace and her current patriotic calm. I am face to face with the Boches just above Verdun and this cocarde brought me great pleasure. The only thing I regret is not to be able to thank myself the fairy with agile figers who made it."[46] Henri Desliens was similarly enthusiastic about his cocarde: "I was thrilled by its loveliness, its grace, by the completely Parisian taste..."[47] Fernand Brantegem asked that Charpentier pass along to "these charming midinettes and Parisian workingwomen" his "sincere congratulations and deepest thanks for the taste that they brought to the fashioning of these superb cocardes."[48] Yet another soldier addressed a poem "to Mimi Pinson" in thanks for his cocarde: "It is your grace and your songs that she keeps in her folds | It is the soul of France and her light laughter... in a bit of ribbon, you give us Paris!"[49] When requests for cocardes went unanswered, some solders wrote again, still hoping to receive "this keepsake that reminds me of my Paris from which I have so long been exiled."[50] A group of twenty-two sailors, most from the *région parisienne*, wrote the OMP in 1915 requesting "a souvenir from our beloved Paris, arriving in the form of a work by our most adorable Mimi Pinsons."[51] Two

[42] Letter from N. Rey, 19 Feb. 1917. FC, No. 474 (b) *Remerciements des soldats du front pour envoi de 'cocardes' et courrier du Front.*

[43] Military postcard from André Cuny, sous-lieutenant, 26 Nov. 1915. FC, No. 474, *Mimi Pinson (Guerre 1914–1918) Demandes de Cocardes.*

[44] J. Nardin, 60eme Artillerie, 28eme Batterie. FC, No. 474.

[45] Rearick, *The French in Love and War*, 19, 30.

[46] Letter from Ch. Cognault to the OMP, 2 May 1916. FC, No. 474 (b) *Remerciements.*

[47] Letter from Henri Desliens to Gustave Charpentier, 15 Apr. 1916. FC, No. 474 (b).

[48] Letter from Fernand Brantegem to the OMP, 17 May 1916. FC, No. 474 (b).

[49] Anonymous, "À Mimi Pinson," 10 Feb. 1916, FC, No. 474 (b). Also reprinted in *Correspondence inédites à des musiciens français 1914–1918*, 269–70.

[50] Letter to OMP, 12 May 1916. FC, No. 474 (b).   [51] Letter, 14 Nov. 1915. FC, No. 474 (b).

self-proclaimed "Parisian sparrows at the Front," Pascal Gaudry and Henri Retiveau, wrote in December 1915 to "Dear Mimi Pinson" after learning of the cocardes campaign: "ingenious and graceful" and evidence of her "talents", "these little masterpieces will remind us of something other than the dreadful skeletal ashes that occupy our woods. They will remind us of Paris!"[52] In the midst of such horrors, soldiers took strength from a flirtation, both remembered and renewed, that spoke to the very *patrimoine* for which they fought in the trenches.

The cocarde campaign, for all of its high-flung jingoism, concentrated considerable erotic attention on the body of the Parisian garment worker—using her appealing corporeality to incarnate homefront comforts, French taste, and gender order. Yves Pourcher discusses wartime Paris as not only "military heart" of the country but also as an erotic tableau where the balance between debauchery and wartime release was constantly under scrutiny.[53] Tens of thousands of soldiers on leave came in and out of Paris by train during the war years, often experiencing the city for the first time, and often as sexual tourists in "Paris putain." Workingwomen were part of the sensual attraction of the city—and perhaps a safer outlet for sexual frustration than prostitutes or foreigners. So prevalent was the idea of wartime Paris as a sexual playground specifically hosting idylls between soldiers and midinettes, that this trope entered into a criminal court case in the suburbs of Paris in 1915. A merchant named Guimelli, accused of stealing automobile parts from British military installations, defended himself by insisting that the stolen goods had been gifts from British soldiers as recompense for translating their correspondence with amorous garment workers, "countless letters from 'Mimi Pinsons' looking for affairs."[54]

The spectacle and erotic potential of the midinette's body as wartime comfort carried over into wartime films, songs, poems, and vaudeville shows that imagined a romantic, physical connection between Mimi Pinson and the *poilu*.[55] In the 1915 film *Le Roman de la Midinette*, film star Musidora plays Jeanne Bernard, a woman who is "one of those delicious Parisian workingwomen that we have baptized with the graceful name Midinettes."[56] Jeanne, the sickly daughter of a sergeant killed in battle, is recuperating in a provincial chateau and corresponding with a lonely soldier named Pierre, who, as a foundling, has no family. The affectionate letters from this unknown midinette brighten his spirit, and ultimately save his

[52] Letter from Pascal Gaudry and Henri Retiveau to the OMP, 30 Nov. 1915. FC, No. 474.

[53] Yves Pourcher, *Les Jours de guerre: la vie des français au jour le jour entre 1914 et 1918* (Paris, 1994), 36, 169, 174.

[54] "Chronique des Tribunaux: Sur la plainte des Anglais," *Le Journal* (25 Apr. 1915), 2.

[55] Mimi Pinson functioned similarly to the heroine of a popular wartime song "Quand Madelon." See Charles Rearick in "Madelon and the men—in war and memory," *French Historical Studies* 17 (1992), 1001–34. On the sexual imagery and erotic longing of wartime songs see Anne Simon-Carrère, *Chanter la Grand Guerre: les 'poilus' et les femmes* (Seyssel, 2014).

[56] *Le Roman de la midinette: scénario* (Paris: Établissements Gaumont, 1915) BNF IFN-53007148 numerisé.

life. Once recovered, he finds Jeanne on her deathbed, and they share their first and only kiss.

The production of songs featuring midinettes, already popular in the pre-war years, continued apace during the war, and consistently focused on the body of the female garment worker as a source of gaiety and romantic escape for front soldiers. René de Buxeuil and Virgile Thomas's 1917 march "Les Midinettes" avoided all references to the war, and instead reveled in the now-traditional imagery of female garment workers as gay, hardworking, and seducible.[57] The song follows the garment workers as they walk to work, and sing along the boulevards, "gay and stylish," while we (the auditors) gaze on dreamily, "all men are besotted | With the midinettes of Paris." The third verse finds the midinettes heading off ("gaily" once more) on a Sunday excursion to the country, where they cavort with lovers under the trees—resulting in a final verse in which a midinette becomes pregnant and marries. The only nod toward the national significance of all of this cheerful laboring, singing, and procreating comes in the last line: "While merry | They're serious | And work for the Country…" 1916's "Tommy et Mimi Pinson" imagined a romance between a midinette and a British soldier on leave in Paris. Here, Mimi's kisses are described in the refrain as a patriotic duty: "In front of all the passers-by, | She doesn't care… it's for a soldier, | Mimi Pinson gives what she has!"[58]

1916's "Si j'étais midinette, ou, Ah! Tais toi," written and performed by the comic *chansonnier* Georgius, has a man imagining himself as a midinette, to bawdy comic effect.[59] Written in one of the darkest years of the war, this light piece accompanied by piano has a male singer reject dreams of becoming an artist, an aviator, or even an emperor, and instead wants only to be a "trottin." He pictures himself "graceful and stylish," lifting his skirt to show off "lovely calves." The song descends into some lewd jokes about the kind of midinette Georgius would make, and ends with his seduction and impregnation by a male lover. In the final verse, he breastfeeds his newborn, and then offers a drink from his breasts to a passing soldier who eyes him. The body and the embodying of the midinette are sources of natalist sexual release and gaiety.

The cocarde initiative, thus, was created out of and understood within this context of an eroticized rapport between Parisian garment workers and front soliders. The catalogue and the inaugural speeches for the exhibit at the Petit Palais

[57] "Les Midinettes." Crée par L. Montagné; chanté par Lucette, Yseyola, Drussy, Andrée Suterre. Paroles de René de Buxeuil & Virgile Thomas. Musique de Léon Montagné (Paris: Imp. Ch. Joly, 1917). BNF-L, 4-VM7-10 (3224).

[58] H. Christiné, "Tommy et Mimi Pinson," Paroles et musique de H. Christiné (Paris: Imprimerie Cavel, 1916). BNF-L, FOL VM7-13514.

[59] G. Guibourg dit Georgius, "Si j'étais midinette, ou, Ah! Tais toi." Music by R. Mercier and H. Piccolini (Paris, 1916). BNF-LFOL-VM7-13823.

envisioned the cocardes as physical manifestations of a romantic connection. Prefect of the Seine Marcel Delanney explained the importance of the cocardes in his speech to the assembled female workers and guests at the opening of the Exposition: "Our soldiers are fighting for a grand and sublime lady: France...But these valliant men need to have their lady personified and need their lady to smile at them and affirm for them the constance of her thought..."[60] Maurice Le Blond invited those in attendance to conjure the sensual physicality behind the cocardes: "Let us consider that in each of these, a pious thought, a discreet and tender emotion, a kiss perhaps, has been deposited, and the invincible essence of a parfume we can almost breathe in...Let us admire them like flowers, flowers of hope and victory, innocently blooming, creased, and elegant, in the quivering and fervent fingers of the humble, diligent fairies of immortal Paris."[61] Photographs attest to the presence of soldiers on leave at the exhibit mingling with live Mimi Pinsons; in one postcard, a woman referred to in the caption only as "Mimi Pinson" pins a cocarde to a visiting soldier's lapel. Indeed, the image of Mimi Pinson offering a cocarde or even a kiss to a *poilu* was repeated in statues and songbooks related to the exhibit, including a statue by Charles-Henri Pourquet in which a stoic *poilu* looks off into the distance while a Mimi Pinson kisses him and pins a cocarde to his uniform.[62] Garment workers who took part in the exposition received a diploma depicting Mimi Pinson kissing a soldier as she fastens a cocarde to his lapel. Directly behind the pair, we see soldiers involved in a firefight and bombs exploding alongside a trench, collapsing the distance between homefront and combat by way of physical contact between the *poilu* and the working Parisienne.

Berthe Bontoux went so far as to suggest that the true object of patriotic display and beauty at the cocarde exposition was the workingwoman herself: "Modest midinettes, and all of your sisters in national devotion, to adorn this altar of the Nation, it would be enough to arrange yourselves in front of it, because you are the most radiant flowers that could bloom in its shadow: flowers of blood, beauty, and love—French flowers!"[63] In fact, in order to "augment the attraction of the Exposition," organizers enlisted the major Parisian fashion houses to send one or two workingwomen to sew cocardes in a model workshop at the

[60] "Discours de M. Marcel Delanney, Préfet de la Seine," FC, No. 466.

[61] Maurice Le Blond, "Préface," *Concours des Cocardes de Mimi Pinson: Catalogue, Novembre 1915* (Paris: Palais des Beaux-Arts de la Ville de Paris, 1915), 3–5, 5. Le Blond was a former secretary of the Conservatoire Populaire de Mimi Pinson, and a former *chef du cabinet* for the Minister of Public Instruction.

[62] Charles-Henri Pourquet, "Mimi Pinson décore de sa cocarde nos héroiques combattants," [statue] photographed in Le Blond, *Histoire*, 32. Pourquet was a monument sculpteur responsible for numerous *monuments aux morts*. See DanielSherman, "Art, commerce, and the production of memory in France after World War I," in *Commemorations: The Politics of National Identity*, ed. John R. Gillis (Princeton, 1994), 186–211, 196.

[63] Berthem-Bontoux, *Les Françaises et la grande guerre*, 72.

exposition, "before the eyes of the public," one afternoon per week from 2 to 4 p.m.[64] This spectacular foregrounding of the workingwoman's body as decorative *objet d'art* reflected the widespread use of working female bodies as a sign of the feminine devotion and diligence of the homefront. Parisian seamstress Louise Délétang complained about another wartime philanthropic workshop where unemployed workingwomen sewed bandages and garments for soldiers in front of a large window, "like strange beasts."[65]

The cocardes were seen as a material extension of the sexualized and aestheticized body of the Parisian garment worker, and became an extremely popular means of representing the homefront. A 1915 cover of *La Vie Parisienne* featured an image by Georges Léonnec titled, "Mimi Pinson's Latest Creation: The Cocarde Dress," in which Mimi Pinson, in a transparent bodice, holds her tricolor skirt aloft, making herself into a cocarde. In this striking vision of Parisian haute couture and the erotic potential of the garment worker, Mimi Pinson's tastefulness, sexual availability, and patriotism are inextricable (Figure 6.4).

Wartime representations of the cocarde campaign inevitably staged physical contact between the seamstress and the *poilu*. The romantic possibilities of the campaign were the main plot of the popular light opera *La Cocarde de Mimi Pinson*, produced at Paris's Apollo Theater in 1915.[66] Set in a Parisian couture house, it follows a wartime love triangle involving the shop's owner (the young widow Madame Frivolet), the head seamstress Marie-Louise, and a dashing lieutenant named Jean. While Jean visits the couture workshop on leave, Marie-Louise secretly stitches a cocarde medallion into the lining of his jacket as protective talisman. When the medallion later shields him from a bullet, Jean assumes Frivolet is responsible and promptly proposes marriage. In the final act, Marie-Louise, who, like many of her fellow seamstresses, has become a war nurse, confesses her love to Jean. Ultimately, Frivolet magnanimously cedes the seamstress not only her fiancé but also her share in the couture house.[67]

---

[64]   Form letter from the OMP presumably to couture houses, Paris, Oct. 1915. FC, No. 466.

[65]   Délétang, *Journal d'une ouvrière parisienne pendant la guerre*, 61–2.

[66]   Maurice Ordonneau and Francis Gally, *La Cocarde de Mimi Pinson: opérette en trois actes*, music by Henri Goublier (Paris, 1915). Louis Maillard directed its debut at the Apollo on 25 November 1915. Jenny Syril (Opéra Comique) played Marie-Louise. Thanks to Charles Rearick for pointing me to Goublier's tomb at Père Lachaise, which lists the operetta first among his prominent works. Paris's Théâtre Moncey put on another patriotic operetta in 1915, *La Caporale Mimi Pinson*, which depicted the "amours du soldat Gavroche" and Mimi Pinson, played by Jane Alstein. *La Renaissanc* (9 June 1917), 20. This show included a military parade, and played to packed houses throughout October 1915 (*Le Journal*, 16 Oct. 1915). On the operetta, see Michela Niccolai, "Une infirmière d'opérette: Mimi Pinson et sa cocarde," in *La Grande Guerre en musique: vie et création pendant la première musicales en France Guerre mondiale*, ed. Florence Doé de Maindreville and Stéphan Etcharry (Brussels, 2014), 233–51.

[67]   Jean-Yves LeNaour refers to a "souffle de moralisation" in Parisian theater during the war. "La Première Guerre mondiale et la régénération," *Revue d'histoire du théâtre* 53, No. 3 (2001), 229–39. Mathilde Joseph explores the heroic vision of the *poilu* in the wartime music-hall. "Le Poilu de music-hall: l'image du poilu dans les music-halls parisiens pendant la Grande Guerre," *Guerres mondiales et conflits contemporains* 50, No. 197 (2000), 21–41.

Figure 6.4. Georges Léonnec (1881–1940), "La Dernière Création de Mimi Pinson: La Robe Cocarde," *La Vie Parisienne*, 4 December 1915.

The Apollo's theater director noted that the operetta would be a "living exposition" of "true Mimi Pinsons in flesh and bone."[68] Reviews of the show and the program highlighted the participation of actress Suzie Myriane, herself a

---

[68] "La Cocarde de Mimi-Pinson: Analyse," *Matinée au profit de l'Office départemental des Oeuvres de Guerre de l'Hôtel-de-Ville pour le Ravitaillement des Serbes*, 11 Jan. 1916. FC, No. 470.

former OMP student.[69] Thanks to philanthropic efforts, workers from Parisian couture houses and department stores were provided free tickets to certain performances of the operetta.[70] The *Echo de Paris* observed that the operetta was performed in "an atmosphere overheated by the presence in the theater of numerous Mimi-Pinsons and glorious wounded soldiers."[71] A worker from the Maison Carlier, though she had already seen the show once, sought a ticket in January 1916 for her "*poilu* from the front who is coming for six days."[72] Alice Guyard, a seamstress at the Maison Henriette, requested tickets for herself, several of her colleagues, and "notre petit ami," a soldier they had met through the cocarde initiative.[73] The show was such a success that performances continued through the winter at the Apollo, and in other theaters through the summer of 1916.[74]

In the opening scene, the young apprentice Zoé describes her demonstrations of gratitude to soldiers: "To thank them, I give a smile in passing to any soldiers on leave I meet, and when I happen on one who says, 'She's nice, this cutie, I'd really like to kiss her!' I respond to that, 'Go ahead, old boy! It's for France!' "[75] Indeed, a running joke in the show is that men wishing to kiss the seamstresses must put coins in a collection box for the troops. Zoé explains, "Since the start of the war, we let anyone kiss us, but on the condition that each 'kisser' makes a little offering... We support our nation with the means available to us."[76]

The cocarde initiative, in which the women in the operetta participate enthusiastically, is understood quite thoroughly as a romantic endeavor. The chaste first hand Marie-Louise secretly pines for the owner's son, the dashing Jean, and sings to the cocarde, "Watch over my love... That he will know upon his return | He will find my love... My sweet cocarde of love, | The lover's messenger."[77] For Jean, too, the cocardes are an emblem of romance with an unknown midinette: "Seeing them | We imagine your face."[78] Later, as he seeks out the anonymous creator of the medallion that saved him, he conjures an image of "this sweet girlfriend"; he imagines the "lovely and very blond" midinette who surely created it, "With the most beautiful eyes in the world, | Seductive, golden voice, enchanting smile."[79] In the classic comedic trope, the curtain closes upon three impending weddings between working-class women (who have all become war nurses) and three men

---

[69] "Théâtre-Français: La Cocarde de Mimi-Pinson," *Journal de Rouen*, 24 June 1916. FC, No. 470.

[70] Some employers selected workers to attend the show. See FC, No. 469. *Mimi Pinson (Guerre 1914–1918). Spectacles "Mimi Pinson."*

[71] "Dans les théâtres," *Echo de Paris*, 27 Nov. 1915.

[72] Letter from L. Andrieux, Maison Carlier, to Gustave Charpentier, 26 Jan. 1916. FC, No. 470.

[73] Letter from Alice Guyard to Gustave Charpentier, 3 Feb. 1916. FC, No. 471. *Mimi Pinson (Guerre 1914–1918). Courier concernant le "Cocarde de Mimi-Pinson."*

[74] The show was performed after World War II, and to this day in the Nord. "La Cocarde de Mimi Pinson," *Opérette*, No. 94.

[75] Ordonneau and Gally, *La Cocarde de Mimi Pinson*, 7.   [76] Ibid. 20.

[77] Ibid. 35.   [78] Ibid. 56.   [79] Ibid. 76.

in national service, and with the entire cast singing of the "tri-color cocarde" as an "insignia of hope" and an "emblem of France" which calls all to victory.[80]

Wartime songs also envisioned the cocarde as a path to physical and sentimental connection between women on the homefront and *poilus*. In 1916's "Mimi Pinson met sa Cocarde" by André Piédallu, the cocarde reminds a trench soldier of Mimi's sweetness, beauty, and fidelity to her loves; "While the shellfire explodes and rages, he smiles thinking of you...".[81] "The New Mimi Pinson and her Cocarde" by Edmond Teulet[82] was sold as a songbook with a cover image of a uniformed soldier with his arm in a sling standing proudly while an attractive Mimi Pinson pins a cocarde to his lapel (Figure 6.5). This Mimi wears a short jacket, a fashionably short full skirt, and a jaunty feathered hat over her smartly coiffed hair. The ribbons flying gaily from her hand-muff and jacket and the ruffles of her collar mimic the cocardes decorating the page, making her a living cocarde. Mimi Pinson is again a fashion producer *and* consumer, as well as romantic companion to the trench soldier.

Paul Marinier's 1916 waltz "La Cocarde de Mimi Pinson" took the form of a letter from a Mimi Pinson to a front soldier to whom she is sending "sa coquette cocarde."[83] Marinier dedicated the song to Henri Lescouzères, a 21-year-old corporal killed in combat in Belgium in May 1915.[84] Marinier imagined this song as a profession of love by a young, attractive garment worker (she describes herself as just twenty years old, "pretty in my light dress") for an unknown *poilu*:

> How I adore you and I don't even know you!
> Are you brunette or blond? I really don't care.
> Short or tall? I don't know at all;
> But yes, I know that you are at the war
> That suffices and I like you a lot.
> This is why I am writing you.
> Don't be too surprised by
> These caressing words,
> "I love you!"

The cocarde is a material conduit of the garment worker's sensual presence: "I'm sending you this ribbon | Which decorated my belt just yesterday. | Last night

---

[80] Ibid. 144.

[81] André Piédallu, "Mimi Pinson met sa cocarde," music by Henry Février (Paris: Heugel & Cie, 1916). BNF Louvois FOL-VM7-13420(1–9).

[82] Teulet wrote another song about "the new Mimi Pinson" in 1903. "La Nouvelle Mimi Pinson," *La Lanterne*, 15 Aug. 1903.

[83] Paul Marinier, "La Cocarde de Mimi Pinson" (1916). Music by Paul Marinier and F. Heintz. Répertoire Mayol (Paris, 1916).

[84] "Lescouzeres, Henri," *Mémoire des Hommes—Mort pour la France de la Première Guerre Mondiale* (Ministère de la Défense, 2013). http://www.memoiredeshommes.sga.defense.gouv.fr

Figure 6.5. "La Nouvelle Mimi Pinson et Sa Cocarde."
Source: Bibliothèque de la Ville de Paris, Fonds Charpentier, Dossier 469.

while falling asleep | It's true, I swear! | I put it close to me | And I dreamt of you; | It saw my dream and, my word, | She's not a cold fish | That Mimi Pinson!" Thus, the cocarde, which Mimi wears close to her during an erotic dream, is a substitute for the absent soldier.

Archival evidence indicates that some front soldiers also found an erotic charge in the cocarde campaign. In 1916, Jacques Caplen, an 18-year-old pilot who received a cocarde, won a military contest for a song honoring Mimi Pinson, shortly before he was killed in a training exercise. Caplen meant his song, "Response to Mimi Pinson," as an answer to Marinier's 1916 song—evidence that popular songs of this sort were circulating on the front.[85] Caplen's mother, a Parisian fashion writer known as Comtesse Maud, financed the song's publication. According to her, the song "enjoyed an enormous success" when vaudeville star Lyse Berty began performing it as part of her repertoire. Following Jacques Caplen's wishes, profits from the song were donated "to all the Midinettes as thanks for sending the Cocardes to the courageous combatants."[86] In the song, the cocarde becomes a tactile, sensual link between the theater of war and the homefront. Addressing his anonymous Mimi Pinson, Caplen notes that the "flirtatious cocarde... crimped by your fine little fingers" is enough for him to imagine her, "delicate and lovely, true jewel of Paris." Caplen refers to keeping the cocarde, which "graced your belt just yesterday," close to him when he sleeps, provoking dreams about his unknown pen pal, "wild dreams which are sometimes | Quite hard on the virtue | Of the poor *poilu*..."[87] The sexual innuendo of these lines reflects a common cultural vision of the working-class Parisienne as at once a comforting sexual companion, a joyful laborer, and a symbol of Parisian culture— a vision validated and even celebrated by the teenage soldier's upper-class mother and by the music-hall audiences who made the song a success.

In January 1916, Maurice Marée of the 164ème infantry regiment posed his demand for cocardes for himself and a dozen comrades in the form of a poem to Mimi Pinson. The poilus think "of you always | Parisiennes, our loves," and long to receive the good-luck charms "that make lovers smile."[88] A *poilu* in the 6e Hussard division addressed a poem to Mimi Pinson which applied the three colors of the cocarde to her body: "Blue like Mimi's eyes... | As white as Mimi's

---

[85] Letter to Gustave Charpentier from the Comtesse Maud, "rédactrice au "*Carnet de la Semaine*, à *la Rampe*, etc...", Jan. 1918. FC, No. 471. The stationery was lined in mourning black. Caplen's song was a prizewinner in the "Concours des Auteurs du Front," *Carnet de la Semaine*, 31 Dec. 1916.

[86] Letter to Charpentier from Comtesse Maud, 2 Sept. 1917. FC, No. 471.

[87] Jacques Caplen, "La Cocarde de Mimi-Pinson," printed song lyrics included with letter to Charpentier from Comtesse Maud, 2 Sept. 1917.

[88] Letter from Maurice Marée [Compagnie Hors Rang 164e Régiment d'Infanterie, Secteur Postal 197] to the Oeuvre de Mimi Pinson, 31 Jan. 1916. *Correspondences inédites à des musiciens français 1914–1918*, 268–9.

arms | And then her cherry mouth | Is red, pretty red, | The red of a love that intoxicates | It's Mimi's caress."[89]

A trench newspaper described the cocarde initiative's popularity at the front, with soldiers awarding them to one another; the Mimi cocardes had become "a war medal...quite difficult to obtain." Physical contact with a Mimi Pinson by way of this campaign was imagined and even demanded by this *poilu* journalist: "So sweet midinettes of Paris, here's to you! And here's to Paris!...a kiss and hug are *de rigueur* for all awarding of medals: in the meantime, kiss all of the rue de la Paix for the *poilus!*"[90] Here we see a transfer of erotic energy—from the workers of the garment district to the cocarde, from the cocarde to the soldiers who distribute them to each other, and then from the soldiers back to the midinettes, who are charged with kissing Parisian men in the absence of these particular soldiers.

Numerous letters from front soldiers to Charpentier's OMP reveal that some already knew Mimi Pinsons well, if not individually. Two Parisian soldiers reminisced about their encounters with garment workers in Paris while on leave: "in days past, you robbed these same *Poilus*, pretty bandits," recounting a moment when a Mimi Pinson grabbed some cords from their epaulettes and ran off, laughing, saying "it's good luck."[91] Several Parisian soldiers asked for cocardes, "to bring us a little bit of this Paris where we lived for so long, to bring us a little bit of the grace...of Mimi-Pinsons. It has been such a long time since we could admire Parisiennes coming and going along the streets of the capital."[92] Once again, Mimi Pinson's importance is not her labor, which remains invisible, but her style, allure, and Parisian-ness. Paris-born soldier Jules Delavis requested cocardes for himself and his comrades, all of whom had some prior knowledge of Mimi Pinson: "Our midinettes, and I say 'our' for good reason," since all of his comrades in the trenches had "known" Mimi in some way—either passing through Paris, or, "Supreme gift, to have been, like me, born there..." As such, the *poilus* recognized the value of "these extravagant cocardes that [the midinettes] know so well how to fashion from their agile hands, with so much grace and finesse."[93]

This metropolitan identity, however, was also legible and meaningful to soldiers who were not Parisian. G. Borgers, an infantry sergeant, wrote to the OMP from the trenches in November 1915 and described himself as "a poor *poilu* who knows no more of Paris than six short days on leave there three months ago." He learned of the cocarde initiative of "our dear midinettes" by way of the *Bulletin des Armées*: "[The cocardes] would remind us of Paris and of our dear Parisiennes...lovely

---

[89] Letter from G.D. [Du front, 6e Hussard, 1er escadron—4e peloton] to "Mimi Pinson," in *Correspondences inédites à des musiciens français 1914–1918*, 273.

[90] "L'Ordre de Mimi Pinson," *L'Echo des Gourbis: Journal anti périodiques des tranchés et boyaux— organe des troglodytes du front*, 3 (May 1915).

[91] Letter from Pascal Gaudry and Henri Retiveau to the OMP, 30 Nov. 1915. FC, No. 474.

[92] Letter from "quelques poilus" to the Oeuvre de Mimi Pinson, 14 Nov. 1915. FC, No. 474.

[93] Letter from Jules Delavis to the Oeuvre de Mimi Pinson, Nov. 1915. FC, No. 474.

workingwomen."[94] René-Elie Amar, a sergeant from Algeria serving on the front in the 3e Zouaves, sent his request for a cocarde in the form of a remembrance of the Battle of the Marne. Titled "Zouzous et Mimi-Pinson," this vignette recalls midinettes encouraging troops moving through Paris in the early days of the mobilization in September 1914: "Learning that they were passing through, the Mimi-Pinsons—deliciously sweet—gave them a rapturous welcome—a kiss here—a word there. And our good Zouaves, made exuberant by the enthusiasm, went off to the Marne...many of these Brave Ones, at the sublime call to Victory, would be lost by the evening of 11 September. But they had saved Paris...the most beautiful of flowers, Paris...the pearl of the World—and making the Boche say...'Deutschland nicht Kapout Pâriss!' [The Germans will not get to Paris]"[95] For Amar, French victory in the Marne was inseparable from the defense of Paris as cultural "pearl" and from the erotic energy of the Parisian midinette. Amar was so pleased with the aptness of his *feuillet* that he published it multiple times in the years after the war in the North African veterans' journal *Le Mutilé de l'Algérie* to honor his comrades.[96]

Letters between the homefront and the trenches, as Stéphane Audoin-Rouzeau has chronicled, were an indispensable emotional and physical "bridge" linking soldiers to "the universe of the home front, its attractions counterbalancing resentment accumulated against the population as a whole."[97] Soldiers' letters to the OMP fortified links in a fantasized courtship with midinettes. Indeed, these letters often read more as love letters than institutional correspondence, emphasizing an individual emotional and (possible future) physical connection. Often, soldiers who received cocardes requested the names and addresses of their "generous *donatrices*" so that they could begin a personal correspondence.[98] Léon Jouve, an infantryman in the 413ème, wrote to the OMP in December 1916 asking not for a cocarde, but for a "young and gay" correspondent, "who wanted to have the perfume of her letters mix with the smell of gunpowder and

---

[94] Letter from G. Borgers to the Oeuvre de Mimi Pinson, 28 Nov. 1915. FC, No. 474.

[95] Letter from René-Elie Amar, *Correspondences inédites à des musiciens français 1914–1918*, 274. During the war, Amar served on the governing council of the Association fraternelle des anciens combattants de l'Armée de Paris. He was wounded in the Marne, and later was elevated to the rank of *maréchal des logis* in the 83e artillery regiment (*L'Univers Israélite*, 13 July 1917; 28 Feb. 1919). After the war, he served as the vice president of the Sociétés Patriotiques de Relizane in Algeria, and published in *Le Mutilé de l'Algérie*, *L'Echo d'Alger*, and *L'Afrique du Nord illustré*. He was the son of Abraham Amar, municipal councillor and president of the Association culturelle israélite de Relizane.

[96] René-Elie Amar, "Zouzous et Mimi-Pinsons," *Le Mutilé de l'Algérie: Journal des mutilés, réformés, et blessés de guerre de l'Afrique du Nord* (16 Sept. 1934), 5. See also René-Elie Amar, "Zouzous et Mimi-Pinson," *Le Mutilé de l'Algérie* (25 Jan. 1934).

[97] Stéphane Audoin-Rouzeau, *Men at War, 1914–1918: National Sentiment and Trench Journalism in France during the First World War* (Oxford, 1992), 142.

[98] Letter to OMP, 6 Aug. 1915.

asphyxiating gas…"[99] Pierre Chaffange included a poem in his request for a cocarde rhapsodizing about his "two girlfriends at the front: | Rosalie and Mimi Pinson." ("Rosalie" was the commonly used nickname for the *poilu*'s bayonet.) Mimi Pinson, he writes, is a "dainty workingwoman" who "enchants" him, and makes him dream of bigamy.[100] A song composed by a *poilu* to thank "Mimi Pinson" for her cocarde emphasized the personal connection between these two strangers; in return for the cocarde made by her "skillful fingers," he will fashion her a ring and find a four-leaf clover for her in a field.[101] One letter included some dried flowers and leaves from the front.[102] Another hoped that an imagined addressee, "Dear Maiden," would write him, as he had not heard from his own family in two years: "I will at least be happy to know you are in perfect health and still working for this beautiful oeuvre."[103]

A *poilu* who identified himself as "Charlette" addressed a racy postcard to thank "Chère Mimi Pinson" for her cocarde; the postcard was a color-tinted photograph of a man and a woman, nude from the shoulders up, kissing. The card included a poem titled "The Kiss" which described lovers, "heart against heart": "We give each other a long kiss, and then an even better one." In his note on the back of the card, Charlette indicates that he is sure that his imagined correspondent, the creator of his cocarde, is single and that after the war "a true *poilu* (as I have the honor of being) in giving you his heart, will know how to make you as happy as you surely deserve." He concludes by offering his correspondent "either a ring, or a brooch."[104]

There is evidence in Charpentier's archive that some garment workers conceived of their participation in the cocarde initiative in the same way: a means of establishing a fortifying intimacy with a *poilu*. Some cocardes enclosed locks of hair as part of the "fetish." One worker named Mady sent her own personal good-luck charm—a worn coin hanging from three handmade rings—to the cocarde initiative, in order to protect an unknown *poilu*.[105] Jean Aubray noted that "Certain cocardes contain a strand of hair, a new coin, a cigar, a love note.

---

[99] Carte-lettre a.s. de Léon Jouve, 30 Dec. 1916 to "Mme la Directrice du Cour [sic] de Mimie Pinçon [sic], Boulevard des Capucines, Paris," *Correspondences inédites à des musiciens français 1914–1918*, ed. Sylvie Douche (Paris, 2012), 264. The same phrasing about perfume and asphyxiating gas was used by a soldier in the same regiment and secteur the previous month (letter from Jules Rodier, téléphoniste 413eme d'Infanterie, ibid. 262).

[100] Letter from Pierre Chaffange to Gustave Charpentier, 23 Nov. 1915. FC, No. 474.

[101] "La Marraine," Chanson de remerciement envoyée à Gustave Charpentier par un poilu (signature illegible). Bibliothèque Historique de la Ville de Paris. In *Correspondences inédites à des musiciens français 1914–1918*, 285.

[102] FC, No. 471.

[103] Letter to OMP ("Chère Demoiselle"), 5 May 1916, FC, No. 474 (b).

[104] Letter from "Charlette" to the OMP, 10 Jan. 1916.

[105] "Une fétiche," Exposition de la Cocarde de Mimi Pinson [Carte postale]. CPA-2290 Exposition de la Cocarde de Mimi Pinson [1915]. "Mady donne son vieux porte bonheur car elle est sûre de son efficacité."

Ah! The love notes of Mimi Pinson!" A workingwoman named Andrée Gatineau "braided a lock of her hair with the ribbons in the colors of the Allies," and attached a note: "In sending this, a little bit of Paris flies toward you, soldier, you who defend us. Mimi Pinson is waiting for you."[106] Some cocardes struck one battalion chief as so personal that he wrote the OMP to make sure he understood the intention: "before handing out certain cocardes signed with a name with or without an address, and a lock of fine hair, I would like to know the intention of the *donatrices*."[107]

Nineteen-year-old seamstress Marcelle Niowesielska at the Maison Ory in the Paris suburbs sent packages of hand-knitted socks and sweaters to soldiers throughout the war, and also contributed to the cocarde campaign. She composed a poetic homage to "Our brave *poilus*" in which she insisted that the enclosed cocarde would evoke envy in "more than one boche" and, most important, would bring the *poilu* back, "Close to your mother with the soft eyes | To your fiancée who loves you | And whose kisses are so wild."[108] In October 1915, a seamstress at Boué Soeurs scolded the organizers of the cocarde initiative for exhibiting her handiwork rather than sending the cocardes directly to trench soldiers. In this rare document, a workingwoman expressed her vision of the cocarde campaign, one that also saw the cocarde as a private intimacy between working Parisienne and trench soldier. Signing herself "an anonymous midinette," she wrote on behalf of her comrades in the workshop:

> When we agreed to collaborate with the Cocarde charity, it was because we were pleased by the idea that a small bit of ribbon folded by our shops could carry a little bit of joy to some brave *poilu* who, in receiving it, would feel the heartfelt thought that motivated us. We were told we needed to hurry, that many *poilus* had received their cocardes and had been so happy about them that you wanted to continue the distribution. We were more than a little disappointed to see our humble cocardes remain in shop windows on full view in front of indifferent folks instead of heading toward the ones for whom our hearts had intended them. We are even more so now that we see the Cocarde charity has become a point of competition between our shops rather than reserved purely and simply for our Brave Ones, and we would prefer not to take part any more.[109]

---

[106] Jean Aubray, "Mimi Pinson au Petit Palais," *Liberté*, 11 Nov. 1915. FC, No. 466.

[107] Letter from Émile Lelandais, Chef de Bataillon to the OMP, 22 Oct. 1917. FC, No. 471.

[108] Letter from Marcelle Niowesielska [Maison Ory, Enghien-les-Bain] to Oeuvre de Mimi Pinson, 28 July 1915. According to genealogical work by Michel Bouyeron, Niowesielska was born 31 July 1896 in Paris's 14e arrondissement. She married painter Marcel Bouyeron in August 1922, and died in Neuilly-sur-Seine in 1969. Her granddaughter, Sophie Ververken, shared with the author letters written by soldiers during the war to express gratitude for sweaters, socks, and caps Marcelle had knitted.

[109] Letter to Gustave Charpentier from "Une midinette inconnue qui vous exprime la pensée de ses compagnes," 21 Oct. 1915. FC, No. 471.

She insisted that the Maison Boué worked hard for "our soldiers," without the need for encouragement or publicity. She requested that their cocardes not be exhibited, and, instead, be kept in a "modest" box until they could be sent to the front. She regretted that many soldiers had died while the cocardes were on display in Paris and thus would never benefit from the joy they provided. She concluded with an angry postscript to the letter in which she demanded, from the perspective of the cocardes, "Above all, don't put us on display because our little words were intended to amuse a dear *poilu* and not a crowd of idlers."[110] Here the cocarde is indeed conceived as an intimate connection between this woman and the unknown soldier who will receive her confections. The director of the Maison Redfern relayed a similar sentiment on the part of his workers in a letter to Charpentier that same month, responding to a request by Charpentier that his workers join in a large display of cocardes: "Monsieur Redfern feels that this does not accord with the desired objective of the workingwomen. They made these cocardes, through their own initiative, in the hopes that they would be sent directly to the soldiers."[111]

Much like Santanu Das, I contend that the fantasized intimacy between these workingwomen and soldiers was at once sexual and not.[112] The isolation of the trenches and the fear of France's defeat transmuted a pre-war trope of sexual idyll between young garment workers and bourgeois men into a patriotic vision of union between the homefront and the trenches. The tastefulness and corporeal availability of the Parisienne's body took on magical qualities: the ability to ward off death and defeat, to bring gaiety improbably to the trenches, and to reintegrate a severed nation. Artilleryman George Laure wrote the OMP in November 1915, requesting cocardes that "dear Midinettes" had made with "your charming fingers." The power of the cocarde is imagined by even this *poilu* as a talisman, "a fetish" which "will revive the unsteady." After the victory, "we will create together not a France 'uber alles' but a France that is grand, long-lasting, admired, and respected." He signed off by musing that the *poilus* regretted only that "your delicate hands do not pin this good-luck charm to their chest."[113]

The very materiality of the cocarde as talismanic object to be touched and carried seems to have been the root of its appeal. Soldiers, garment workers, and observers alike were all invested, however whimsically, in the semi-magical capacities of the cocarde, a *fétiche de guerre* that drew its power from the erotic imaginary of the midinette. We have already seen this function of the cocarde in

---

[110] Ibid.

[111] Letter to Gustave Charpentier from Maison Redfern, 14 Oct. 1915, Paris. FC, No. 471.

[112] Santanu Das, "'Kiss me Hardy': intimacy, gender, and gesture in World War I trench literature," *Modernism/modernity* 9, n No. 1 (2002), 51–74.

[113] Letter from George Laure (?) [58e Régiment Artillerie de Campagne, 3e Groupe] to the Oeuvre de Mimi Pinson, 14 Nov. 1915. FC, No. 471. On good-luck objects and superstitions in the trenches see Stéphane Audoi-Rouzeau and Annette Becker, *14–18, Retrouver la Guerre* (Paris, 2000).

Ordonneau and Gally's 1916 operetta. The cocarde created by Marie-Louise not only saves Jean from a bullet, but also plays the role of Cupid for whoever holds it. Marie-Louise endows the medallion with protective powers over "the one that I love": "Little cocarde...you will deflect all danger from him...these little pieces of ribbon which I kiss with all of the strength of my love, will be a talisman for him!"[114] Later, she sings of the protective force of the cocarde, "when made with love": "all of its power will reside | in the gentle kiss of a woman."[115] Marie-Louise's cocarde not only saves lives, but also enacts romantic bewitching, conjuring marital union between Jean and Marie-Louise, Zoé and a wealthy dilettante, and the cook Sophie with a *poilu*.

The cocardes were coveted in the trenches at least in part because of their talismanic touch. Sometimes the wives of front soldiers requested cocardes for their husbands at the front expressly for their protective capacities.[116] One *poilu* wrote to the OMP in 1916: "I like to believe that this sweet good-luck charm will protect me from the dangers of the campaign."[117] Marcel Le Boucher, a 22-year-old medical student serving in the *infirmier militaire* on the front, asked the OMP if "one of your 'Mimi Pinson' girlfriends" could send him "a doll which she will have dressed and which will be for me and for my comrades a real luck-bearing talisman."[118] An unusual request which jars the modern reader—a frontline medic asking a Parisian workingwoman to send a doll to him and his comrades as they tend to the war wounded. And the doll is quite specifically meant to be dressed by a midinette, emphasizing the role of the midinette's fashion acumen in her position as national talisman.

In winter 1918, as Paris became the increasing target of bombardment, a new talisman appeared—the rough homemade pair of dolls in woolen thread known as Nénette et Rintintin that proliferated as good luck charms to protect Parisians from German air raids.[119] Over time, the makeshift dolls were also sent to soldiers on the front. One figure in a skirt, one in pants, attached by a thread, and sometimes accompanied by a baby, these dolls could be found all over France in the final year of the war. Popular lore suggested that the figures had originated as the confection of Parisian midinettes to ward off the German bombers.[120] *Le Carnet de la Semaine* claimed that their creator was an amorous seamstress at Paquin

---

[114] Ordonneau and Gally, *La Cocarde de Mimi Pinson*, 35.   [115] Ibid. 54–5.
[116] FC, No. 474, FC, No. 474 (b).
[117] Letter to the OMP ("Chère Demoiselle"), 5 May 1916. FC, No. 474 (b).
[118] Letter from Marcel Le Boucher, "étudiant en médecine, 22 ans, 4e section d'infirmier militaire, détaché aux fonctions de médecin auxiliaire au groupe de Brancadiers," to the OMP, [undated]. FC, No. 474.
[119] The dolls seem to have been named after a pair of dolls designed by *dessinateur* Francisque Poulbot in 1913.
[120] See a description of the dolls in Marquise de Ravenel, "French fashions: the spirit of Nenette and Rintintin helps Parisians to hold out for victory en route," *The New France: An Illustrated Monthly Magazine of Franco-American Relations* II, No. 6 (Aug. 1918), 172–4.

named Geneviève, and that the dolls had quickly become "the war fetish of Parisian midinettes"[121] Édouard Delabarre reported seeing midinettes wearing the dolls pinned to their bodices during the bombing of Paris.[122]

The connection between the male and female dolls was believed to be crucial to their effectiveness. Illustrator and novelist Pierre Mac Orlan wrote of the dolls: "Separated, they lose their power."[123] American soldier Kenneth MacNichol was told by a French soldier that the love of the midinette who stitched the dolls was critical to their protective power: "It is said that Nenette and Rintintin the First were conceived in the mind of an unknown midinette, and were torn between the curves of her clever fingers to be given to her lover before he went away...there is no doubt that those little puppets had power to make brave men of cowards, and heroes of those who needed no such support. The secret? It was ordained that Nenette and Rintintin should be made with love sewn into every stitch—thence came their virtue. Otherwise they were no more than a wisp of yarn crumpled and twisted resting in a forgotten pocket of a soldier's blouse."[124]

Many found the dolls not only a touching response to the terrors of the war, but also characteristic of Parisian taste. Mac Orlan argued that the dolls were "the clear manifestation of the soul of an entire elegant race that knows how to make beautiful things with a song on their lips...Nénette et Rintintin are a part of the genius of our country."[125] Delabarre saw the dolls as proof that "The gravest events have never suffocated French gaiety" and as a "pleasing vision, a pure and entirely French expression of the disdain that the most fragile and graceful elements of our threatened city have put up against the useless and idiotic brutality of the savages across the Rhine."[126] It is difficult not to draw a corollary between these dolls, wildly popular in the last months of the war, and the cocardes. Both relied on a notion of national unity based on sexual union between midinettes and front soldiers. Each warded off violence and death by way of this eroticized, if vulnerable, link between French men and women. And each was also used as a stand-in for French national taste.

---

[121] "La Défense de Paris," *Le Carnet de la Semaine* (2 June 1918), 3.

[122] Édouard Delabarre, "Nénettes et Rintintins," in *Précis analytique des travaux de l'Académie des sciences, belles-lettres et arts de Rouen pendant l'année 1918* (Rouen, 1919) 697–8.

[123] Pierre Mac Orlan, "Les Petits Soldats de la bonne chance," *La Baïonette* No.157 (4 July 1918), 422. On the importance that the figures remain connected see also Caroline Frevert, "Nenette and Rintintin," *St Nicholas* 46 (Dec. 1918), 119–20.

[124] Kenneth MacNichol, "Nenette and Rintintin," *Advocate of Peace through Justice* 87, No. 5 (May 1925), 275–83, 277. MacNichol, a sergeant in the US forces and a writer for *Stars and Stripes*, had a romance with a young Frenchwoman while in France, followed by a custody controversy when she gave birth to a daughter. *New York Times*, 24 March 1920.

[125] Mac Orlan, "Les Petits Soldats de la bonne chance," 422.

[126] Delabarre, "Nénettes et Rintintins," 697.

The Grisette and the *Poilu*

While slightly updated, the wartime image of Mimi Pinson was one of continuity, a link to a pre-war France unchanged by the cataclysm of the conflict. The Exposition de la Cocarde in 1915 embedded the handiwork of the Parisian *ouvrières* within a longer historical narrative of working-class Frenchwomen's taste and national devotion. Spelling out the laboring Parisienne's storied tradition of service to the Republic in inaugurating the Exposition, Prefect of the Seine Marcel Delanney imagined Mimi Pinson as a timeless defender of French liberty, back to the Revolution of 1830 (quoting Musset on Mimi's "republican heart"), and even the first French Revolution in 1789: "Wasn't [Mimi Pinson] already waging war, back when Liberty, at its dawning, called to citizens to defend the sacred ground of the nation? She waged war, just as you do today, by fashioning, with all her patriot's soul, these innumerable tricolor cocardes intended to show other peoples the new faith…"[127] Here, Mimi's historic role is to call for the defense of the Patrie, and to manufacture tasteful cocardes that will reveal to the world the universal values of the French Revolution. The exposition catalogue declared that in cocardes, "the warrior virtues of the ancestors suddenly will be heard to sing through [these women]."[128] At the exposition, workingwoman Berthe Petit erected a historical "reconstitution" of cocardes dating back to the Revolution of 1789, assembled from documents in the Musée de l'Armée. Thus, the tasteful manufacture of cocardes by working-class Frenchwomen was tied to a legacy of national defense and republican faith.

While the cocarde exhibit represented garment workers as modish sweethearts, it also cloaked them in the garb of historical memory, the nineteenth-century *grisette*. Musset's poem about Mimi was cited in multiple speechs from the exhibition. In fact, other than the Paquin-draped *coquette* (Figure 6.3), the only representations of Mimi Pinson in the exhibition were markedly nineteenth-century figures. The panel of the Magasins du Louvre featured two Mimi Pinsons—one seated on a stool fashioning a cocarde and wearing a long, flowered dress with puffed sleeves and lace collar; another in a voluminous gown, puffed sleeves, a large ribbon headdress, and delicate slippers (Figure 6.6). Both figures call to mind the romantic styles of the Parisienne of the 1830s rather than the midinette of 1915, though they tower above twentieth-century scenes of war: bayonet-wielding *poilus*, trucks, planes, and zeppelins.

---

[127] "Discours de M. Marcel Delanney, Préfet de la Seine," *Discours prononcés à l'Inauguration de l'Exposition de la "Cocarde de Mimi Pinson" au Palais des Beaux-Arts de la Ville de Paris*, 11 Nov. 1915. FC, No. 466. The speech was also excerpted in "Les Cocardes de Mimi Pinson," *Le Radical*, 12 Nov. 1915. See newsreel of the event, *Une Exposition artistique féminine en l'honneur de nos poilus* (Paris, 1915). www.gaumontpathearchives.com, Ref. No. 1546GJ 00003.

[128] *Concours des Cocardes de Mimi-Pinson, Novembre 1915, Catalogue* (Palais des Beaux-Arts de la Ville de Paris, 1915). FC, No. 468, *Mimi Pinson (Guerre, 1914–1918)*.

Figure 6.6. "Exposition de la Cocarde de Mimi Pinson, 9. Grands Magasins du Louvre—Maison Jenny," 1915.

Source: Bibliothèque de la Ville de Paris, Fonds Charpentier, Dossier 469.

A prominent lifesized diorama in the exposition depicted "Mimi Pinson in her boutique," a mid-nineteenth-century female wax figure in long dress, frilly apron, lace fichu, and demure bonnet standing in the doorway of an ivy-covered wood shack. A bird cage hangs in the doorway, and the window is decorated with nineteenth-century fashion prints and flowers. Mimi turns coquettishly and holds a tricolor cocarde. *L'Excelsior* admired the "exquisite evocation" and "adorable reconstitution" of "Mimi Pinson, flowerseller" alongside the church of St Martin.[129] Of course, this lifelike "reconstitution" was nothing of the sort. Musset's fictional Mimi Pinson frequented the Latin Quarter, not St Martin's 3rd arrondissement, and she was a seamstress, not a flowerseller. So, if this diorama's significance lay not in its historical recreation of a fictional character, why this detailed *mise en scène*? This was an assemblage of signs meant to evoke a particular version of the Parisian working class, and a particular, pre-twentieth-century version of French labor. This supposed flowerseller has multiple hat boxes—a clear signifier in this period for a midinette and garment labor. Likewise, the caged bird, first identified with Mimi Pinson in Bayard and Dumanoir's 1845 play *Mademoiselle Mimi Pinson*, was frequently used to stand in for midinettes, the "pinsons" of Paris, with their delicate appetites, song, and decorative appeal.

---

[129] "Mimi Pinson dans sa boutique," *Excelsior: Journal Illustré Quotidien* (9 Dec. 1915), 10.

The cocarde exposition also included a display titled "Some Mementos of 1830: Musset's Room," furnished by Madame Lardin de Musset, along with the Garde-Meubles National and a group called "the Mussettistes." This scene featured furniture and bibelots from mid-nineteenth-century romanticism—a portrait of Musset, one of Chopin's pianos, etc. A seemingly odd display for an exposition dedicated to celebrating the heroes of the current war and their homefront admirers, the Musset mementos would have been legible to viewers steeped in a national culture which seamlessly connected Parisian midinettes with pre-twentieth-century romantic dalliance and tasteful cultural production. For exposition visitors, the links between the bayonet of the Altar of the Nation and Chopin's piano, between Mimi Pinson's puffed sleeves and the zeppelins behind her, would have been self-evident. The soldiers understood that the precious accoutrements of romantic artistic production were signs of French civilization itself, in no small way a perfect rendering of the stakes of the war. The link between the trenches and this cultural patrimony was the body of the Parisian garment worker, a living conduit between the beleaguered *poilu* and the abstract ideals of *Patrie* for which he sacrificed his youth. The cocarde exposition thus gave monumental play to Mimi Pinson as attractive cypher of a French national identity rooted in nostalgic longing.

Maurice Le Blond, a former functionary in the Ministry of Public Instruction and one of the exposition organizers, demonstrated the way the nostalgic reson-ance of Mimi Pinson was transformed in the war years to speak to a loyal and newly serious French public. He suggested that "today's Mimi-Pinson"—listening to lectures, attending meetings at the union hall—would be unrecognizable to Musset. Still, the Mimi Pinson of 1915 had "stayed a simple pretty girl, smiling, impulsive, disinterested, capable of all caprices, but also susceptible to the most unexpected devotion. Thus, it is true that the permanent character of the race survives and carries on in spite of superficial transformations!"[130] In "our current pinsonettes," one could glimpse the "traditional silhouette, the classic figure of the *grisette* of yesteryear. Improvident and carefree, coquette and poor, they know, in spite of everything, how to preserve a sense of citizenship, a sympathetic and charitable spirit..." At the outbreak of the war, these "valiant and patriotic" young women had sung the "warrior virtues of our ancestors."[131] He compared the Mimi Pinsons to the "intrepid" *poilus* in whom one could still ascertain the "virtues that led to the glory of their ancestors, the volunteers of [1792]..."[132] Here, young workingwomen are, unusually, elevated alongside combat soldiers for their

---

[130] Maurice Le Blond, "Préface," *Concours des Cocardes de Mimi Pinson*, 3.

[131] Ibid. 4. These speeches were reprinted in press coverage of the event, and appended in their entirety in the OMP's official *Histoire de Mimi Pinson*. See "Les Cocardes de Mimi Pinson," *Le Radical*, 12 Nov. 1915, and Le Blond, *Histoire*, 35.

[132] Le Blond, "Préface," *Concours des Cocardes de Mimi Pinson*, 3. This line refers to the men who enlisted in the French revolutionary army during war with Austria and Prussia in 1792.

patriotic valor, their feminine courage and civic devotion evinced only by their wistful immutability.

Beyond the exposition, the cocardes were understood within a field of patriotic nostalgia. Reporting in 1916 on the OMP boutique where cocardes were sold by midinettes to benefit war wounded, Michel Georges-Michel reassured readers concerned that the Paris and France of old were lost in the war: "But yes, it's Mimi Pinson! Mimi Pinson lives still!"[133] Edmond Teulet's popular wartime song "The New Mimi Pinson and her Cocarde," presumably inspired by the OMP initiative, provided new lyrics to an 1846 song "Mimi Pinson," by Frédéric Bérat (in which Bérat set Musset's words to music).[134] Lines about Mimi's cocarde being pinned to the horizon-blue caps of front soldiers were accompanied by a nostalgic nineteenth-century melody—a comforting frame which updates but does not fundamentally overturn older models of female devotion and picturesque submission.

Beyond the cocarde campaign, the wartime midinette was employed as a sign of continuity, the perseverance of both pre-war insouciance and French cultural ascendancy. In 1918, playwright Maurice Rostand composed a poetic ode to Paris unchanged despite the war.[135] While he admits that many have left Paris, true Parisians have remained, especially "the supple midinette," whistling on the sidewalk and falling effortlessly into a love affair. Published in La Baïonnette in June 1918, the poem's airiness is somewhat forced; Rostand claims that after four years of cataclysm and bloodshed, and a winter during which Paris was the target of frequent bombings, "Nothing has changed." Rostand juxtaposes the amorous midinette on the streets of Paris with politicians, hommes des lettres, and literary characters like Les Misérables' Gavroche. The seducible garment worker is made a piece with a vital cultural patrimony which, for France to survive, must remain unchanged.

Reimagining Mimi Pinson as an attractive, jolly, and undemanding companion as well as a patriotic and hard-working tastemaker may have offered journalists, philanthropists, and even soldiers a helpful narrative for organizing the trauma of the war years. The insistence and persistence of this image during wartime may also, however, indicate just how unsettled both gender and class hierarchies were perceived to have become in this period—with the new Mimi Pinson one (ultimately unsuccessful) attempt to stem changes in the labor force and in French society

---

[133] Michel Georges-Michel, "Mimi-Pinson," L'Excelsior, 19 Nov. 1916. FC, No. 466. Mimi Pinson (Guerre, 1914–1918) La Cocarde de Mimi Pinson: organisation, magasin.

[134] Edmond Teulet, "La Nouvelle Mimi Pinson et sa cocarde" (Paris: Marcel Labbé) FC, No. 469. Frédéric Bérat, "Mimi Pinson: paroles d'Alfred Musset" (Paris: J. Meissonnier, 1846). This was not the first time that Teulet had taken up the subject; he authored a song in 1903 also titled "La Nouvelle Mimi Pinson," La Lanterne (15 Aug. 1903), 2. Teulet hosted a performance of the song at a convalescent home for blinded soldiers in October 1915. "Nouvelles théâtrales," La Lanterne (4 Oct. 1915), 2. In 1926, he was interviewed as part of a discussion about the destruction of the Maison de Mimi Pinson. A.L., "Au sujet d'une vieille maison: de Mimi Pinson à Louise," L'Intransigeant, 3 Sept. 1926.

[135] Maurice Rostand, "A la grosse Bërtha," La Baïonnette (6 June 1918), 366.

in general which had been underway well before the outbreak of hostilities. The new Mimi Pinson embodied not only a nostalgic vision of French femininity, but also a nostalgic vision of French industry—a labor force of skilled artisans devising wonders of handmade ingenuity.

Mimi Pinson Infirmière

During the war years, Charpentier's Oeuvre de Mimi Pinson also organized a volunteer nursing corps, an initiative which failed to capture the degree of public interest and approval sparked by the cocarde campaign. A brief examination of this nursing corps offers both useful comparison and striking contrast to the reception of the cocarde initiative. Charpentier's nursing corps originated from the unsuccessful effort of a number of Parisian workingwomen to join military health services as volunteers. When these women offered "their tenderness and their devotion" to the military, according to Le Blond, they were rebuffed, and this "setback had left them heartbroken and incensed."[136] The OMP responded by arranging a free nurse training program for unemployed Parisian workingwomen at the Hôpital Boucicaut. Instructors recommended the strongest students for a month-long hospital internship in Paris. The OMP assumed the costs of providing and laundering the required uniform, and of a daily lunch allowance. Some OMP members embarked upon door-to-door campaigns to fundraise for the program.[137] After several months of service in a military hospital, interns were admitted to the "corps des infirmières libres du Ministre de la Guerre."[138] The first OMP nurses departed for service in military hospitals in February 1915,[139] taking on an array of tasks from darning socks to tending to typhoid patients to assisting with physiotherapy. More than 800 women signed up to serve as OMP nurses, ranging in age from women in their fifties and sixties to teenagers.[140]

The OMP also seems to have handled the processing of unemployment benefits for their nurses while they were on assignment, and some OMP nurses benefited from a small government salary. In February 1915, Charpentier successfully lobbied the Ministry of War to give the nurses of the OMP the status of "Croix Rouge auxiliare" (so that they could take advantage of the half-price train tickets offered by the railways to war-wounded aid organizations).[141] That same month, Prefect Delanney announced that Mimi Pinsons serving as nurses away from Paris would

---

[136] Le Blond, *Histoire*, 29.

[137] See "Rapport de Marguerite Bourguin à Monsieur Charpentier," FC, No. 462.

[138] "Oeuvre de Guerre des infirmireres de MIMI PINSON: Extrait du Règlement," 1917. FC, No. 463. *Mimi Pinson (Guerre, 1914–1918) Infirmières-Hôpitaux militaires.*

[139] This was reported in "Mimi Pinson infirmière," *Le Figaro*, 4 Feb. 1915.

[140] See letters from OMP nurses to Charpentier and Charpentier's registration lists, FC, Nos. 465 and 478.

[141] Letter from the Ministère de la Guerre to Gustave Charpentier, 16 Feb. 1915. FC, No. 463.

have their unemployment benefits extended.[142] The Ministry of War declared the OMP nursing corps an official "oeuvre de guerre" in February 1917.

The OMP nursing corps revealed, for observers, worrisome cracks in the *union sacrée* and became an opportunity for talking about class solidarity and for further critiquing the leisured *bourgeoises* of the Croix Rouge. Margaret Darrow has demonstrated the difficulty all women faced in carving out a place in the national mobilization, and she references some contemporary criticism of the Croix Rouge "for shutting out the vocation and nursing talent of less well-to-do women." Nurses also faced suspicion about war nursing as a route to emancipation, social status, and even sexual pleasure for bored women.[143]

OMP nurses were often contrasted with the bourgeois and aristocratic ladies of the Croix Rouge. Charpentier played upon this distinction when he asked donors to fund nursing uniforms for Mimi Pinsons: "Finally, here are some women who know how to work."[144] Le Blond suggested that garment workers wished to serve because they better understood men of their class: "Isn't it, they protested, their brothers, their fiancés who are battling over there, in the Artois, in the Argonne?...Don't they know better than many others how to care for a laborer, a son of the People, shivering on his bed from fever and pain?"[145] He noted that OMP nurses, who knew grueling daily labor, "joyfully take on the most off-putting, the most difficult jobs, with a preference for serving the critically wounded, those suffering from tetanus and typhus, those consumed by delirium or the horror of convulsions."[146]

OMP nurses met resistance in military hospitals and in the press. In the spring of 1915, Charpentier wrote an indignant reply to a hospital director who had refused the services of the Mimi Pinsons: "I do not see in your response your usual courtesy toward our kind Parisiennes...What are they asking for? To be received as the Ladies of the Red Cross are..." Charpentier nonetheless assured the hospital director that after the war, "There is absolutely no possibility that Mimi Pinson will abandon her métier to become an orderly or a professional nurse."[147] By the summer of 1915, Charpentier protested the rejection of OMP nurses in certain military hospitals to the Under-Secretary of State at the Ministry of War, Justin Godart. Charpentier described the "true injustice" of treating OMP nurses as interlopers trying to usurp the authority of the Red Cross. In Amiens, the Inspector General of the Service de Santé "has banned our nurses, prescribing

[142] "Oeuvre de Mimi Pinson: Mimi Pinson infirmière," *L'Humanité* (12 Feb. 1915), 4.

[143] Darrow, *French Women and the First World War*, 145–6. Katrin Schultheiss critiques accounts of nursing in this period for imagining "an undifferentiated professional 'category' of nurse"; the French nursing corps "was comprised of women and men from a wide range of social and professional backgrounds..." *Bodies and Souls: Politics and the Professionalization of Nursing in France, 1880–1922* (Cambridge, MA, 2001).

[144] Letter from Gustave Charpentier, 1916. FC, No. 463.

[145] Le Blond, "Préface," *Concours des Cocardes de Mimi-Pinson: Catalogue*, 4.   [146] Ibid. 5.

[147] Letter from Gustave Charpentier, 22 May 1915, to "Monsieur le Directeur."

that only the ladies of the Société de Secours aux blessés be employed." In spite of this treatment, he wrote, Mimi Pinson, "fortified by her patriotic zeal," "managed to gain the "esteem and confidence of the medical personnel and the gratitude of the wounded and ill..." Charpentier pleaded with the Under-Secretary of State to intervene: "The Parisian workingwomen demand nothing more than the strict right to devote themselves to the noble victims of the war...You have given such proof of your democratic faith, you will not allow the humiliation of these little humble souls that quiver in unison with the hearts of our heroes..."[148] Charpentier wrote to another official in the Ministry of War that same month, declaring that the exclusion of the Mimi Pinsons from the military hospital in Amiens was a "measure that shatters the *union sacrée* in precisely the place where Frenchwomen should be able to make friends."[149] Charpentier wrote Godart once more the following month, asking again that he intervene in this "affront."[150] By the following spring, OMP nurses were working once more at Amiens.

For some, these working-class nurses were women whose primary contribution to the war effort was their supposed attractiveness. One hospital director said as much in a letter to Charpentier requesting a half dozen nurses from his program, all "agreeable enough in silhouette and face. That's very important. I've noticed that ugly girls raise the temperature of the sick."[151] A journalist for the *Cri de Paris* examined a document listing the available Mimi Pinson nurses, divided into the most intelligent and the sturdiest. He imagined a third category, "those who are not particularly sturdy nor particularly intelligent" but are "deliciously lovely. The pleasure of looking at them will comfort our soldiers better than the most assiduous treatment."[152] Pierre Bonhomme, writing in *Le Radical* in November 1914, counseled OMP nurses that their national service role was rooted in their attractiveness and gaiety: "Your job as a nurse is to be pretty...to be gay...It's to babble like a finch [*pinson*]...It's to be a light and a joy in the sick wards. Leave the expert bandaging to the fine ladies; your innocent warbling...will be a good remedy for the wounded."[153] Bonhomme highlighted the distinct class contribution of the OMP nurses, a welcome comfort to the brave working-class soldiers who had put down their tools to pick up a rifle: "all the proletarian-soldiers of the Republic at war will identify with their diligent little sister."[154] While many references to the ladies of the Croix Rouge suggested the potential social

---

[148] Letter from Gustave Charpentier to Justin Godart, Sous-Secretaire d'État au Ministres de la Guerre (Service de Santé), Paris, 24 Aug. 1915. FC, No. 463.

[149] Letter from Gustave Charpentier to Monsieur Persil, Chef Adjoint du Cabinet du Ministre de la Guerre, Aug. 1915. FC, No. 463. Charpentier indicated that, in part, the Mimi Pinsons at Amiens were removed after being publicized in *Le Journal*.

[150] Charpentier to Godart, 24 Aug. 1915.

[151] Letter from André Couvreur, Amiens, Hôpital Temporaire. FC, No. 463.

[152] "Mimi-Pinson," *Le Cri de Paris* [undated]. FC, No. 463.

[153] Pierre Bonhomme, "Le Bonnet de Mimi Pinson," *Le Radica* (22 Nov. 1914), 1.   [154] Ibid.

benefits of upper-class women caring for lower-class soldiers, commentaries like this suggest a marked anxiety about the class interactions of the military hospital.

Numerous observers represented the Mimi Pinsons' wartime service not as a continuation of grueling pre-war labor, but rather as a transformation of a frivolous girl into a serious caregiver. Formerly, Mimi Pinson had been an amusing sexual adventure for bourgeois youth. Now, she was a protective fetish and erotically charged fortifier of the nation's soldiers, a transformation which erased the realities of sweated labor. *Cri de Paris*, reporting on the OMP nurses, noted that with the coming of the war, "The merry seamstress has changed into a sister of charity."[155] Le Blond marked an analogous change: "These delicate Parisiennes, these children of the *faubourg*, once upon a time happy-go-lucky, prone to frivolity and coquetry, have metamorphosed into attentive and merciful sisters..."[156] Considering that the women who signed up for the OMP's nursing program were servants, factory workers, and seamstresses, many of them in their forties and fifties, this description of carefree flirts demonstrates a curiously rosy impression of pre-war labor which makes sense only within the context of the period's conflation of French workingwomen's labor and decorative function.

Raymond Séris and Jean Aubry in *Les Parisiens pendant l'état de siège* (1915), devoted a chapter to "Les Midinettes" and noted a similar transformation, in which the garment workers of the Rue de la Paix, used to romantic entanglements, make-up, and fashion, have seen an end to frivolity with the war. They pointed to the OMP as the best example of this transformation. Before the war, the OMP taught workingwomen how to "entertain themselves honestly... to let their youth bloom." Now, Mimi Pinson "was dreaming of caring for the wounded and of replacing the rose in her bodice with a red cross."[157] Ever *rêveuse*, the romantic midinette has at least channeled her amorous gaiety into patriotic service.

In Ordonneau and Gally's operetta *La Cocarde de Mimi Pinson*, the seamstresses sing of their conversion from scatterbrained pleasure lovers to serious patriots. Once they had been called "frivolous" and "light-hearted," only content to "prattle, | Flirt, sparkle." But once the war came, they had bid farewell to "lace and ribbons... laughter, amusements... fashion and pleasures." The "little playthings of yesterday" had grown up in their "nurse's smock."[158] Once again, as in press coverage of garment workers' strikes, the pop cultural representation of a frivolous and even leisured midinette effaced sweated garment labor and labor activism. Laughter and frivolous amusement characterize the ideal midinette before her patriotic transfiguration during the war. Her work in Parisian couture is virtually invisible in this rendering, as she appears more as a customer of Parisian fashion than creator.

---

[155] "Mimi-Pinson," *Le Cri de Paris*. FC, No. 463.   [156] Le Blond, *Histoire*, 30.

[157] Séris and Aubry, *Les Parisiens pendant l'état de siège*, 98.

[158] Ordonneau and Gally, *La Cocarde de Mimi Pinson*, 116–17.

What of the women who served as OMP nurses during the war? Their own assessment of their national role balanced popular representations of the garment worker with a defiant sense of their right to join the nursing effort at the level of respect as Croix Rouge ladies. Correspondence between OMP nurses on assignment in military hospitals and Charpentier in Paris indicate that the Mimi Pinsons recognized that they were being assigned different kinds of work than Red Cross nurses. A former OMP member wrote Charpentier to recommend a young woman for the nursing initiative, and framed this desire as a right denied the lower classes. This young woman had been searching for "all possible ways to devote herself to the wounded and had always been prevented from doing so because this devotion is a luxury beyond her means."[159] Suzanne Morel, a Mimi Pinson serving as a nurse in 1917, was more candid. While she liked caring for wounded soldiers, she told Charpentier she was considering leaving the service: "The sisters [of the Red Cross] make our lives impossible ... not only do we take care of the ill but we must do many other tasks outside of our official duties."[160] Marie-Louise Jeunesse, a 29-year-old Parisian seamstress tending to soldiers at Uriage les Bains in September 1915, complained to Charpentier that while she had trained as a nurse, the chief physician said he had assigned her as a seamstress to work in the laundry: "I responded that I hadn't come with that intention."[161]

Despite this complaint, Jeunesse wrote that she and the other Mimi Pinsons "have formed a little workshop, a very cheerful one, I assure you. I mend shirts and socks, and I do it gladly even because it is still working for the wounded." She had found a group of "good comrades" with whom she experienced "an extraordinary gaiety."[162] Jeunesse's letters thus reverted to the cultural frame of sunny Mimi Pinson and her fairy fingers. OMP nurse Pauline Guérin wrote of taking part in musical get-togethers at the hospital, and articulated the difficulty of maintaining the midinette's characteristic cheer in the face of the horrors of the war wounded: "I am so happy to bring them some gaiety! But what sadness I hide behind my smile, and what a painful impression the sight of this audience of wounded men: arms in slings, pale heads wrapped in bandages..." Thinking of these men and those who would never return from war, Guérin exclaimed, "I have to muster all my courage to maintain a smiling face. I sing though, and the emotion that grips me makes my voice even more stirring." She attested to being "ecstatically moved" by this "call to duty and this love of the *Patrie*."[163]

OMP nurses were keenly aware of public interest in their service. Mathilde, a Mimi Pinson serving at Amiens' military hospital in March 1916, learned that an

[159] Letter to Gustave Charpentier, 31 Dec. 1914. FC, No. 463.

[160] Letter from Suzanne Morel to Gustave Charpentier, 6 Sept. 1917. FC, No. 465.

[161] Letter from Marie-Louise Jeunesse to Gustave Charpentier, Uriage les Bains, 9 Sept. 1915. FC, No. 465. *Mimi Pinson (Guerre, 1914–1918) Lettres de Mimi Pinson infirmières à Gustave Charpentier.*

[162] Ibid.

[163] Pauline Guérin to Gustave Charpentier, 7 Oct. 1914, Mermanville-sur-mer. FC, No. 465.

army major had published an article on the OMP nurses, and hoped that Charpentier could track it down.[164] Jeunesse thanked Charpentier for sending along articles about the OMP, which she read with "great pleasure."[165] When a nurse named Alice learned from family in Paris that her nursing citation was being displayed in the Mimi Pinson boutique in Paris under an incorrect first name, she asked Charpentier to rectify the error.[166]

OMP nurses often included requests in their letters that Charpentier send them freshly laundered uniforms, replacement badges, or money. They were also unabashed about sharing the touristic outings that they enjoyed during these nursing assignments. Jeunesse wrote of daytrips around the spa town of Uriage les Bains, where she worked, as well as into nearby Grenoble, and sent Charpentier numerous postcards from Uriage and the nearby Belledonne mountains. She even enclosed a photograph of herself in one letter to show, she said, how "favorable" the weather in Uriage was to her health. When Charpentier disappointed OMP nurses, they were quick to point this out. Jeunesse once scolded Charpentier for not including a personal note with a replacement badge he had sent at her request.[167]

Mimi Pinson Marguerite Bourguin went door to door in Paris and its suburbs to solicit materials and funds from garment trade merchants, department stores, banks, and government ministries to fund the OMP nursing program. She noted that many potential donors mistook the Mimi Pinsons for "singers or dancers, or muses even";[168] several tailors believed they were clients. When the women's identity is made clear, the response often was one of patronizing affection for "the little Pinsonettes or the little Midinettes," "that we were three midinettes too sweet to refuse," and "how I like them, the little Mimi Pinsons, I can't ever do enough for them."[169]

Bourguin's report demonstrates the satisfaction that workingwomen took in serving the war effort in such a public way. She saw this experience as transformative: "It took the arrival of the war for me to learn to understand people's character. I learned confidence, boldness, to back down from nothing, which would serve me well one day."[170] When the director of L'Illustration responded to Bourguin's plea with a 100-franc donation, she recalled, "I was overcome with joy... my heart was

---

[164] Letter from Mathilde to Camille Willay, Amiens, 16 Mar. 1916. FC, No. 465.

[165] Letter from Marie-Louise Jeunesse, Hôpital Militaire d'Uriage les Bains, to Gustave Charpentier, 13 Sept. 1915. FC, No. 465. For information on Jeunesse, see FC, No. 478 Mimi-Pinson (Guerre 1914–1918) (b) Répertoire Infirmières.

[166] Alice P. to Gustave Charpentier, Secteur 8, 10 Nov. [no year]. FC, No. 465.

[167] Marie-Louise Jeunesse to Gustave Charpentier, Postcard ["Dauphiné—Massif Belledonne"] from Uriage, 1915. FC, No. 465.

[168] Marguerite Bourguin, "Rapport de Marguerite Bourguin à Monsieur Charpentier," FC, No. 462: Mimi Pinson, Guerre 1914–1918, 5.

[169] Ibid, 2, 6, 6.   [170] Ibid. 1.

bursting, my legs wobbled."[171] Bourguin describes exploring her "beloved Capital," being chased by suspicious concierges, and developing strategies for gaining entry to various offices. Yet through it all, she insists, "the essential thing for us was to obtain what we desired."[172]

While the OMP nurses were popularly imagined as cheerfully resigned to their work, they were able to push slightly beyond the limits of this cultural role during the war using the organization set up in their name. They procured a role for themselves in the national war effort which allowed them to take advantage of free nursing programs and to take up positions in military hospitals around France, often far from home. Nonetheless, the relative public indifference to the OMP's nursing program as compared to the wide resonance of the cocarde initiative indicates that certain forms of working-class feminine patriotism may have been more culturally palatable than others as France attempted to weather the cataclysm of the Great War.

[171] Ibid. 9.   [172] Ibid. 8.

Conclusion

In February 2012, a minor scandal erupted around a proposed statue in the affluent Parisian suburb of Nogent-sur-Marne. The town wanted to honor its long-standing Italian immigrant community by erecting a statue of a nineteenth-century female *plumassière* (featherworker) from Nogent's prominent ostrich feather manufacturing industry at the turn of the century.[1] The Valnurèse (as the statue was titled) was an attractive woman wearing a calf-length dress with puffed sleeves, apron, heeled boots, and carrying ostrich feathers, a diminutive and pleasing belle époque vision two meters high and cast in bronze.[2] Aesthetically, the statue could easily be taken for a belle époque creation like the Mimi Pinson of the Canal St Martin.

As sculptor Élisabeth Cibot began the project, Nogent's mayor, Jacques J. P. Martin, suggested using France's telegenic first lady, the former model and Italian heiress Carla Bruni-Sarkozy as inspiration for the *plumassière*'s face. In suggesting a monument to the woman he called "the most Italian of Frenchwomen," Martin, a member of President Sarkozy's UMP, was seen to be currying favor with the leader of his political party on the eve of a contentious presidential election. Nogentais and Socialist politicians alike decried the choice as "grotesque," and hardly representative of either the Italian community in France or of French workers.[3] By the time the statue was unveiled in September 2012, Bruni-Sarkozy's husband had been voted out of the Elysée, a real estate developer had taken over all costs for the statue, and its private inauguration ceremony drew a handful of protesters. Martin's speech highlighted the "exceptional" nature of the Italian community in Nogent, remarkable for their homogeneity and their success: "the Italo-nogentais are completely French citizens."[4] The *plumassières* of Nogent, who fashioned "hats or clothes for elegant ladies," were remarkable, he said, both for the large role the industry played in Nogent, and because it had provided "a form of social ascent" for Italian women.

The week after the statue's unveiling, another, more successful, effort at nationalist nostalgia was erected in Nogent, this time a statue of the "last French *poilu*,"

---

[1] A male mason had been the original conception of the piece, as tribute to the Italian immigrants who worked in construction in Nogent.

[2] The statue took its name from the Nure valley in Italy from which many of Nogent's Italian immigrants hailed.

[3] *Agence France Presse*, 12 Feb. 2012.

[4] Speech by Jacques J. P. Martin, Maire de Nogent-sur-Marne, "Inauguration de la Résidence 'La Petite Italie'. 21 septembre 2012."

Working Girls: Sex, Taste, and Reform in the Parisian Garment Trades, 1880–1919. Patricia Tilburg, Oxford University Press (2019). © Patricia Tilburg.
DOI: 10.1093/oso/9780198841173.001.0001

Italian immigrant Lazare Ponticelli, who had immigrated to Nogent as a child and fought for France in the First World War, before founding a prosperous industrial chimney company with his brothers.[5] When Ponticelli died at the age of 110 in 2008, he was given a national funeral at the Hôtel des Invalides. In both installations, two model immigrants are made to represent the contributions of all Italian immigrants to the glory of the French Republic, one as French first lady and multimillionaire, one as diligent veteran and prosperous *citoyen*. Both statues were commissioned as part of Nogent's "Petite Italie," a major development complex of residential and commercial buildings at least partially inspired by the Italian villages whence many Nogentais had emigrated in the nineteenth century.[6] One must understand these commemorative efforts in the context of decades of French immigration policy which favored European arrivals over immigrants from outside of Europe, especially former French colonies in North Africa, and which made immigrant women increasingly vulnerable.[7] Indeed, in the years in which "La Valnurèse" was conceived and executed, Sarkozy and his government instituted several controversial laws tightening restrictions on immigration in France and insisting upon the assimilation of immigrant populations. The Parisian midinette and Nogent's Valnurèse were both feminine, white, nostalgic, and cheerful versions of the French labor force. Yet the ridicule aimed at the Valnurèse targeted none of those characteristics. The Valnurèse's Europeanness/whiteness, her air of sentimental nostalgia, and her feminine attractiveness all made the statue a palatable symbol of civic and national pride, and an appealing fantasy of immigration in the Republic. But critics rejected the association of this image with an upper-class woman, Bruni-Sarkozy. As a woman with tremendous economic power who also seemed to leverage her physical attractiveness to win substantial social and political power, Bruni-Sarkozy muddled the useful symbolic function of the turn-of-the-century garment worker. Commentators on the Left and Right seemed entirely comfortable with a highly romanticized, eroticized, and nostalgic commemoration of sweated labor, and only balked that Bruni-Sarkozy's class made the fantasy unsustainable. Socialist politician William Geib complained, "It is sad for the women who worked in this métier...Carla Bruni must have seen more feathers on ostriches and in fashion shows than in factories."[8] But Geib seemed untroubled by the monument's prettified and nostalgic version of labor history, not to mention the sanitized and politically useful vision of the "good immigrant" (hardworking, attractive, white, and European).

[5] Ponticelli Frères is now a multinational corporation headquartered in the Marne valley, and still owned by the Ponticelli family.

[6] http://www.pss-archi.eu/immeubles/FR-94052-55194.html

[7] Catherine Raissiguier, *Reinventing the Republic: Gender, Migration, and Citizenship in France* (Stanford, 2010), 57–63.

[8] "La Statue de Carla qui fait jaser," *Le Parisien*, 12 Feb. 2012.

This book has followed the Parisian midinette up to strikes of the immediate postwar period in 1919. The subsequent interwar decades saw a radically transformed French workplace, as trends only nascent in the French economy before the war became dominant. Before World War I, some 60 per cent of workers in France were employed by businesses with fewer than 100 employees. By the 1920s, a majority of workers were in businesses employing more than 100 people. The more traditional garment industry was increasingly outdated next to rationalizing and "aggressive food, automobile, and metalworking industries."[9] French industry saw increasing numbers of colonial, non-white immigrant laborers in the workforce alongside white Frenchwomen.[10] While immigrant women were a small part of the labor force, they were "especially prominent in the textile and garment industries."[11] In a *coup de grâce* to Vieux Paris, the city walls were demolished in 1919.[12]

In the face of this new economic, social, and urban landscape, interwar artists, performers, and writers mourned the passing of the midinette, as their grandfathers had mourned the grisette. In the closing paragraph of Stéphane Manier's 1933 novel *Midinettes*, the narrator, a writer who spends his free time watching and courting the seamstresses in his neighborhood, notes the disappearance of his upstairs neighbor Mathilde, a talented "first hand" in a couture workshop. Has she moved, found a lover, changed jobs? Her older co-worker, Madame Beauvard, assumes the worst: "She responded to me with the pitiable, resigned solemnity of soldiers who survive the war: 'She was very ill. At this point, she must be dead. What do you want? The midinettes last only a *déjeuner de soleil.*'"[13] The novel, a sentimental study of Paris's young workingwomen from the perspective of male admirers, thus ends with a sentence, that, out of context, would seem to be emphatically gloomy—the disappearance and probable death of a young woman—and perhaps even a pointed critique of the economic fragility of this class of workers. But in fact Manier closes his novel with Mathilde's apparent death as part of a wistful, apolitical affirmation of a certain Paris—a decidedly romantic vision of the tasteful elegance of the French garment industry and its female workers. Manier here deploys a nineteenth-century expression, "déjeuner de soleil," to do so, a phrase with its roots in the world of fashion (meaning fabric that has had its color degraded or "eaten" by exposure to sunlight). Mathilde's premature death is shrugged off as a picturesque if melancholic aside, collapsing the bodily insecurity of the garment worker with the changeability of fashion. Manier combines his query about Mathilde with an elegy for the capital's eternal midinette: "The midinettes, anonymous and discreet little sisters of our great

---

[9] Laura Levine Frader, *Breadwinners and Citizens: Gender and the Making of the French Social Model* (Durham, NC, 2008), 9.
[10] Ibid.   [11] Ibid. 43.   [12] Rearick, *Paris Dreams*, 47.
[13] Stéphane Manier, *Midinettes* (Paris, 1933), 249. Emphasis in original.

artists, were, in the city, 500,000 little lights... Without them, Paris would no longer be Paris. To allow the midinettes to perish would be to let the charm of Paris be extinguished."[14] As we have come to see over the course of this study, a melodramatic recollection of the traditional garment worker was standard practice for male writers from the beginning of the previous century. Such valedictions reified the personal and national values of masculine, bourgeois youth, at the expense of real workingwomen who were relegated to imagined lives of picturesque anonymity and discretion.

Interwar midinettes themselves built upon their decades of activism, taking to the front lines of labor militancy once again in the year leading up to the Popular Front and the Matignon Accords. They initiated important strikes in 1935 that helped launch the movement of May and June 1936.[15] In 1935, *L'Humanité* called upon underpaid needle workers in Nantes to "imitate the Parisian midinettes" by unionizing.[16] In 1936, columnist Léa Maury drew frequent connections between the Popular Front's midinette and previous workingwomen's garment trade militancy: "Like their little sisters in 1917, the midinettes of 1936 are no less resolved to conquer: for bread, for peace."[17] Maury interviewed an old "midinette" who connected the activism of that year to her strikes as a young garment worker in 1917, 1919, and 1923, recalling those earlier strikes as "an episode in our protest struggle... The mainstream press tried to throw discredit on our movement. But we remained firm."[18] Here, the midinette was once again a figure evoking the past, but now a past of successful labor action rather than frivolous romance.[19] Garment union secretary Fernand Bellugue agreed: "when the midinettes have had enough, they fight, and hard. All of the improvements to their lot they have obtained by fighting. How many times have they been on the forefront of the battle in these protest fights." They had even managed, he reminded readers, to win labor rights during wartime.[20] Press coverage of this strike generally applauded the midinettes without expressing surprise at their activism and without describing the sexual allure of the women. Indeed, several years later, under the Nazi occupation, writer André Salmon called out the "egotism" and "real ignorance about the lot of the workingwoman" in the "cheap sham poetry celebrating *cousettes* and milliners lunching on a sack of fries and sharing their

---

[14] Ibid. 245.   [15] Didry, "Les Midinettes, avant-garde oubliée du prolétariat," 79.

[16] "À la Société Parisienne de Confection à Nantes, une ouvrière a gagné 20 francs on six jours," *L'Humanité* (22 Dec. 1935), 5. "Syndiquez-vous, groupez-vous, imitez les midinettes parisiennes..."

[17] Maury, "Quand les midinettes en ont assez!," *Le Figaro* (10 May 1936), 5.

[18] Léa Maury, "Quand les midinettes descendent dans la rue," *L'Humanité* (11 May 1936), 5. Didry quotes from this article as well, "Les Midinettes, avant-garde oubliée du prolétariat," 83. Maury (1905–43) later was mortally wounded fighting for the French Resistance.

[19] Maury, "Quand les midinettes en ont assez!," 5.

[20] Bellugue, quoted in Maury, "Quand les midinettes en ont assez!" 5. Bellugue was deported by the Nazis, and died in Germany in 1944.

bread with the sparrows. But, in 1941, there are no more fries...and the sparrows make do as they can, that is, badly. The midinettes too."[21]

Outside of labor activism, interwar midinettes-turned-grand-couturiers like Jeanne Lanvin and Madeleine Vionnet used their own economic success to argue on behalf of the protection of Parisian tastemakers like themselves, while also transforming their companies to offer progressive working conditions. Vionnet's workers benefited from free medical care, night classes, paid maternity leave, a childcare center, and a fund for each employee's children.[22] Vionnet embraced the notion of Parisian fashion production, even that of the lowliest *ouvrière*, as art, and was one of the first to fight to protect Parisian taste and skill by way of trademarks and copyright infringement suits. In 1922, she helped found the Association pour la Defense des Arts plastiques et appliqués which aimed to help protect the "artistic creations" of fashion houses by assisting members with the paperwork required for registering a trademark. As journalist Henry Hugault put it in a profile of Vionnet in 1930, "Vionnet considered herself to be an artist at heart. In her fierce battle against the 'copyists,' she seemed to have been seeking recognition for her work, an irrefutable proof of its artistic value. 'It is not so much damages and interests we want: above all, we want respect for our intellectual property.' "[23] The interwar period also saw the creation of a Syndicat de la protection artistique des industries saisonnières specifically established to combat design theft.[24] Vionnet offered a full-throated defense of the taste and labor of the Parisienne in interviews with André Beucler in 1930:

> What have we done to protect our creative genius, to protect from pillagers a material and spiritual treasure that may be about to slip from our grasp? To save the future of Paris? Almost nothing...Plans to "defend French fashion" are under study. It's about time because there is another risk...counterfeiting in France, under the noses of genuine fashion houses, and distributed abroad, not only creating unfair competition in Paris and beyond, but also, because of shoddy execution, forever damaging our reputation for quality and discrediting a magnificent work. The requirements of haute couture are actually small...Yet it is essential. Otherwise, Paris will become lazy in the long term, then crass, useless to the world.[25]

This former midinette understood the global renown of Parisian couture as personally, professionally, and nationally significant, and made an argument for

---

[21] André Salmon, "L'Injuste Condition des midinettes," *Le Petit Parisien*, 8 June 1941.

[22] Delauche, "Une belle oeuvre et une bonne oeuvre, les apprenties de Madeleine Vionnet," *Moniteur de l'exportation et la revue artistique réunis* (Dec. 1923), 8.

[23] Henry Hugault, "Une campagne d'assainissement, défendons nos artistes," *Le Figaro*, 12 Aug. 1930.

[24] Green, *Ready-to-Wear*, 81.

[25] André Beucler, "Chez Madeleine Vionnet," in *Madeleine Vionnet*, ed. Pamela Golbin, 285. Beucler was contracted to write a book about Maison Vionnet in 1930 which never seems to have been published.

the protection of Parisian designs that linked skilled labor and the place of France in the twentieth-century global economy. This "material and spiritual treasure" is guaranteed by a workforce whose livelihood and skill are respected.

Beyond Paris's workingwomen, as Claire Oberon Garcia demonstrates, interwar Paris was also an imagined and lived landscape for many non-white, non-Parisian subjects, as the "distant metropole shaped the colonized subject's sense of self and objects of desire through textbooks, products consumed, and the formal and informal rules that govern social relations."[26] Francophone literary scholars have been particularly attentive to the power and legacy of the broader Parisian imaginary across France and the French empire.[27] How might the monumental, omnipresent Mimi Pinson have constructed and inflected the experience of non-white or non-French workers in Paris and elsewhere in the Hexagon? The celebration of Paris as the center of French civilization and taste embodied by a young white Frenchwoman must be understood as a political act as much as a cultural one.

In the fall of 2017, Carla Bruni-Sarkozy made news once again when she weighed in on the global activism around sexual harassment and sexual assault following revelations of decades of abuse of women by Hollywood mogul Harvey Weinstein. Spurred by the Twitter hashtag #metoo, French feminists, actors, and journalists mobilized around the phrase, "#BalanceTonPorc" ("Denounce Your Pig"). Bruni-Sarkozy was one of a number of French celebrities to express support for the movement. While insisting that women be made to feel they could come forward, Bruni-Sarkozy also remarked that "In the world of fashion, there isn't an enormous share of sexual abuse..."[28] Indeed, a familiar polemic resulted from the flowering of #metoo's French varietal, as #BalanceTonPorc was decried by some for going too far and for threatening an essential part of French identity. One hundred prominent professional Frenchwomen (writers, artists, journalists, physicians, and academics, and the actress Catherine Deneuve) pushed back against the revelations of #BalanceTonPorc. The signatories insisted upon the "freedom to bother" ("liberté d'importuner") as an essential corollary to "sexual freedom" ("la liberté sexuelle"), and argued on behalf of the necessity of "galanterie."[29] Charlotte Belaich in *Libération* asked, "Is seduction *à la française* in danger?" and answered with a short history of the concept of France as a nation uniquely

[26] Claire Oberon Garcia, "Remapping the metropolis: theorizing Black women's subjectivities in interwar Paris," in *Black French Women and the Struggle for Equality, 1848–2016*, ed. Félix Germain and Silyane Larcher (Lincoln, NB, 2018).

[27] See *Paris, Capital of the Black Atlantic: Literature, Modernity, and Diaspora*, ed. Jeremy Braddock and Jonathan Eburne (Baltimore, 2013), especially Braddock and Eburne, "Introduction," 1–14, and Dawn Fulton, "Interurban Paris: Alain Mabanckou's *Invisible Cities*," 330–49.

[28] Marion Royer, "Carla Bruni sur le harcèlement sexuel: 'Il faut dire aux femmes qu'elles peuvent parler,'" *Gala*, 16 Oct. 2017.

[29] "Nous défendons une liberté d'importuner, indispensable à la liberté sexuelle," 8 Jan. 2018, *Le Monde*. http://www.lemonde.fr/idees/article/2018/01/09/nous-defendons-une-liberte-d-importuner-indispensable-a-la-liberte-sexuelle_5239134_3232.html#joLxUKU6SrY1JWeA.99

concerned with an "asymmetry between the sexes."[30] In an interview in January 2018, historian Joan Scott noted the predictability and historicity of the manifesto: "It is the continuation of a tradition in which French national identity and seduction are linked."[31]

Despite the vigorous defense of "seduction à la française" by some, in the wake of #metoo, French unions and newspapers launched calls for action against workplace harassment,[32] and the French government moved ahead with new legislation against "sexist and sexual violence," including proposed fines for street harassment.[33] A 2018 report released by the Fondation Jean-Jaurès and the Fondation européenne d'Études progressistes demonstrated that 86 per cent of French women had been insulted or subjected to aggression on the street. The most vulnerable to such harassment were "young women with low incomes living in cities or *banlieue populaire*."[34]

This book has traced the historical contingency of a specific idea of French working-class feminine sexuality and its deployment in political, economic, and cultural discourse as a constraining force on women's and workers' emancipation. The twinned erotic submission and tasteful appeal of the fantasized working-class woman made her a curiously sexualized national icon in early twentieth-century France, culturally omnipresent yet politically and economically dominated. It is important to consider how this historically specific and politically conservative vision of garment workers might inform twenty-first-century questions of sweated garment labor globally, not simply in France. The Clean Clothes Campaign, a global alliance dedicated to "improving and empowering workers in the global garment and sportswear industries," estimated in 2015 that three-quarters of garment workers worldwide are female, and that the industry employs 60 to 75 million people.[35] Garment production by and large is driven by retailers and brands in the developed world (Europe, the USA, and Japan), who outsource the bulk of production to the least developed or developing nations in the world. Many garment workers, especially women and migrant workers, are embedded in

---

[30] Charlotte Belaich, "La 'séduction à la française' est-elle en danger?" *Libération*, 11 Jan. 2018.

[31] Cécile Daumas, "Joan Scott: 'La séduction comme trait d'identité nationale française est un mythe,'" *Libération*, 26 Jan. 2018.

[32] Francine Aizicovici, "Harcèlement sexuel chez les ouvrières, 'la peur de perdre son travail,'" *Le Monde*, 23 Nov. 2017; "Lettre ouverte: #BalanceTonPorc à l'inspection du travail...ou pas?," 19 Oct. 2017. https://www.cnt-tas.org/2017/10/19/lettre-ouverte-balancetonporc-inspection-du-travail-sexisme-ministere-travail/

[33] "Marlène Schiappa: 'Les Premières Amendes contre le harcèlement de rue seront mises à l'automne,'" *Le Parisien*, Propos recueillis par Florence Méréo, 29 July 2018.

[34] Carine Janin, "Harcèlement de rue: 86% des Françaises déjà insultées ou agressées," *Ouest-France*, 20 Nov. 2018.

[35] Lina Stotz and Gillian Kane, "Global garment industry factsheet," *Clean Clothes Campaign*, 2015. https://cleanclothes.org/resources/publications/factsheets/general-factsheet-garment-industry-february-2015.pdf

the "informal economy," that is workers who "'are not protected under the legal and regulatory frameworks' and are 'characterised by a high degree of vulnerability.'"[36] Such an economy, granted on a far smaller scale, would have been familiar to the Parisian midinette of 1900. Her history offers a cautionary tale of the power of cultural narratives to sexualize, romanticize, and stifle female workers' efforts to improve their working and living conditions. Piercing such narratives is all the more urgent now that the great majority of global garment labor is done by women who do not share an apartment landing with an amorous bourgeois journalist eager to tell her tale (however romanticized), but who live far from the commercial centers where their production is consumed.

[36] Ibid. 9.

Bibliography

Archives

Archives Nationales de France (AN)
Archives de Paris
Archives de la Préfecture de Police de Paris (APPP)
Bibliothèque de l'Opéra
Bibliothèque du Musée des Arts Décoratifs: Mode et Textile
Bibliothèque Forney
Bibliothèque Historique de la Ville de Paris
   Fonds Marie-Louise Bouglé: Fonds Jeanne Bouvier
   Fonds Gustave Charpentier (FC)
Bibliothèque Marguerite Durand (BMD)
Bibliothèque Nationale de France
   BNF Richelieu, Arts du Spectacle (BNF-R)
   BNF Richelieu, (Louvois) Musique (BNF-L)
Centre de Recherches des Archives nationales
Gaumont Pathé Archives
Musée de la Mode et du Textile

Selected Periodicals

La Bataille syndicaliste, 1911–1920
L'Humanité, 1910–1918
Le Journal de Mimi Pinson, 1908
Le Populaire, 1918–1920
Le Temps, 1885–1926

Primary Sources

Acker, Paul. *Oeuvres sociales des femmes.* Paris: Librarie Plon, 1908.
Alexandre, Arsène. *Les Reines de l'aiguille, modistes et couturières. Études Parisiennes.* Illustrations by François Courboin. Paris: Belin, 1902.
Artus, Louis. *Les Midinettes: comédie en quatre actes* (Paris: Émile-Paul, 1912).
Audoux, Marguerite. *Marie-Claire.* Paris: Fasquelle, 1910.
Audoux, Marguerite. *L'Atelier de Marie-Claire.* Paris: Charpentier, 1920.
Bacquet, A. *Mémoire présenté à Messieurs les députés pour l'obtention de droits de douane sur les fleurs et feuillages artificiels de fabrication étrangère.* Paris: Louis Jeanrot, c.1908–1917.

Barrès, Maurice. *Le Coeur des femmes de France: extraits de la "Chroniques de la Grande Guerre."* Paris: Plon, 1928.

Baüer, Gérard. *Recensement de l'amour à Paris.* Paris: Le Livre, 1922.

Béarnais, Jean. *Nouvelle Mimi Pinson: roman d'amour inédit.* Montrouge: L'Imprimerie Moderne, 1929.

Beauvallet, Léon and Lemercier de Neuville, *Les Femmes de Murger.* Paris: Charlieu et Huillery, 1864.

Benoist, Charles. *Les Ouvrières de l'aiguille à Paris: notes pour l'étude de la question sociale.* Paris: L. Chailley, 1895.

Berthem-Bontoux [Berthe-Marie Bontoux]. *Les Françaises et la Grande Guerre.* Paris: Bloud et Gay, 1917.

Bodève, Simone. *Clo.* Paris: Henri Jouve, 1908.

Bodève, Simone. *Celles qui travaillent* (Paris: Ollendorff, 1913).

Bonneff, Léon, and Maurice Bonneff. *Les Métiers qui tuent: enquête auprès des syndicats ouvriers sur les maladies professionnelles.* Paris: Bibliographie sociale, 1900.

Bonneff, Léon, and Maurice Bonneff. *La Vie tragique des travailleurs: enquêtes sur la condition économique et morale des ouvriers et ouvrières d'industrie.* Paris: Jules Rouff & Cie, 1911.

Bouvier, Jeanne. *Mes Mémoires: ou 59 années d'activité industrielle, sociale et intellectuelle d'une ouvrière, 1876–1935.* Paris: La Découverte/Masperom 1983.

Brunhes, Henriette, *La Ligue Sociale d'Acheteurs: rapport présenté par Madame Jean Brunhes, dans la séance du 10 novembre 1903.* Paris: Félix Alcan, 1903.

Carette, Georges. *Exposition Franco-Britannique de Londres, 1908: Section Française, Classe 85: Rapport.* Paris: Comité Français des Expositions à l'Étranger, 1909.

Chadourne, André. *Le Quartier latin.* Paris: E. Dentu, 1884.

Charpentier, Gustave. *Gustave Charpentier: lettres inédites à ses parents.* Ed. Françoise Andrieux. Paris: Presses Universitaires de France, 1984.

Charpentier, Gustave. *Louise* (libretto), *French Opera Libretti*, Vol. III. New York: Leyerle, 2005.

Clément, P. de. *Cousette: roman d'amour inédit.* (Paris: Éditions modernes, 1928).

Colette, "Le 'Beau langage,'" *L'Excelsior*, 27 November 1917, in *Cahiers Colette*, No. 14. Société des Amis de Colette, 1992.

Colette, *Une Parisienne dans la Grande Guerre, 1914–1918* (Paris: L'Herne, 2014).

Compain, Louise. *La Femme dans les organisations ouvrières.* Paris: V. Giard & E. Brière, 1910.

Davy, Charlotte. *Une Femme...* Paris: Eugène Figuière, 1927.

Decourcelle, A., and J. Barbier, *Jenny l'ouvrière: drame en cinq actes.* Paris: Librairie théatrale, 1850.

Delabarre, Édouard. "Nénettes et Rintintins," in *Précis analytique des travaux de l'Académie des sciences, belles-lettres et arts de Rouen pendant l'année 1918.* Rouen: Imprimerie Cagniard, 1919, pp. 697–8.

Délétang, Louise. *Journal d'une ouvrière parisienne pendant la guerre.* Paris: E. Figuière, 1936.

Descaves, Lucien, Léon Hennique, Octave Mirbeau, Gustave Geffroy, J. H. Rosny, Paul Margueritte, Léon Daudet, Justin Rosny, Jules Renard, and Elémir Bourges. *The Colour of Paris: Historical, Personal & Local*, ed. Lucien Descaves. London: Chatto & Windus, 1908.

Desfossez, Alfred. *Les Midinettes: drame en 5 actes et 7 tableaux.* Paris: C. Joubert, 1904.

Desprez, Ernest. "Les Grisettes de Paris," in *Paris, ou Le Livre des cent et un, Tome 6.* Paris: Ladvocat, 1832.

Diraison-Seylor, Olivier. *Irène, grande première, roman.* Paris: L'Édition, 1916.

Donnay, Maurice. *La Parisienne et la guerre*. Paris: Georges Crés, 1916.

Douche, Sylvie, ed. *Correspondences inédites à des musiciens français, 1914–1918*. Paris: L'Harmattan, 2012.

Drumont, Édouard. *La Fin d'un monde: étude psychologique et sociale*. Paris: Savine, 1889.

Du Maroussem, Pierre. *La Petite Industrie: salaires et durées du travail, Tome II: Le vêtement à Paris*. Paris: Office du Travail, 1896.

Dumas, F. G., ed. *The Franco-British Exhibition: Illustrated Review, 1908*. London: Chatto & Windus, 1908.

Famchon, René. *Exposition Franco-Britannique de Londres, 1908: Section Française, Groupe XIIIB, Classe 86, Industries des Accessoires du Vêtement: Rapport*. Paris: Comité Français des Expositions à l'Étranger, 1910.

Fargue, Léon-Paul. *Le Piéton de Paris de Léon-Paul Fargue, illustré par Valdo Barbey*. Paris: Henri Lefebvre, 1948.

The Franco-British Exhibition: Official Souvenir. London: Hudson & Kearns, 1908.

Franco-British Exhibition in London, 1908. Catalogue of the Special Exhibition of the City of Paris and of the Department of the Seine. Paris: Chaix, 1908.

Froment, Madame. *Ouvrières Parisiennes*. Tract of L'Action Populaire: Publication bimensuelle, deuxième série, No. 9. Professions et Métiers, II. Lille: Imprimerie de l'Action Populaire, 1903.

Gérard, Claire. "La Fleur artificielle: une visite aux fées qui font le printemps," *Le Petit Journal*, 3 April 1908, 1.

Gérard, Claire. *Condition de l'ouvrière parisienne dans l'industrie de la fleur artificielle (Musée Social: Mémoires et Documents)*. Paris: Arthur Rousseau, 1909.

Gérard, Claire. "Les Industries feminines anglaises: la lutte contre la chomage." *Musée Social: Mémoires et Documents: Supplément aux Annales* (June 1909), 133–68.

Guilbert, Yvette. *The Song of My Life: My Memories*. London: G. G. Harrap, 1929.

Guiraud, Gaston. *P'tite gueule: roman*. Paris: Fasquelle, 1938.

Gustave Charpentier reçoit son épee d'academicien, Paris: Gaumont Pathé, 1914. www.gaumontpathearchives.com, Ref. No. 1409GJ 00008.

Guyot, Yves, and G.-Roger Sandoz, *Exposition Franco-Britannique de Londres, 1908: Rapport général, Tome II*. Paris: Comité français des expositions à l'étranger, 1908.

Haussonville, Comte d' [Gabriel-Paul-Othenin de Cleron]. *Salaires et misères de femmes*. Paris: Calmann Lévy, 1900.

Heim de Balsac, Frédéric, and Édouard Agasse-Lafont, *Le Dépistage du saturnisme latent par l'examen du sang*. Paris: Duruy, 1909.

Henrey, Mrs Robert [née Madeleine Gal]. *The Little Madeleine: The Autobiography of a Young Girl in Montmartre*. London: Dent, 1951.

Hepp, Alexander. *Les Anges parisiens*. Paris: E. Dentu, 1886.

Huart, Louis, *Physiologie de la Grisette, vignettes de Gavarni*. Brussels: Moen, 1841.

Huart, Louis, and Gavarni. *La Grisette*. Paris: Aubert, 1850.

Institut scientifique de recherches économiques et sociales, Paris, and Gabrielle Letellier. *Enquêtes sur le chômage*. Paris: Recueil Sirey, 1938.

Janin, Jules. "La Grisette," in *Les Français peints par eux-mêmes: encyclopédie morale du dix-neuvième siècle, Tome 1*. Paris: L. Curmer, 1840.

Ladoucette, Edmond. *Les Amours de "Mimi-Pinson."* Paris: J. Tallandier, 1904.

La Fontaine, Jean de. *Joconde ou l'infidelité des femmes, nouvelles en vers tirée de Boccace et de l'Arioste*. Paris: C. Barbin, 1665.

Lannoy, A.-P. de. *Les Plaisirs et la vie de Paris (guide du flâneur)*. Paris: Librairie L. Borel, 1900.

Lannoy, Pierre de. *Modiste et grande dame, roman inédit*. Paris, 1919.

La Question des veillées devant la commission départementale du travail du département de la Seine. Extraits des procès-verbaux des séances, 1900–1901. Paris: Imprimerie Chaix, 1901.

Le Blond, Maurice. *Histoire de Mimi Pinson*. Paris: Jules Logier, 1916.

Le Rouge, Gustave, *Le Crime d'une midinette*. Paris: Éditions Nilsson, 1900.

Les "Midinettes": Restaurants coopératifs d'ouvrières. Société anonyme à capital et à personnel variables. Paris: Imprimerie Nouvelle (association ouvrière), 1905.

Les Tribulations de Mlle Flore, couturière en robe. Clermont: Imprimerie de Vaissière et Perol, 1834.

Lesueur, Daniel. "La Parisienne," in *La Beauté de Paris*. Paris: La Renaissance de l'Art Français et des Industries de Luxe, 1919, pp. 289–92.

Loti, Pierre. *Soldats bleus: Journal intime 1914–1918*. Paris: La Table Ronde, 1998.

Lourdelet, Ernest. *Les Emotions de midinette: saynéte en vers*. Chez l'auteur: Paris, 1914.

Kleeck, Mary Van. *Artificial Flower Makers*. New York: Survey Associates, 1913.

Maday, André de. *Les Femmes et les Tribunaux de Prud'hommes*. Neuchâtel: Attinger Frères, 1917.

Manier, Stéphane. *Midinettes*. Paris: Librairie de la Revue Française, 1933.

Mendès, Catullle, and Reynaldo Hahn, *La Fête chez Thérèse: ballet-pantomime en deux actes*. Paris: Heugel, 1910.

Michaud, René. *J'avais vingt ans: un jeune ouvrier au début du siècle*. Paris: Éditions Syndicalistes, 1967.

Milhaud, Caroline. *L'Ouvrière en France: sa condition présent, les réformes nécessaires*. Paris: Félix Alcan, 1907.

Milhaud, Caroline. *Enquête sur le travail à domicile dans l'industrie de la fleur artificielle*. Office du Travail, Ministère du Travail et de la Prévoyance sociale. Paris: Imprimerie Nationale, 1913.

Monnier, Henri. *Les Grisettes, dessinées d'après nature*. Paris: H. Gaugain, 1829.

Montorgueil, Georges. *La Vie des boulevards: Madeleine-Bastille*. Illustrations by Pierre Vidal. Paris: Libraries-Imprimeries Réunies, 1896.

Montorgueil, Georges. *La Parisienne, peinte par elle-même*, illustrations by Henry Somm. Paris: Librairie L. Conquet, 1897.

Montorgueil, Georges. *La Vie à Montmartre*. Paris, 1899.

Montorgueil, Georges. *Midi: le déjeuner des petites ouvrières (les minutes Parisiennes)*. Paris: P. Ollendorff, 1899.

Musset, Alfred de. *Frédéric et Bernerette*. Paris: Dumont, 1840.

Musset, Alfred de. "Mademoiselle Mimi Pinson. Profil d'une grisette," in *Diable à Paris*, Vol. 1. Paris: Hetzel, 1845.

Nordau, Max. "The Quartier Latin," in *Paris Sketches from the German of Max Nordau*. Chicago: Laird and Lee, 1895. Originally *Pariser Studien und Bilder*, Leipzig: Duncker, 1878.

Office central des Oeuvres de bienfaisance, *Paris Charitable et Bienfaisant*. Paris: Librairie Plon, 1912.

Office du Travail. *Enquête sur le travail à domicile dans l'industrie de la fleur artificielle*. Paris Impr. Nationale, 1913.

Ordonneau, Maurice, and Arthur Verneuil, *Mimi Pinson: vaudeville-opérette en trois actes*. Musique by Michiels. Paris: Tresse, 1882.

Ordonneau, Maurice, and Francis Gally, *La Cocarde de Mimi Pinson: opérette en trois actes*, Music by Henri Goublier. Paris: Choudens, 1915.

Oxenford, John. *The Book of French Songs*. London: Frederick Warne & Co., 1877.

Pawlowski, Auguste. *Les Plaisirs et la vie de Paris: guide du flaneur*. Paris: L. Borel, 1900.

Pawlowski, Auguste. *Les Syndicats féminins et les syndicats mixtes en France: leur organisation, leur action professionelle, économique, et sociale, leur avenir.* Paris: Librairie Félix Alcan, 1912.

Perret, Léonce, dir., *Oscar et Kiki la midinette.* Paris: Gaumont Pathé, 1913. 1913CNCGFIC 00038 1/280441, Gaumont Pathé Archives, www.gaumontpathearchives.com.

Pichardie, Delphin. *Considérations sur l'intoxication saturnine et en particulier la paralysie chez les ouvrières en fleurs artificielles: thèse pour le doctorat en médecine...*, Paris: Université de Paris, PhD Diss., 1901.

Pratz, Claire de. *France from Within.* London: Hodder and Stoughton, 1912.

Richards, Charles R. *Art in Industry.* New York: Macmillan, 1929.

Roger, Noëlle. *Les Carnets d'une infirmière.* Paris: Attinger frères, 1915.

Rondot, Natalis. *Rapport sur les objets de parure, de fantaisie et de goût, fait à la commission française du jury international de l'Exposition universelle de Londres.* Paris: Imprimerie impériale, 1854.

Saint-Ursanne, René. *La Grève des midinettes, comédie en un acte pour jeunes filles.* Paris: Flammarion, 1925.

Sand, George. *Horace.* Paris: De Potter, 1842.

Séris, Raymond, and Jean Aubry. *Les Parisiens pendant l'état de siège.* Paris etc.: Berger-Levrault, 1915.

Sibre, Georges, and Albert Verse. *Couturière sans aiguilles: vaudeville-opérette en un acte.* Paris: C. Joubert, 1905.

Silvestre, Armand. *Guide Armand Silvestre de Paris et de ses environs et de l'Exposition de 1900.* Paris: Éditeurs Méricant, 1900.

Simon, Jules. *L'Ouvrière.* Paris: Hachette, 1861.

Simon, Jules. *Exposition universelle de 1878: rapports du jury international.* Paris: Imprimerie nationale, 1880.

Sommerville, Frankfort, G. Fraipont, Lucien Gautier, Raphaël Kirchner, Maurice de Lambert, A. Marcel-Clement, and G Riom. *The Spirit of Paris.* London: Adam & Charles Black, 1913.

Stoullig, Edmond. *Les Annales du théâtre et de la musique: vingt-septième année, 1900.* Paris: Ollendorf, 1901.

Teulet, Edmond. *Chansons du siècle dernier.* Preface by Jules Claretie. Paris: Éditions du Grillon, 1901.

Une Exposition artistique féminine en l'honneur de nos poilus. Paris: Gaumont Pathé, 1915. www.gaumontpathearchives.com, Ref. No. 1546GJ 00003.

Vernières, André. *Camille Frison, ouvrière de la couture,* 29–30. Paris: Librairie Plon, 1908.

Walton, William. *Paris from the Earliest Period to the Present Day.* Philadelphia, G. Barrie & Son, 1902.

Worth, Gaston. *La Couture et la confection des vêtements de femme.* Paris: Imprimerie Chaix, 1895.

Secondary Sources

Adams, Christine. *Poverty, Charity, and Motherhood: Maternal Societies in Nineteenth-Century France.* Urbana: University of Illinois Press, 2010.

Albert, Anaïs. "Les Midinettes parisiennes à la Belle Époque: bon goût ou mauvais genre?" *Histoire, Économie, et Société* (September 2013), 61–74.

Alexander, Lynn M. *Women, Work, and Representations: Needlewomen in Victorian Art and Literature*. Athens, OH: Ohio University Press, 2003.

Amossy, Ruth. "Types ou stéréotypes? Les 'physiologies' et la littérature industrielle." *Romantisme* 19, No. 64 (1989), 113–23.

Andrieux, Françoise, "Les ouvrières parisiennes chantent et dansent dans les banlieues (1903–1939)," in *La Banlieue en fête: de la marginalité urbaine à l'identité culturelle*. Eds. Noëlle Gérome, Danielle Tartakowsky, and Claude Willard. Saint-Denis: Presses universitaires de Vincennes, 1988, pp. 233–43.

Antier, Chantal. *Les Femmes dans la Grande Guerre*. Saint-Cloud: Éditions 14–18 Soteca, 2011.

Ardis, Ann L. *New Women, New Novels Feminism and Early Modernism*. New Brunswick: Rutgers University Press, 1990.

Aubert, Louis. *Notice sur la vie et les travaux de Gustave Charpentier*. Paris: Firmin-Didot, 1956.

Audoin-Rouzeau, Stéphane, *Men at War, 1914–1918: National Sentiment and Trench Journalism in France during the First World War*. Oxford: Berg, 1992.

Audoin-Rouzeau, Stéphane. *La Grande Guerre: 1914–1918*. Paris: Gallimard, 1998.

Audoin-Rouzeau, Stéphane, and Annette Becker. *14–18, Retrouver la guerre*. Paris: Gallimard, 2000.

Auslander, Leora. "Perceptions of beauty and the problem of consciousness: Parisian furniture makers," in *Rethinking Labor History*. Ed. Lenard Berlanstein. Urbana: University of Illinois, 1993, pp. 149–81.

Auslander, Leora. *Taste and Power: Furnishing Modern France*. Los Angeles: University of California Press, 1996.

Avrane, Colette. *Ouvrières à domicile: le combat pour un salaire minimum sous la Troisième République*. Rennes: PU Rennes, 2013.

Bard, Christine. *Les Filles de Marianne: histoire des féminismes: 1914–1940*. Paris: Fayard, 1995.

Barlow, Tani E., Madeleine Yue Dong, Uta G. Poiger, Priti Ramamurthy, Lynn M. Thomas, and Alys Eve Weinbaum, "The modern girl around the world: a research agenda and preliminary findings," *Gender & History* 17, No. 2 (August 2005), 245–94.

Barrows, Susanna. *Distorting Mirrors: Visions of the Crowd in Late Nineteenth-Century France*. New Haven: Yale University Press, 1981.

Bass-Krueger, Maude. "From the 'union parfaite' to the 'union brisée': the French couture industry and the *midinettes* during the Great War," *Costume* 47, No. 1 (2013), 28–44.

Becker, Jean-Jacques. *The Great War and the French People*. Translated by Arnold Pomerans. Dover, NH: Bloomsbury Academic, 1986.

Beetham, Margaret, and Ann Heilmann. *New Woman Hybridities: Femininity, Feminism, and International Consumer Culture, 1880–1930*. New York: Routledge, 2004.

Bellanger, Claude, Jacques Godechot, Pierre Guiral, and Fernand Terrou, eds. *Histoire générale de la presse française, Tome III: de 1871 à 1940*. Paris: Presses Universitaires de France, 1972.

Bellet, Roger, ed. *Paris aux XIXe siècle: aspects d'un mythe littéraire*. Lyon: Presses Universitaires de Lyon, 1984.

Benjamin, Walter. "Paris, the capital of the nineteenth century," in *The Arcades Project*, translated by Howard Eiland and Kevin McLaughlin. Cambridge, MA: The Belknap Press of Harvard University Press, 1999.

Berlanstein, Lenard R. *The Working People of Paris, 1871–1914*. Baltimore: The Johns Hopkins University Press, 1984.

Berlanstein, Lenard R., ed. *Rethinking Labor History*. Urbana: University of Illinois Press, 1993.

Blay, Philippe. "Quand Mimi Pinson croise ciboulette: Gustave Charpentier et Reynaldo Hahn," in *Gustave Charpentier et son temps*, ed. Michela Niccolai and Jean-Christophe Branger. Saint-Etienne: Publications de l'Université de Saint-Etienne, 2013, pp. 89–104.

Bordo, Susan. *Unbearable Weight: Feminism, Western Culture, and the Body*. Los Angeles: University of California Press, 2003.

Bouchard, Anne-Marie. "'Les Midinettes révolutionnaires': prostitution et grand soir dans la presse subversive (1890–1910)," *Médias 19* [online] Guillaume Pinson (dir.), 2013.

Bowlby, Rachel. *Just Looking: Consumer Culture in Dreiser, Gissing, and Zola*. New York: Methuen, 1985.

Boxer, Marilyn J. "Women in industrial homework: the flowermakers of Paris in the Belle Epoque," *French Historical Studies* 12, No. 3 (Spring 1982), 401–423.

Boxer, Marilyn J. "Protective legislation and home industry: the marginalization of women workers in late nineteenth- and early twentieth-century France," *Journal of Social History* 20, No. 1 (1 October 1986), 45–65.

Boym, Svetlana. *The Future of Nostalgia*. New York: Basic Books, 2002.

Branger, Jean-Christophe, and Michaela Niccolai, eds. *Gustave Charpentier et son temps*. L'Université de St Etienne, 2013.

Brouland, Guillaume Doizy Pierre. *La Grande Guerre des cartes postales*. Paris: Hugo, 2013.

Bruegel, Martin. "Le Genre du déjeuner: alimentation et travail dans le Paris de la Belle Époque," *Food & History* 14, Nos. 2–3 (2016), 21–50.

Burgat, Florence. *La Protection de l'animal*. Paris: Presses universitaires de France, 1997.

Cabanes, Bruno. "Negotiating intimacy in the shadow of war (France, 1914–1920s): new perspectives in the cultural history of World War I," *French Politics, Culture & Society* 31, No. 1 (2013), 1–23.

Castagnès, Gilles. *Les Femmes et l'esthéthique de la féminité dans l'oeuvre de Musset*. Bern: Peter Lang, 2004.

Chabot, Joceline. *Les Débuts du syndicalisme féminin chrétien en France, 1899–1944*. Lyon: Presses Universitaires Lyon, 1998.

Charron, Hélène, *Les Formes de l'illégimité intellectuelle: les femmes dans les sciences sociales françaises, 1890–1940*. Paris: CNRS Éditions, 2013.

Chenut, Helen Harden. *The Fabric of Gender: Working-Class Culture in Third Republic France*. University Park: Penn State University Press, 2005.

Cherry, Deborah. "Surveying seamstresses," *Feminist Arts News* 9 (1983), 27–9.

Chessel, Marie-Emmanuelle. "Le Genre de la consommation en 1900. Autour de la Ligue Sociale d'acheteurs," *L'Année sociologique* 61, No. 1 (2011), 125–49.

Chessel, Marie-Emmanuelle. *Consommateurs engagés à la Belle Epoque: La Ligue sociale d'acheteurs*. Paris: Les Presses de Sciences Po, 2012.

Chevalier, Louis. *Les Parisiens*. Paris: Hachette, 1967.

Chevalier, Louis. *Laboring Classes and Dangerous Classes: In Paris During the First Half of the Nineteenth Century*. Trans. Frank Jellinek. New York: Howard Fertig, 1973.

Clayson, Hollis. *Paris in Despair: Art and Everyday Life under Siege (1870–1871)*. Chicago: University of Chicago Press, 2002.

Coffin, Judith G. *The Politics of Women's Work: The Paris Garment Trades, 1750–1915*. Princeton: Princeton University Press, 1996.

Coombes, Annie E. *Reinventing Africa: Museums, Material Culture and Popular Imagination in Late Victorian and Edwardian England*. New Haven: Yale University Press, 1997.

Coons, Lorraine. *Women Home Workers in the Parisian Garment Industry, 1860–1915*. New York: Garland Publishing, 1987.

Coons, Lorraine. "'Neglected sisters' of the women's movement: the perception and experience of working mothers in the Parisian garment industry, 1860–1915," *Journal of Women's History* 5, No. 2 (1993), 50–74.

Cronier, Emmanuelle. *Permissionnaires dans la Grande Guerre*. Paris: Belin, 2013.

Crowston, Clare Haru. *Fabricating Women: The Seamstresses of Old Regime France, 1675–1791*. Durham, NC: Duke University Press Books, 2001.

Daniel, Ute. *The War from Within: German Women in the First World War*. Oxford and New York: Berg Publishers, 1997.

Darrow, Margaret H. "French volunteer nursing and the myth of war experience in World War I," *The American Historical Review* 101, No. 1 (1 February 1996), 80–106.

Darrow, Margaret H. *French Women & the First World War: War Stories of the Homefront*, Oxford and New York: Berg, 2000.

Das, Santanu. "'Kiss me Hardy': intimacy, gender, and gesture in World War I trench literature," *Modernism/modernity* 9, No. 1 (2002), 51–74.

Datta, Venita. *Heroes and Legends of Fin-de-Siècle France: Gender, Politics, and National Identity*. Cambridge University Press, 2011.

David, Alison Matthews. *Fashion Victims: The Dangers of Dress Past and Present*. New York: Bloomsbury, 2015.

Davis, Mary. *Classic Chic: Music, Fashion, and Modernism*. Los Angeles: University of California Press, 2006.

Decouflé, André-Clément. "Histoire de l'Office du Travail: une 'administration de mission' avant la lettre," *Travail et Emploi* 22 (1984), 45–54.

DeGroat, Judith A. "The public nature of women's work: definitions and debates during the Revolution of 1848," *French Historical Studies* 20, No. 1 (Winter 1997), 31–47.

DeGroat, Judith A. "Virtue, vice and revolution: representations of Parisian needlewomen in the mid-nineteenth century," in *Famine and Fashion: Needlewomen in the Nineteenth Century*. ed. Beth Harris. Burlington, VT: Ashgate, 2005, pp. 201–14.

DeGroat, Judith A. "Women in the Paris manufacturing trades at the end of the long eighteenth century," in *Women and Work in Eighteenth-Century France*, ed. Nina Kushner and Daryl Hafter. Baton Rouge: Louisiana State University Press, 2015, pp. 202–22.

DeJean, Joan. *The Essence of Style: How the French Invented High Fashion, Fine Food, Chic Cafés, Style, Sophistication and Glamour*. New York: Free Press, 2005.

Dell, Simon. "The consumer and the making of the 'Exposition Internationale des Arts Décoratifs et Industriels Modernes,' 1907–1925," *Journal of Design History* 12, No. 4 (1999), 311–25.

Delmas, Marc. *Gustave Charpentier et le lyrisme français*. Paris: Librairie Delagrave, 1931.

Didry, Claude. "Les Midinettes, avant-garde oubliée du proletariat," *LHS L'Homme et la société* 3, Nos. 189–90 (2013), 63–86.

Dijkstra, Bram. *Idols of Perversity: Fantasies of Feminine Evil in Fin-de-Siècle Culture*. New York: Oxford University Press, 1986.

Dixmier, Élisabeth, and Michel Dixmier. *L'Assiette au Beurre: revue satirique illustrée, 1901–1912*. Paris: François Maspero, 1974.

Dollard, Catherine L. *The Surplus Woman: Unmarried in Imperial Germany, 1871–1918*. New York: Berghahn Books, 2009.

Downs, Laura Lee. "Women's strikes and the politics of popular egalitarianism in France, 1916–1918," in *Rethinking Labor History*. Urbana: University of Illinois Press, 1993, pp. 114–48.

Downs, Laura Lee. *Manufacturing Inequality: Gender Division in the French and British Metalworking Industries, 1914–1939*. Ithaca: Cornell University Press, 1995.

D'Souza, Aruna, and Tom McDonough. *The Invisible Flâneuse? Gender, Public Space and Visual Culture in Nineteenth Century Paris*. Manchester: Manchester University Press, 2008.

Dubasque, François. "Le Quotidien (1923–1936), instrument de conquête électorale et relais d'influence," *Le Temps des médias* 12, No. 1 (2009), 187–202.

Dubesset, Mathilde, Françoise Thébaud, and Catherine Vincent, "The female munitions workers of the Seine," in *The French Homefront, 1914–1918*. ed. Patrick Fridenson. Oxford: Berg, 1992.

Dymond, Anne. "Embodying the nation: art, fashion, and allegorical women at the 1900 Exposition Universelle," *RACAR: Revue d'art canadienne/Canadian Art Review* 36, No. 2 (2011), 1–14.

Eksteins, Modris. *Rites of Spring: The Great War and the Birth of the Modern Age*. New York: Mariner Books, 2000.

Enstad, Nan. *Ladies of Labor, Girls of Adventure: Working Women, Popular Culture, and Labor Politics at the Turn of the Twentieth Century*. New York: Columbia University Press, 1999.

Erbeznik, Elizabeth. "Workers and wives as legible types in Eugène Sue's *Les Mystères de Paris*," *Nineteenth-Century French Studies* 41, No. 1 (2012), 66–79.

Farber, Paul Lawrence. *Discovering Birds: The Emergence of Ornithology as a Scientific Discipline, 1760–1850*. Baltimore: The Johns Hopkins University Press, 1996.

Fell, Alison S. *French and Francophone Women Facing War*. New York: Peter Lang, 2009.

Felski, Rita. *The Gender of Modernity*. Cambridge, MA: Harvard University Press, 1995.

Ferguson, Eliza Earle. *Gender and Justice: Violence, Intimacy, and Community in Fin-de-Siècle Paris*. Baltimore: The Johns Hopkins University Press, 2010.

Frader, Laura Levine. *Breadwinners and Citizens: Gender and the Making of the French Social Model*. Durham, NC: Duke University Press, 2008.

Fridenson, Patrick, ed. *The French Home Front, 1914–1918*. Trans. Bruce Little. Providence, RI: Bloomsbury Academic, 1993.

Fuchs, Rachel G. *Poor & Pregnant in Paris: Strategies for Survival in the Nineteenth Century*. New Brunswick: Rutgers University Press, 1992.

Fulcher, Jane F. "Charpentier's operatic 'Roman musical' as read in the wake of the Dreyfus Affair," *19th-Century Music* 16, No. 2 (1992), 161–80.

Fulton, Dawn. "Interurban Paris: Alain Mabanckou's *Invisible Cities*," in *Paris, Capital of the Black Atlantic: Literature, Modernity, and Diaspora*, ed. Jeremy Braddock and Jonathan Eburne. Baltimore: The Johns Hopkins University Press, 2013, pp. 330–49.

Fussell, Paul. *The Great War and Modern Memory*. New York: Oxford University Press, 2000.

Gallagher, Catherine. *The Industrial Reformation of English Fiction: Social Discourse and Narrative Form, 1832–1867*. Chicago: The University of Chicago Press, 1985.

Gamber, Wendy. *The Female Economy: The Millinery and Dressmaking Trades, 1860–1930*. Urbana-Champaign: University of Illinois Press, 1997.

Garreau, Bernard-Marie. *Marguerite Audoux: la couturière des lettres*. Paris: Tallandier, 1991.

Gillis, John R. *Commemorations: The Politics of National Identity*. Princeton: Princeton University Press, 1996.

Grayzel, Susan. " 'The souls of soldiers': civilians under fire in First World War France," *The Journal of Modern History* 78 (September 2006), 588–622.

Grazia, Victoria de. "Beyond time and money," *International Labor and Working-Class History* No.43 (1993), 24–30.

Geppert, Alexander. *Fleeting Cities: Imperial Expositions in Fin-de-Siècle Europe*. New York: Palgrave Macmillan, 2013.

Green, Nancy L. *The Pletzl of Paris: Jewish Immigrant Workers in the Belle Epoque*. New York: Holmes & Meier, 1986.

Green, Nancy L. *Ready-to-Wear and Ready-to-Work: A Century of Industry and Immigrants in Paris and New York*. Durham, NC: Duke University Press, 1997.

Grout, Holly. *The Force of Beauty: Transforming French Ideas of Femininity in the Third Republic*. Baton Rouge: LSU Press, 2015.

Guilbert, Madeleine. *Les Femmes et l'organisation syndicale avant 1914*. Paris: Éditions du Centre National de la Recherche Scientifique, 1966.

Guillais-Maury, Joëlle. "La Grisette," in *Madame ou Mademoiselle? Itinéraires de la solitude féminine 18e–20e siècle*, ed. Michelle Perrot. Paris: Montalba, 1984, pp. 233–52.

Gullace, Nicoletta F. *The Blood of Our Sons: Men, Women, and the Renegotiation of British Citizenship During the Great War*. New York: Palgrave Macmillan, 2002.

Gullickson, Gay L. *Unruly Women of Paris: Images of the Commune*. Ithaca: Cornell University Press, 1996.

Haine, W. Scott. "Privacy in public: comportment of working-class women in late nineteenth-century Parisian proletarian cafés," *Proceedings of the Annual Meeting of the Western Society of French History* 14 (1987), 204–12.

Haine, W. Scott. "The priest of the proletarians: Parisian café owners and the working class, 1820–1914," *International Labor and Working-Class History* 45 (Spring 1994), 16–28.

Haine, W. Scott. *"The World of the Parisian Café: Sociability among the French Working Class, 1789–1914*. Baltimore: The Johns Hopkins University Press, 1996.

Hamerton, Katherine. "Eroticizing women's taste in the 1740s: containing the Enlightenment," Western Society for French History Annual Meeting (Quebec City, November 2008).

Hamerton, Katherine. "A feminist voice in the Enlightenment salon: Madame de Lambert on taste, sensibility, and the feminine mind," *Modern Intellectual History* 7, No. 2 (2010), 209–38.

Harris, Beth. *Famine and Fashion: Needlewomen in the Nineteenth Century*. Burlington, VT: Ashgate, 2005.

Harvey, David. *Paris, Capital of Modernity*. New York: Routledge, 2003.

Hertz, Neil. "Medusa's head: male hysteria under political pressure," *Representations* 4 (1983), 27–54.

Higonnet, Margaret R., ed. *Behind the Lines: Gender and the Two World Wars*. New Haven: Yale University Press, 1987.

Hilden, Patricia. *Working Women and Socialist Politics in France, 1880–1914: A Regional Study*. Oxford: Clarendon Press, 1986.

Hilden, Patricia. "Women and the labour movement in France, 1869–1914," *The Historical Journal* 29, No. 4 (1986), 809–32.

Hiner, Susan. *Accessories to Modernity: Fashion and the Feminine in Nineteenth-Century France*. Philadelphia: University of Pennsylvania Press, 2010.

Hiner, Susan. "Picturing the Catherinette: reinventing tradition for the postcard age," in *French Cultural Studies for the Twenty-First Century*, ed. Masha Belenky, Kathryn Kleppinger, and Anne O'Neil-Henry. Newark: University of Delaware Press, 2017, pp. 119–52.

Hoover, Kathleen O'Donnell. "Gustave Charpentier," *The Musical Quarterly* 25, No. 3 (July 1939), 334–50.

Horne, Janet R., *A Social Laboratory for Modern France: The Musée Social and the Rise of the Welfare State*. Durham, NC: Duke University Press, 2001.

Huebner, Steven. "Between anarchism and the box office: Gustave Charpentier's 'Louise,'" *19th-Century Music* 19, No. 2 (1 October 1995), 136–60.

Huebner, Steven. *French Opera at the Fin de Siècle: Wagnerism, Nationalism, and Style.* New York: Oxford University Press, 1999.

Huss, Marie-Monique. *Histoires de famille: cartes postales et culture de guerre.* Paris: Noesis, 2000.

Iskin, Ruth E. *Modern Women and Parisian Consumer Culture in Impressionist Painting.* Cambridge: Cambridge University Press, 2007.

Iskin, Ruth E. "The flâneuse in French fin-de-siècle posters: advertising images of modern women in Paris," in *The Invisible Flâneuse? Gender, Public Space and Visual Culture in Nineteenth Century Paris*, ed. Aruna D'Souza and Tom McDonough. Manchester: Manchester University Press, 2008, pp. 113–28.

Jackson, Shannon. *Lines of Activity: Performance, Historiography, Hull-House Domesticity.* Ann Arbor: University of Michigan Press, 2000.

Jones, Jennifer. *Sexing La Mode: Gender, Fashion and Commercial Culture in Old Regime France.* New York: Berg, 2004.

Joseph, Mathilde. "Le Poilu de music-hall: l'image du poilu dans les music-halls parisiens pendant la Grande Guerre," *Guerres mondiales et conflits contemporains: revue d'histoire* 197 (2000), 23–42.

Kalba, Laura. *Color in the Age of Impressionism: Commerce, Technology, and Art.* University Park: Penn State University Press, 2017.

Kelly, Barbara L., ed. *French Music, Culture, and National Identity, 1870–1939.* Rochester, NY: University of Rochester Press, 2008.

Kelly, Debra, and Tom Jackson. "The Franco-British Exhibition of 1908: legacies and memories one hundred years on," *Synergies* 2 (2009), 11–23.

Kelly, Dorothy. *Reconstructing Woman: From Fiction to Reality in the Nineteenth-Century Novel.* University Park: Penn State University Press, 2007.

Kershaw, Angela, "Proletarian women, proletarian writing: the case of Marguerite Audoux," in *A "Belle Époque"? Women in French Society and Culture, 1890–1914*, ed. Diana Holmes and Carrie Tarr. New York: Berghahn, 2006, pp. 253–69.

Knibiehler, Yvonne, Marcel Bernos, Elisabeth Ravoux-Rallo, and Eliane Richard. *De la pucelle à la minette: les jeunes filles, de l'âge classique à nos jours.* Paris: Messidor/Temps Actuels, 1983.

Knight, Donald R. *The Exhibitions, Great White City, Shepherds Bush, London: 70th Anniversary, 1908–1978.* New Barnet: The author, 1978.

Koven, Seth. *Slumming: Sexual and Social Politics in Victorian London.* Princeton: Princeton University Press, 2006.

Kranidis, Rita. *The Victorian Spinster and Colonial Emigration: Contested Subjects.* New York: St Martin's Press, 1999.

Kushner, Nina, and Daryl M. Hafter. *Women and Work in Eighteenth-Century France.* Baton Rouge: Louisiana State University Press, 2015.

Lacassin, Francis. *A la recherche de l'empire caché: mythologie du roman populaire.* Paris: Julliard, 1991.

Laprade, Maxime. "Haute couture et expositions universelles, 1900–1925," *Apparence(s)* 7 (2017). Online.

Lathers, Marie. "The social construction and deconstruction of the female model in 19th-century France," *Mosaic: A Journal for the Comparative Study of Literature* 29, No. 2 (1996), 23–52.

Lathers, Marie. *Bodies of Art: French Literary Realism and the Artist's Model.* Lincoln: University of Nebraska Press, 2001.

Ledger, Sally. "Gissing, the shopgirl and the New Woman," *Women* 6, No. 3 (1995), 263–74.

Lehning, James R. *To Be a Citizen: The Political Culture of the Early French Third Republic.* Ithaca: Cornell University Press, 2001.

Leighten, Patricia. "The world turned upside down: Modernism and anarchist strategies of inversion in *L'Assiette au Beurre*," *Journal of Modern Periodical Studies* 4, No. 2 (2013), 133–70.

Lemercier, Claire. "Looking for 'industrial confraternity': small-scale industries and institutions in nineteenth-century Paris," *Enterprise & Society* 10, No. 2 (June 2009), 304–34.

LeNaour, Jean-Yves. "La Première Guerre mondiale et la régéneration," *Revue d'histoire du théâtre* 53, No. 3 (2001), 229–39.

Lescart, Alain. *Splendeurs et misères de la grisette: évolution d'une figure emblématique.* Paris: H. Champion, 2008.

Lhuissier, Anne, *Alimentation populaire et réforme social: les consommations ouvrières dans le second XIXe siècle.* Paris: Éditions de la Maison des sciences de l'homme, 2007.

Little, Bruce. *The French Home Front, 1914–1918.* New York: Berg, 1993.

Luciani, Jean, and Robert Salais, "Matériaux pour la naissance d'une institution: l'Office du travail (1890–1900)," *Genèses: Sciences sociales et histoire* 2 (1990), 83–108.

McBride, Theresa M. "A woman's world: department stores and the evolution of women's employment, 1870–1920," *French Historical Studies* 10, No. 4 (1 October 1978), 664–83.

McEachern, Patricia. *Deprivation and Power: The Emergence of Anorexia Nervosa in Nineteenth-Century French Literature.* Westport: Greenwood Press, 1998.

Macleod, Jenny, and Pierre Purseigle. *Uncovered Fields: Perspectives in First World War Studies.* Boston: Brill, 2004.

McMillan, James, *France and Women, 1789–1914: Gender, Society and Politics.* New York: Routledge, 1999.

McWilliam, Neil. "Conflicting manifestations: Parisian commemoration of Joan of Arc and Etienne Dolet in the early Third Republic," *French Historical Studies* 27, No. 2 (Spring 2004), 381–418.

McWilliam, Rohan. "The melodramatic seamstress: interpreting a Victorian penny dreadful," in *Famine and Fashion: Needlewomen in the Nineteenth Century*, ed. Beth Harris. Burlington: Ashgate, 2005, pp. 99–114.

Magraw, Roger. *A History of the French Working Class, Vol. II: Workers and the Bourgeois Republic.* Oxford: Blackwell, 1992.

Maindreville, Florence Doé de, and Stéphan Etcharry. *La Grande Guerre en musique: vie et création musicales en France pendant la Première Guerre mondiale.* New York: Peter Lang, 2014.

Mansker, Andrea. "'Vive Mademoiselle'! The politics of singleness in early twentieth-century French feminism," *Feminist Studies* 33, No. 3 (Fall 2007), 632–58.

Mansker, Andrea. *Sex, Honor and Citizenship in Early Third Republic France.* New York: Palgrave Macmillan, 2011.

Martin, Morag. *Selling Beauty: Cosmetics, Commerce, and French Society, 1750—1830.* Baltimore: The Johns Hopkins University Press, 2009.

Maynes, Mary Jo. *Taking the Hard Road: Life Course in French and German Workers' Autobiographies in the Era of Industrialization.* Chapel Hill: University of North Carolina Press, 1995.

Merriman, John M. *The Red City: Limoges and the French Nineteenth Century.* New York: Oxford University Press, 1985.

Mesch, Rachel. *Having It All in the Belle Epoque: How French Women's Magazines Invented the Modern Woman.* Redwood City: Stanford University Press, 2013.

Michie, Helena. *Flesh Made Word: Female Figures and Women's Bodies*. New York: Oxford University Press, 1990.

Mitchell, Robin. "'Ourika mania': interrogating race, class, space, and place in early nineteenth-century France," *African and Black Diaspora* 10, No. 1 (2017), 85–95.

Monjaret, Anne. "La Sainte-Catherine dans la couture: une fête au féminin," *Ethnologie Française* 16, No. 4 (1 October 1986), 361–78.

Monjaret, Anne. "La Sainte-Catherine à Paris de la fin du dix-neuvième siècle à nos jours: ethnographie d'une fête urbaine et professionelle." Université de Paris-Nanterre, 1992.

Monjaret, Anne. *La Sainte-Catherine: culture festive dans l'entreprise*. Paris: Éditions du C.T.H.S., 1997.

Monjaret, Anne, and Séverine Dessajan, Francine Fourmaux, Michela Niccolai, and Mélanie Roustan, *Le Paris des "midinettes": mise en culture de figures féminines, XIX–XXIème siècles, ethnologie des traces et mémoires d'ouvrières parisiennes*. Rapport Final, Mairie de Paris, Enseignement Superieur & Recherche, Programme de recherche sur la Ville de Paris Patrimoine, La mémoire ouvrière et ses marques dans le paysage urbain, son inscription dans la ville, 2008.

Monjaret, Anne, and Michela Niccolai. "La midinette en chansons: représentations masculines d'un idéal féminin populaire (1830-1939)," in *Représentations: Le genre à l'œuvre, Tome 3*, ed. Melody Jan-Ré. Paris: L'Harmattan, 2012, pp. 101–16.

Monjaret, Anne. "À l'ombre des jeunes filles en pierre. Des ouvrières dans les jardins parisiens," *Ethnologie française* XLII, No. 3 (2012), 503–15.

Monjaret, Anne, and Michela Niccolai. "Elle trotte, danse et chante, la midinette! Univers sonore des couturières parisiennes dans les chansons (XIXe–XXe siècles)," *L'Homme*, No. 215–16 (2015), 47–79.

Mosse, George L. "Caesarism, circuses, and monuments," *Journal of Contemporary History* 6, No. 2 (1 January 1971), 167–82.

Naquet, Emmanuel. "La Société d'études documentaires et critiques sur la guerre. Ou la naissance d'une minorité pacifiste au sein de la Ligue des Droits de l'Homme," *Matériaux pour l'histoire de notre temps* 30, No. 1 (1993), 6–10.

Naquet, Emmanuel. *Pour l'humanité: La Ligue des droits de l'homme de l'affaire Dreyfus à la défaite de 1940*. Rennes: Presses Universitaires de Rennes, 2014.

Nesci, Catherine. *Le Flâneur et les flâneuses: les femmes et la ville à l'époque romantique*. Grenoble: ELLUG, 2007.

Neulander, Joelle. "Model detectives: modernity, femininity, and work in interwar romance comic strips," *Proceedings of the Western Society for French History* 37 (2009), 283–303.

Niccolai, Michela. *La Dramaturgie de Gustave Charpentier*. Turnhout: Brepols, 2011.

Niccolai, Michela, and Jean-Christophe Branger, *Gustave Charpentier et son temps*. Saint-Etienne: Publications de l'Université de Saint-Etienne, 2013.

Niccolai, Michela. "Une Infirmière d'opérette: Mimi Pinson et sa cocarde," in *La Grande Guerre en musique: vie et création pendant la première musicales en France Guerre mondiale* ed. Florence Doé de Maindreville and Stéphan Etcharry. Brussels: Peter Lang, 2014, pp. 233–51.

Noiriel, Gérard. *Workers in French Society in the 19th and 20th Centuries*. New York: Berg, 1990.

Noiriel, Gérard. *Les Ouvriers dans la société française, XIXe–XXe siècle*. Paris: Éditions du Seuil, 2002.

Oberon Garcia, Claire. "Remapping the metropolis: theorizing Black women's subjectivities in interwar Paris," *Black French Women and the Struggle for Equality, 1848–2016*, ed. Félix Germain and Silyane Larcher. Lincoln: University of Nebraska Press, 2018.

Offen, Karen. "Exploring the sexual politics of French republican nationalism," in *Nationhood and Nationalism in France*, ed. Robert Tombs (London: Routledge, 1991), 195–209.

Offen, Karen. *Debating the Woman Question in the French Third Republic, 1870–1920*. Cambridge: Cambridge University Press, 2018.

Omnès, Catherine. *Ouvrières parisiennes: marchés du travail et trajectoires professionelles au 20e siècle*. Paris: Éditions de l'École des Hautes Études en Sciences Sociales, 1997.

O'Neil-Henry, Anne. *Mastering the Marketplace: Popular Literature in Nineteenth-Century France*. Lincoln: University of Nebraska Press, 2017.

Pairault, François. *Images de poilus: la Grande Guerre en cartes postales*. Paris: Tallandier, 2003.

Palmiste, Clara. "L'Utilisation de la mémoire de l'esclavage dans les revendications des feminists guadeloupéennes (1918–1921)," *Sextant* 25 (2008), 43–54.

Parsons, Deborah L. *Streetwalking the Metropolis: Women, the City, and Modernity*. New York: Oxford University Press, 2000.

Pasler, Jann. *Composing the Citizen: Music as Public Utility in Third Republic France*. Berkeley: University of California Press, 2009.

Peiss, Kathy. *Cheap Amusements: Working Woman and Leisure in Turn of the Century New York*. Philadelphia: Temple University Press, 1986.

Perrot, Michelle. "Les Ouvriers en grève (France, 1871–1890)," *Le Mouvement Social* No. 82 (1973), 3–16.

Perrot, Michelle. *Les Femmes, ou, Les silences de l'histoire*. Paris: Flammarion, 1998.

Petro, Patrice. *Joyless Streets: Women and Melodramatic Representation in Weimar Germany*. Princeton: Princeton University Press, 1989.

Piquet, Elisabeth. *Les Fleurs du mal: les maladies professionnelles des ouvriers en fleurs artificielles, France, 1829–1919*. Université de Valenciennes, 2014.

Pollock, Griselda. *Vision and Difference: Femininity, Feminism, and Histories of Art*. New York: Routledge, 1988.

Pomfret, David M. "'A muse for the masses': gender, age, and nation in France, fin de siècle," *American Historical Review* 109, No. 5 (December 2004), 1439–74.

Poole, Mary Ellen. "Gustave Charpentier and the Conservatoire Populaire de Mimi Pinson," *19th-Century Music* 20 (1997), 231–52.

Portis, Larry. "A profound witness: the work of the Bonneff brothers," *Radical History Review* 36 (Fall 1986), 149–50.

Pourcher, Yves. *Les Jours de guerre: la vie des français au jour le jour 1914–1918*. Paris: Plon, 1994.

Preiss, Nathalie, and Claire Scamaroni, eds. *Elle coud, elle court, la grisette!* [exposition catalogue], Maison de Balzac, 14 October 2011–15 January 2012. Paris: Paris Musées, 2011. Bibliothèque des Arts Décoratifs.

Pulju, Rebecca J. *Women and Mass Consumer Society in Postwar France*. Cambridge: Cambridge University Press, 2011.

Purseigle, Pierre. *Mobilisation, sacrifice et citoyenneté: Angleterre–France, 1900–1918*. Paris: Belles Lettres, 2013.

Raissiguier, Catherine. *Reinventing the Republic: Gender, Migration, and Citizenship in France*. Stanford: Stanford University Press, 2010.

Raithorn, Judith. "Le Mouvement ouvrier contre la peinture au plomb. Stratégie syndicale, expérience locale et transgression du discours dominant au début du XXe siècle," *Politix* 3, No. 91 (2010), 7–26.

Raithorn, Judith. "The banning of white lead: French and American experiences in a comparative perspective (early twentieth century)," in *A History of the Workplace: Environment and Health at Stake*. New York: Routledge, 2015, pp. 27–46.

Rearick, Charles. "Festivals in modern France: the experience of the Third Republic," *Journal of Contemporary History* 12, No. 3 (1 July 1977), 435–60.

Rearick, Charles. "Madelon and the men—in war and memory," *French Historical Studies*, 17 (1992), 1001–34.

Rearick, Charles. *The French in Love and War: Popular Culture in the Era of the World Wars*. New Haven: Yale University Press, 1997.

Rearick, Charles. *Paris Dreams, Paris Memories: The City and its Mystique*. Stanford: Stanford University Press, 2011.

Rebérioux, Madeleine. *La République radicale? 1898–1914*. Paris: Éditions du Seuil, 1975.

Rémy, Tristan. *Georges Wague: le mime de la Belle Époque*. Paris: Georges Girard, 1964.

Rifkin, Adrian. *Street Noises: Parisian Pleasure, 1900–40*. New York: Manchester University Press, 1995.

Robert, Jean-Louis. "Women and work in France during the First World War," in *The Upheaval of War: Family, Work, and Welfare in Europe, 1914–1918*, ed. Richard Wall and Jay Winter. Cambridge: Cambridge University Press, 1988, pp. 251–66.

Robert, Jean-Louis. *Les Ouvriers, la patrie, et la révolution, Paris, 1914–1919*. Paris: Belles Lettres, 1995.

Roberts, Mary Louise. *Civilization without Sexes: Reconstructing Gender in Postwar France, 1917–1927*. Chicago: University of Chicago Press, 1994.

Roberts, Mary Louise. *Disruptive Acts: The New Woman in Fin-de-Siècle France*. Chicago: University of Chicago Press, 2002.

Ross, James. "Messidor: republican patriotism and the French revolutionary tradition in Third Republic opera," in *French Music, Culture, and National Identity, 1870–1939*, ed. Barbara L. Kelly, Rochester, NY: University of Rochester Press, 2008, pp. 112–30.

Salin, Sandra. *Women and Trade Unions in France: The Tobacco and Hat Industries, 1890–1914*. New York: Peter Lang, 2014.

Sanson, Rosemonde. " 'La 'Fête de Jeanne d'Arc' en 1894: controverse et célébration," *Revue d'Histoire Moderne et Contemporaine* 20, No. 3 (July–September 1973), 444–63.

Schultheiss, Katrin. *Bodies and Souls: Politics and the Professionalization of Nursing in France, 1880–1922*. Cambridge, MA: Harvard University Press, 2001.

Schweitzer, Sylvie, *Les Femmes ont toujours travaillé: une histoire de leurs métiers, XIXe et XXe siècle*. Paris: Éditions Odile Jacob, 2002.

Scott, Joan Wallach. *Gender and the Politics of History*. New York: Columbia University Press, 1999.

Seigel, Jerrold. *Bohemian Paris: Culture, Politics, and the Boundaries of Bourgeois Life*. Baltimore: The Johns Hopkins University Press, 1986.

Sheridan, Geraldine. *Louder Than Words: Ways of Seeing Women Workers in Eighteenth-Century France*. Lubbock: Texas Tech University Press, 2009.

Sherman, Daniel. "Art, commerce, and the production of memory in France after World War I," in *Commemorations: The Politics of National Identity*, ed. John R. Gillis. Princeton: Princeton University Press, 1994, pp. 186–211.

Shorter, Edward. "The First Great Increase in Anorexia Nervosa," *Journal of Social History* 21, No. 1 (Fall 1987), 69–96.

Silverman, Debora. *Art Nouveau in Fin-de-Siècle France: Politics, Psychology and Style*. Los Angeles: University of California Press, 1989.

Silverman, Debora. "The 'New Woman', feminism, and the decorative arts in fin-de-siècle France," in *Eroticism and the Body Politic*, ed. Lynn Hunt. Baltimore: The Johns Hopkins University Press, 1991, pp. 144–63.

Simon-Carrère, Anne. *Chanter la Grande Guerre: les 'poilus' et les femmes*. Seyssel: Champ Vallon, 2014.

Sirop, Dominique. *Paquin. Suivi du catalogue de l'Exposition 'Paquin—Une Retrospective de 60 ans de Haute Couture' organisée par le Musée Historique des Tissus de Lyon, Decembre 1989–Mars 1990*. Paris: Adam Biro, 1989.

Sonn, Richard D. *Sex, Violence, and the Avant-Garde: Anarchism in Interwar France*. University Park: Penn State University Press, 2010.

Sowerwine, Charles. "Le Groupe féministe socialiste, 1899–1902," *Le Mouvement social* 90 (January–March 1975), 87–120.

Sowerwine, Charles. *Sisters or Citizens?: Women and Socialism in France since 1876*. Cambridge: Cambridge University Press, 1982.

Sowerwine, Charles. "Workers and women in France before 1914: the debate over the Couriau affair," *The Journal of Modern History* 55, No. 3 (1983), 411–41.

Sowerwine, Charles. *France since 1870: Culture, Politics and Society*. New York: Palgrave, 2001.

Sowerwine, Charles. "La Politique, 'cet élément dans lequel j'aurais voulu vivre': l'exclusion des femmes est-elle inhérente au républicanisme de la Troisième République?," *CLIO: Histoire, Femmes, et Sociétés* 24 (2006), 171–94.

Sowerwine, Charles. "Bouvard, Stéphanie," in *Dictionnaire des féministes: France, XVIIIe–XXIe siècle*. Paris: Presses Universitaires, 2017, pp. 202–4.

Spang, Rebecca L. *The Invention of the Restaurant: Paris and Modern Gastronomic Culture*. Cambridge, MA: Harvard University Press, 2000.

Steele, Valerie. *Paris Fashion: A Cultural History*. Oxford: Oxford University Press, 1988.

Stewart, Mary Lynn. *Women, Work, and the French State: Labour Protection and Social Patriarchy, 1879–1919*. Montreal: McGill-Queen's Press, 1989.

Stewart, Mary Lynn. *For Health and Beauty: Physical Culture for Frenchwomen, 1880s–1930s*. Baltimore: The Johns Hopkins University Press, 2001.

Stewart, Mary Lynn. *Dressing Modern Frenchwomen: Marketing Haute Couture, 1919–1939*. Baltimore: The Johns Hopkins University Press, 2008.

Stewart, Mary Lynn, and Nancy Janovicek, "Slimming the female body? Re-evaluating dress, corsets, and physical culture in France, 1890s–1930s," *Fashion Theory: The Journal of Dress, Body & Culture* 5, No. 2 (June 2001), pp. 173–93.

Stone, Judith. *The Search for Social Peace, 1890–1914*. Albany: State University of New York Press, 1985.

Stovall, Tyler. *Paris and the Spirit of 1919: Consumer Struggles, Transnationalism and Revolution*. New York: Cambridge University Press, 2012.

Sullivan, Courtney Ann. "Classification, containment, contamination, and the courtesan, the grisette, lorette, and demi-mondaine in nineteenth-century French fiction," PhD Dissertation, University of Texas, Austin, 2003.

Sweeney, Regina M. *Singing Our Way to Victory: French Cultural Politics and Music during the Great War*. Middleton: Wesleyan University Press, 2001.

Thébaud, Françoise. *La Femme au temps de la Guerre de 14*. Paris: Stock/Laurence Pernoud, 1986.

Thompson, Victoria. "Splendeurs et miseres des journalistes: female imagery and the commercialization of journalism in July Monarchy France," *Proceedings of the Annual Meeting of the Western Society for French History* 23 (1996), 361–8.

Thompson, Victoria. *The Virtuous Marketplace: Women and Men, Money and Politics in Paris, 1830–1870*. Baltimore: The Johns Hopkins University Press, 2000.

Tickner, Lisa. *The Spectacle of Women: Imagery of the Suffrage Campaign, 1907–14*. Chicago: University of Chicago Press, 1988.

Tiersten, Lisa. *Marianne in the Market: Envisioning Consumer Society in Fin-de-Siècle France*. Los Angeles: University of California Press, 2001.

Tilburg, Patricia. *Colette's Republic: Work, Gender, and Popular Culture in France, 1870–1914*. New York: Berghahn Books, 2009.

Tilburg, Patricia. "Mimi Pinson goes to war," *Gender & History* 23, No. 1 (April 2011), 92–110.

Tilburg, Patricia. "'Sa coquetterie tue la faim': garment workers, lunch reform, and the Parisian midinette, 1896–1933," *French Historical Studies* 38, No. 2 (2015), 281–309.

Torigian, Michael. *Every Factory a Fortress: The French Labor Movement in the Age of Ford and Hitler*. Athens: Ohio University Press, 1999.

Traugott, Mark. *The French Worker: Autobiographies from the Early Industrial Era*. Berkeley: University of California Press, 1993.

Troy, Nancy. "The theatre of fashion: staging haute couture in early 20th-century France," *Theatre Journal* 53 (2001), 1–32.

Troy, Nancy. *Couture Cultures: A Study in Modern Art and Fashion*. Cambridge, MA: MIT Press, 2003.

Vahe, Isabelle. "Jeanne Mélin (1877–1964): une féministe radicale pendant la grande guerre," in *Les Femmes face à la guerre*, ed. Alison Fell. New York: Peter Lang, 2009, pp. 85–100.

Valenze, Deborah. *The First Industrial Woman*. Oxford: Oxford University Press, 1995.

Vanier, Henriette. *La Mode et ses métiers: frivolités et luttes des classes, 1830–1870*. Paris: Armand Colin, 1960.

Videbien, Marie. "Bouvard, Stéphanie," in *Dictionnaire des féministes: France, XVIIIe–XXIe siècle* [online] (Université d'Angers, 2017). http://blog.univ-angers.fr/dictionnairefeministes/2017/07/04/bouvard-stephanie/

Viet, Vincent. *Les Voltigeurs de la république: l'inspection du travail en France jusqu'en 1914*, Vols. 1 and 2. Paris: CNRS Éditions, 1994.

Walkley, Christina. *The Ghost in the Looking Glass: The Victorian Seamstress*. London: P. Owen, 1981.

Walkowitz, Judith R. *City of Dreadful Delights: Narratives of Sexual Danger in Late-Victorian London*. Chicago: University of Chicago Press, 1992.

Walton, Whitney. "'To triumph before feminine taste': bourgeois women's consumption and hand methods of production in mid-nineteenth-century Paris," *Business History Review* 60 (Winter 1986), 541–63.

Walton, Whitney. *France at the Crystal Palace: Bourgeois Taste and Artisan Manufacture in the Nineteenth Century*. Los Angeles: University of California Press, 1992.

Whorton, James. *The Arsenic Century: How Victorian Britain Was Poisoned at Home, Work, and Play*. New York: Oxford University Press, 2010.

Williams, Rosalind. *Dream Worlds: Mass Consumption in Late Nineteenth-Century France*. Los Angeles: University of California Press, 1982.

Wilson, Elizabeth, *The Sphinx in the City: Urban Life, the Control of Disorder, and Women*. Los Angeles: University of California Press, 1991.

Winter, Jay, and Jean-Louis Robert. *Capital Cities at War: Paris, London, Berlin, 1914–1919*. Cambridge: Cambridge University Press, 1999.

Winter, Jay, and Jean-Louis Robert. *Capital Cities at War: Paris, London, Berlin 1914–1919*, *Volume 2: A Cultural History*. Cambridge: Cambridge University Press, 2007.

Winter, Jay, and Richard Wall, eds. *The Upheaval of War: Family, Work, and Welfare in Europe, 1914–1918*. Cambridge: Cambridge University Press, 1988.

Wolff, Janet. "The invisible flâneuse: women and the literature of modernity," *Theory, Culture & Society* 2, No. 3 (1985), 37–46.

Wolff, Stéphane. *Un Demi-siècle d'opéra comique (1900–1950): les oeuvres, les interprètes*. Paris: Éditions André Bonne, 1953.

Young, Robert J. *Under Siege: Portraits of Civilian Life in France During World War I.* New York: Berghahn Books, 2001.

Yvorel, Jean-Jacques. "De Delacroix à Poulbot, l'image du gamin de Paris," *Revue d'histoire de l'enfance 'irrégulière'* 4 (2002), 39–72.

Zancarni-Fournel, Michelle. "Femmes, genre et syndicalisme pendant la Grande Guerre," in *Combats des femmes, 1914–1918: les françaises, pillier de l'effort de guerre.* Paris: Éditions Autrement, 2004, pp. 98–110.

Zdatny, Steven. *Fashion, Work, and Politics in Modern France.* New York: Palgrave Macmillan, 2006.

Zeisler, Wilfried. *L'Objet d'art et de luxe français en Russie (1881–1917): fournisseurs, clients, collections et influences.* Paris: Mare & Martin Editions, 2014.

Zylberberg-Hocquard, Marie-Hélène. *Féminisme et syndicalisme en France.* Paris: Éditions Anthropos, 1978.

Zylberberg-Hocquard, Marie-Hélène. *Femmes et feminisme dans le mouvement ouvrier français.* Paris: Éditions ouvrières, 1981.

Zylberberg-Hocquard, Marie-Hélène. "L'Ouvrière dans les romans populaires du XIXe siècle," *Revue du Nord* 63, No. 250 (July–September 1981), 603–36.

Zylberberg-Hocquard, Marie-Hélène, and Slava Liszek, "Marie-Claire ou la voix des couturières," in *Le Roman social: littérature, histoire et mouvement ouvrier.* Paris: Les Éditions de l'Atelier, 2002, pp. 39–46.

Index

For the benefit of digital users, indexed terms that span two pages (e.g., 52–53) may, on occasion, appear on only one of those pages.